Look! I'm all grown up! —♫
So hand-some! ♥
SZZZTT

Four Knights of the Apocalypse

4

Nakaba Suzuki Presents

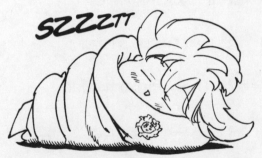

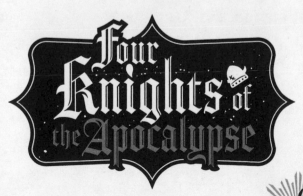

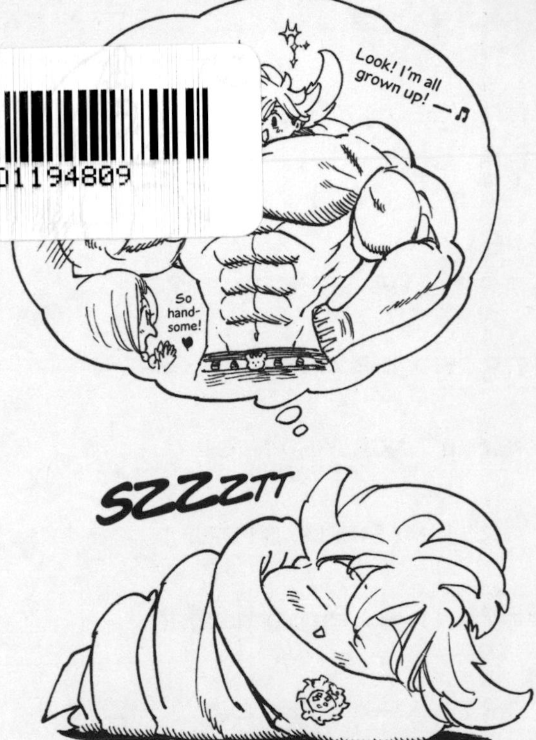

❖ Contents ❖

Four Knights
Of The Apocalypse

Four Knights of the Apocalypse

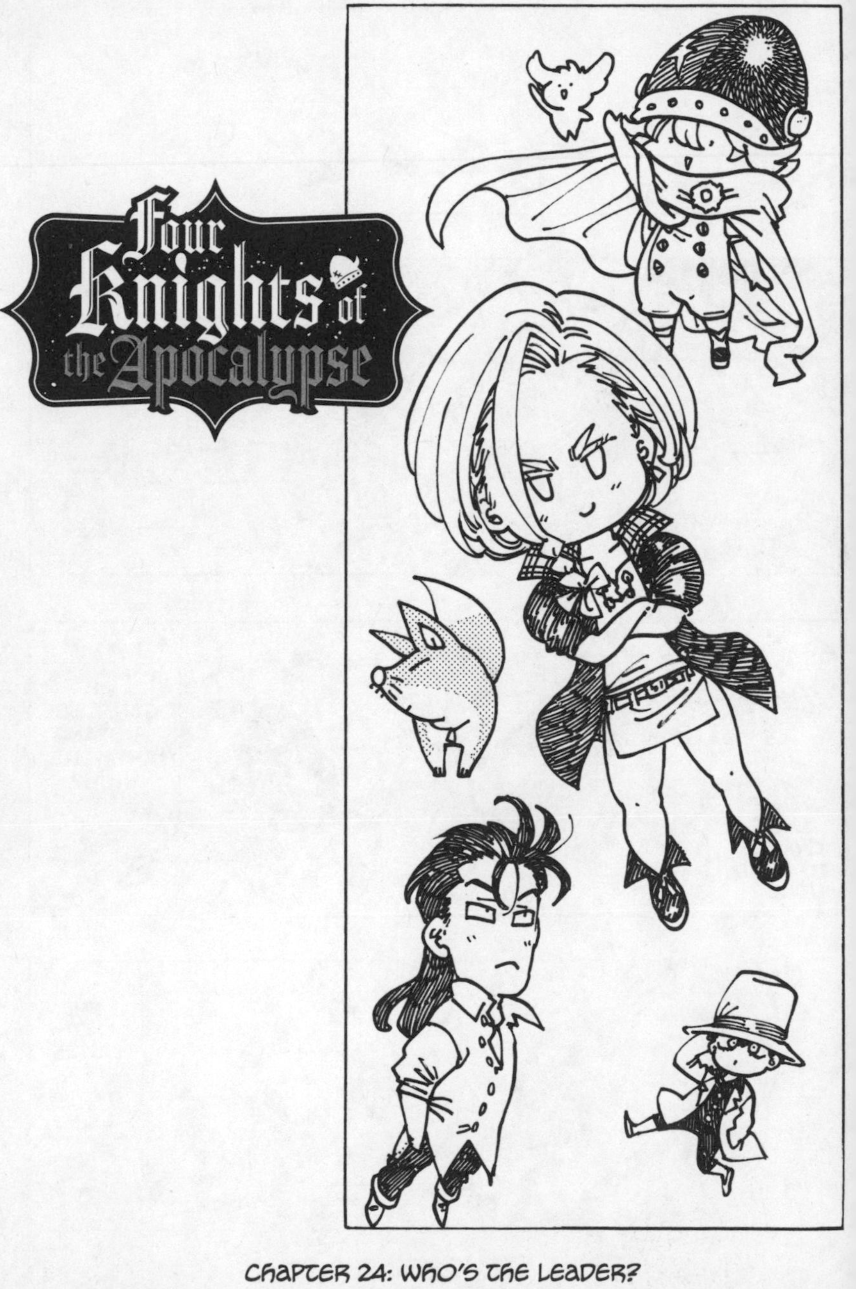

CHAPTER 24: WHO'S THE LEADER?

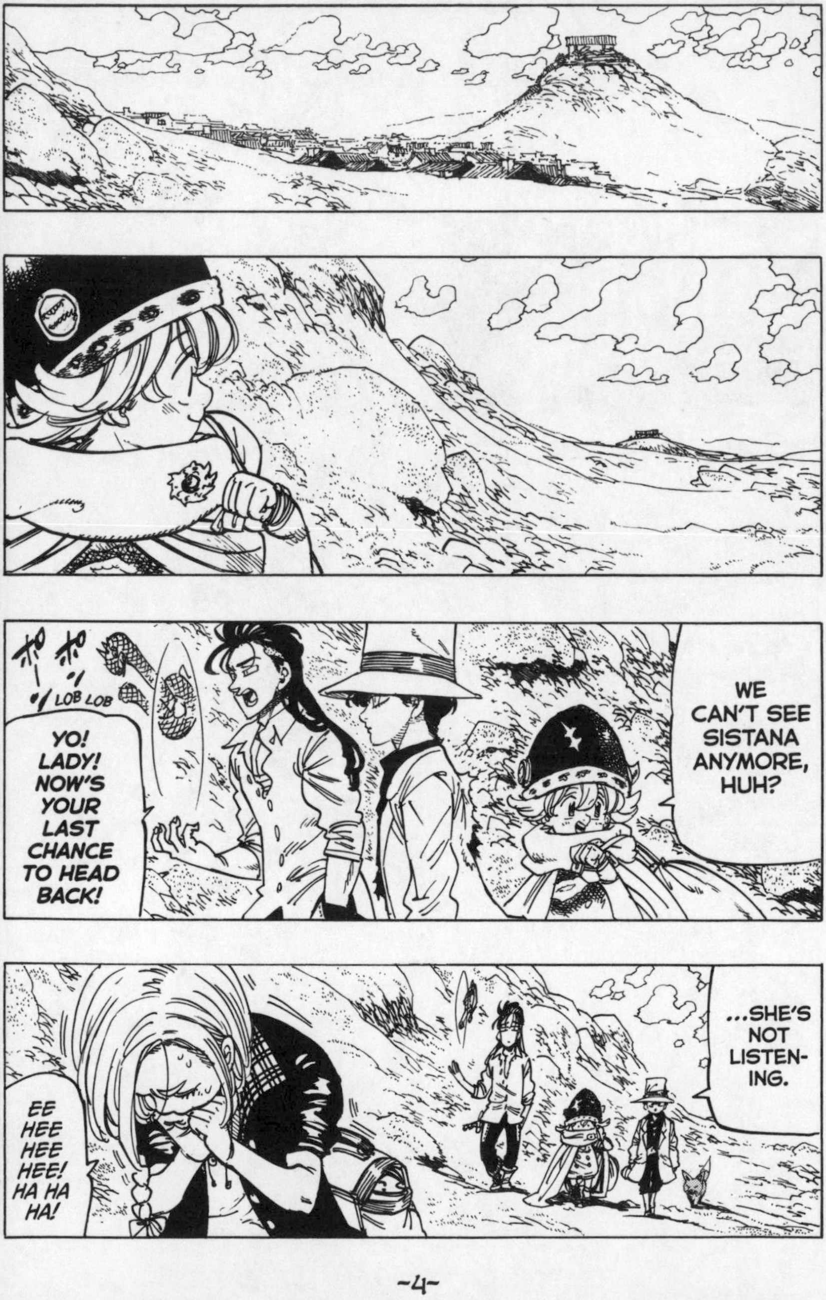
WE CAN'T SEE SISTANA ANYMORE, HUH?
LOB LOB
YO! LADY! NOW'S YOUR LAST CHANCE TO HEAD BACK!
...SHE'S NOT LISTEN-ING.
EE HEE HEE HEE! HA HA HA!

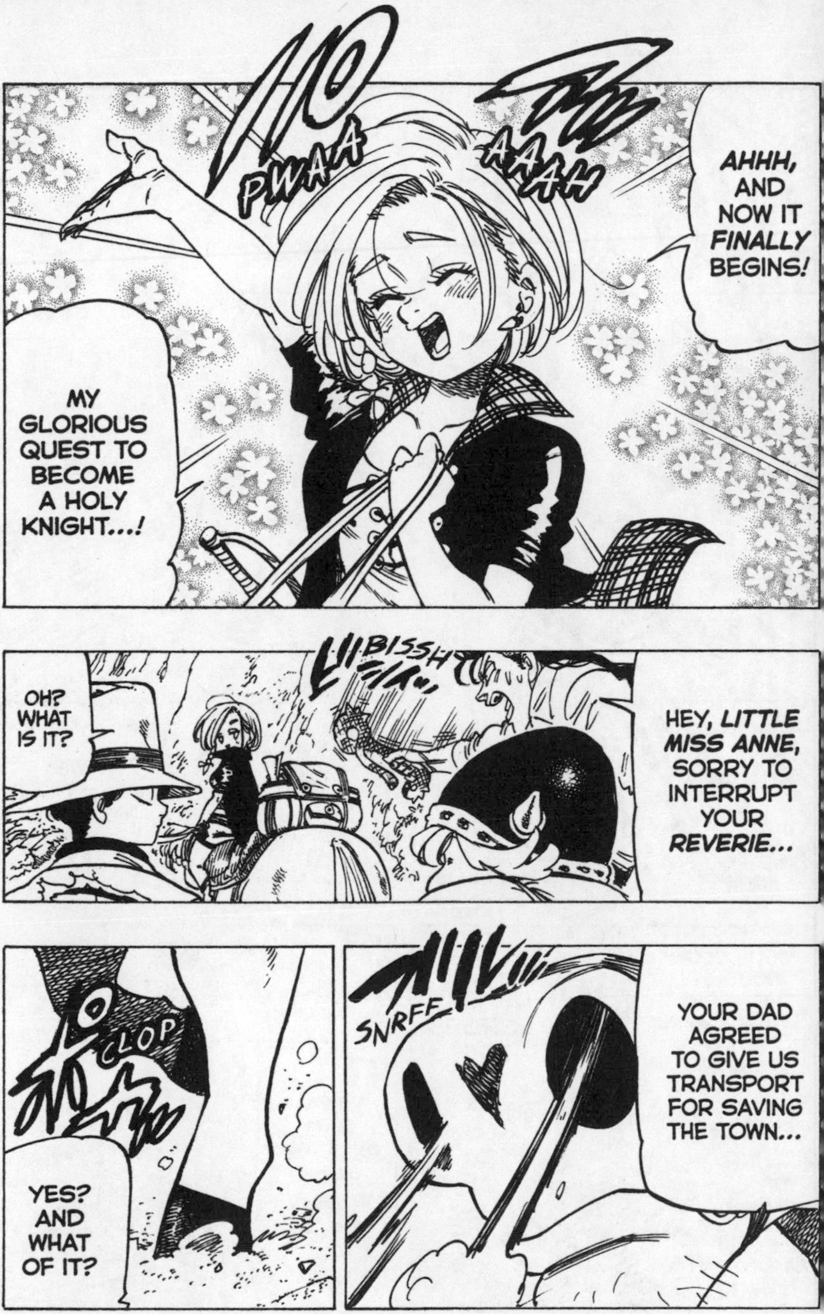
PWAAA
AAAH
AHHH, AND NOW IT *FINALLY* BEGINS!
MY GLORIOUS QUEST TO BECOME A HOLY KNIGHT...!
HEY, *LITTLE MISS ANNE*, SORRY TO INTERRUPT YOUR *REVERIE*...
BISSH
OH? WHAT IS IT?
SNRFF
YOUR DAD AGREED TO GIVE US TRANSPORT FOR SAVING THE TOWN...
CLOP
YES? AND WHAT OF IT?

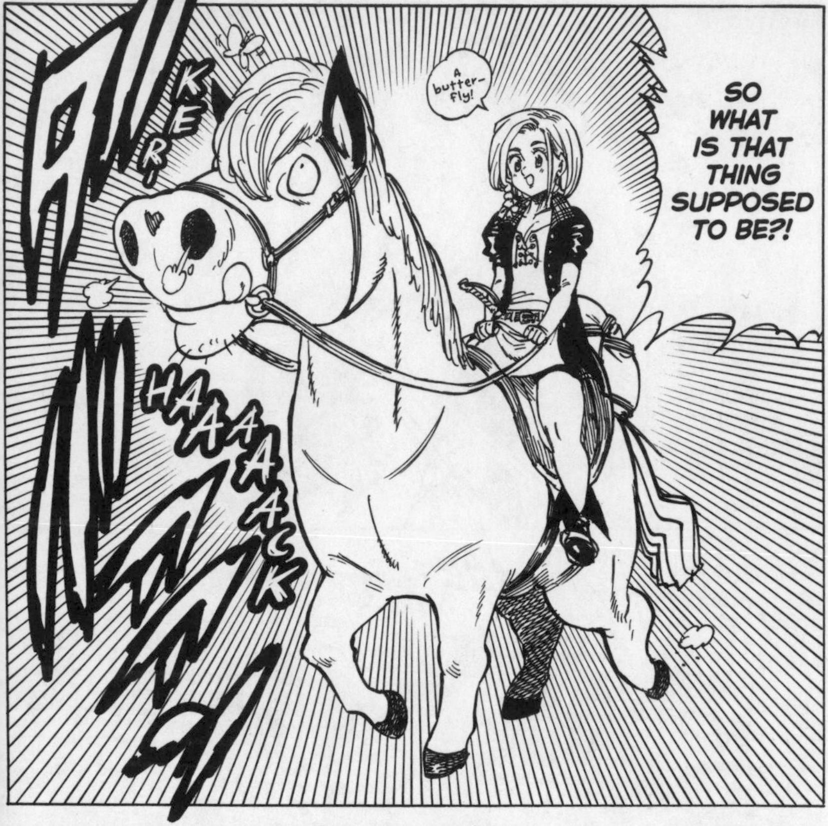
SO WHAT IS THAT THING SUPPOSED TO BE?!
A butter-fly!
KERI
HAAAAACK

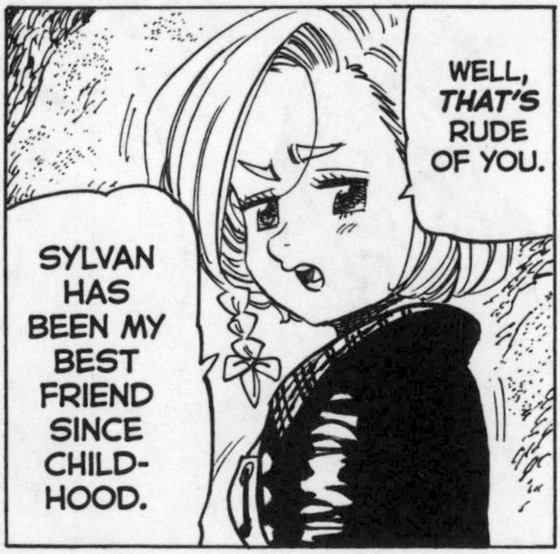
WELL, *THAT'S* RUDE OF YOU.
SYLVAN HAS BEEN MY BEST FRIEND SINCE CHILD-HOOD.

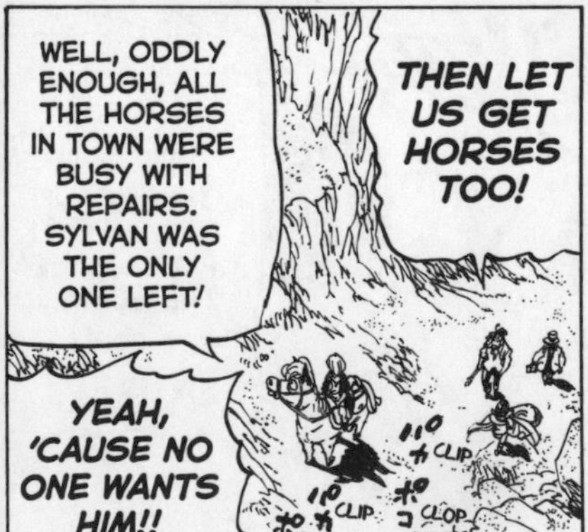
THEN LET US GET HORSES TOO!
WELL, ODDLY ENOUGH, ALL THE HORSES IN TOWN WERE BUSY WITH REPAIRS. SYLVAN WAS THE ONLY ONE LEFT!
YEAH, 'CAUSE NO ONE WANTS HIM!!
パカ CLIP
ポコ CLOP
パカ CLIP
ポコ CLOP

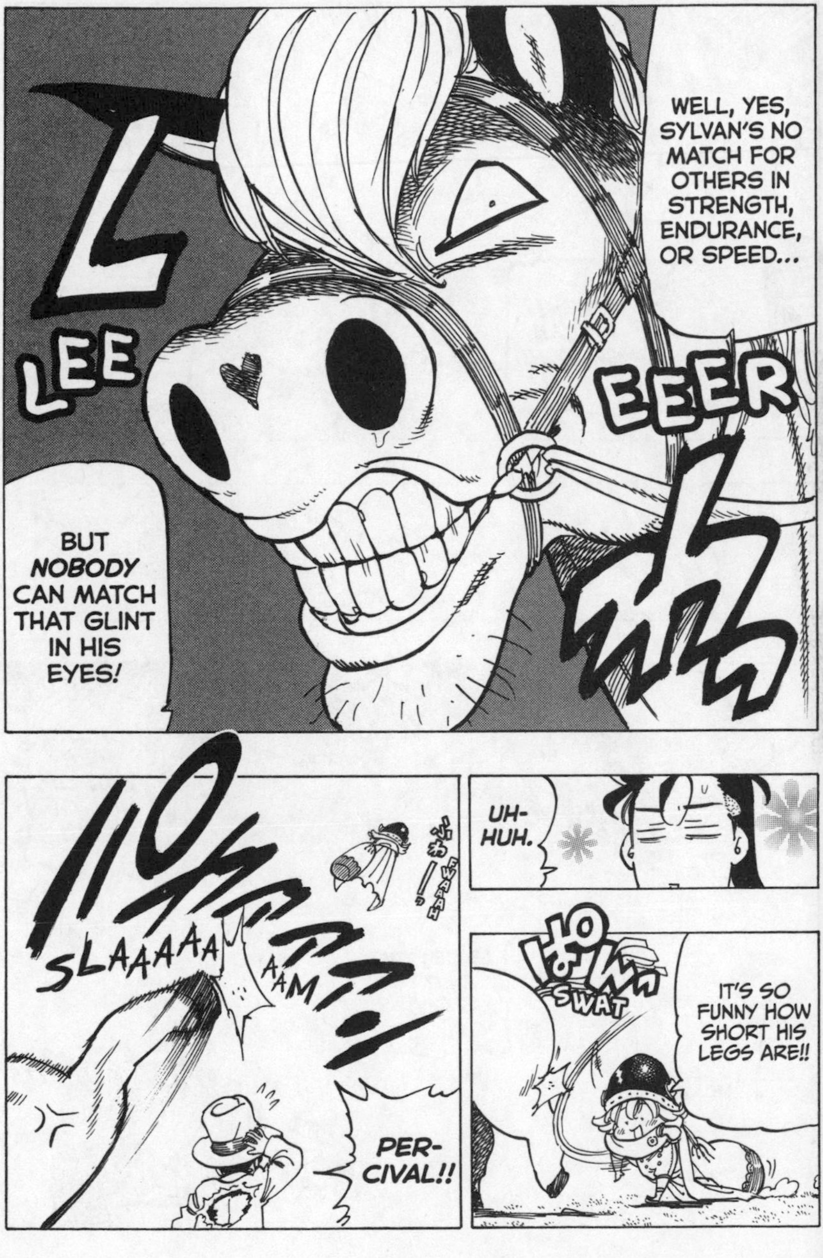
WELL, YES, SYLVAN'S NO MATCH FOR OTHERS IN STRENGTH, ENDURANCE, OR SPEED...
LEE
EEER
BUT NOBODY CAN MATCH THAT GLINT IN HIS EYES!
UH-HUH.
IT'S SO FUNNY HOW SHORT HIS LEGS ARE!!
SWAT
WAAAH
SLAAAAA
AAM
PER-CIVAL!!

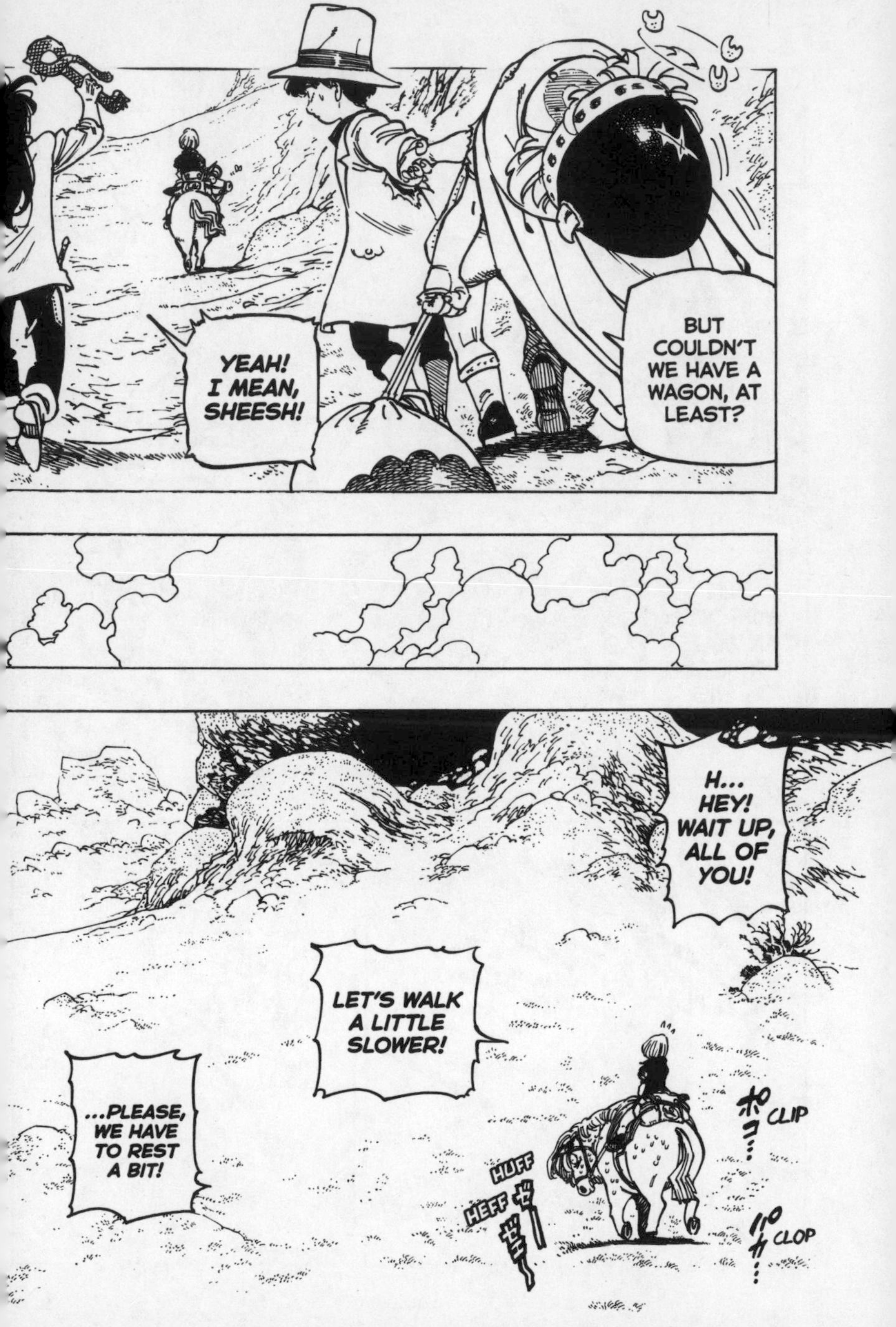
BUT COULDN'T WE HAVE A WAGON, AT LEAST?
YEAH! I MEAN, SHEESH!
H... HEY! WAIT UP, ALL OF YOU!
LET'S WALK A LITTLE SLOWER!
CLIP
CLOP
HUFF
HEFF
...PLEASE, WE HAVE TO REST A BIT!

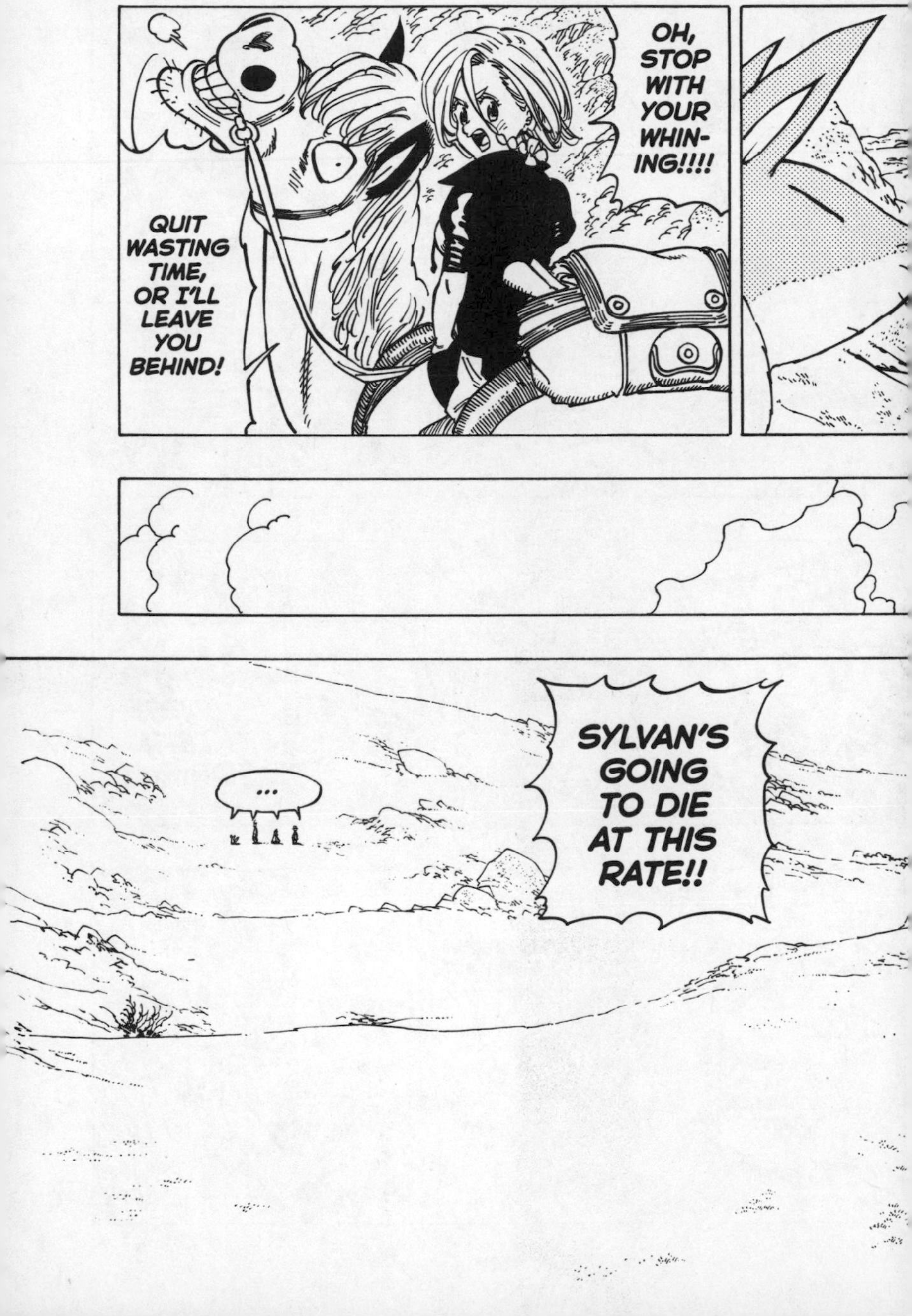
OH, STOP WITH YOUR WHINING!!!!
QUIT WASTING TIME, OR I'LL LEAVE YOU BEHIND!
SYLVAN'S GOING TO DIE AT THIS RATE!!
...

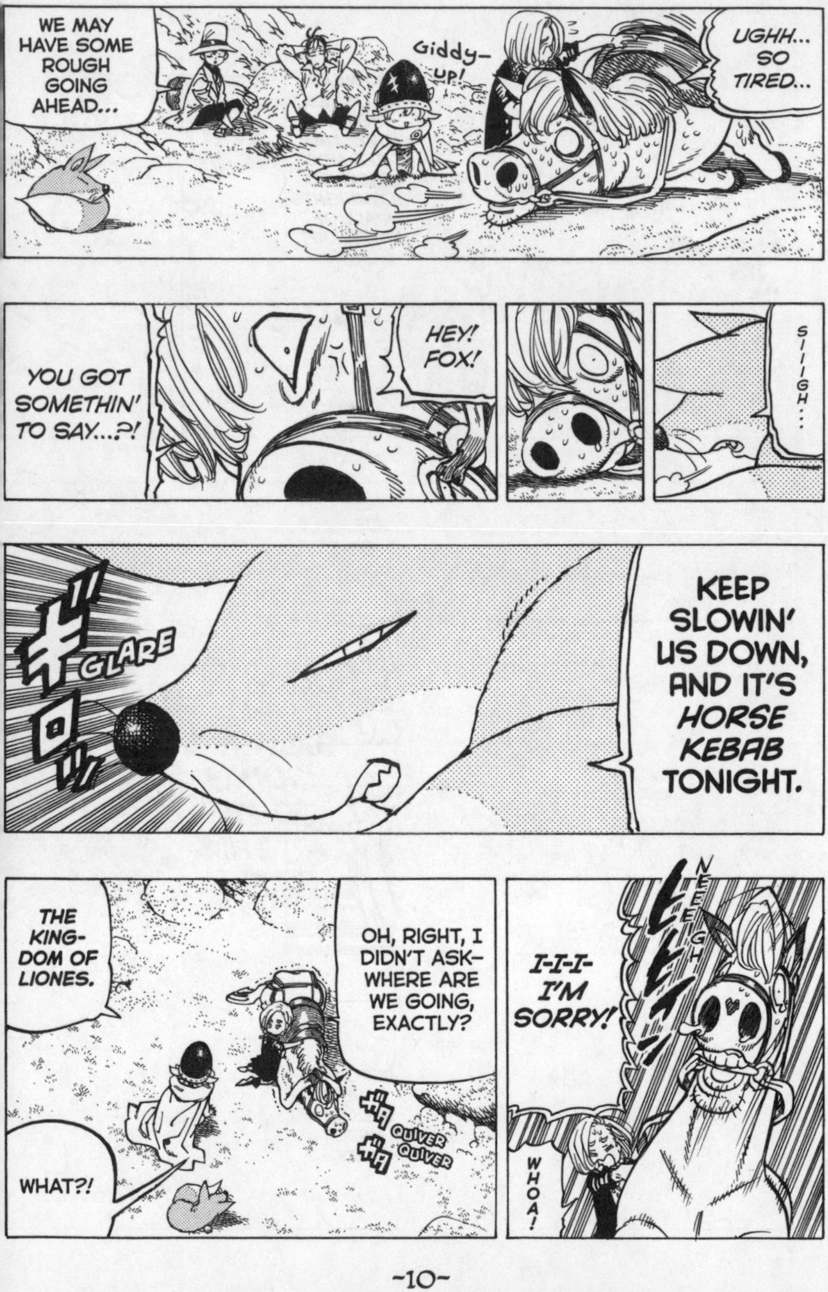

UGHH... SO TIRED...
Giddy-up!
WE MAY HAVE SOME ROUGH GOING AHEAD...
SIIIGH...
HEY! FOX!
YOU GOT SOMETHIN' TO SAY...?!
KEEP SLOWIN' US DOWN, AND IT'S HORSE KEBAB TONIGHT.
GLARE
NEEEEIGH
I-I-I-I'M SORRY!
WHOA!
OH, RIGHT, I DIDN'T ASK—WHERE ARE WE GOING, EXACTLY?
THE KING-DOM OF LIONES.
QUIVER QUIVER
WHAT?!

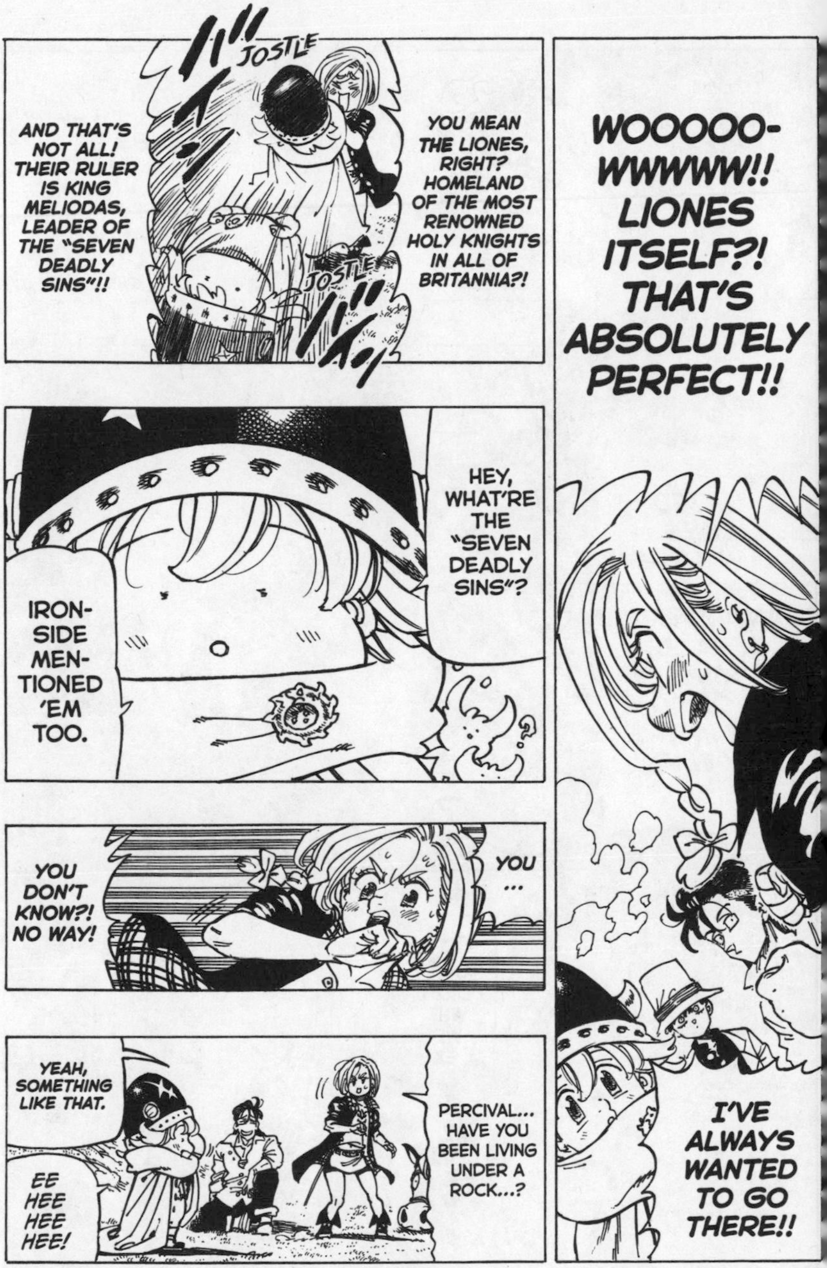
WOOOOO-WWWWW!! LIONES ITSELF?! THAT'S ABSOLUTELY PERFECT!!
I'VE ALWAYS WANTED TO GO THERE!!
JOSTLE
YOU MEAN THE LIONES, RIGHT? HOMELAND OF THE MOST RENOWNED HOLY KNIGHTS IN ALL OF BRITANNIA?!
JOSTLE
AND THAT'S NOT ALL! THEIR RULER IS KING MELIODAS, LEADER OF THE "SEVEN DEADLY SINS"!!
HEY, WHAT'RE THE "SEVEN DEADLY SINS"?
IRON-SIDE MEN-TIONED 'EM TOO.
YOU ...
YOU DON'T KNOW?! NO WAY!
PERCIVAL... HAVE YOU BEEN LIVING UNDER A ROCK...?
YEAH, SOMETHING LIKE THAT.
EE HEE HEE HEE!

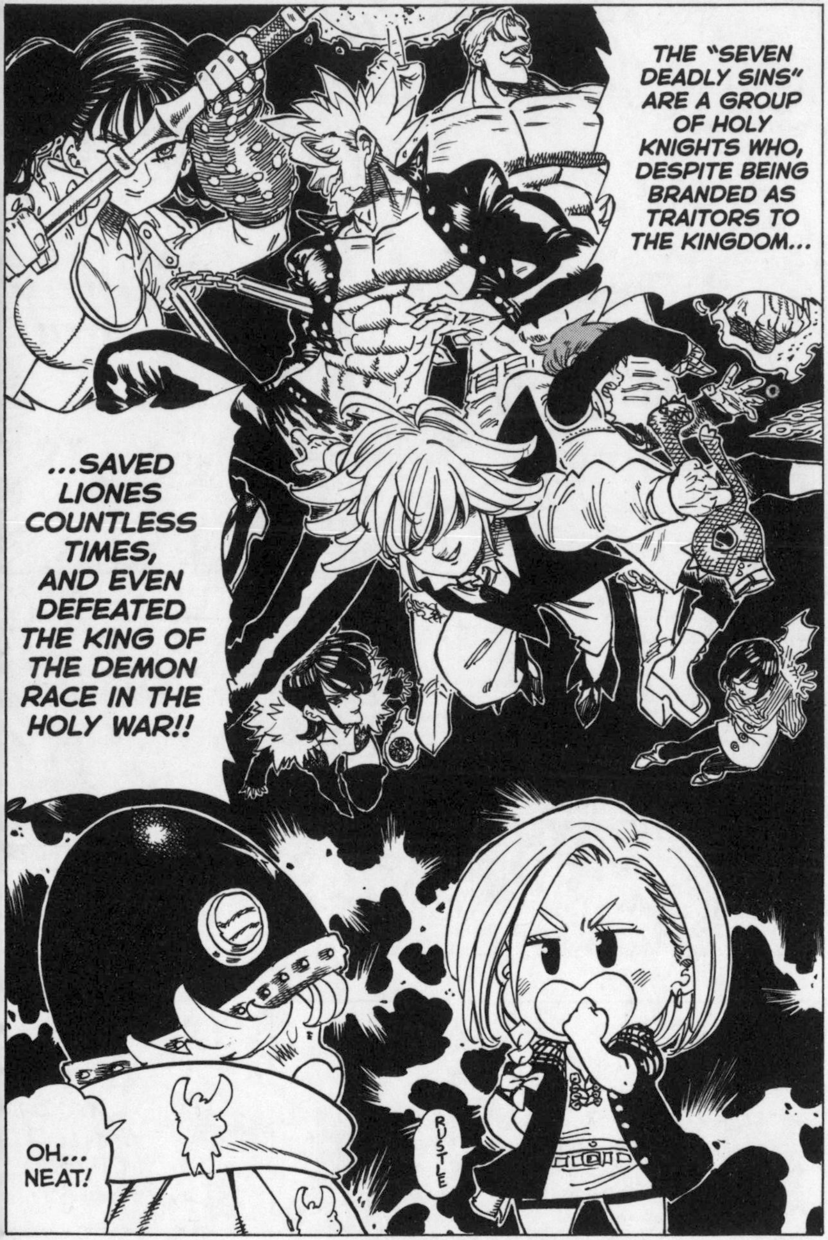
THE "SEVEN DEADLY SINS" ARE A GROUP OF HOLY KNIGHTS WHO, DESPITE BEING BRANDED AS TRAITORS TO THE KINGDOM...
...SAVED LIONES COUNTLESS TIMES, AND EVEN DEFEATED THE KING OF THE DEMON RACE IN THE HOLY WAR!!
RUSTLE
OH... NEAT!

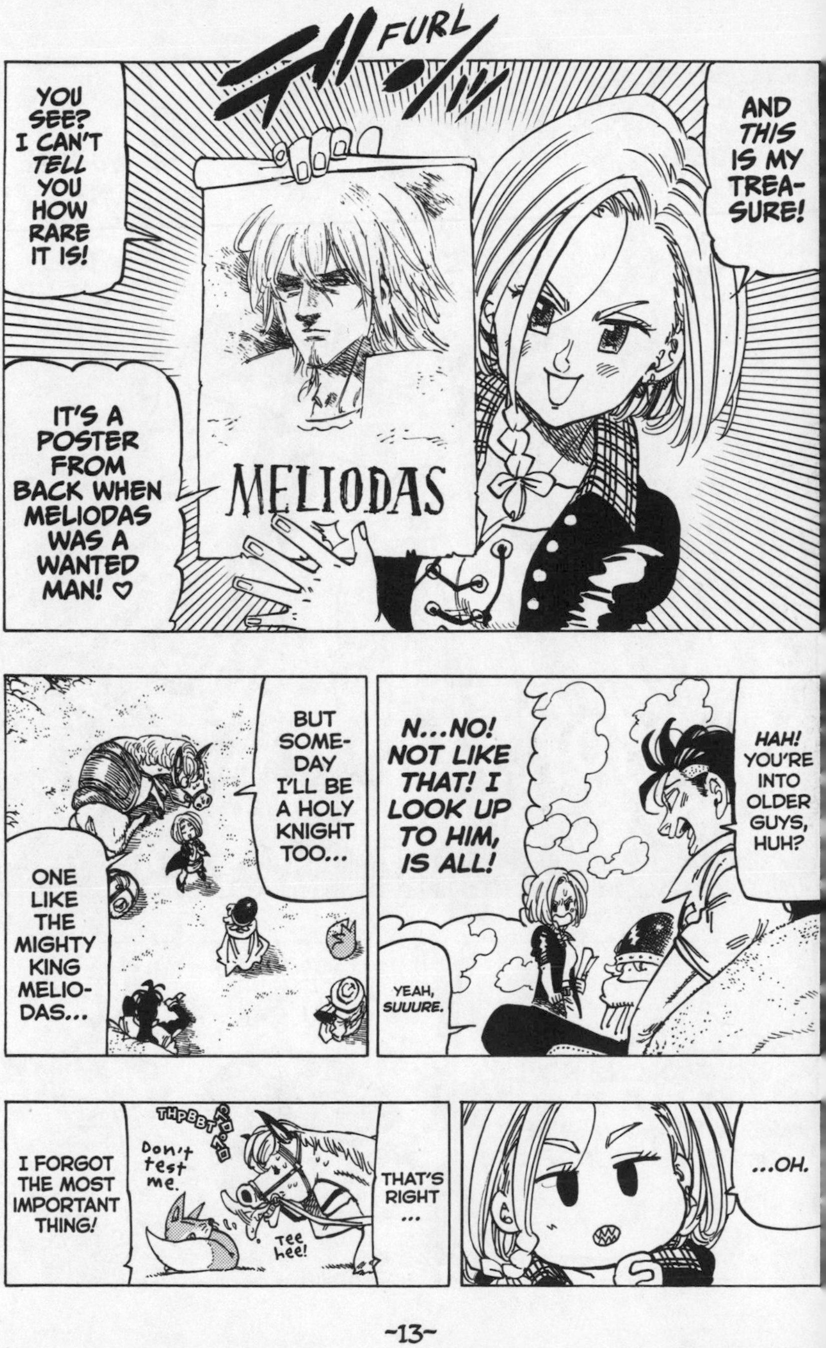
FURL
AND THIS IS MY TREASURE!
YOU SEE? I CAN'T TELL YOU HOW RARE IT IS!
MELIODAS
IT'S A POSTER FROM BACK WHEN MELIODAS WAS A WANTED MAN! ♡
HAH! YOU'RE INTO OLDER GUYS, HUH?
N...NO! NOT LIKE THAT! I LOOK UP TO HIM, IS ALL!
YEAH, SUUURE.
BUT SOME-DAY I'LL BE A HOLY KNIGHT TOO...
ONE LIKE THE MIGHTY KING MELIO-DAS...
...OH.
THAT'S RIGHT ...
THPBBT
Don't test me.
Tee hee!
I FORGOT THE MOST IMPORTANT THING!

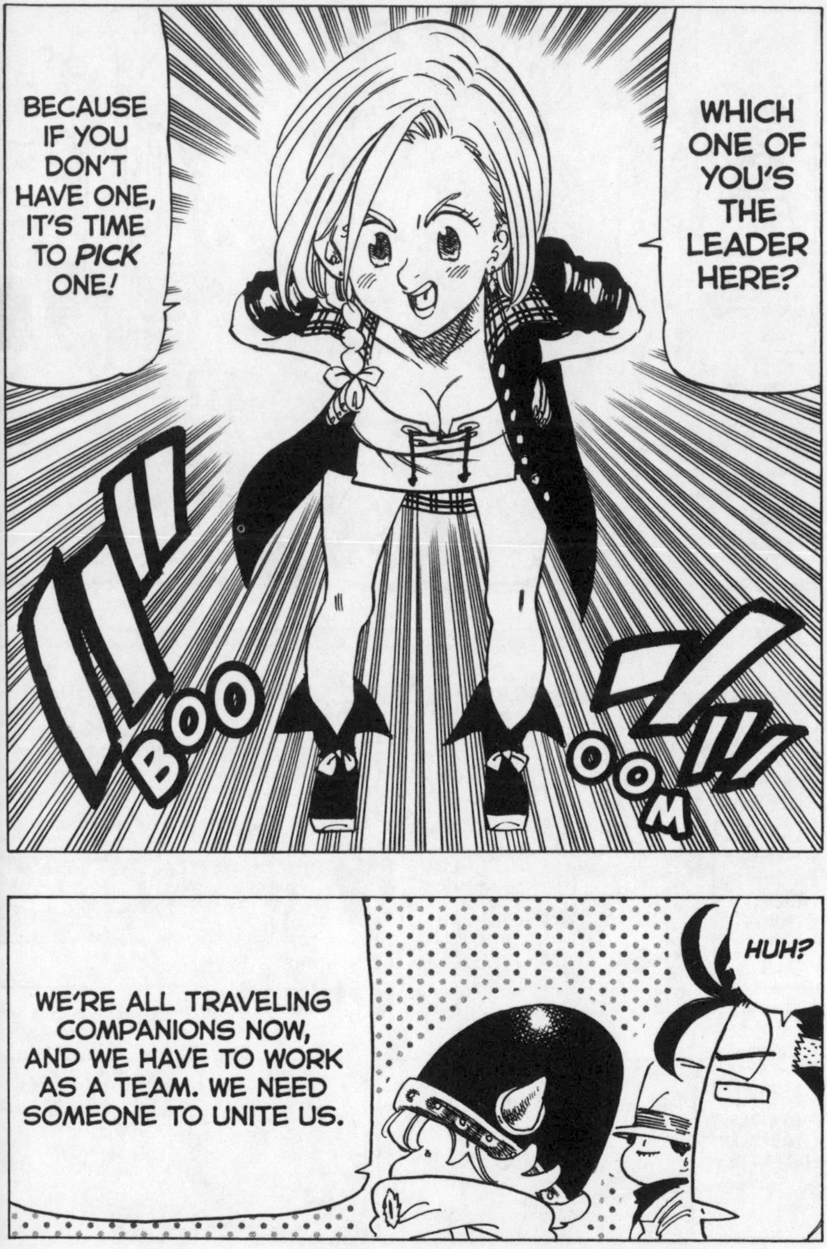
WHICH ONE OF YOU'S THE LEADER HERE?
BECAUSE IF YOU DON'T HAVE ONE, IT'S TIME TO *PICK* ONE!
BOOOOM
HUH?
WE'RE ALL TRAVELING COMPANIONS NOW, AND WE HAVE TO WORK AS A TEAM. WE NEED SOMEONE TO UNITE US.

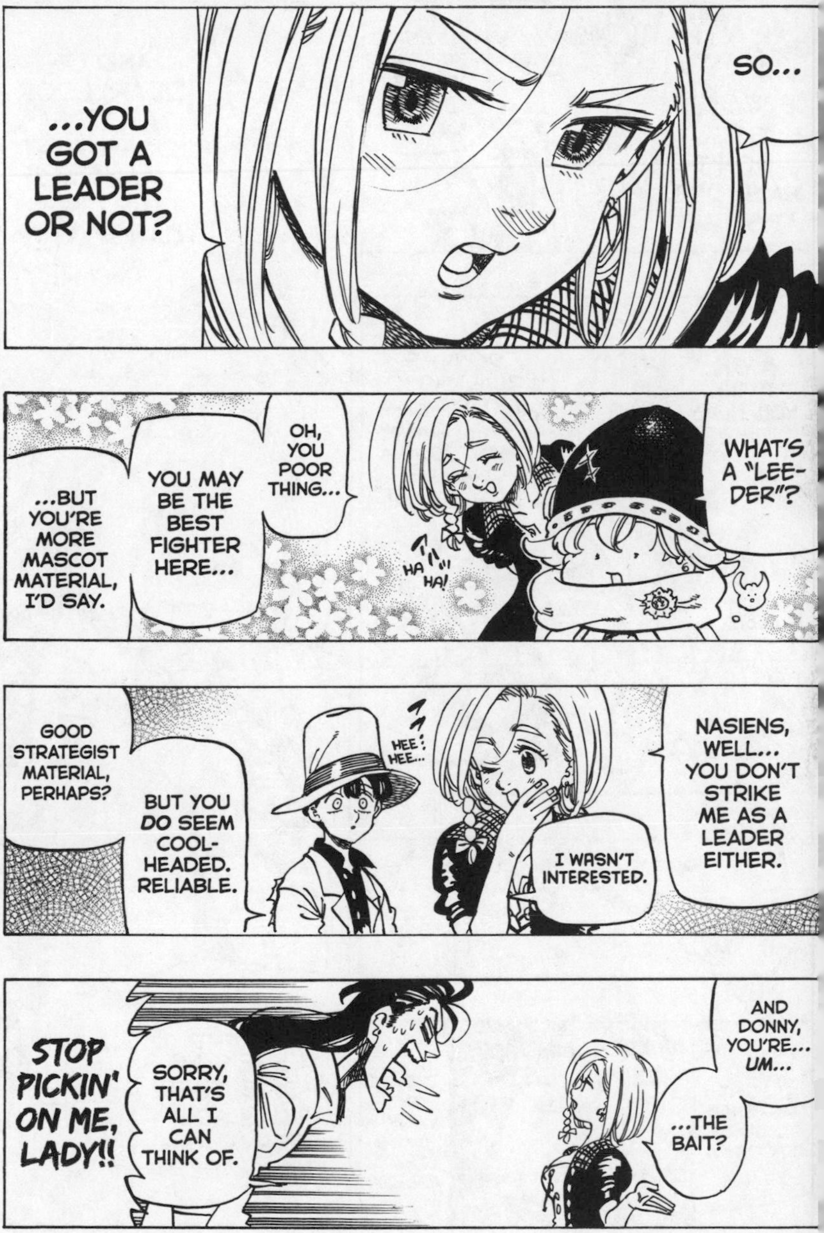
SO...
...YOU GOT A LEADER OR NOT?
WHAT'S A "LEE-DER"?
HA HA!
OH, YOU POOR THING...
YOU MAY BE THE BEST FIGHTER HERE...
...BUT YOU'RE MORE MASCOT MATERIAL, I'D SAY.
NASIENS, WELL... YOU DON'T STRIKE ME AS A LEADER EITHER.
I WASN'T INTERESTED.
HEE HEE...
BUT YOU *DO* SEEM COOL-HEADED. RELIABLE.
GOOD STRATEGIST MATERIAL, PERHAPS?
AND DONNY, YOU'RE... *UM...*
...THE BAIT?
SORRY, THAT'S ALL I CAN THINK OF.
STOP PICKIN' ON ME, LADY!!

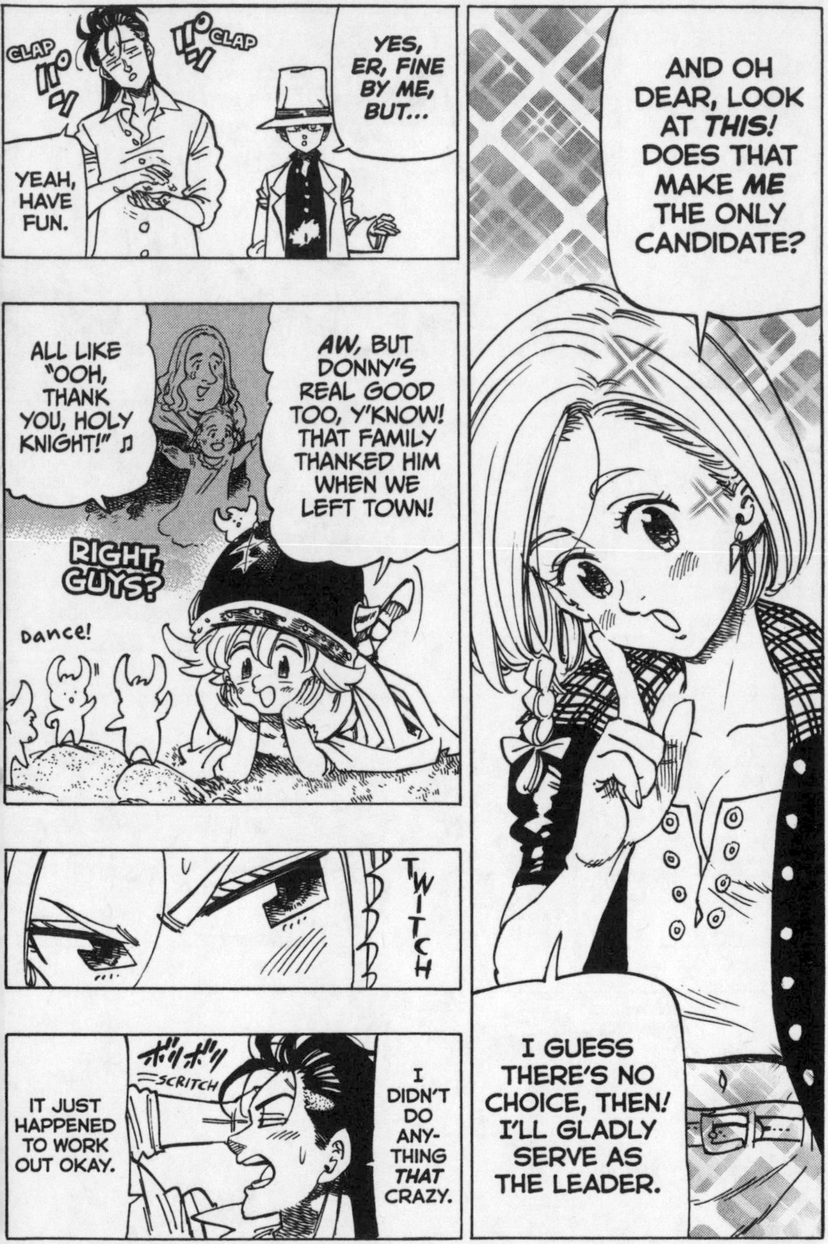
AND OH DEAR, LOOK AT *THIS!* DOES THAT MAKE *ME* THE ONLY CANDIDATE?
I GUESS THERE'S NO CHOICE, THEN! I'LL GLADLY SERVE AS THE LEADER.
YES, ER, FINE BY ME, BUT...
CLAP
CLAP
YEAH, HAVE FUN.
AW, BUT DONNY'S REAL GOOD TOO, Y'KNOW! THAT FAMILY THANKED HIM WHEN WE LEFT TOWN!
ALL LIKE "OOH, THANK YOU, HOLY KNIGHT!" ♫
RIGHT, GUYS?
Dance!
TWITCH
I DIDN'T DO ANY-THING *THAT* CRAZY.
SCRITCH
IT JUST HAPPENED TO WORK OUT OKAY.

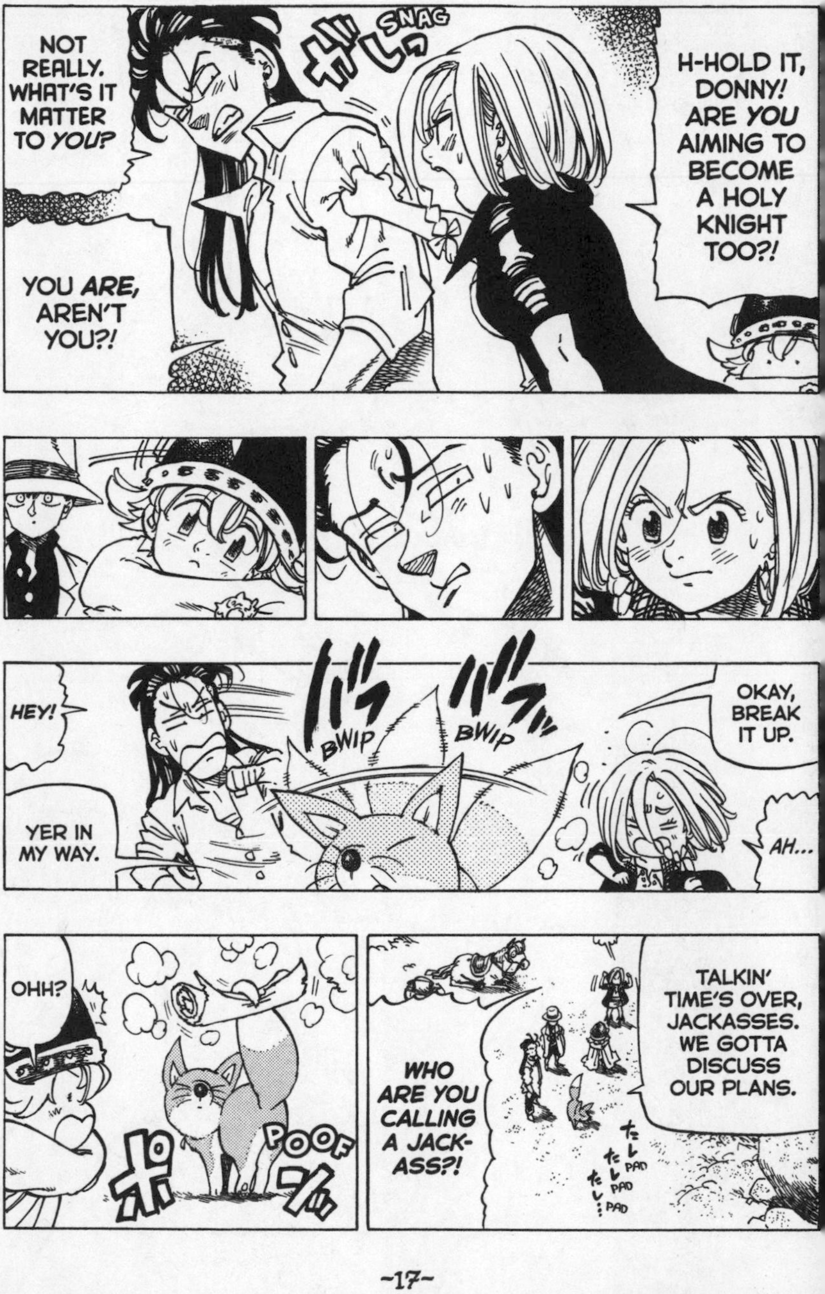

H-HOLD IT, DONNY! ARE *YOU* AIMING TO BECOME A HOLY KNIGHT TOO?!
SNAG
NOT REALLY. WHAT'S IT MATTER TO *YOU*?
YOU *ARE*, AREN'T YOU?!
OKAY, BREAK IT UP.
BWIP
BWIP
HEY!
AH...
YER IN MY WAY.
TALKIN' TIME'S OVER, JACKASSES. WE GOTTA DISCUSS OUR PLANS.
WHO ARE YOU CALLING A JACK-ASS?!
PAD
PAD
PAD
POOF
OHH?

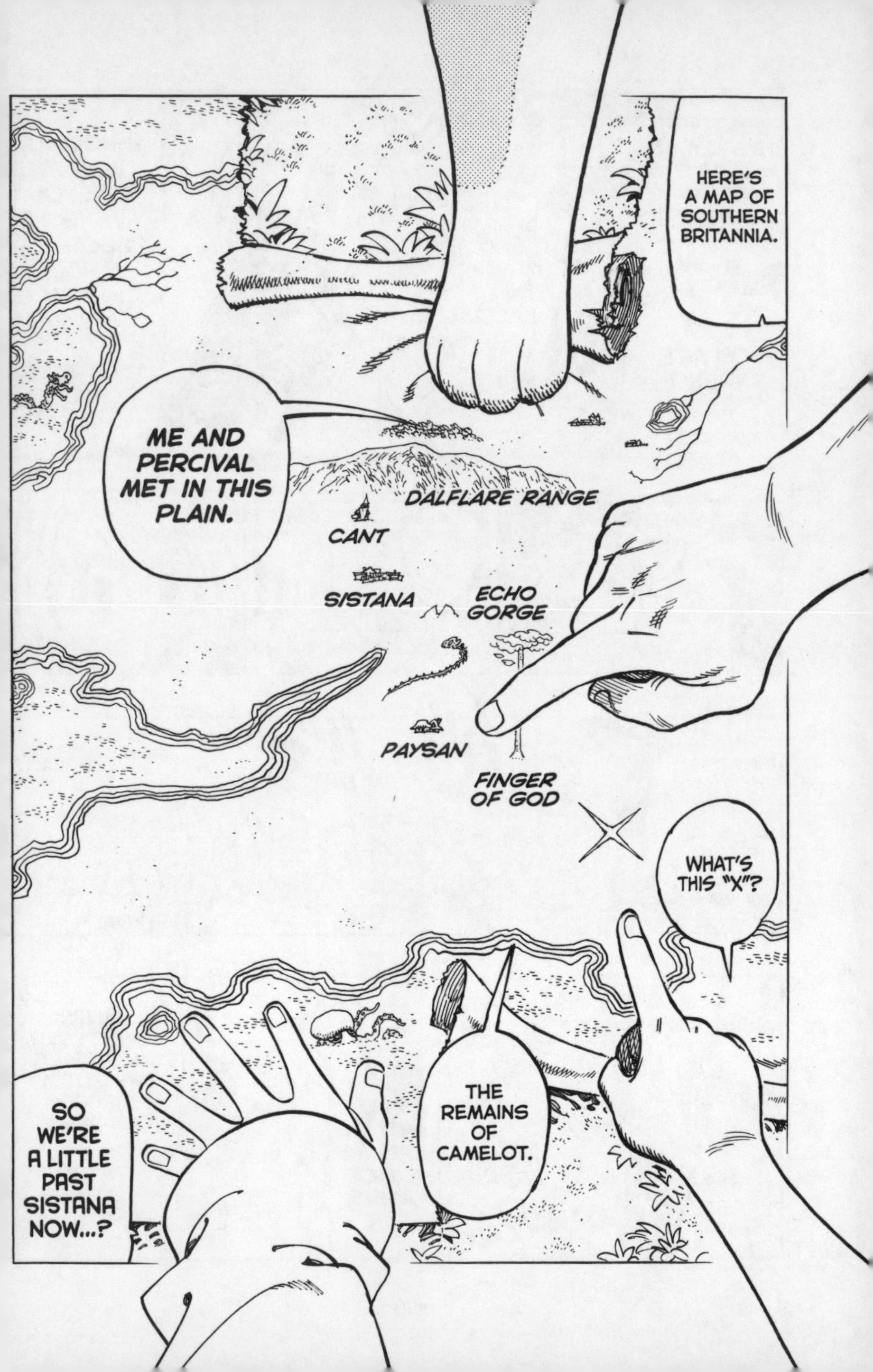
HERE'S A MAP OF SOUTHERN BRITANNIA.
ME AND PERCIVAL MET IN THIS PLAIN.
DALFLARE RANGE
CANT
SISTANA
ECHO GORGE
PAYSAN
FINGER OF GOD
WHAT'S THIS "X"?
THE REMAINS OF CAMELOT.
SO WE'RE A LITTLE PAST SISTANA NOW...?

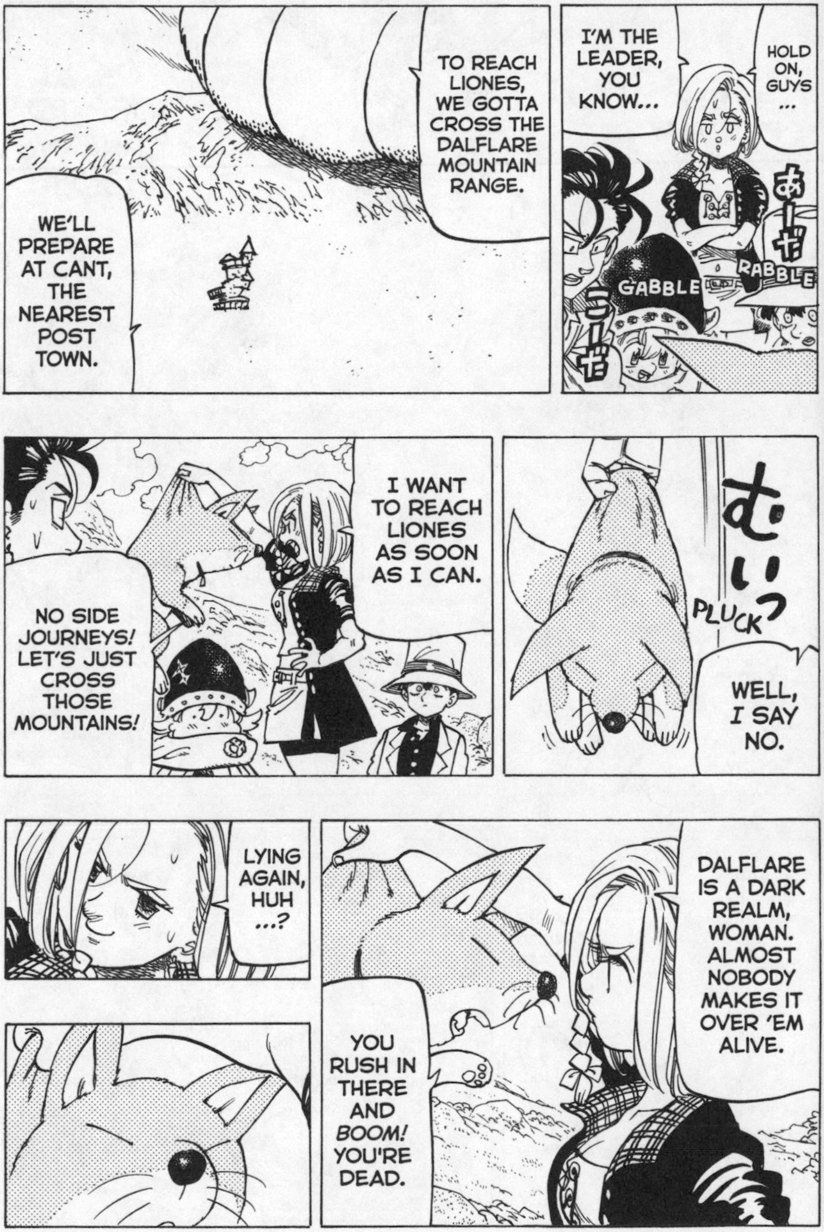
HOLD ON, GUYS ...
I'M THE LEADER, YOU KNOW...
RABBLE
GABBLE
TO REACH LIONES, WE GOTTA CROSS THE DALFLARE MOUNTAIN RANGE.
WE'LL PREPARE AT CANT, THE NEAREST POST TOWN.
むいっ
PLUCK
WELL, I SAY NO.
I WANT TO REACH LIONES AS SOON AS I CAN.
NO SIDE JOURNEYS! LET'S JUST CROSS THOSE MOUNTAINS!
DALFLARE IS A DARK REALM, WOMAN. ALMOST NOBODY MAKES IT OVER 'EM ALIVE.
YOU RUSH IN THERE AND *BOOM!* YOU'RE DEAD.
LYING AGAIN, HUH ...?

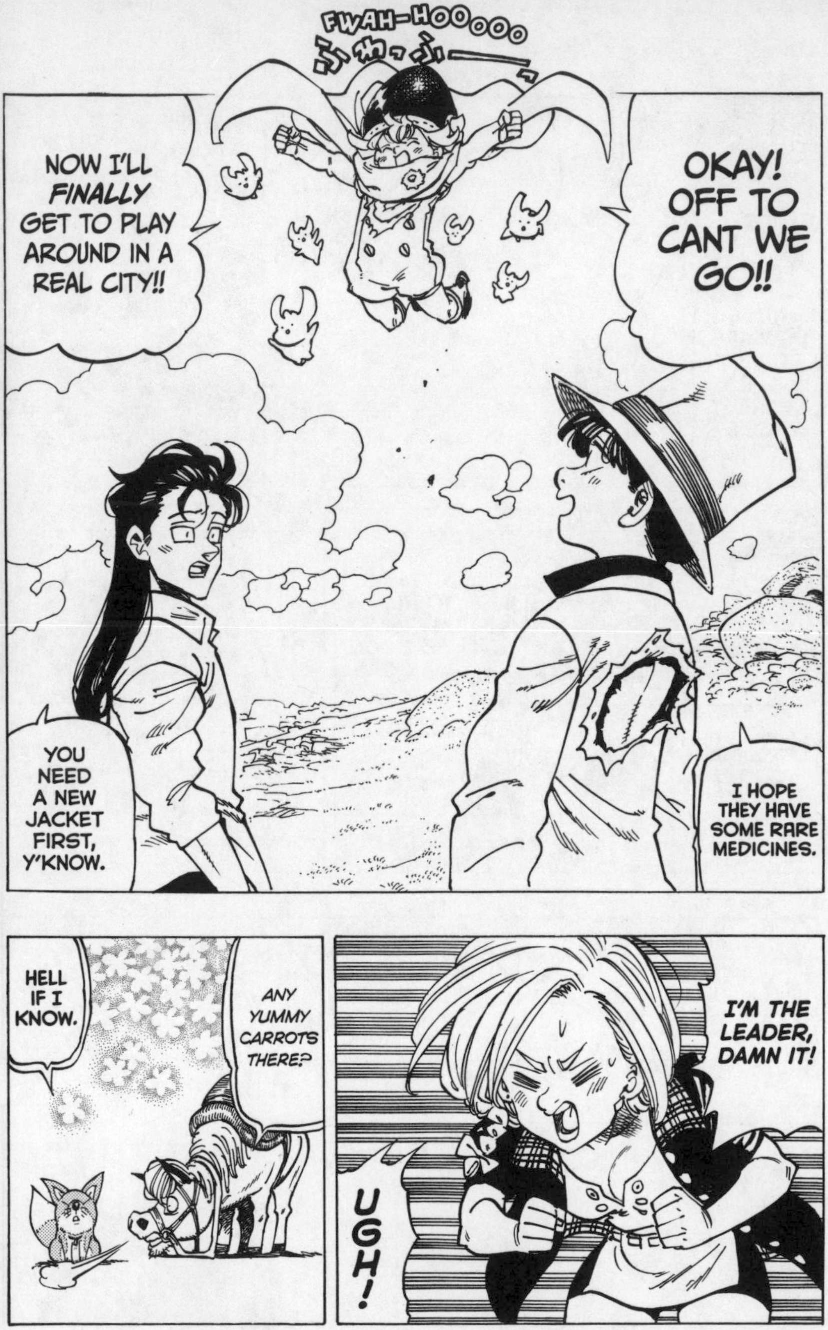
OKAY! OFF TO CANT WE GO!!
FWAH-HOOOOOO
NOW I'LL FINALLY GET TO PLAY AROUND IN A REAL CITY!!
I HOPE THEY HAVE SOME RARE MEDICINES.
YOU NEED A NEW JACKET FIRST, Y'KNOW.
I'M THE LEADER, DAMN IT!
UGH!
ANY YUMMY CARROTS THERE?
HELL IF I KNOW.

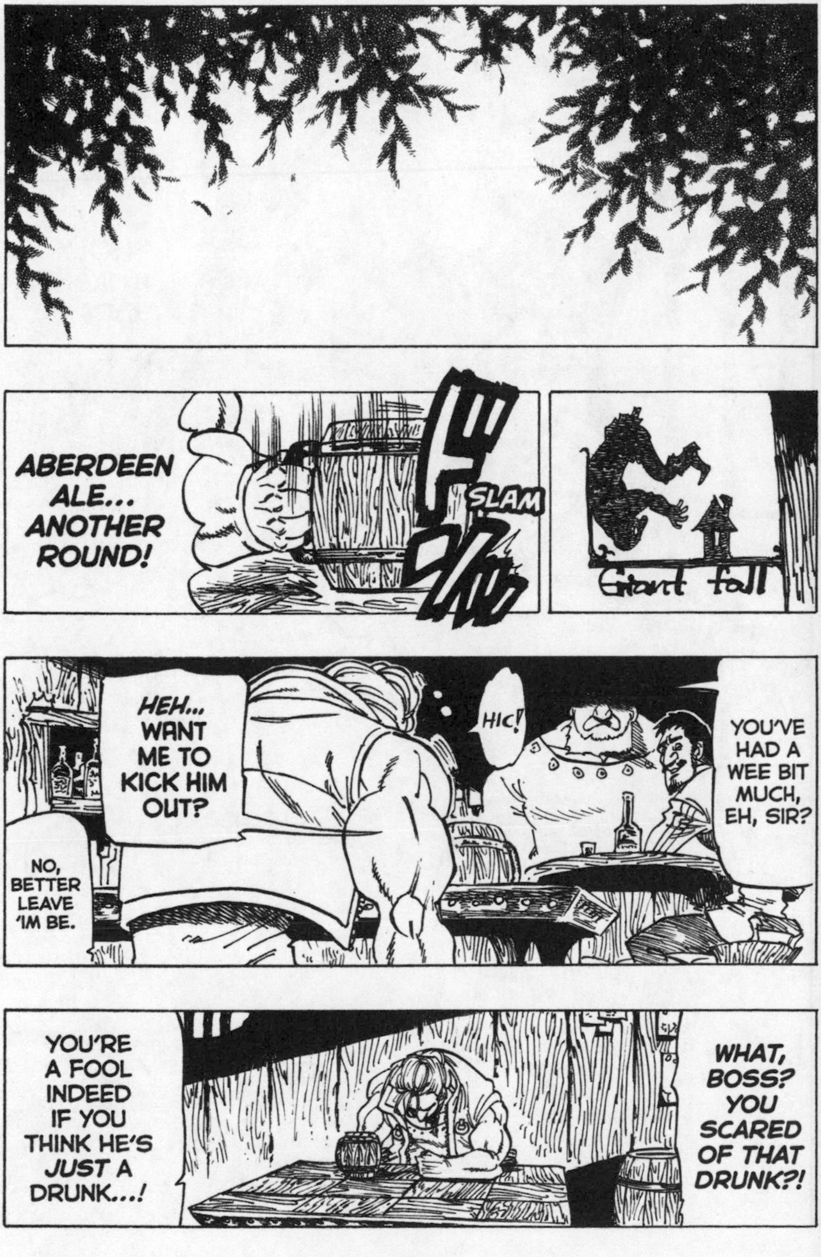
Giant fall
SLAM
ABERDEEN ALE... ANOTHER ROUND!
YOU'VE HAD A WEE BIT MUCH, EH, SIR?
HIC!
HEH... WANT ME TO KICK HIM OUT?
NO, BETTER LEAVE 'IM BE.
WHAT, BOSS? YOU SCARED OF THAT DRUNK?!
YOU'RE A FOOL INDEED IF YOU THINK HE'S *JUST* A DRUNK...!

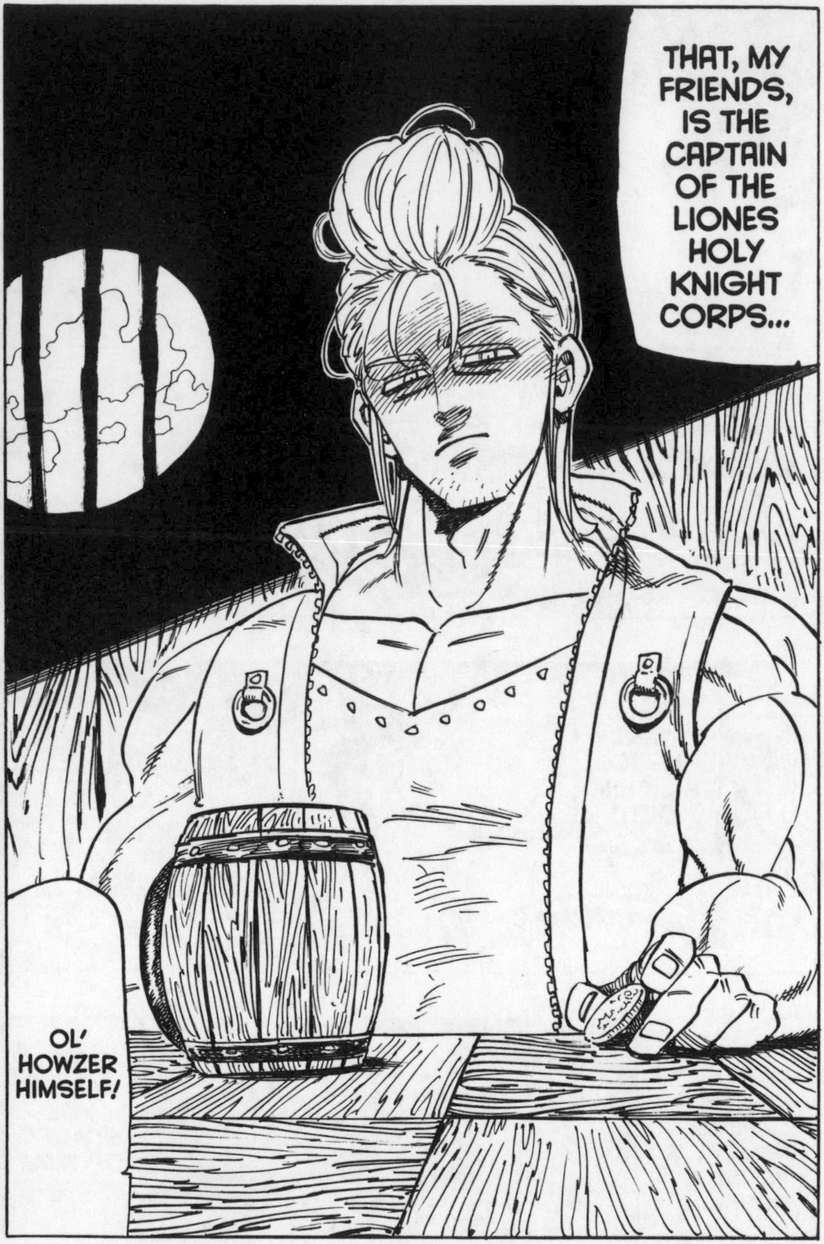
THAT, MY FRIENDS, IS THE CAPTAIN OF THE LIONES HOLY KNIGHT CORPS...
OL' HOWZER HIMSELF!

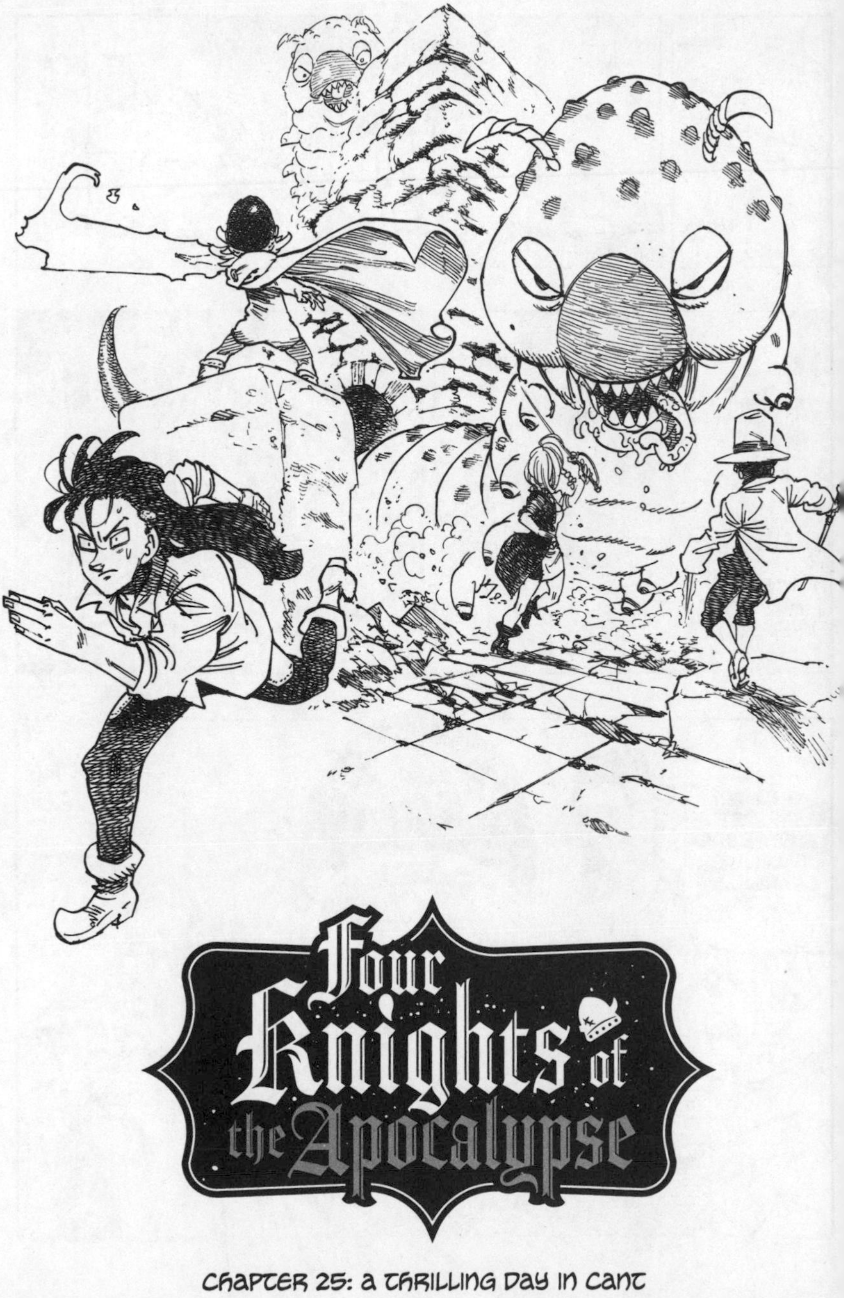

Four Knights of the Apocalypse

Chapter 25: A Thrilling Day in Cant

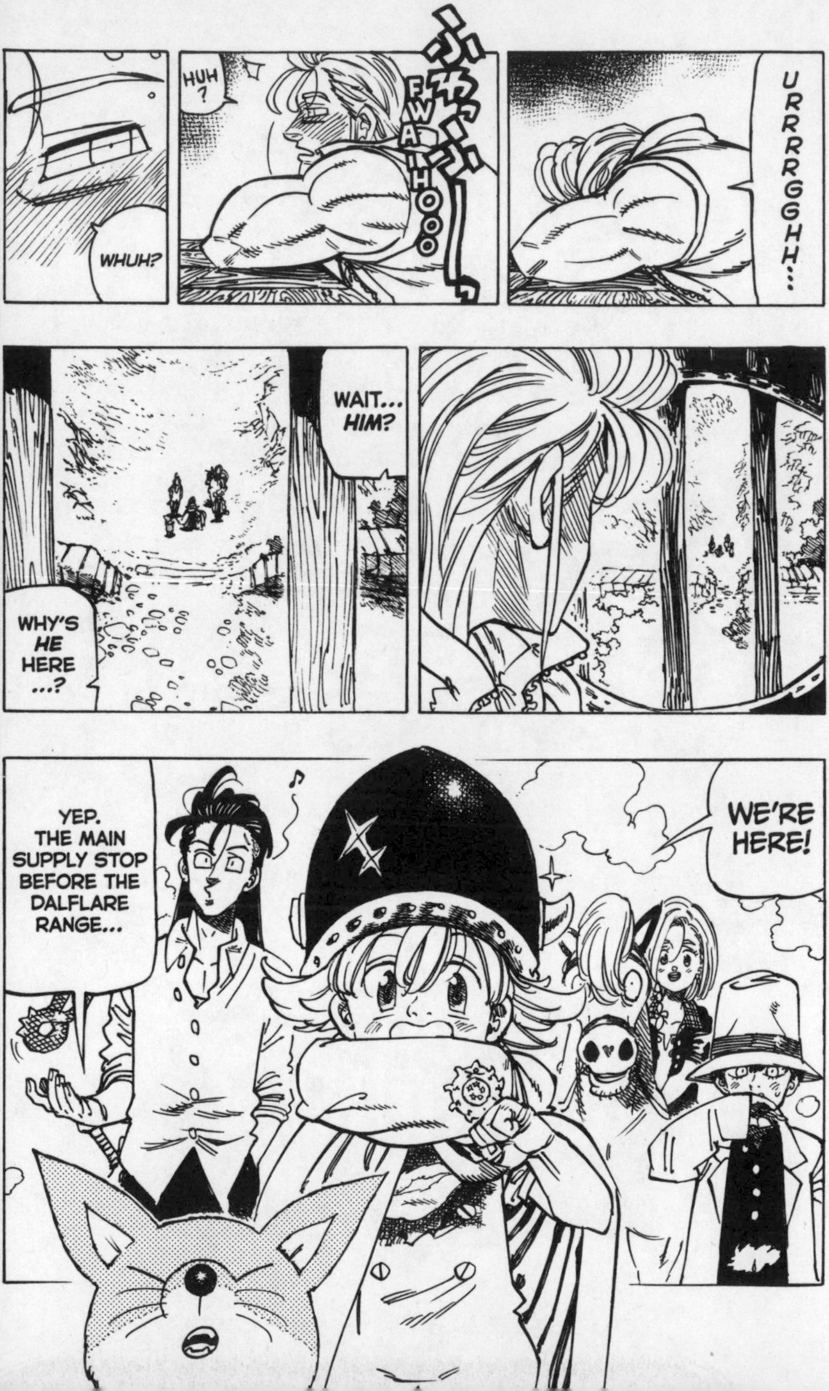
URRRRGGHH...
HUH?
FWAHOOO
WHUH?
WAIT... HIM?
WHY'S HE HERE ...?
WE'RE HERE!
YEP. THE MAIN SUPPLY STOP BEFORE THE DALFLARE RANGE...

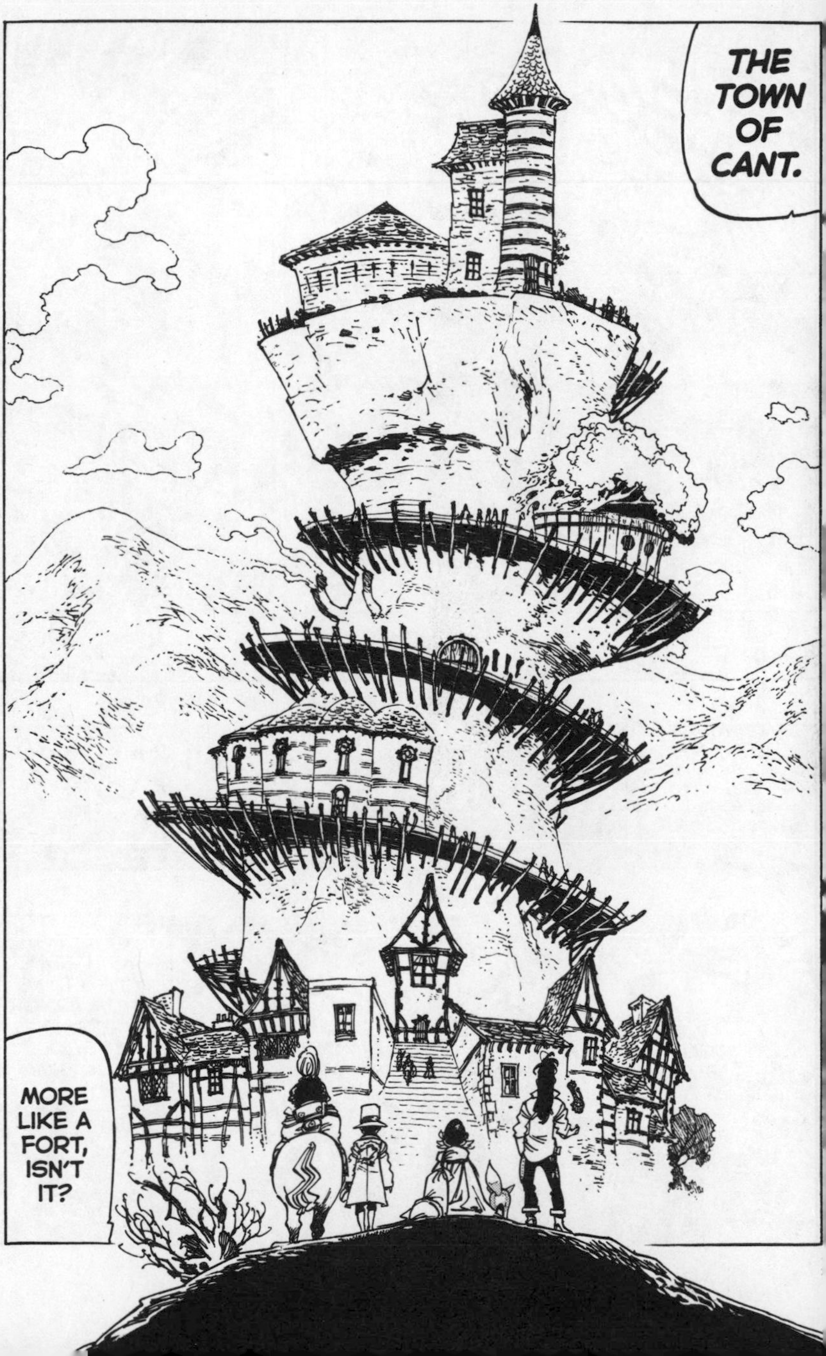
THE TOWN OF CANT.
MORE LIKE A FORT, ISN'T IT?

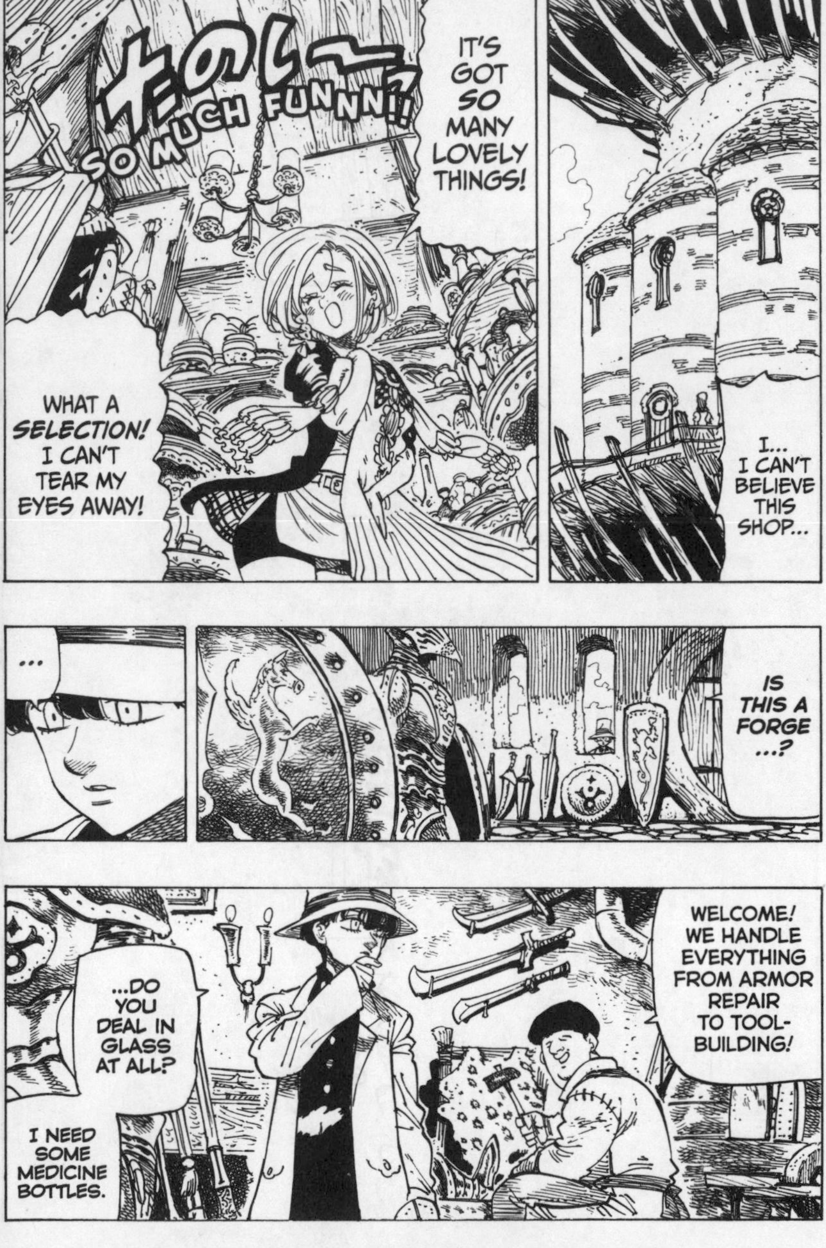
I... I CAN'T BELIEVE THIS SHOP...
たのし～
SO MUCH FUNNN!!
IT'S GOT SO MANY LOVELY THINGS!
WHAT A SELECTION! I CAN'T TEAR MY EYES AWAY!
IS THIS A FORGE ...?
...
WELCOME! WE HANDLE EVERYTHING FROM ARMOR REPAIR TO TOOL-BUILDING!
...DO YOU DEAL IN GLASS AT ALL?
I NEED SOME MEDICINE BOTTLES.

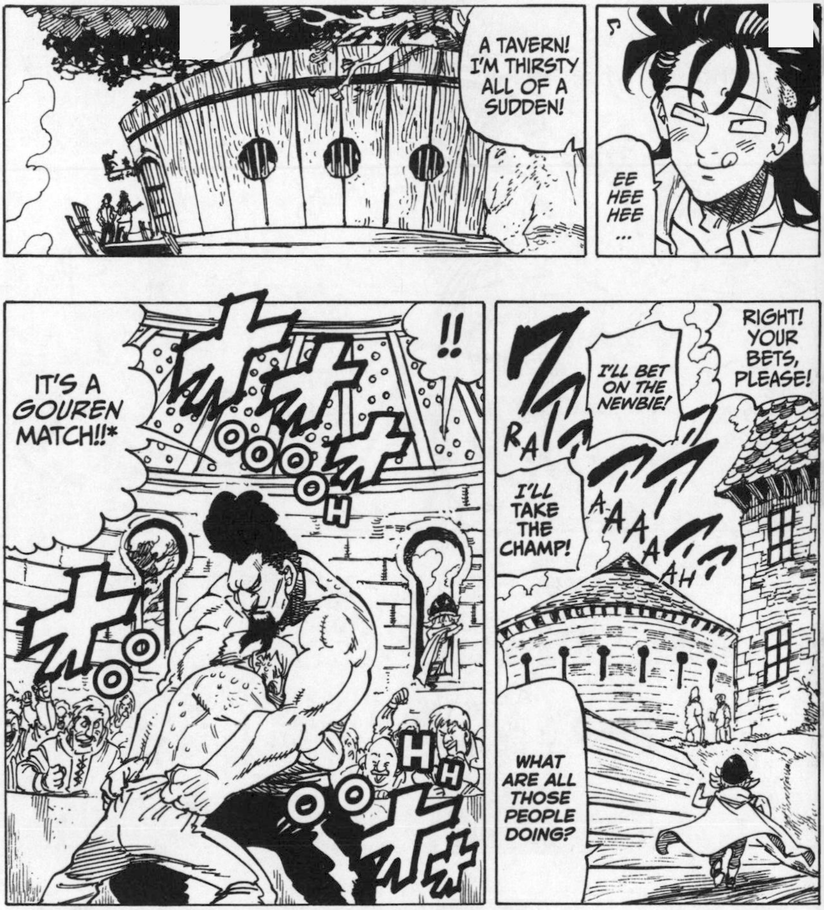
EE HEE HEE ...
A TAVERN! I'M THIRSTY ALL OF A SUDDEN!
RIGHT! YOUR BETS, PLEASE!
I'LL BET ON THE NEWBIE!
I'LL TAKE THE CHAMP!
RAAAAAAAH
WHAT ARE ALL THOSE PEOPLE DOING?
!!
IT'S A GOUREN MATCH!!*
OOOOOH
OOOHH

* A FORM OF TOPLESS WRESTLING ORIGINATING IN CELTIC LANDS.

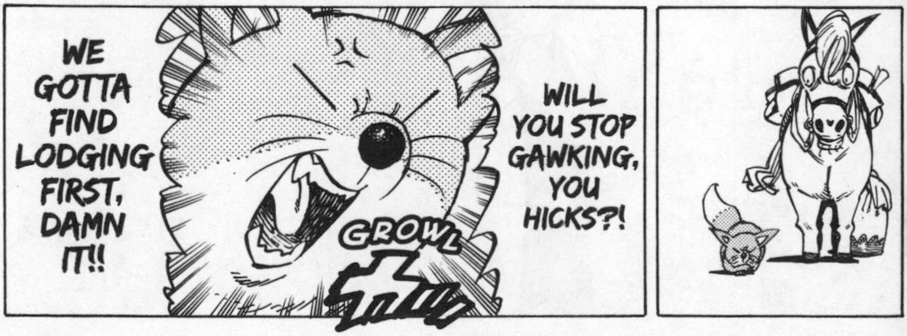
WILL YOU STOP GAWKING, YOU HICKS?!
WE GOTTA FIND LODGING FIRST, DAMN IT!!
GROWL

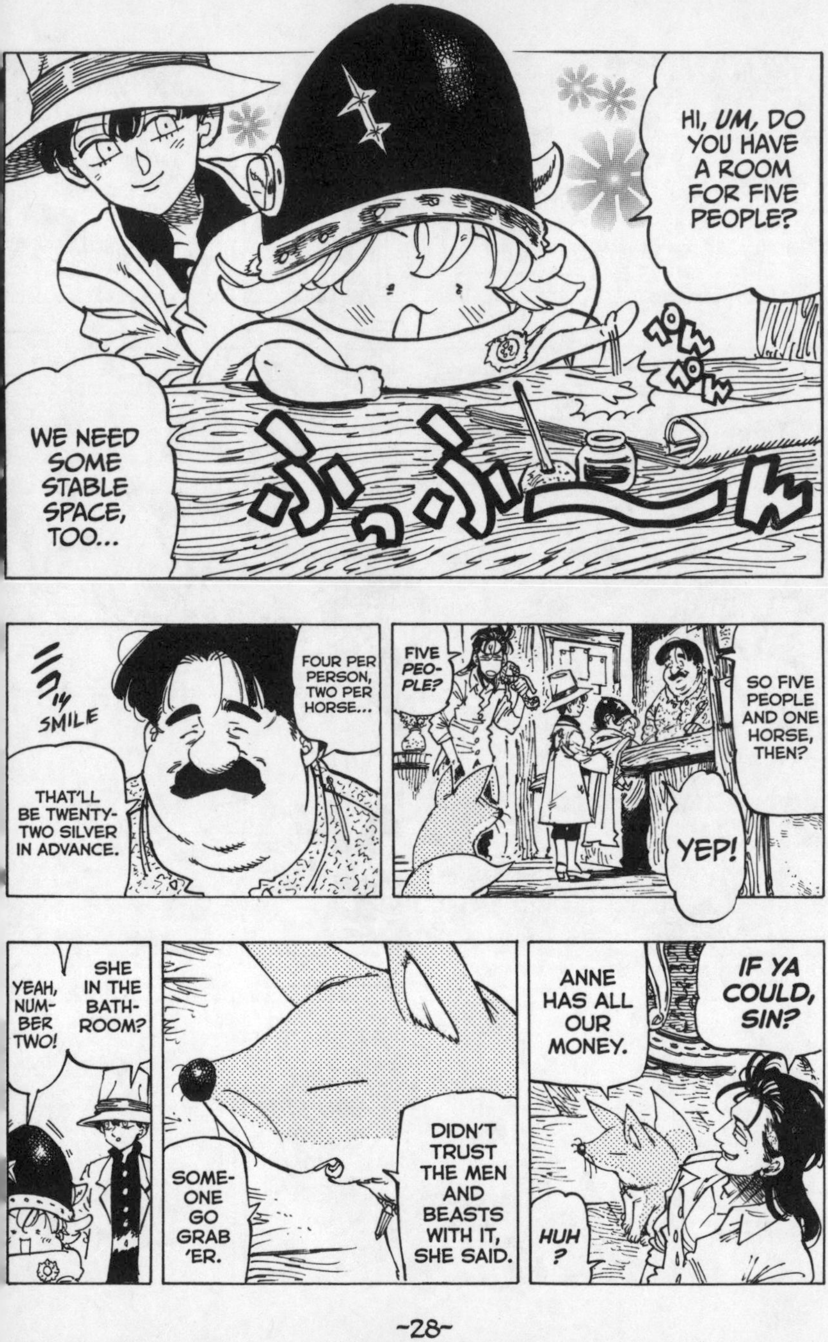
HI, UM, DO YOU HAVE A ROOM FOR FIVE PEOPLE?
TOW TOW
ふっふーん
WE NEED SOME STABLE SPACE, TOO...
SO FIVE PEOPLE AND ONE HORSE, THEN?
FIVE PEOPLE?
YEP!
FOUR PER PERSON, TWO PER HORSE...
ニコッ SMILE
THAT'LL BE TWENTY-TWO SILVER IN ADVANCE.
IF YA COULD, SIN?
ANNE HAS ALL OUR MONEY.
HUH?
DIDN'T TRUST THE MEN AND BEASTS WITH IT, SHE SAID.
SOME-ONE GO GRAB 'ER.
SHE IN THE BATH-ROOM?
YEAH, NUM-BER TWO!

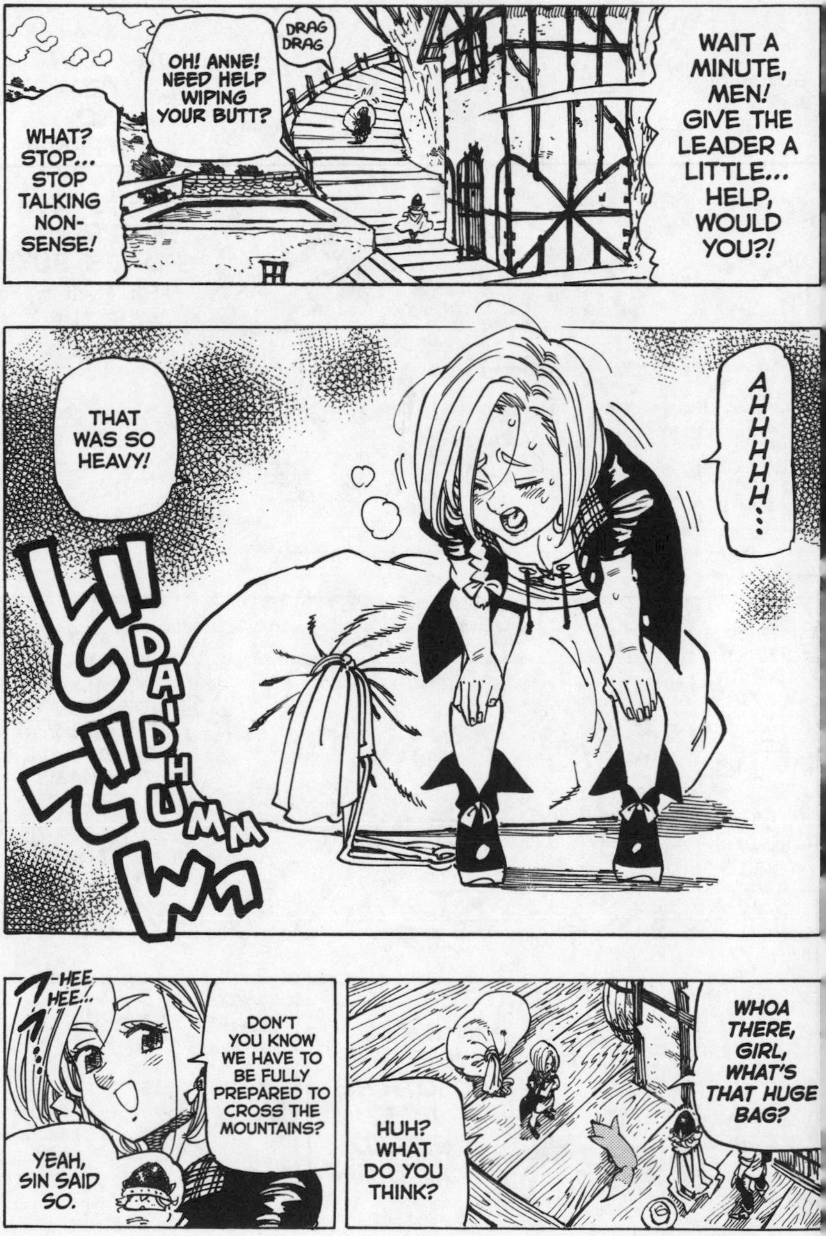
WAIT A MINUTE, MEN! GIVE THE LEADER A LITTLE... HELP, WOULD YOU?!
DRAG DRAG
OH! ANNE! NEED HELP WIPING YOUR BUTT?
WHAT? STOP... STOP TALKING NONSENSE!
AHHHHH...
THAT WAS SO HEAVY!
DA-DHUMM
WHOA THERE, GIRL, WHAT'S THAT HUGE BAG?
HUH? WHAT DO YOU THINK?
DON'T YOU KNOW WE HAVE TO BE FULLY PREPARED TO CROSS THE MOUNTAINS?
-HEE HEE...
YEAH, SIN SAID SO.

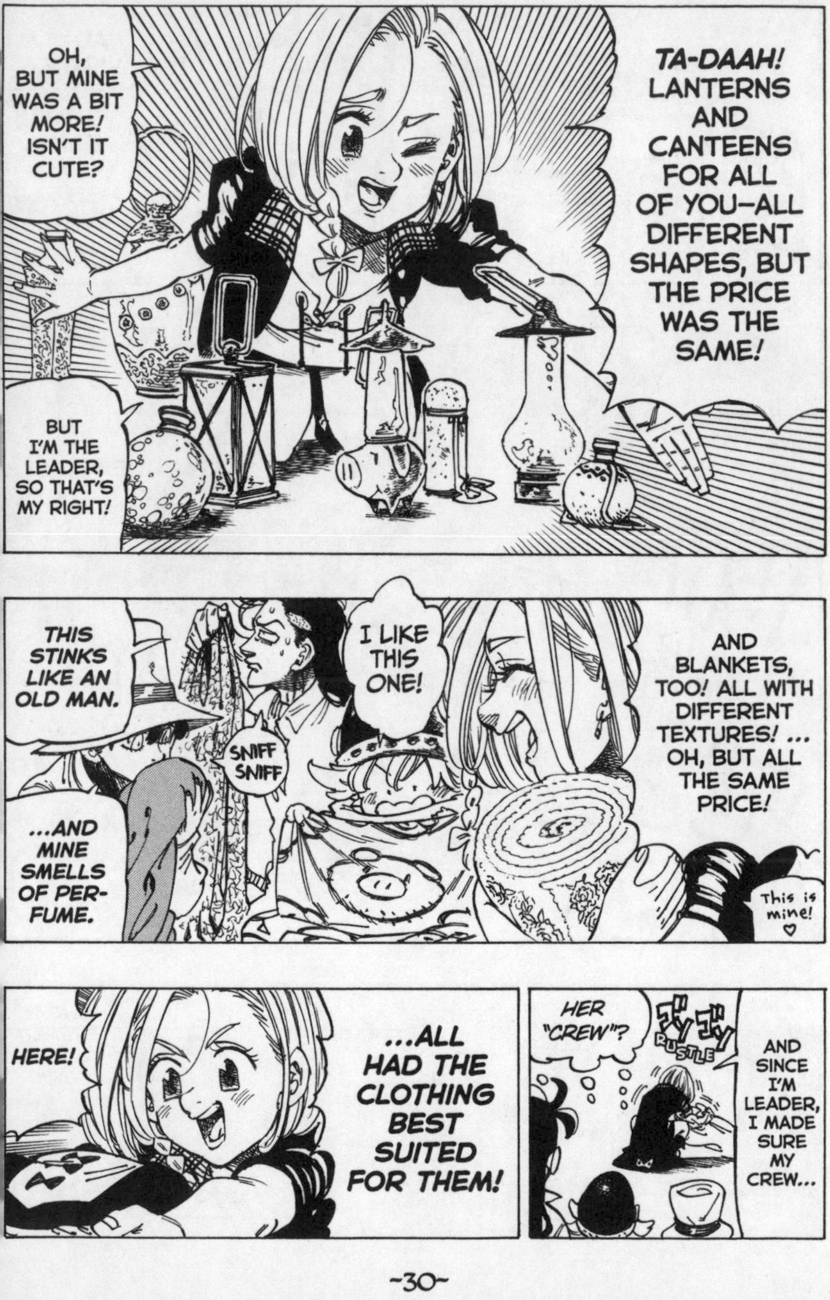
TA-DAAH! LANTERNS AND CANTEENS FOR ALL OF YOU—ALL DIFFERENT SHAPES, BUT THE PRICE WAS THE SAME!
OH, BUT MINE WAS A BIT MORE! ISN'T IT CUTE?
BUT I'M THE LEADER, SO THAT'S MY RIGHT!
AND BLANKETS, TOO! ALL WITH DIFFERENT TEXTURES! ... OH, BUT ALL THE SAME PRICE!
This is mine! ♡
I LIKE THIS ONE!
SNIFF SNIFF
THIS STINKS LIKE AN OLD MAN.
...AND MINE SMELLS OF PERFUME.
AND SINCE I'M LEADER, I MADE SURE MY CREW...
HER "CREW"?
RUSTLE
...ALL HAD THE CLOTHING BEST SUITED FOR THEM!
HERE!

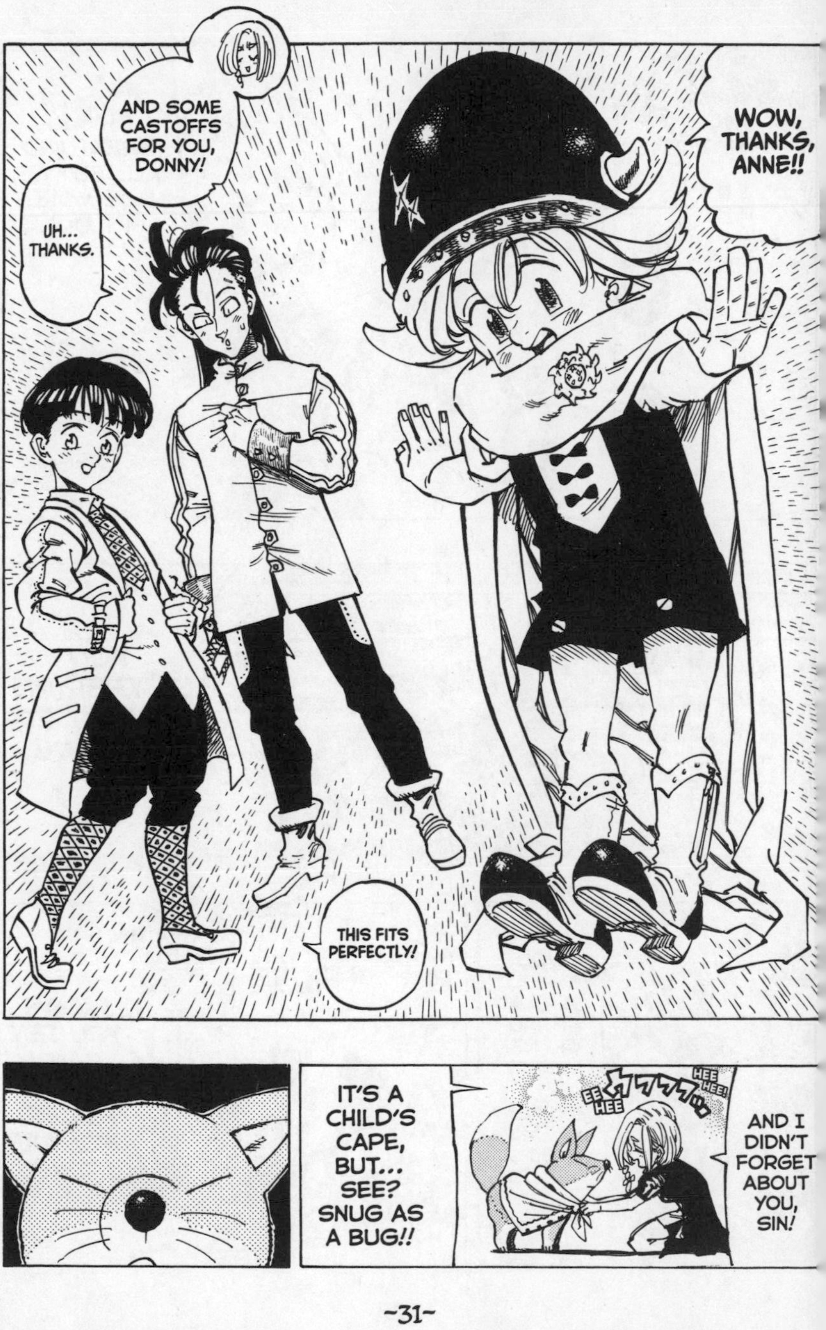
WOW, THANKS, ANNE!!
AND SOME CASTOFFS FOR YOU, DONNY!
UH... THANKS.
THIS FITS PERFECTLY!
AND I DIDN'T FORGET ABOUT YOU, SIN!
HEE HEE!
EE HEE
IT'S A CHILD'S CAPE, BUT... SEE? SNUG AS A BUG!!

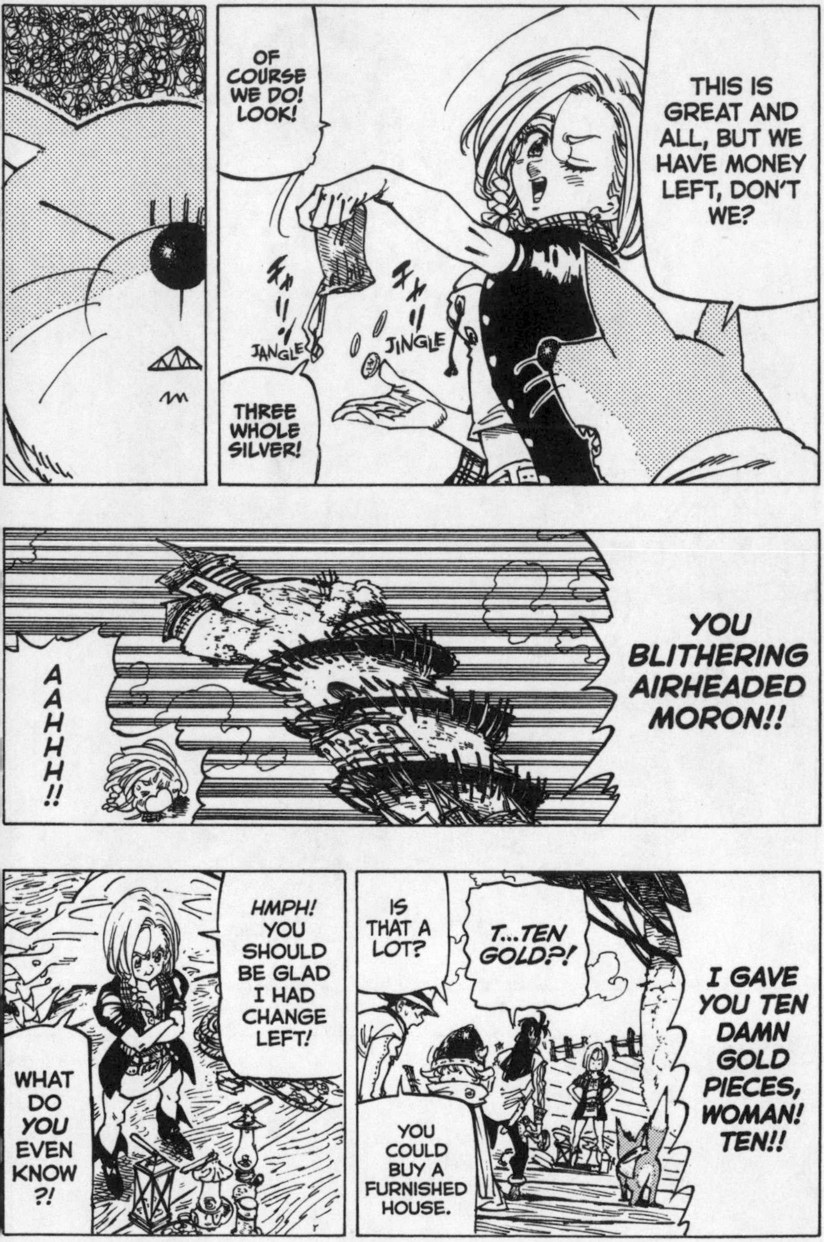
THIS IS GREAT AND ALL, BUT WE HAVE MONEY LEFT, DON'T WE?
OF COURSE WE DO! LOOK!
JINGLE
JANGLE
THREE WHOLE SILVER!
YOU BLITHERING AIRHEADED MORON!!
AAHHH!!
I GAVE YOU TEN DAMN GOLD PIECES, WOMAN! TEN!!
T...TEN GOLD?!
IS THAT A LOT?
YOU COULD BUY A FURNISHED HOUSE.
HMPH! YOU SHOULD BE GLAD I HAD CHANGE LEFT!
WHAT DO YOU EVEN KNOW?!

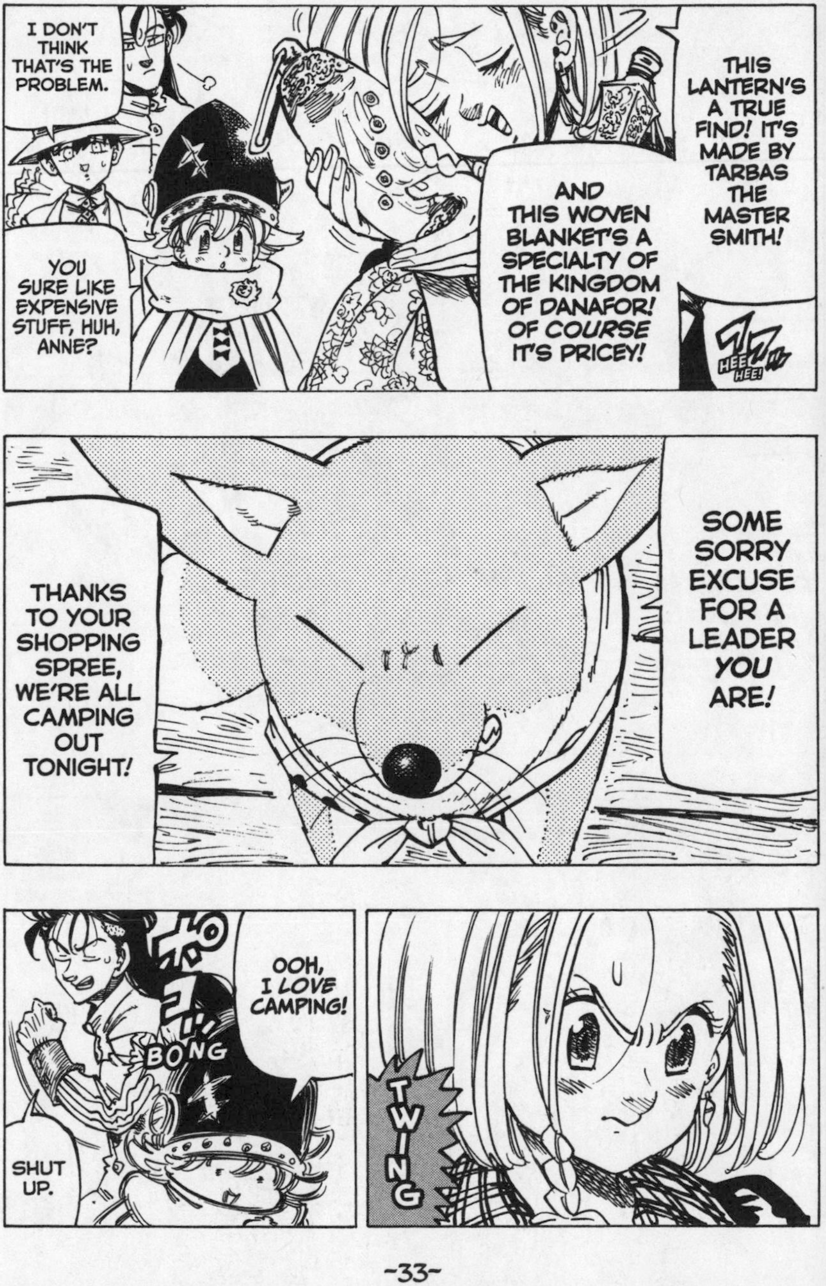
THIS LANTERN'S A TRUE FIND! IT'S MADE BY TARBAS THE MASTER SMITH!
HEE HEE!
AND THIS WOVEN BLANKET'S A SPECIALTY OF THE KINGDOM OF DANAFOR! OF COURSE IT'S PRICEY!
I DON'T THINK THAT'S THE PROBLEM.
YOU SURE LIKE EXPENSIVE STUFF, HUH, ANNE?
SOME SORRY EXCUSE FOR A LEADER YOU ARE!
THANKS TO YOUR SHOPPING SPREE, WE'RE ALL CAMPING OUT TONIGHT!
TWING
OOH, I LOVE CAMPING!
BONG
SHUT UP.

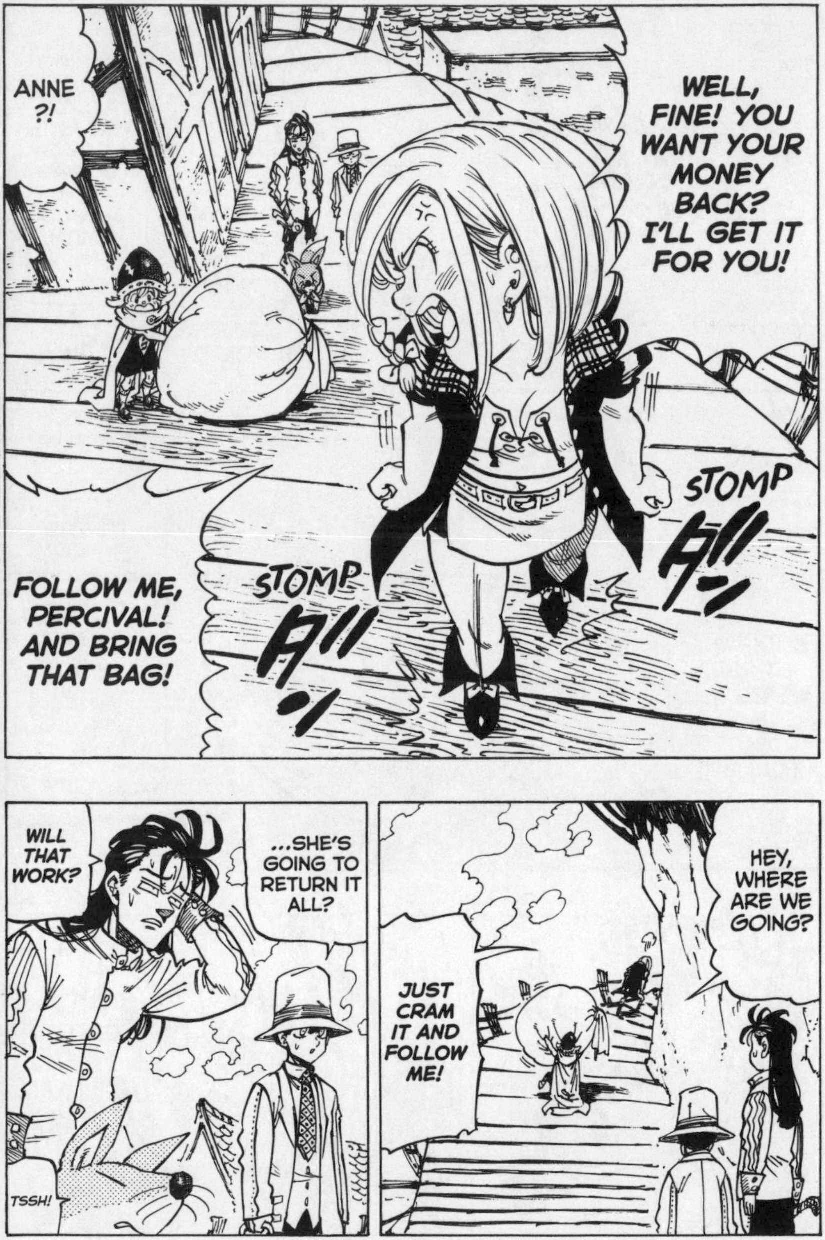
WELL, FINE! YOU WANT YOUR MONEY BACK? I'LL GET IT FOR YOU!
ANNE ?!
STOMP
STOMP
FOLLOW ME, PERCIVAL! AND BRING THAT BAG!
HEY, WHERE ARE WE GOING?
JUST CRAM IT AND FOLLOW ME!
...SHE'S GOING TO RETURN IT ALL?
WILL THAT WORK?
TSSH!

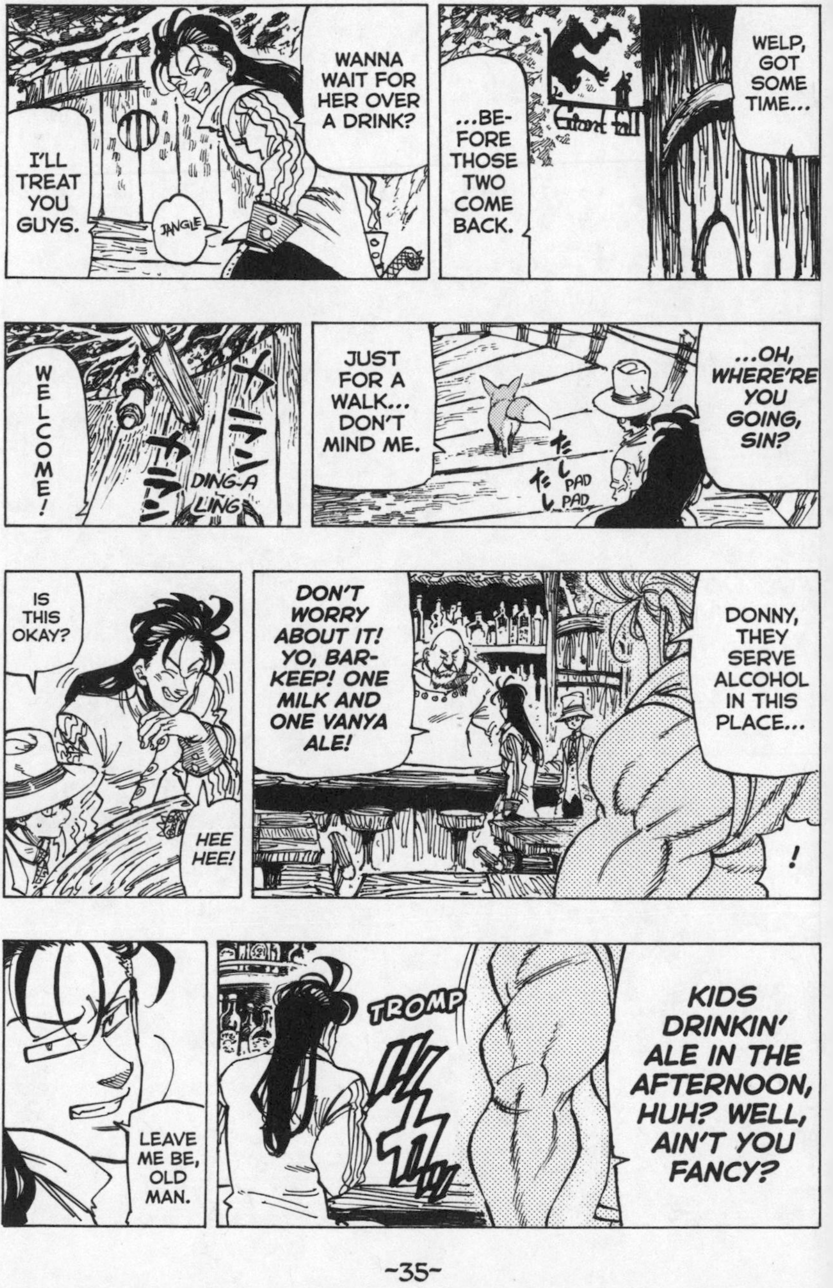
WELP, GOT SOME TIME...
...BE-FORE THOSE TWO COME BACK.
WANNA WAIT FOR HER OVER A DRINK?
I'LL TREAT YOU GUYS.
JANGLE
...OH, WHERE'RE YOU GOING, SIN?
JUST FOR A WALK... DON'T MIND ME.
たし たし
PAD PAD
WELCOME!
カラン カラン
DING-A LING
DONNY, THEY SERVE ALCOHOL IN THIS PLACE...
!
DON'T WORRY ABOUT IT! YO, BAR-KEEP! ONE MILK AND ONE VANYA ALE!
IS THIS OKAY?
HEE HEE!
KIDS DRINKIN' ALE IN THE AFTERNOON, HUH? WELL, AIN'T YOU FANCY?
TROMP
LEAVE ME BE, OLD MAN.

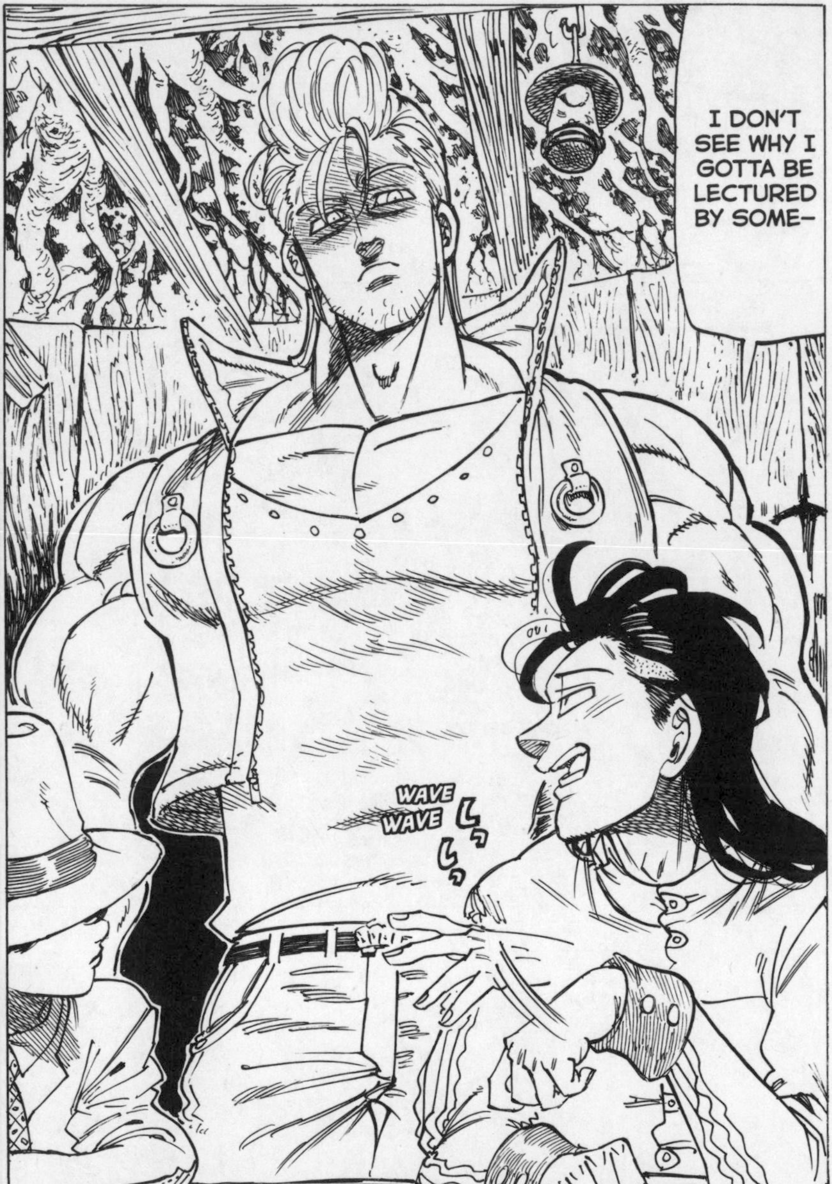
I DON'T SEE WHY I GOTTA BE LECTURED BY SOME–
WAVE WAVE

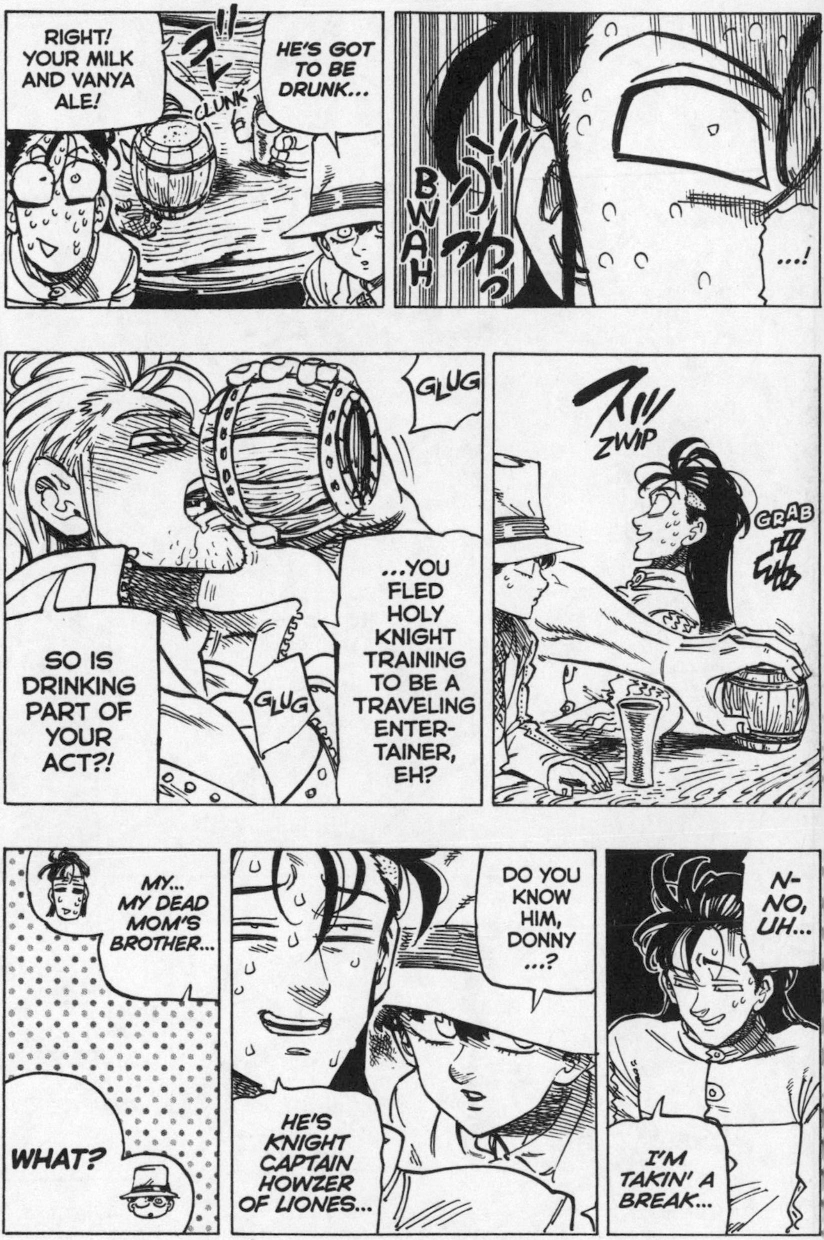
BWAH
...!
HE'S GOT TO BE DRUNK...
CLUNK
RIGHT! YOUR MILK AND VANYA ALE!
ZWIP
GRAB
GLUG
...YOU FLED HOLY KNIGHT TRAINING TO BE A TRAVELING ENTER-TAINER, EH?
SO IS DRINKING PART OF YOUR ACT?!
GLUG
N-NO, UH...
I'M TAKIN' A BREAK...
DO YOU KNOW HIM, DONNY ...?
HE'S KNIGHT CAPTAIN HOWZER OF LIONES...
MY... MY DEAD MOM'S BROTHER...
WHAT?

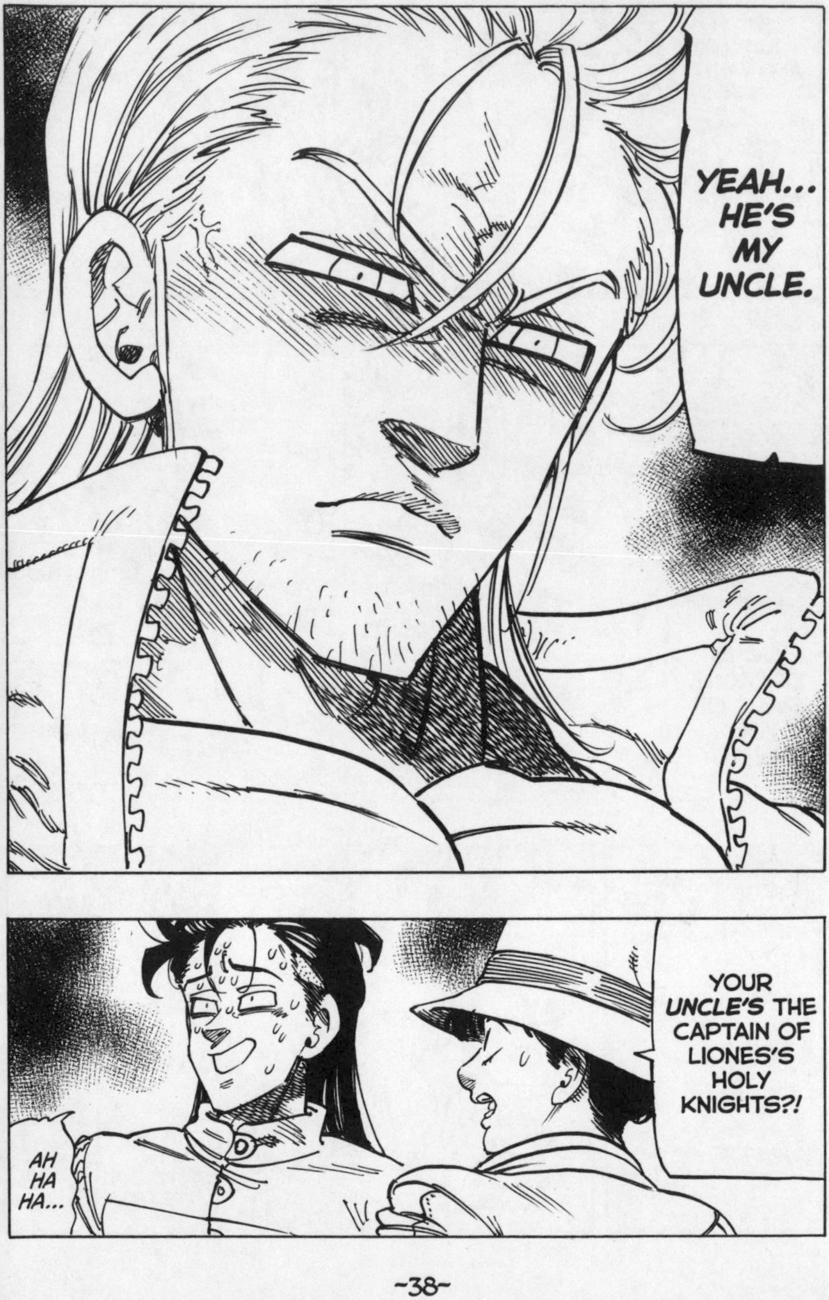
YEAH... HE'S MY UNCLE.
YOUR *UNCLE'S* THE CAPTAIN OF LIONES'S HOLY KNIGHTS?!
AH HA HA...

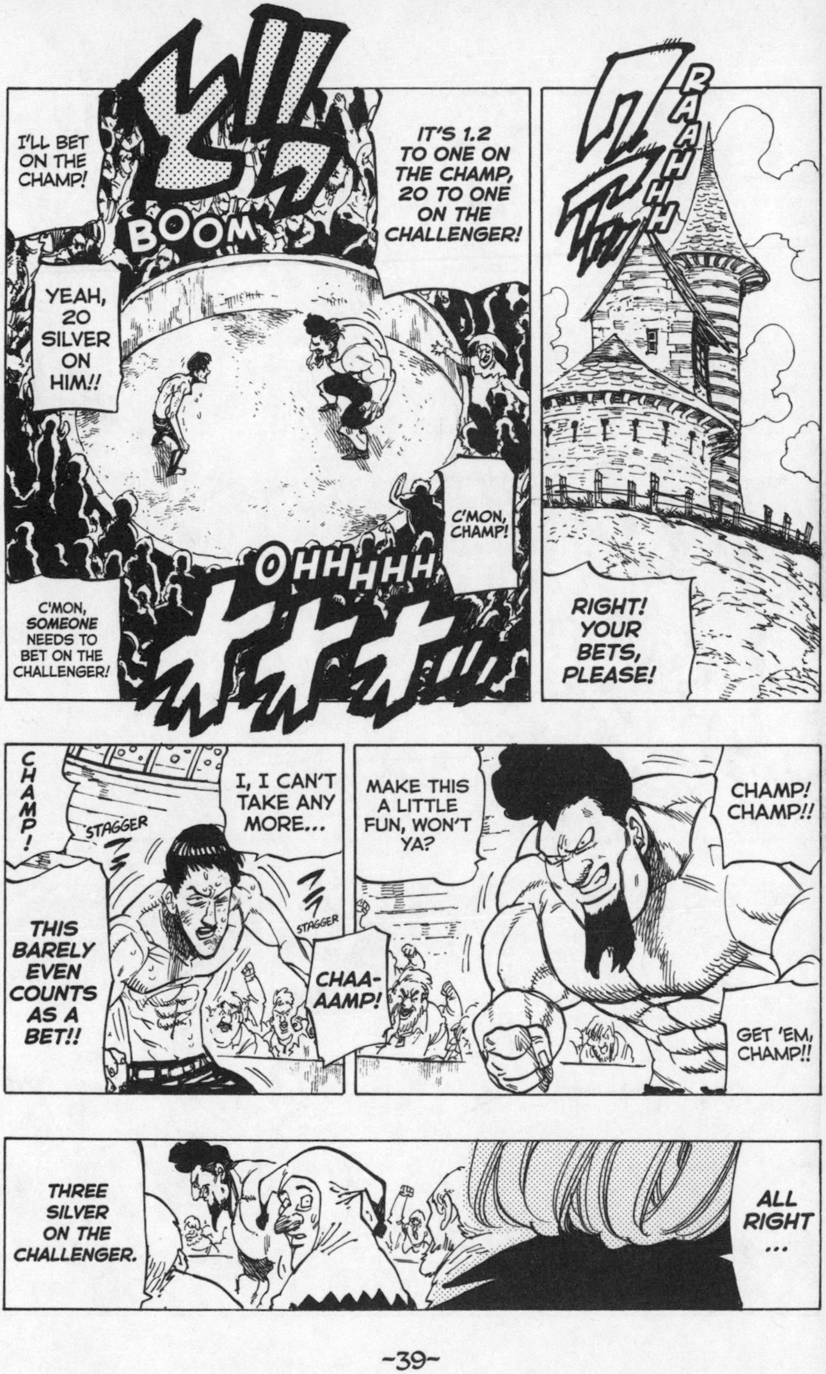
RAAHHHH
RIGHT! YOUR BETS, PLEASE!
IT'S 1.2 TO ONE ON THE CHAMP, 20 TO ONE ON THE CHALLENGER!
BOOM
I'LL BET ON THE CHAMP!
YEAH, 20 SILVER ON HIM!!
C'MON, CHAMP!
OHHHHHH
C'MON, SOMEONE NEEDS TO BET ON THE CHALLENGER!
CHAMP! CHAMP!!
MAKE THIS A LITTLE FUN, WON'T YA?
GET 'EM, CHAMP!!
I, I CAN'T TAKE ANY MORE...
CHAMP!
STAGGER
STAGGER
CHAA-AAMP!
THIS BARELY EVEN COUNTS AS A BET!!
ALL RIGHT ...
THREE SILVER ON THE CHALLENGER.

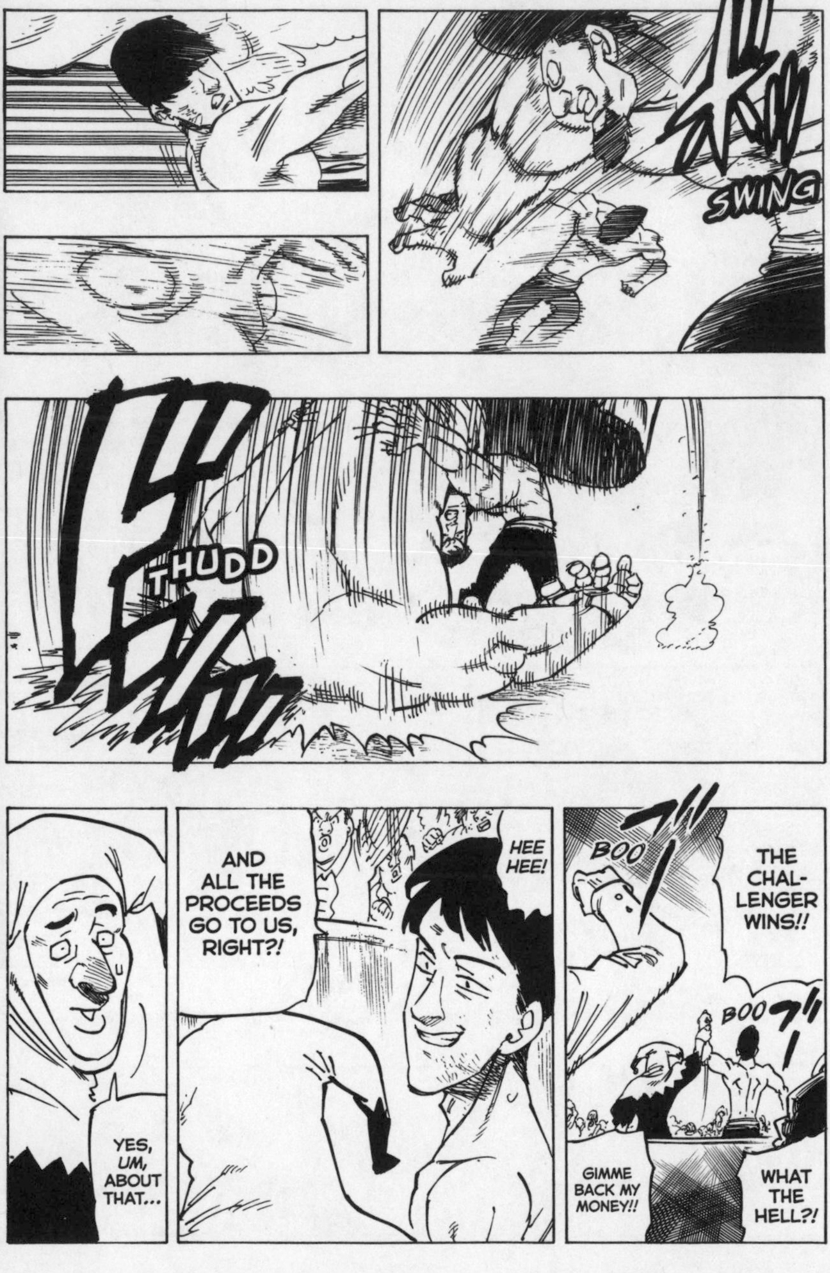
SWING
THUDD
THE CHAL-LENGER WINS!!
BOO
BOO
WHAT THE HELL?!
GIMME BACK MY MONEY!!
HEE HEE!
AND ALL THE PROCEEDS GO TO US, RIGHT?!
YES, UM, ABOUT THAT...

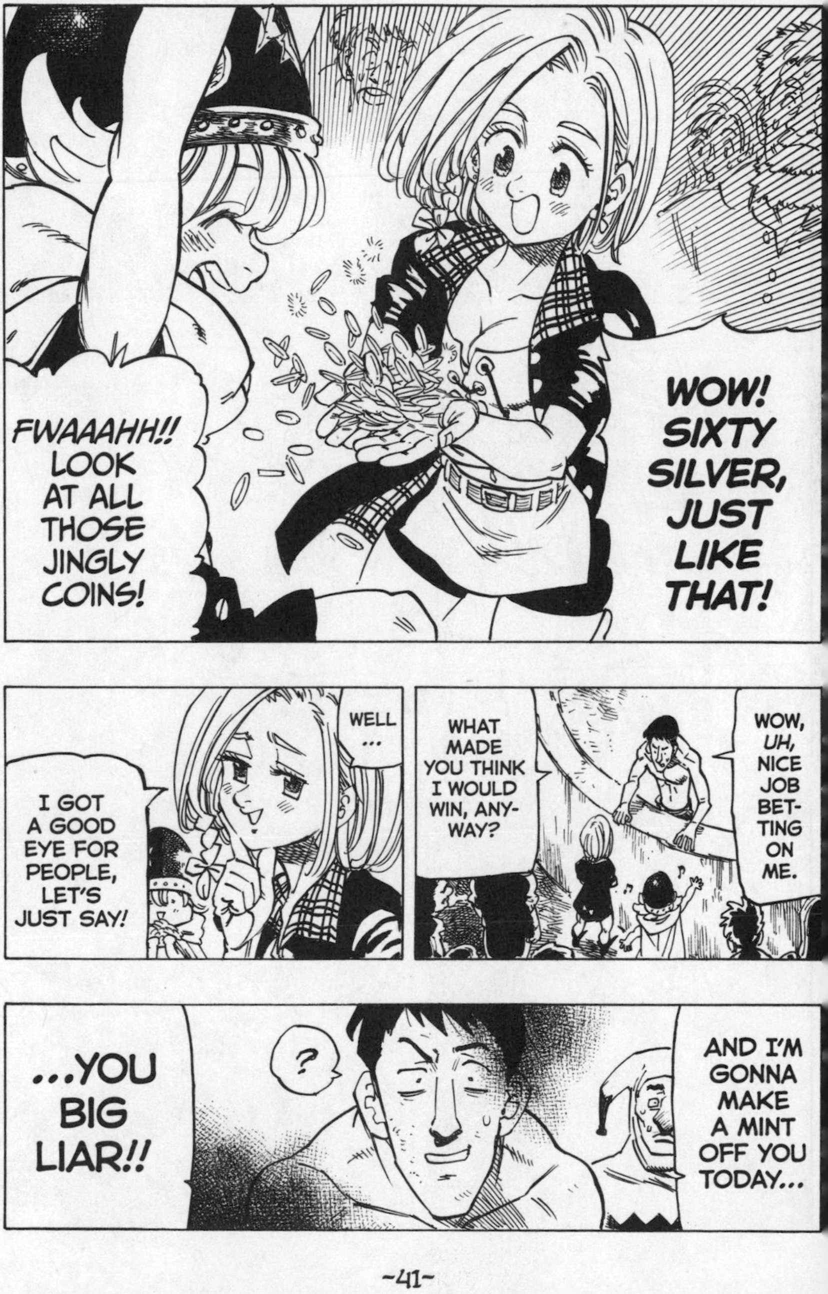
WOW! SIXTY SILVER, JUST LIKE THAT!
FWAAAHH!! LOOK AT ALL THOSE JINGLY COINS!
WOW, UH, NICE JOB BETTING ON ME.
WHAT MADE YOU THINK I WOULD WIN, ANYWAY?
WELL ...
I GOT A GOOD EYE FOR PEOPLE, LET'S JUST SAY!
AND I'M GONNA MAKE A MINT OFF YOU TODAY...
?
...YOU BIG LIAR!!

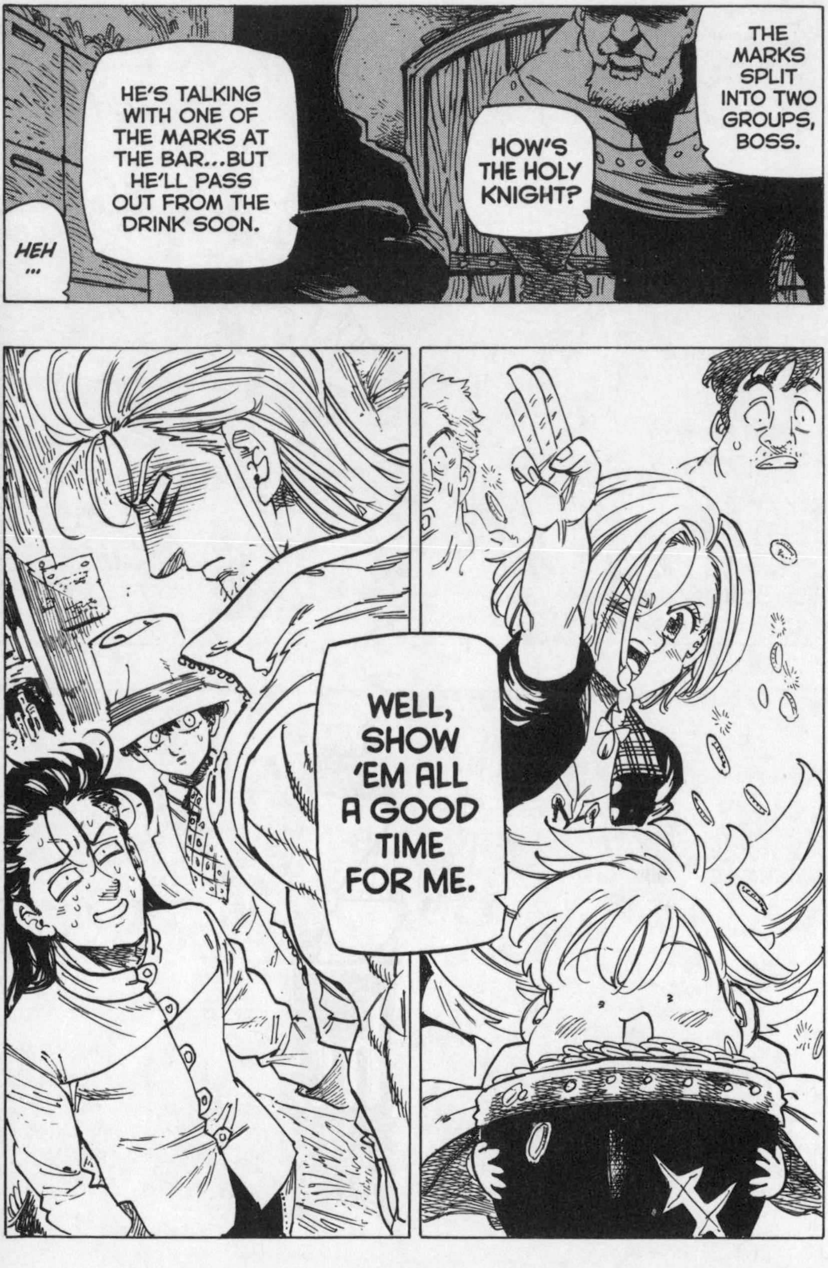
THE MARKS SPLIT INTO TWO GROUPS, BOSS.
HOW'S THE HOLY KNIGHT?
HE'S TALKING WITH ONE OF THE MARKS AT THE BAR...BUT HE'LL PASS OUT FROM THE DRINK SOON.
HEH ...
WELL, SHOW 'EM ALL A GOOD TIME FOR ME.

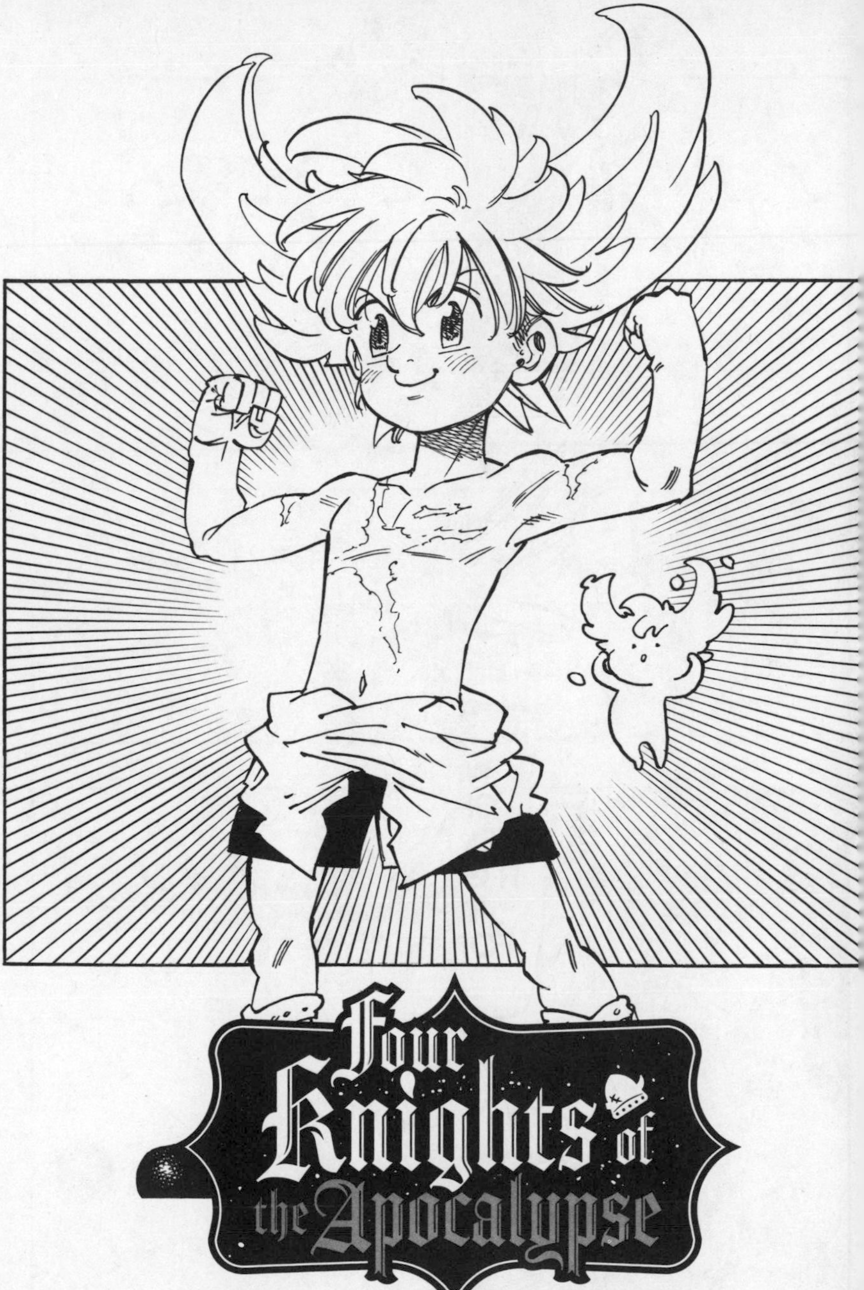
Four Knights of the Apocalypse

CHAPTER 26: UNCLE AND NEPHEW

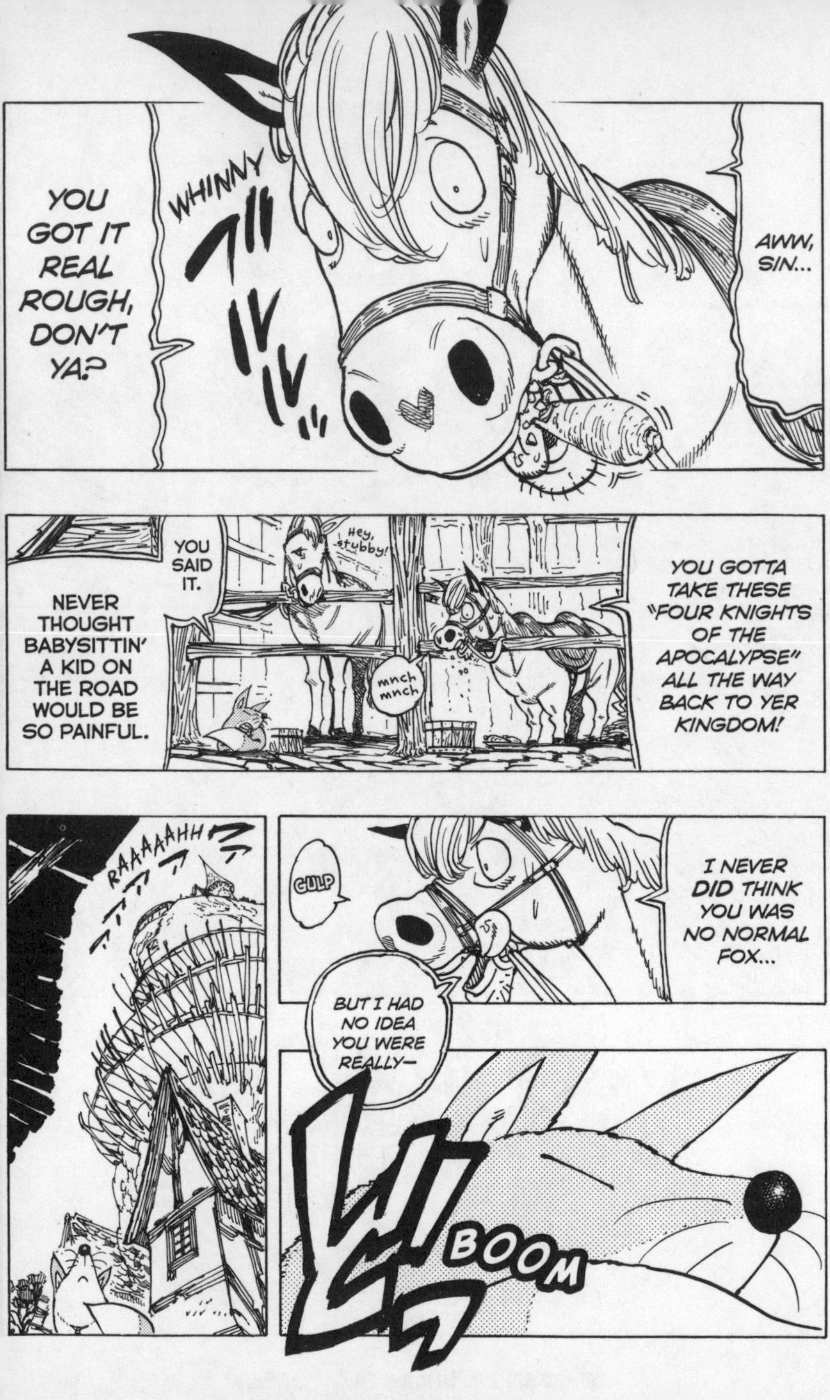
AWW, SIN...
WHINNY
YOU GOT IT REAL ROUGH, DON'T YA?
YOU GOTTA TAKE THESE "FOUR KNIGHTS OF THE APOCALYPSE" ALL THE WAY BACK TO YER KINGDOM!
Hey, stubby!
YOU SAID IT.
mnch mnch
NEVER THOUGHT BABYSITTIN' A KID ON THE ROAD WOULD BE SO PAINFUL.
I NEVER DID THINK YOU WAS NO NORMAL FOX...
GULP
BUT I HAD NO IDEA YOU WERE REALLY—
BOOM
RAAAAAHH

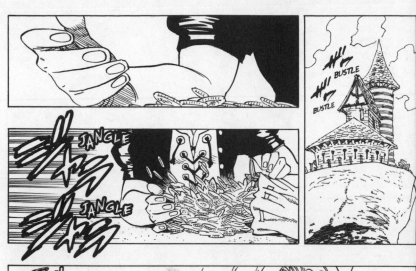

JANGLE

JANGLE

BUSTLE

BUSTLE

JANGLE

RIGHT, FOLKS...

I'LL JUST BE TAKIN' THIS. ♡

ALL RIGHT!

THAT'S ALL THE GOUREN FOR TODAY, PERCIVAL!

OOF!

GASP

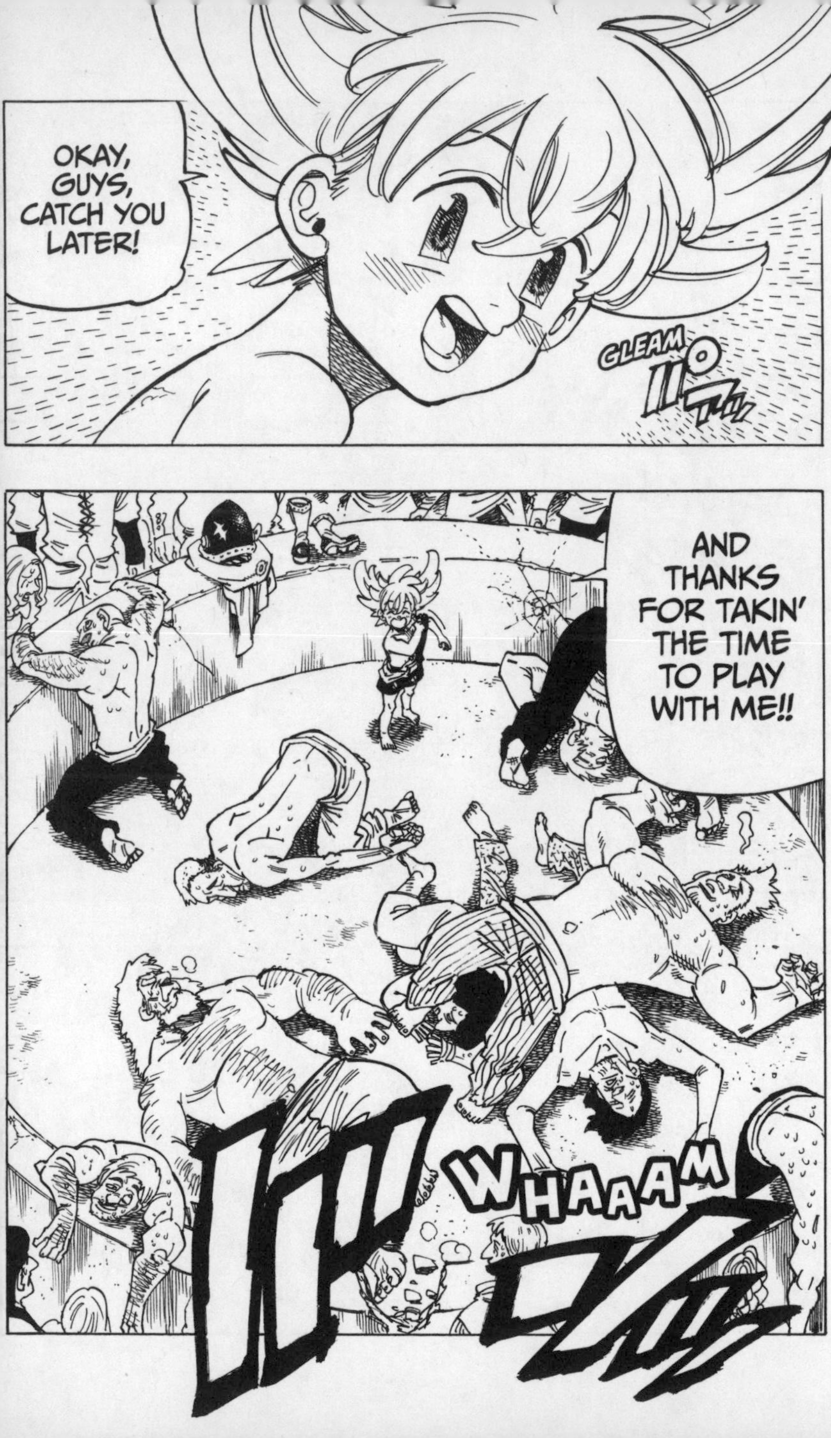
OKAY, GUYS, CATCH YOU LATER!
GLEAM
AND THANKS FOR TAKIN' THE TIME TO PLAY WITH ME!!
WHAAAM

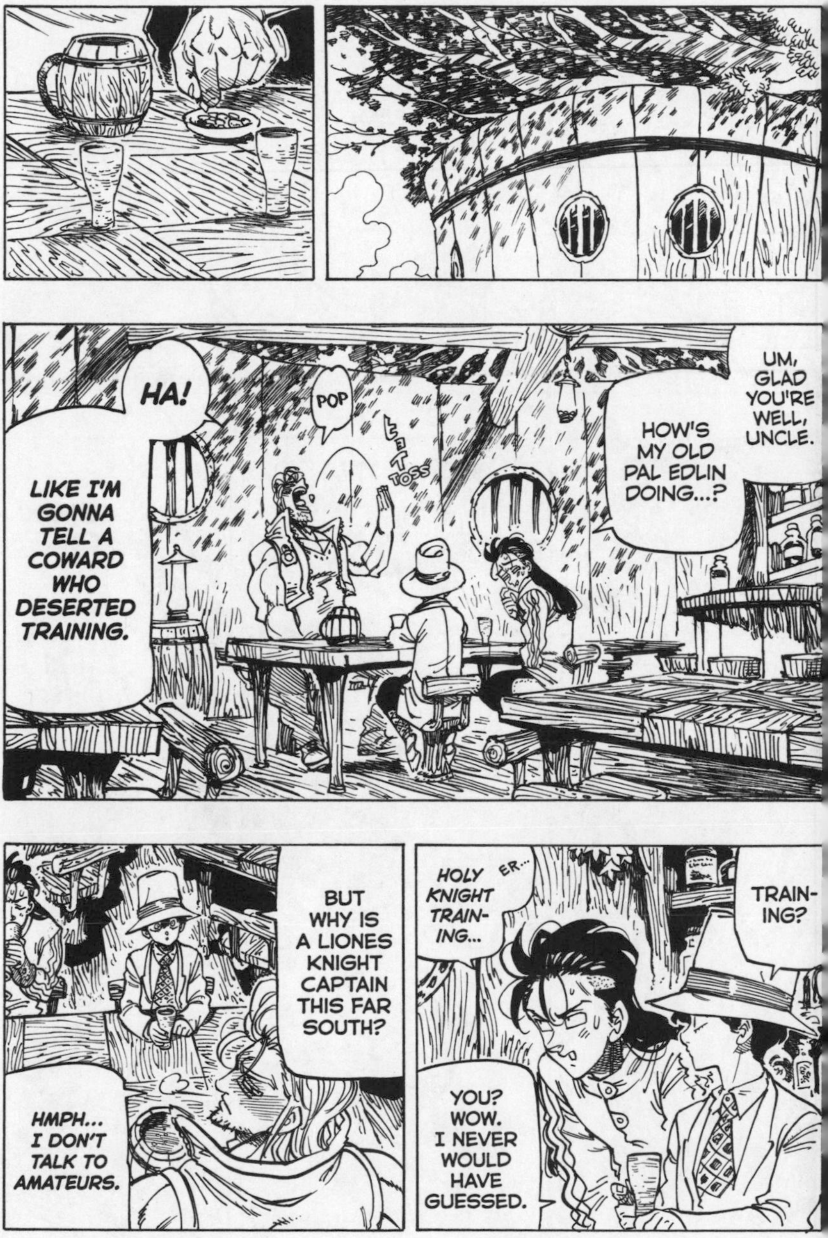
UM, GLAD YOU'RE WELL, UNCLE.
HOW'S MY OLD PAL EDLIN DOING...?
TOSS
POP
HA!
LIKE I'M GONNA TELL A COWARD WHO DESERTED TRAINING.
TRAIN-ING?
ER...
HOLY KNIGHT TRAIN-ING...
YOU? WOW. I NEVER WOULD HAVE GUESSED.
BUT WHY IS A LIONES KNIGHT CAPTAIN THIS FAR SOUTH?
HMPH... I DON'T TALK TO AMATEURS.

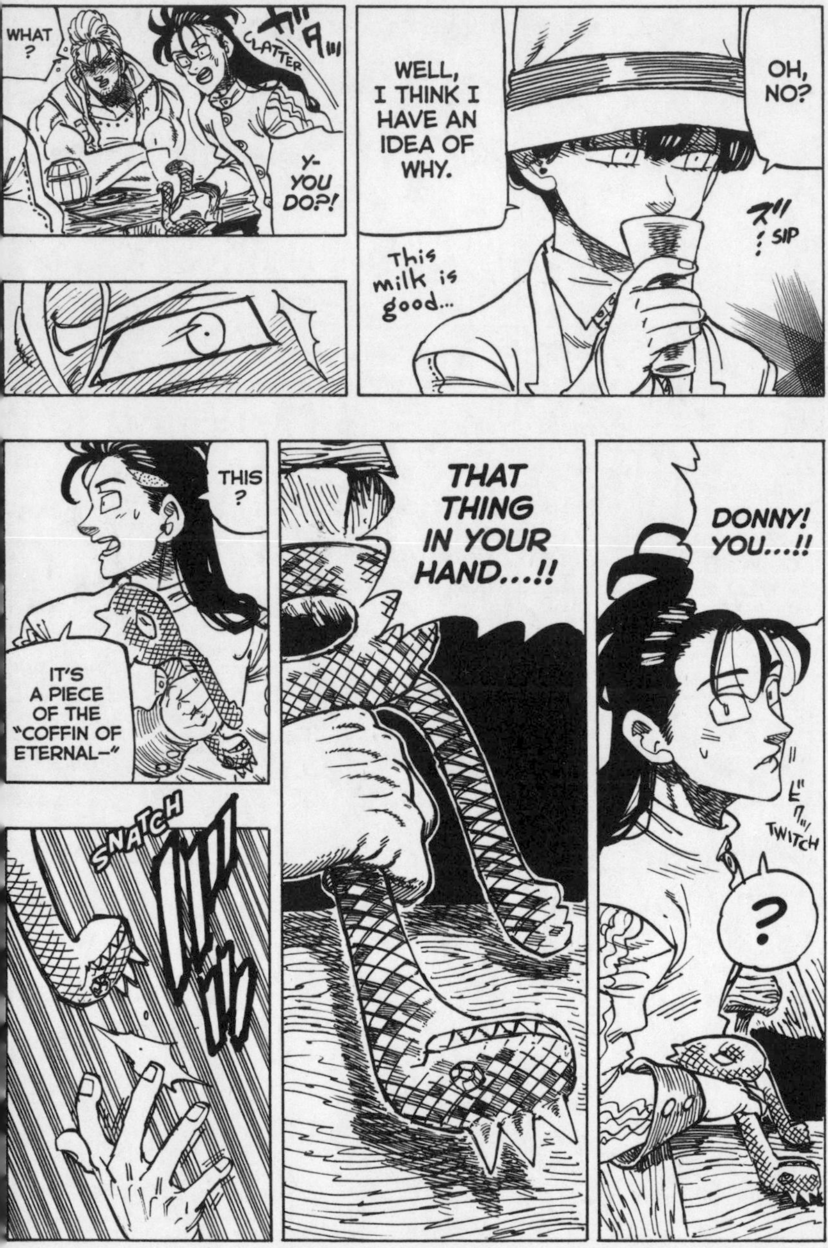
OH, NO?
WELL, I THINK I HAVE AN IDEA OF WHY.
SIP
This milk is good...
CLATTER
Y-YOU DO?!
WHAT?
DONNY! YOU...!!
TWITCH
?
THAT THING IN YOUR HAND...!!
THIS?
IT'S A PIECE OF THE "COFFIN OF ETERNAL—"
SNATCH

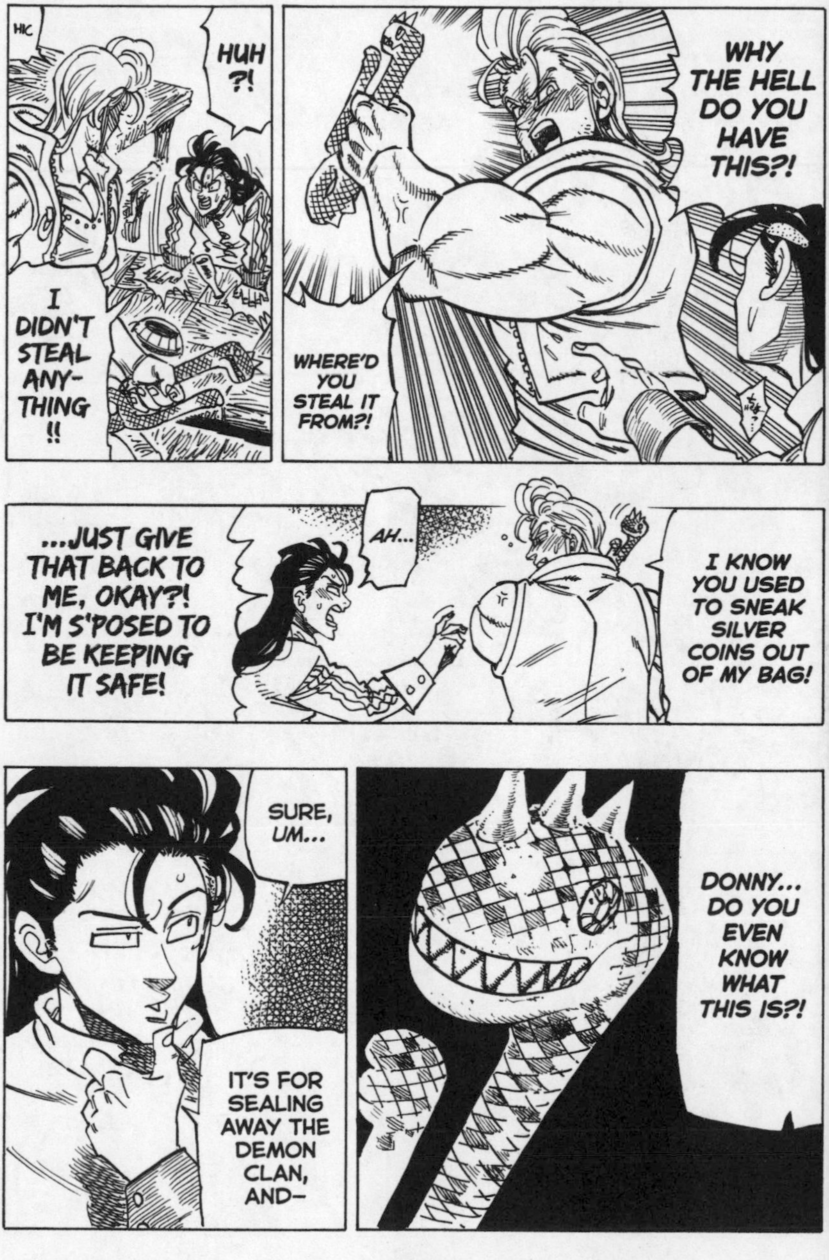
WHY THE HELL DO YOU HAVE THIS?!
WHERE'D YOU STEAL IT FROM?!
HIC
HUH ?!
I DIDN'T STEAL ANY-THING !!
I KNOW YOU USED TO SNEAK SILVER COINS OUT OF MY BAG!
AH...
...JUST GIVE THAT BACK TO ME, OKAY?! I'M S'POSED TO BE KEEPING IT SAFE!
DONNY... DO YOU EVEN KNOW WHAT THIS IS?!
SURE, UM...
IT'S FOR SEALING AWAY THE DEMON CLAN, AND–

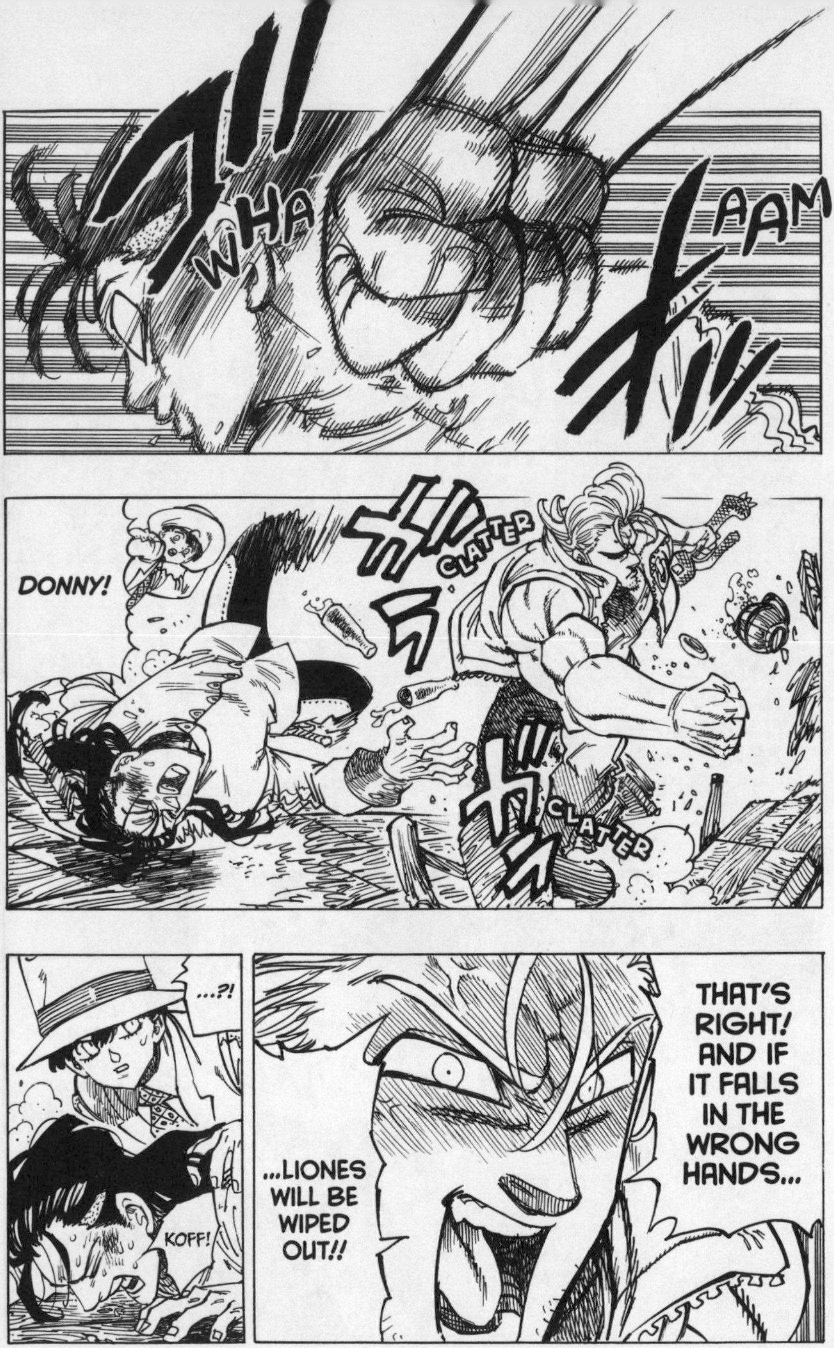
WHA
AAM
CLATTER
DONNY!
CLATTER
THAT'S RIGHT! AND IF IT FALLS IN THE WRONG HANDS...
...LIONES WILL BE WIPED OUT!!
...?!
KOFF!

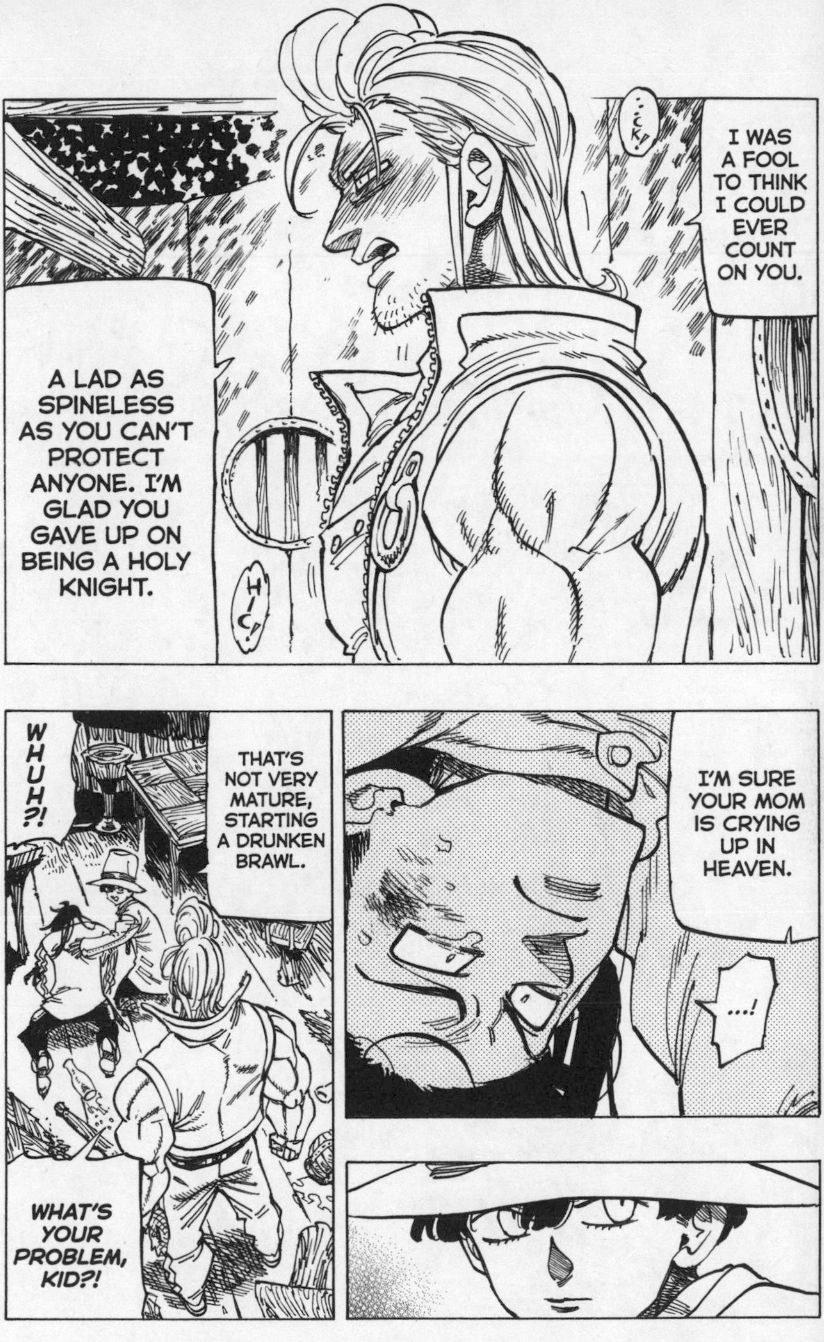
I WAS A FOOL TO THINK I COULD EVER COUNT ON YOU.
...CK!
A LAD AS SPINELESS AS YOU CAN'T PROTECT ANYONE. I'M GLAD YOU GAVE UP ON BEING A HOLY KNIGHT.
HIC!
I'M SURE YOUR MOM IS CRYING UP IN HEAVEN.
...!
THAT'S NOT VERY MATURE, STARTING A DRUNKEN BRAWL.
WHUH?!
WHAT'S YOUR PROBLEM, KID?!

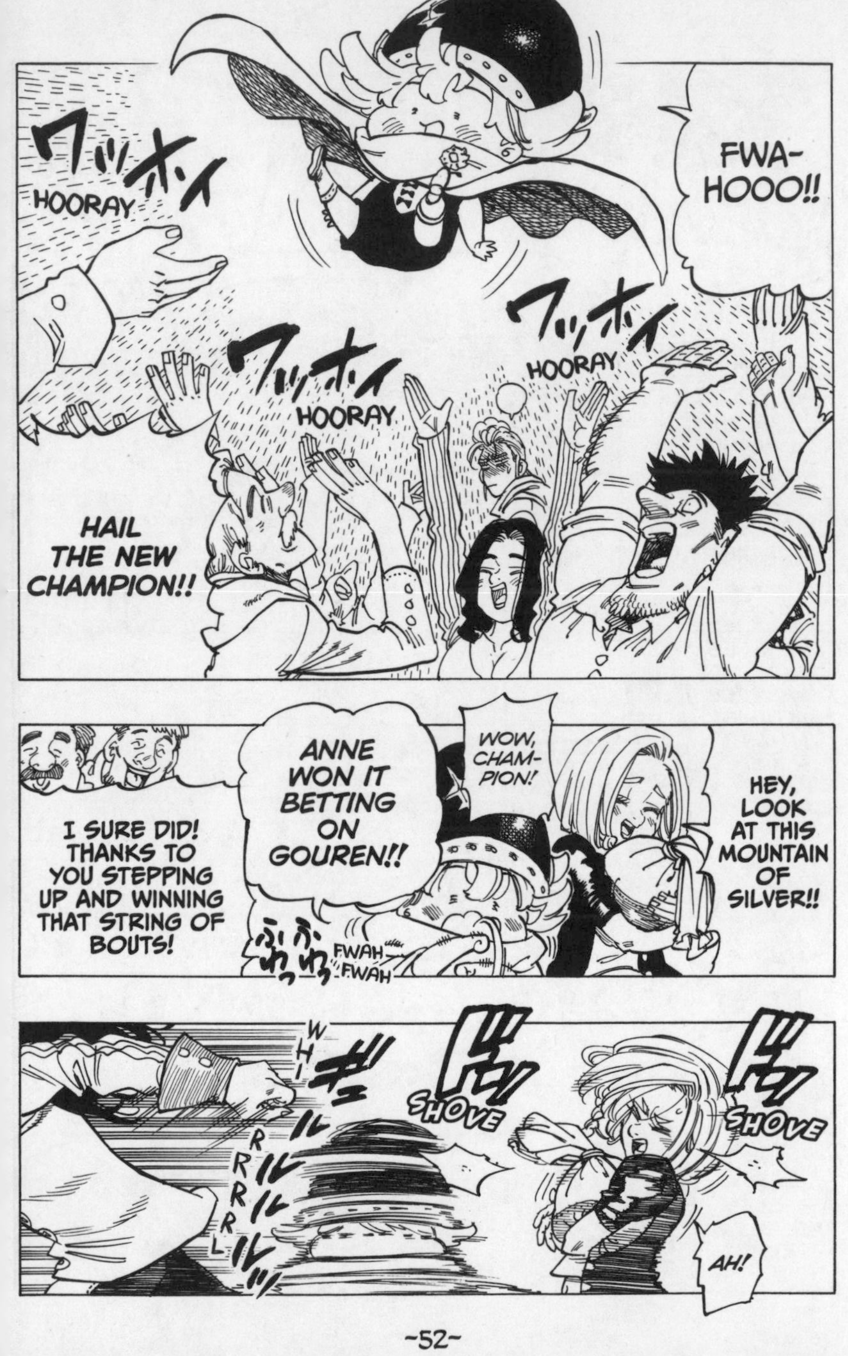
FWA-HOOO!!
ワッホイ
HOORAY
ワッホイ
HOORAY
ワッホイ
HOORAY
HAIL THE NEW CHAMPION!!
HEY, LOOK AT THIS MOUNTAIN OF SILVER!!
WOW, CHAMPION!
ANNE WON IT BETTING ON GOUREN!!
I SURE DID! THANKS TO YOU STEPPING UP AND WINNING THAT STRING OF BOUTS!
ふわっふわっ
FWAH-FWAH
ドン
SHOVE
AH!
ドン
SHOVE
ギュルルルル
WHIRRRRL

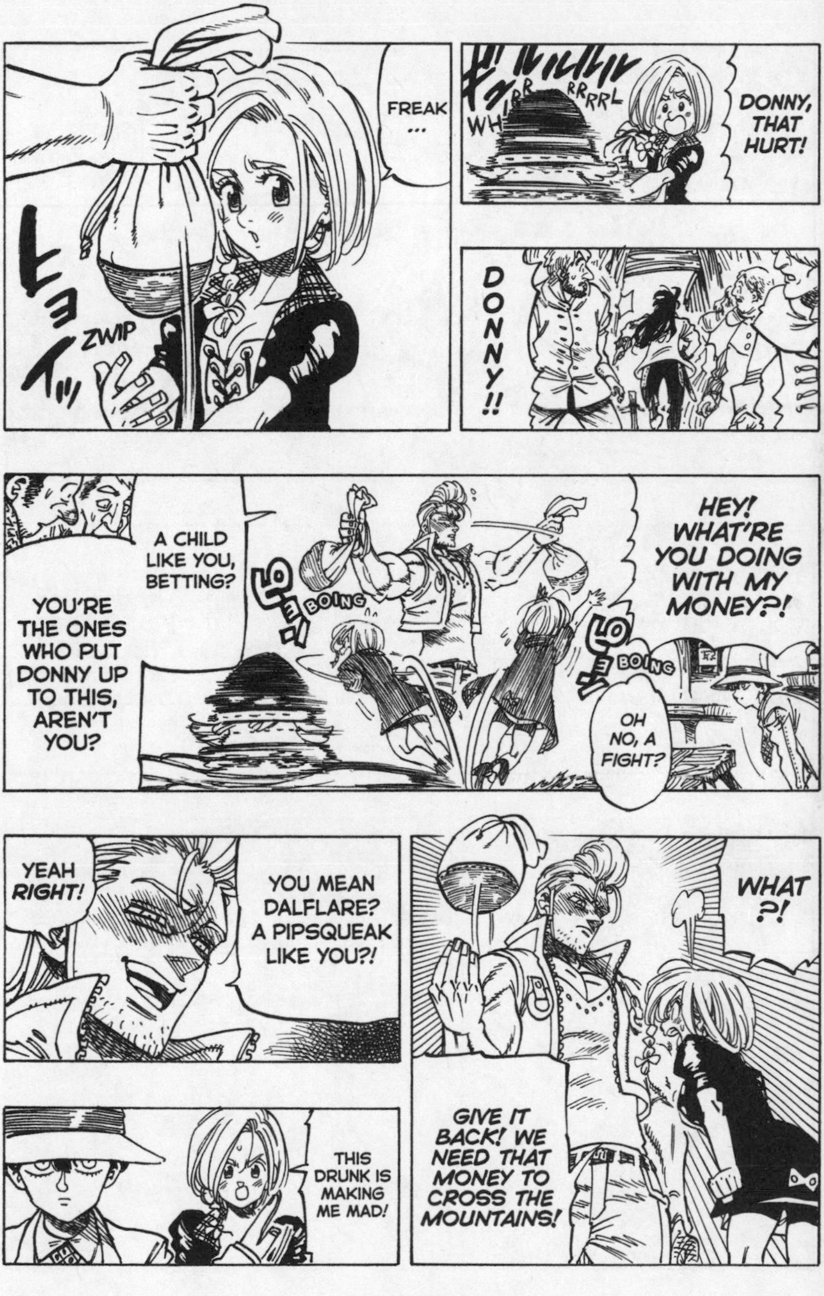
DONNY, THAT HURT!
WHIRRRRRRL
DONNY!!
FREAK ...
ZWIP
HEY! WHAT'RE YOU DOING WITH MY MONEY?!
OH NO, A FIGHT?
BOING
BOING
A CHILD LIKE YOU, BETTING?
YOU'RE THE ONES WHO PUT DONNY UP TO THIS, AREN'T YOU?
WHAT ?!
GIVE IT BACK! WE NEED THAT MONEY TO CROSS THE MOUNTAINS!
YOU MEAN DALFLARE? A PIPSQUEAK LIKE YOU?!
YEAH RIGHT!
THIS DRUNK IS MAKING ME MAD!

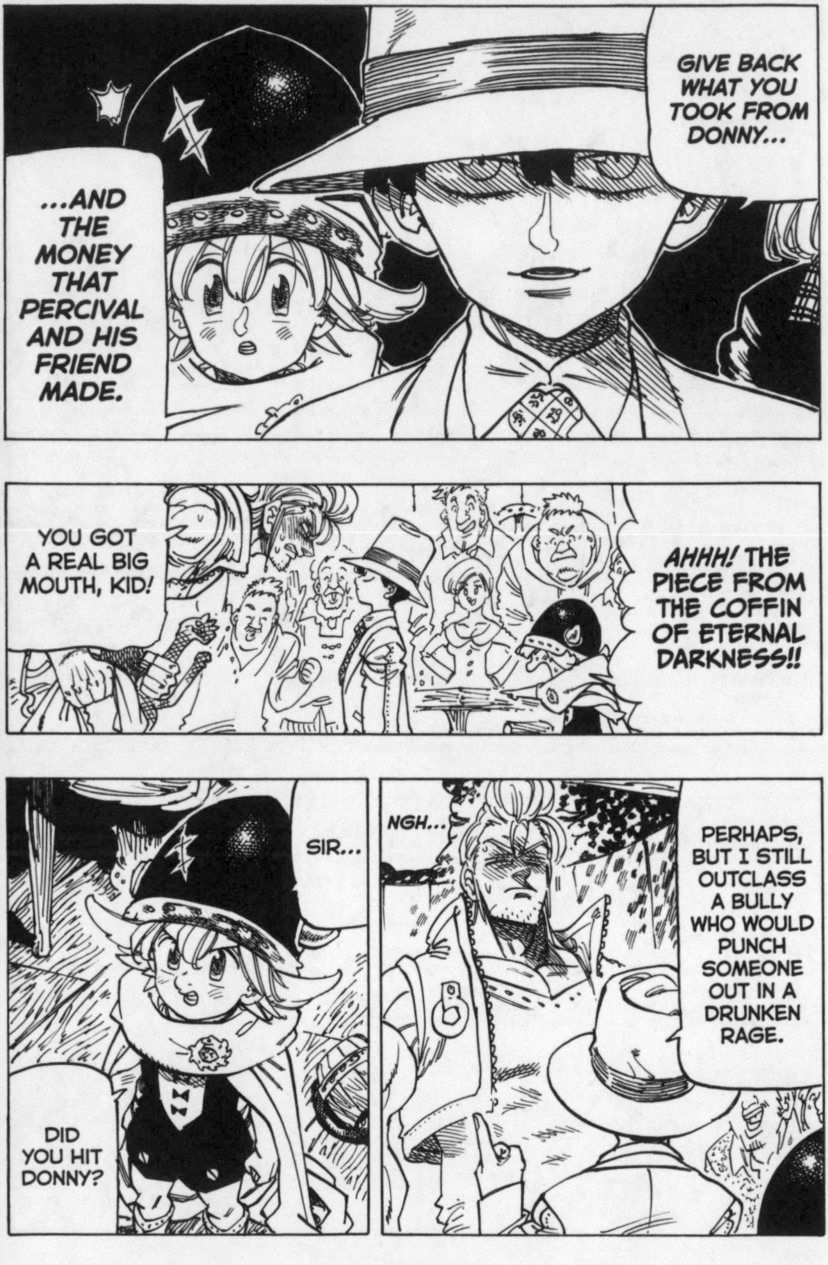
GIVE BACK WHAT YOU TOOK FROM DONNY...
...AND THE MONEY THAT PERCIVAL AND HIS FRIEND MADE.
AHHH! THE PIECE FROM THE COFFIN OF ETERNAL DARKNESS!!
YOU GOT A REAL BIG MOUTH, KID!
PERHAPS, BUT I STILL OUTCLASS A BULLY WHO WOULD PUNCH SOMEONE OUT IN A DRUNKEN RAGE.
NGH...
SIR...
DID YOU HIT DONNY?

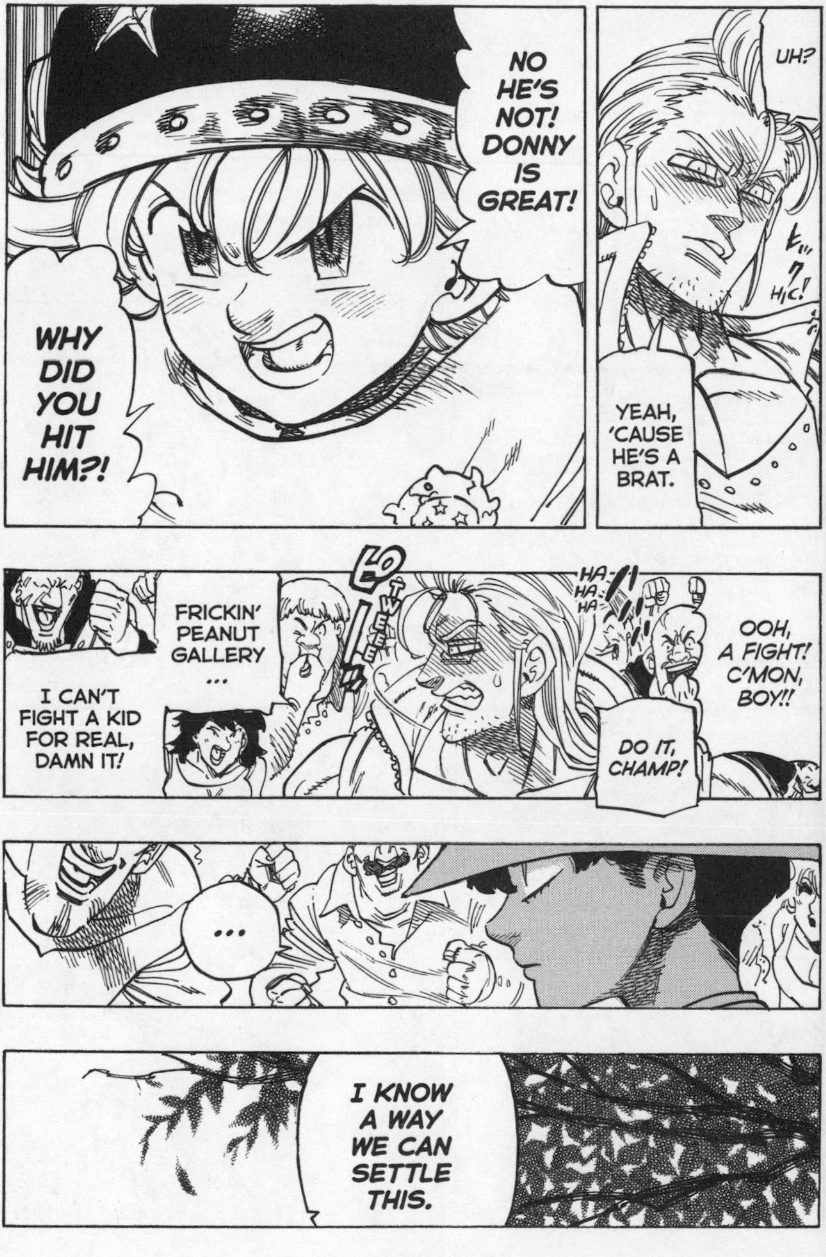
UH?
HIC!
YEAH, 'CAUSE HE'S A BRAT.
NO HE'S NOT! DONNY IS GREAT!
WHY DID YOU HIT HIM?!
OOH, A FIGHT! C'MON, BOY!!
HA-HA-HA
DO IT, CHAMP!
TWEE
FRICKIN' PEANUT GALLERY ...
I CAN'T FIGHT A KID FOR REAL, DAMN IT!
...
I KNOW A WAY WE CAN SETTLE THIS.

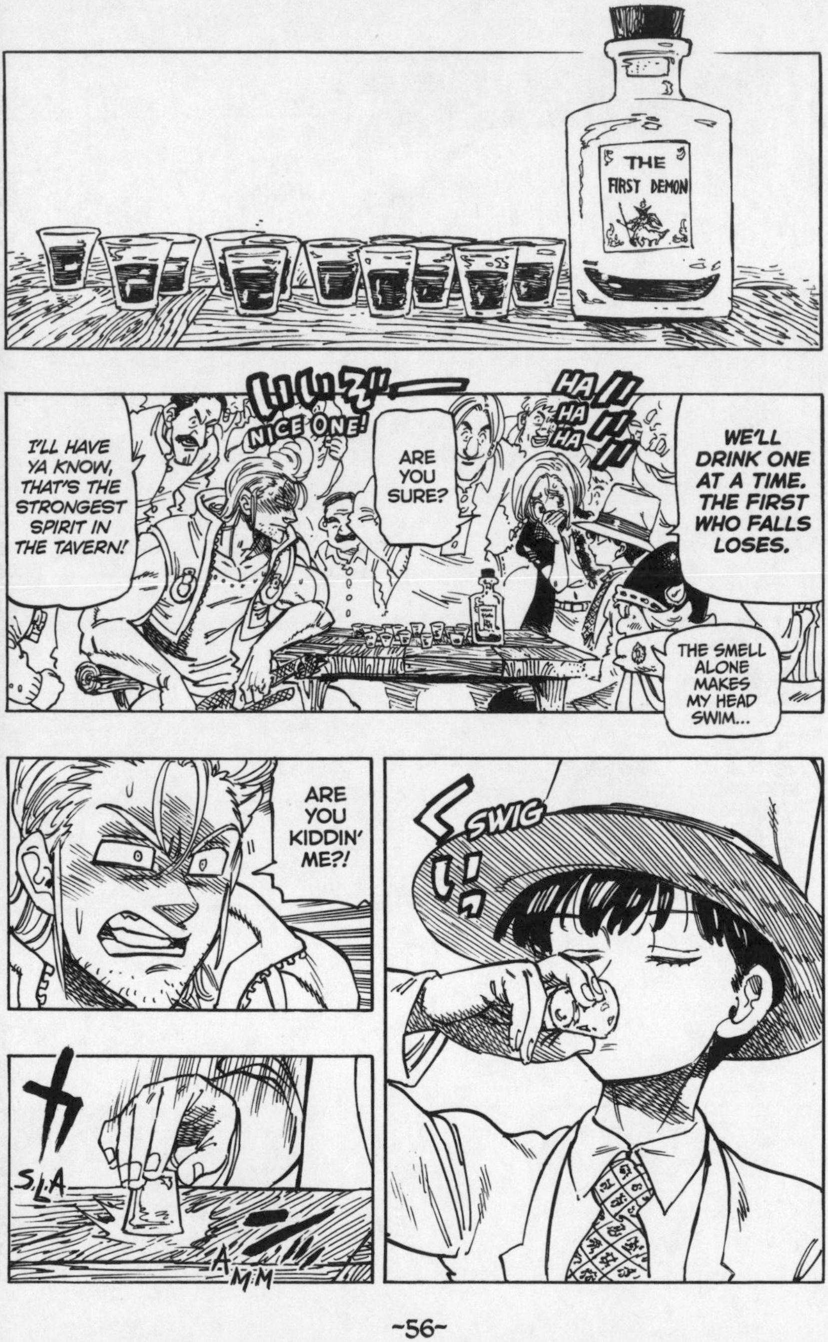
THE FIRST DEMON
HA HA HA
WE'LL DRINK ONE AT A TIME. THE FIRST WHO FALLS LOSES.
THE SMELL ALONE MAKES MY HEAD SWIM...
ARE YOU SURE?
NICE ONE!
I'LL HAVE YA KNOW, THAT'S THE STRONGEST SPIRIT IN THE TAVERN!
SWIG
ARE YOU KIDDIN' ME?!

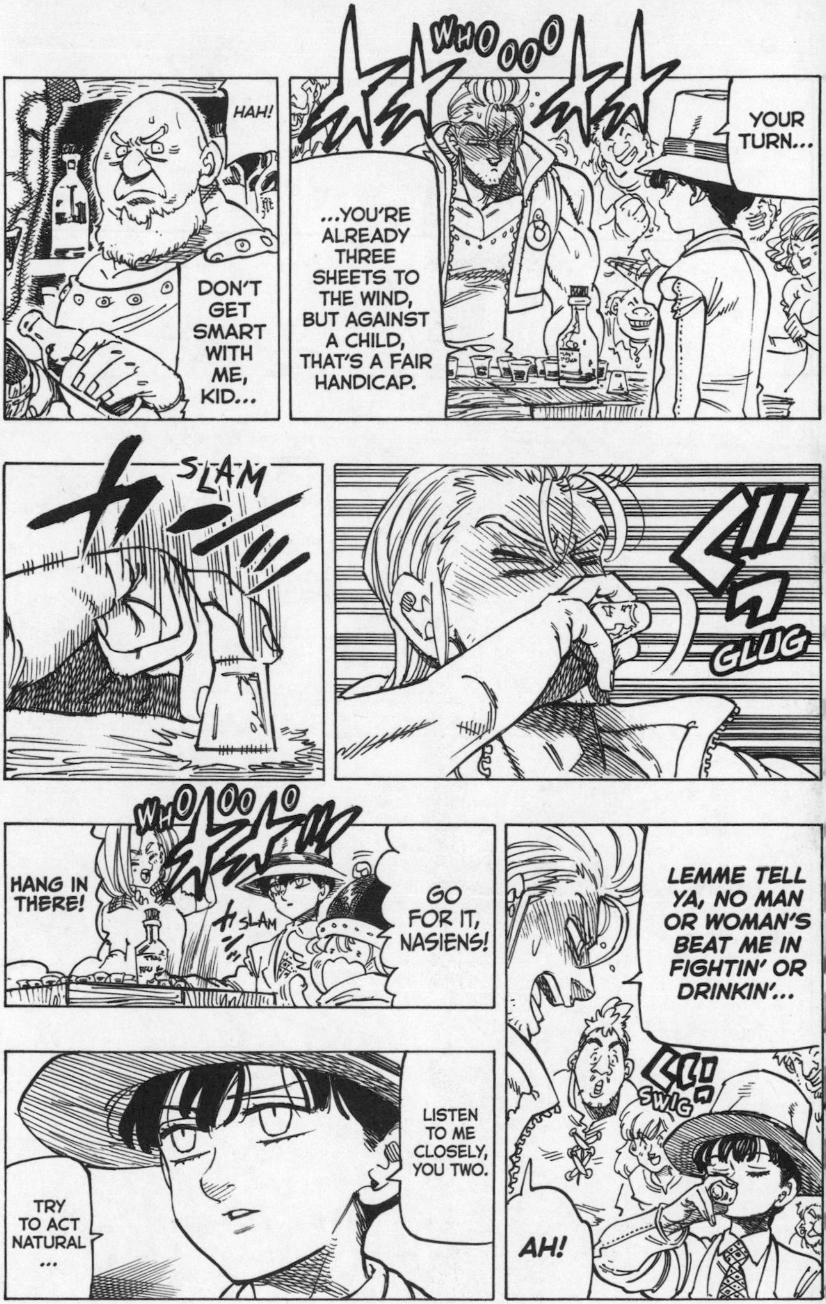
WHOOOO
YOUR TURN...
...YOU'RE ALREADY THREE SHEETS TO THE WIND, BUT AGAINST A CHILD, THAT'S A FAIR HANDICAP.
HAH!
DON'T GET SMART WITH ME, KID...
GLUG
SLAM
LEMME TELL YA, NO MAN OR WOMAN'S BEAT ME IN FIGHTIN' OR DRINKIN'...
SWIG
AH!
WHOOOOO
GO FOR IT, NASIENS!
SLAM
HANG IN THERE!
LISTEN TO ME CLOSELY, YOU TWO.
TRY TO ACT NATURAL ...

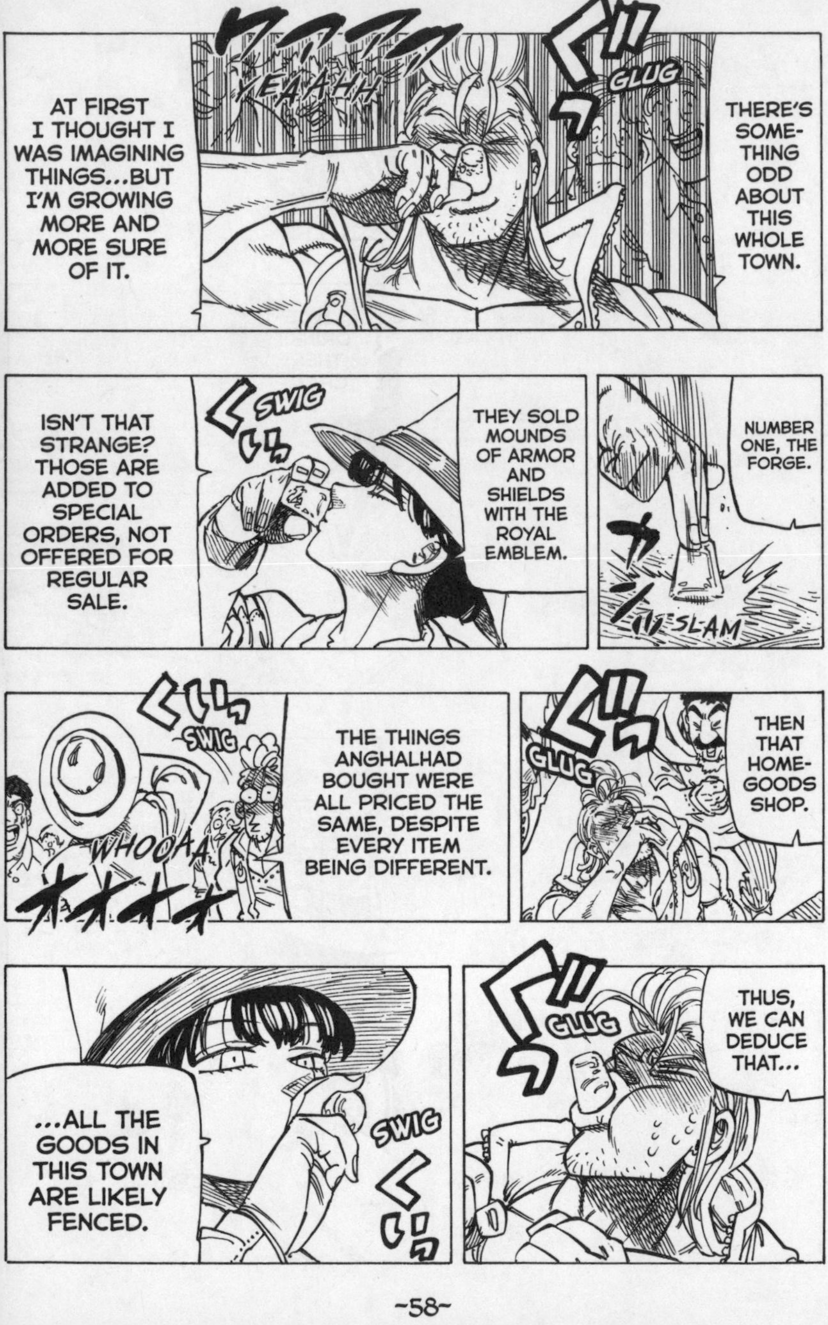
GLUG
THERE'S SOME-THING ODD ABOUT THIS WHOLE TOWN.
YEAAHH
AT FIRST I THOUGHT I WAS IMAGINING THINGS...BUT I'M GROWING MORE AND MORE SURE OF IT.
NUMBER ONE, THE FORGE.
SLAM
THEY SOLD MOUNDS OF ARMOR AND SHIELDS WITH THE ROYAL EMBLEM.
SWIG
ISN'T THAT STRANGE? THOSE ARE ADDED TO SPECIAL ORDERS, NOT OFFERED FOR REGULAR SALE.
GLUG
THEN THAT HOME-GOODS SHOP.
THE THINGS ANGHALHAD BOUGHT WERE ALL PRICED THE SAME, DESPITE EVERY ITEM BEING DIFFERENT.
SWIG
WHOOAA
GLUG
THUS, WE CAN DEDUCE THAT...
SWIG
...ALL THE GOODS IN THIS TOWN ARE LIKELY FENCED.

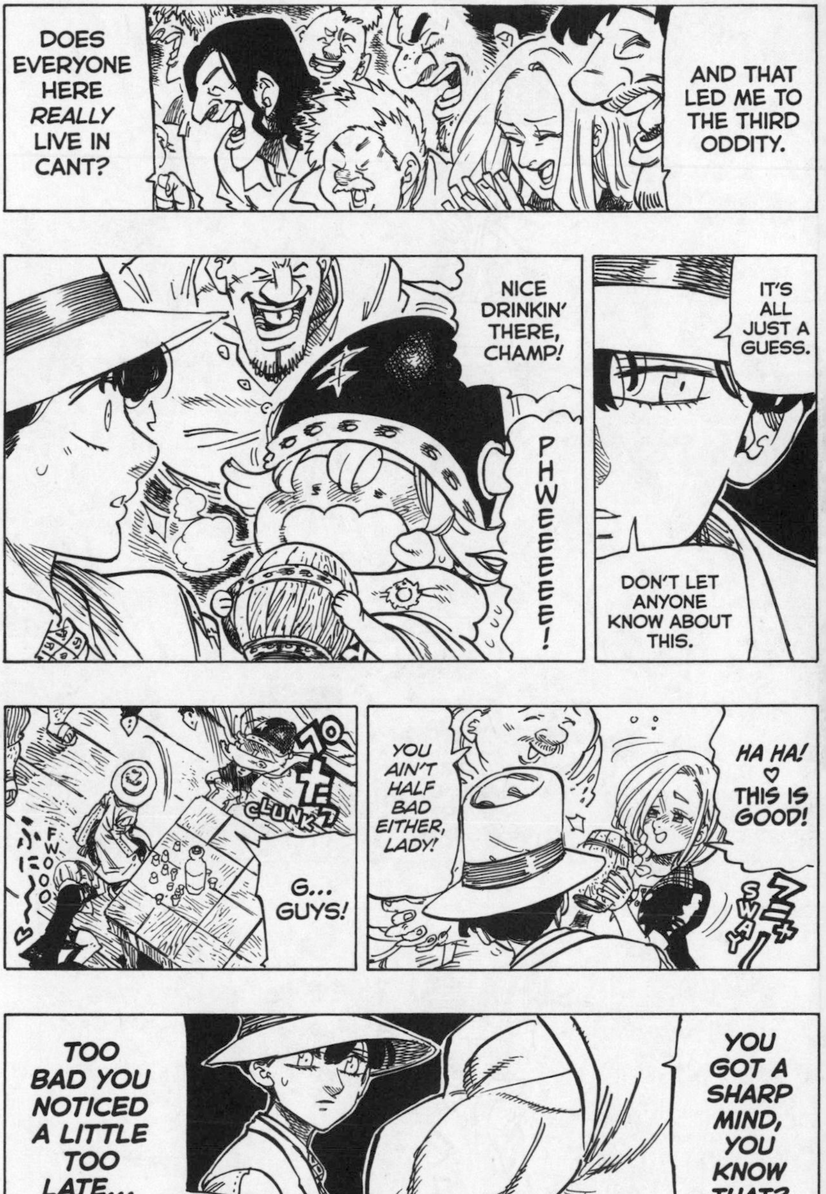
AND THAT LED ME TO THE THIRD ODDITY.
DOES EVERYONE HERE *REALLY* LIVE IN CANT?
IT'S ALL JUST A GUESS.
DON'T LET ANYONE KNOW ABOUT THIS.
NICE DRINKIN' THERE, CHAMP!
PHWEEEEEE!
HA HA! ♡ THIS IS GOOD!
SWAY
YOU AIN'T HALF BAD EITHER, LADY!
CLUNK
G... GUYS!
FWOOO
YOU GOT A SHARP MIND, YOU KNOW THAT?
TOO BAD YOU NOTICED A LITTLE TOO LATE...

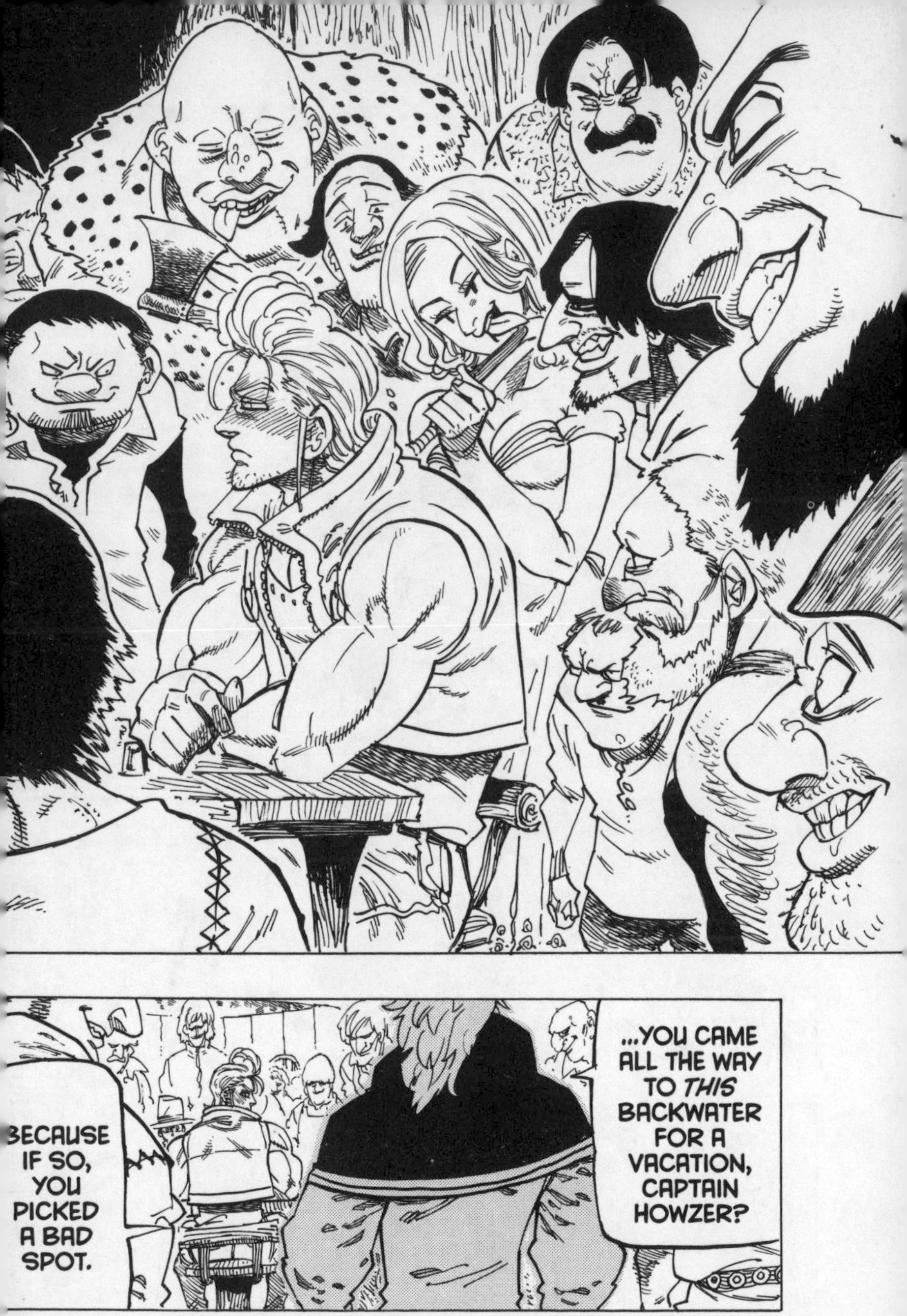
...YOU CAME ALL THE WAY TO *THIS* BACKWATER FOR A VACATION, CAPTAIN HOWZER?
BECAUSE IF SO, YOU PICKED A BAD SPOT.

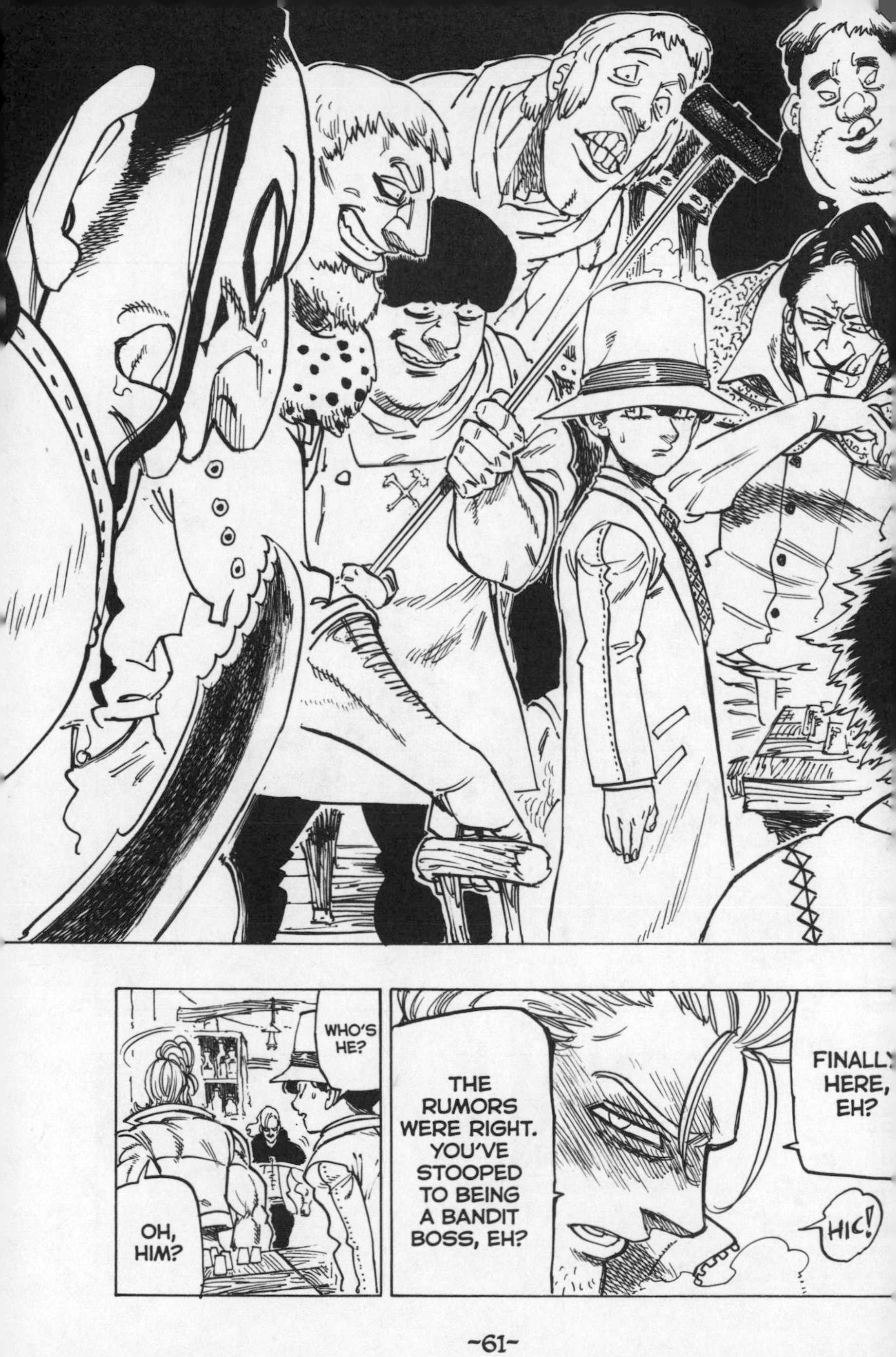
FINALLY HERE, EH?
THE RUMORS WERE RIGHT. YOU'VE STOOPED TO BEING A BANDIT BOSS, EH?
HIC!
WHO'S HE?
OH, HIM?

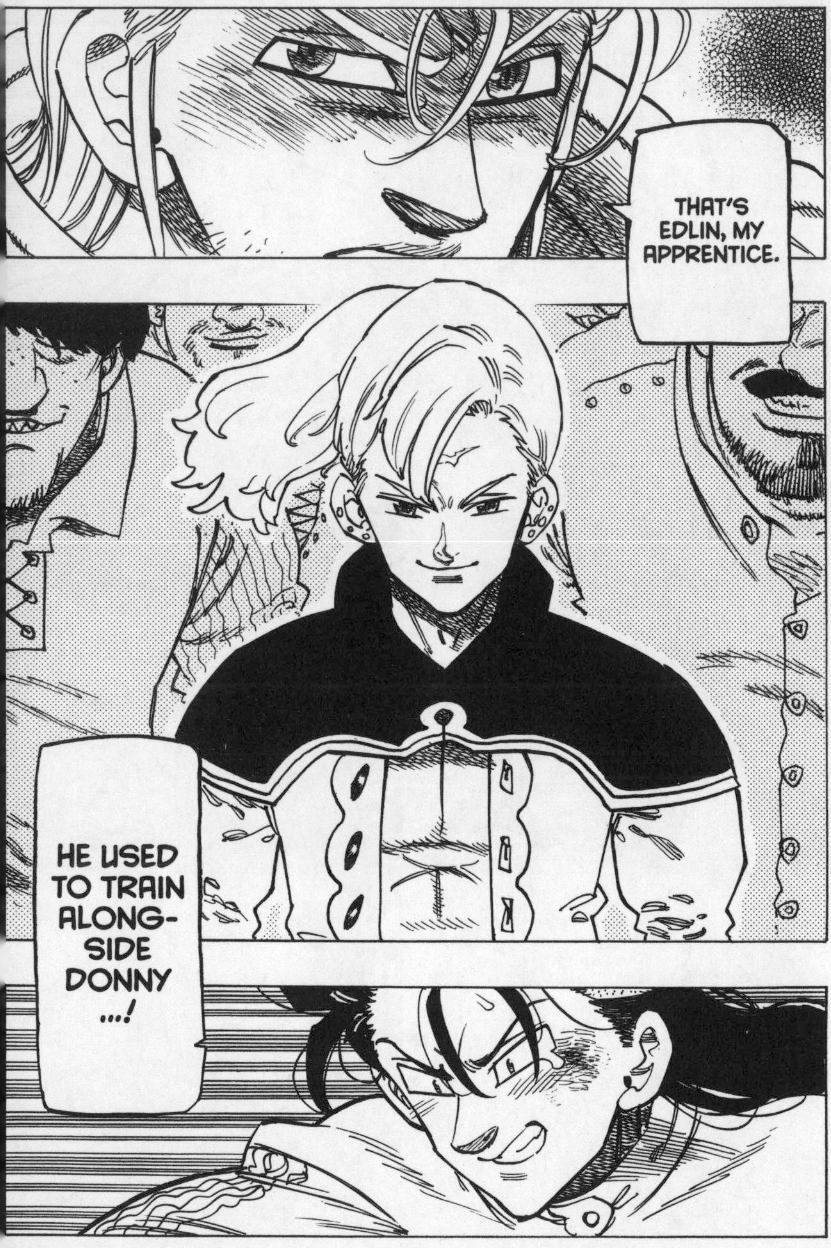
THAT'S EDLIN, MY APPRENTICE.
HE USED TO TRAIN ALONG-SIDE DONNY ...!

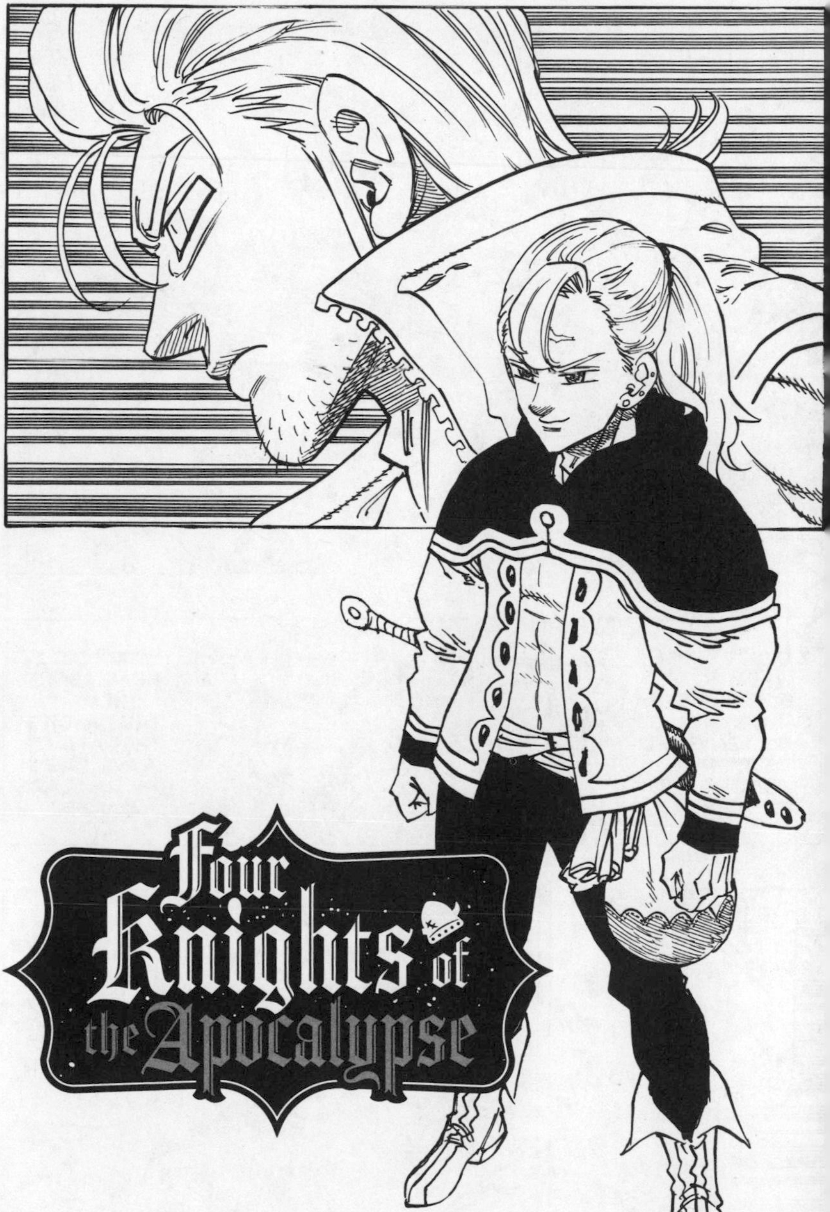
Four Knights of the Apocalypse

CHAPTER 27: MASTER AND PUPIL

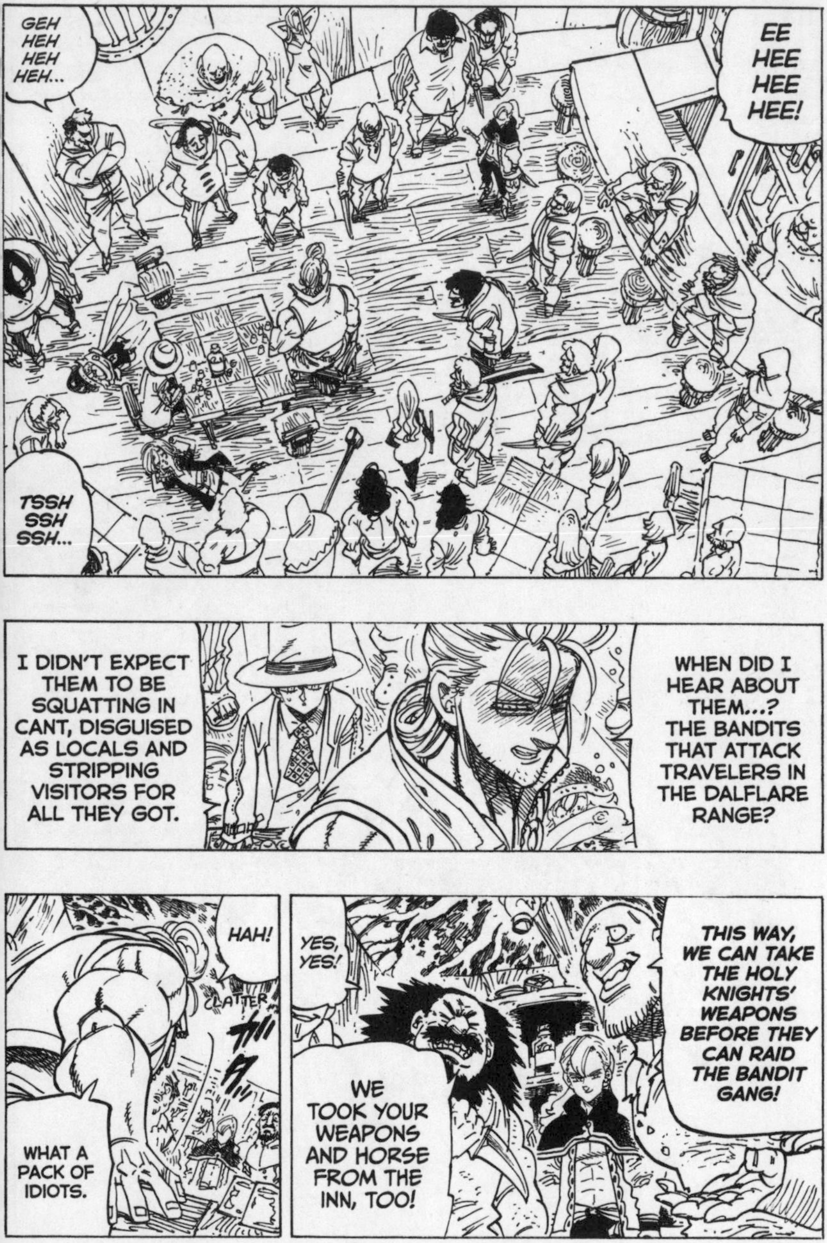

EE HEE HEE HEE!
GEH HEH HEH HEH...
TSSH SSH SSH...
WHEN DID I HEAR ABOUT THEM...? THE BANDITS THAT ATTACK TRAVELERS IN THE DALFLARE RANGE?
I DIDN'T EXPECT THEM TO BE SQUATTING IN CANT, DISGUISED AS LOCALS AND STRIPPING VISITORS FOR ALL THEY GOT.
THIS WAY, WE CAN TAKE THE HOLY KNIGHTS' WEAPONS BEFORE THEY CAN RAID THE BANDIT GANG!
YES, YES!
WE TOOK YOUR WEAPONS AND HORSE FROM THE INN, TOO!
HAH!
CLATTER
WHAT A PACK OF IDIOTS.

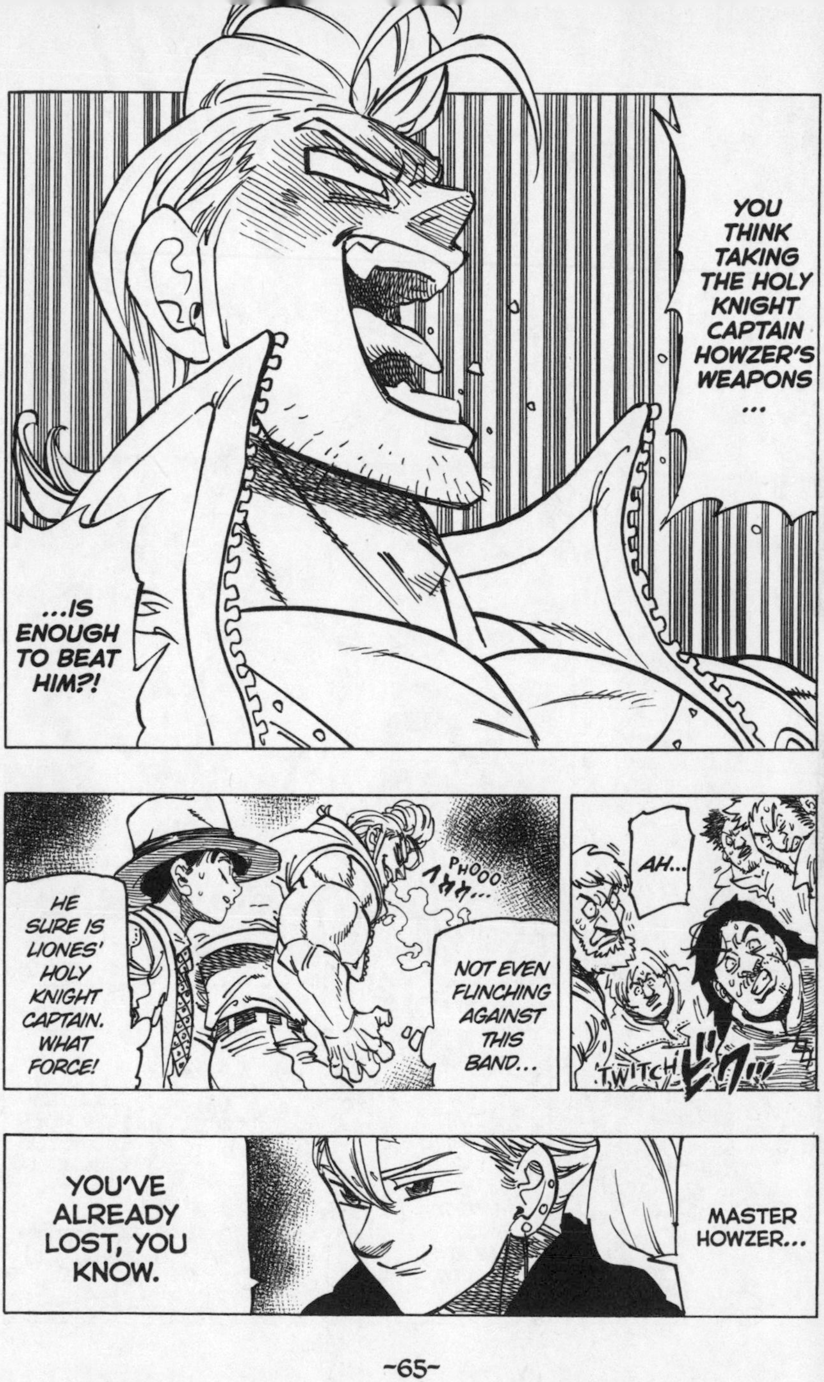
YOU THINK TAKING THE HOLY KNIGHT CAPTAIN HOWZER'S WEAPONS ...
...IS ENOUGH TO BEAT HIM?!
AH...
TWITCH
PHOOO...
NOT EVEN FLINCHING AGAINST THIS BAND...
HE SURE IS LIONES' HOLY KNIGHT CAPTAIN. WHAT FORCE!
MASTER HOWZER...
YOU'VE ALREADY LOST, YOU KNOW.

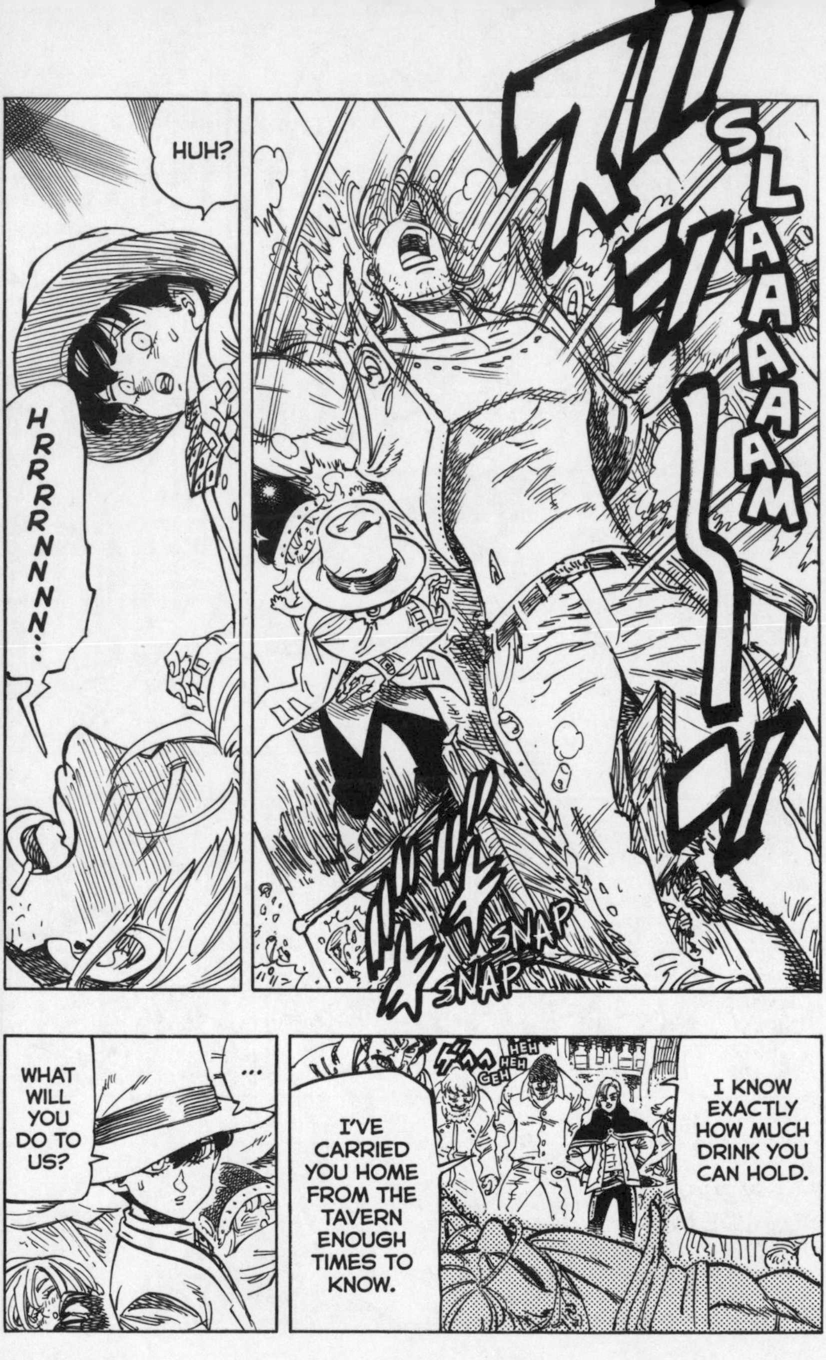
SLAAAAAM
SNAP
SNAP
HUH?
HRRRRNNNNN...
I KNOW EXACTLY HOW MUCH DRINK YOU CAN HOLD.
HEH HEH GEH
I'VE CARRIED YOU HOME FROM THE TAVERN ENOUGH TIMES TO KNOW.
...
WHAT WILL YOU DO TO US?

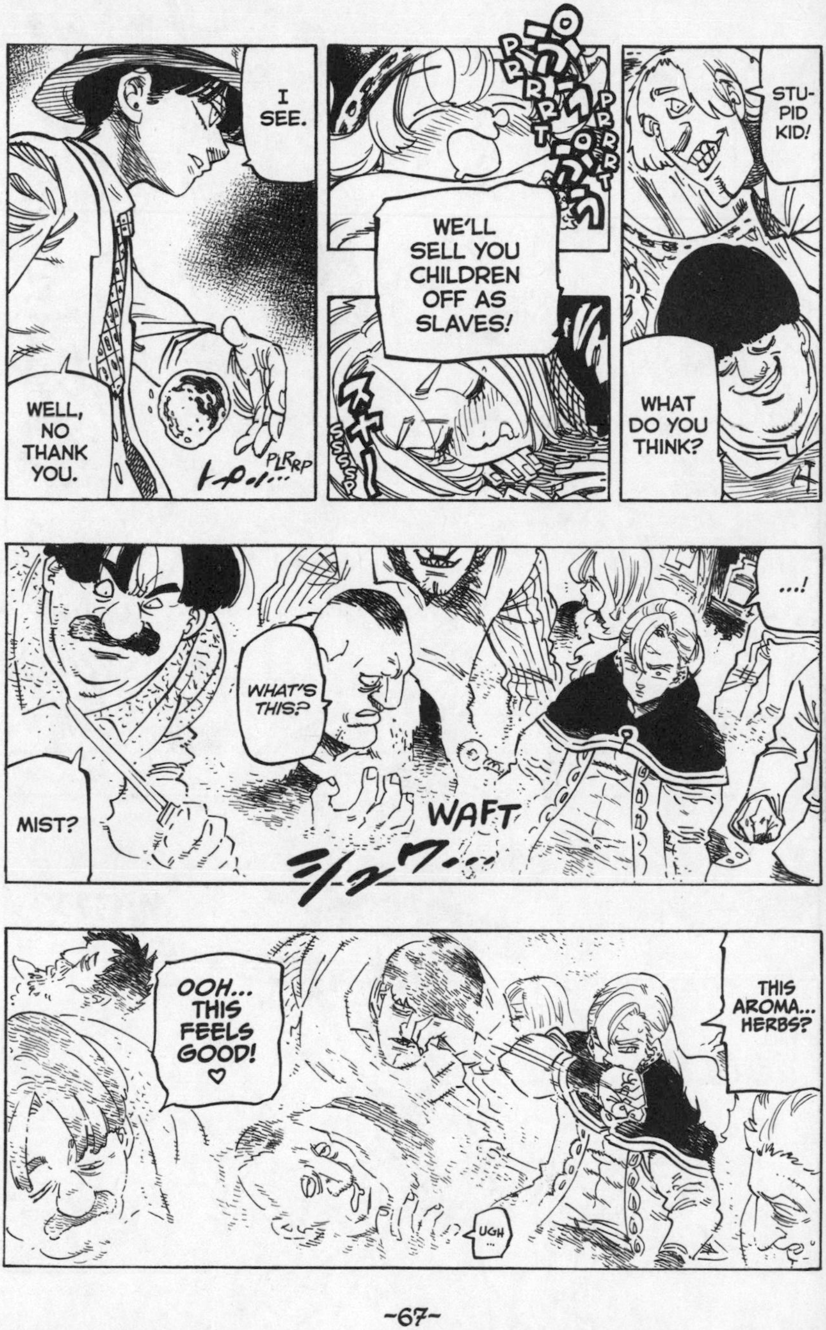
STU-PID KID!
WHAT DO YOU THINK?
PRRRT
PRRRT
WE'LL SELL YOU CHILDREN OFF AS SLAVES!
SSSSP
I SEE.
WELL, NO THANK YOU.
PLRRP
...!
WHAT'S THIS?
WAFT
MIST?
THIS AROMA... HERBS?
UGH...
OOH... THIS FEELS GOOD! ♡

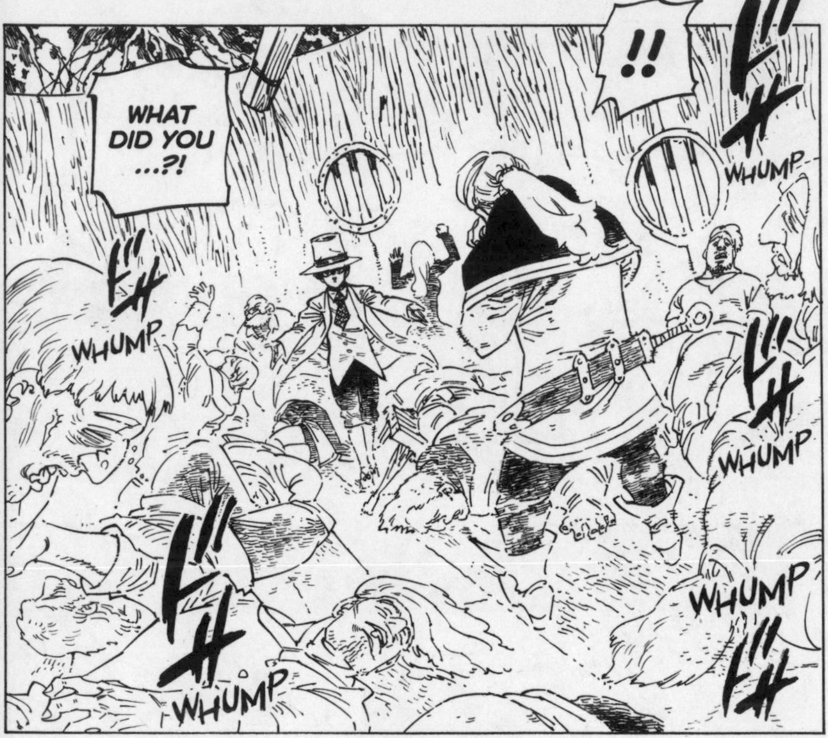
!!
WHUMP
WHAT DID YOU ...?!
WHUMP
WHUMP
WHUMP
WHUMP

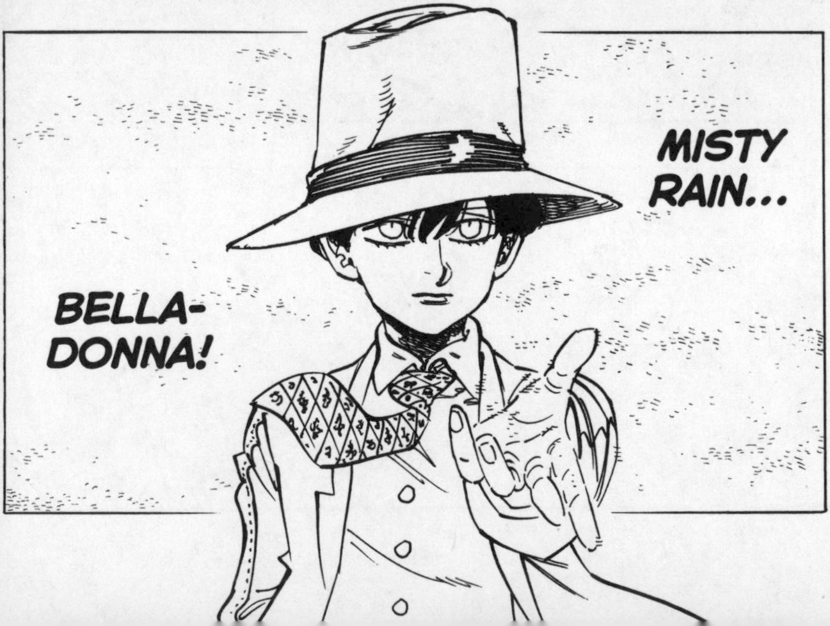
MISTY RAIN...
BELLA-DONNA!

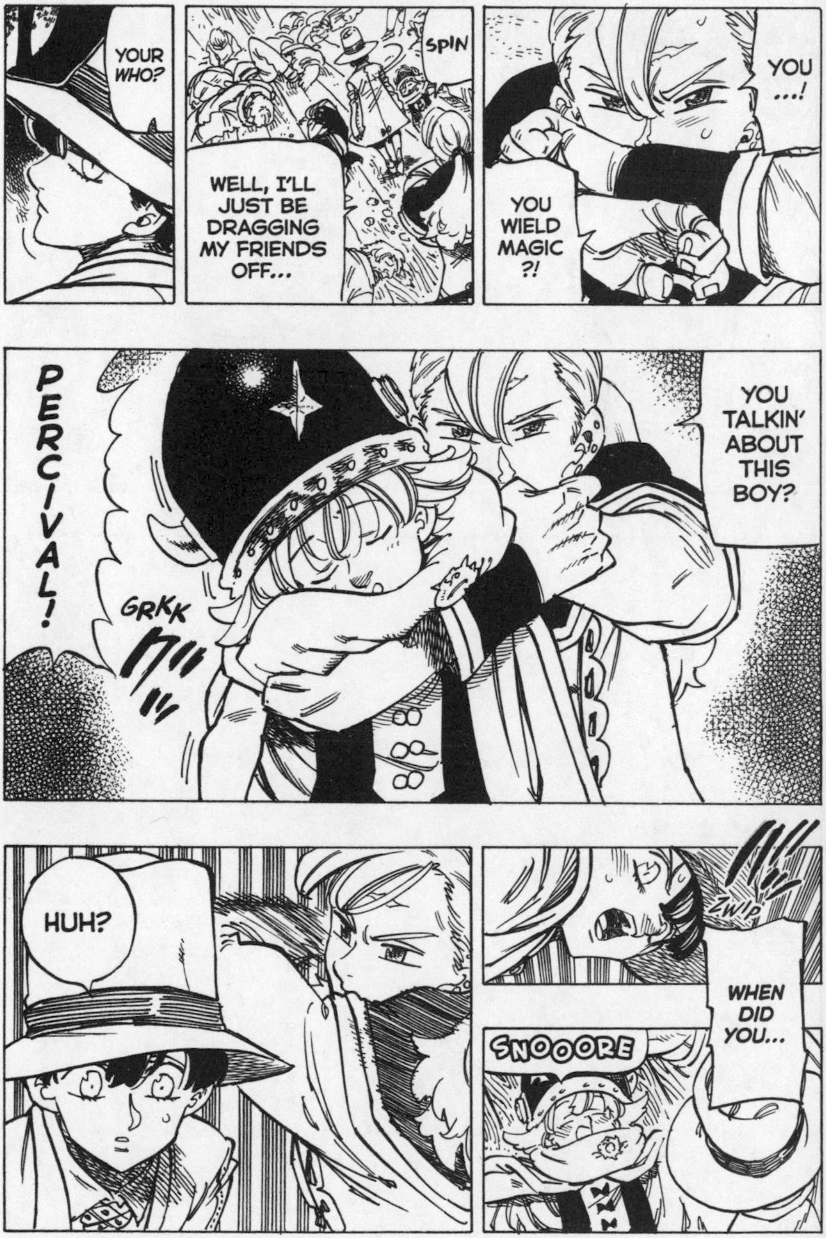
YOU ...!
YOU WIELD MAGIC ?!
SPIN
WELL, I'LL JUST BE DRAGGING MY FRIENDS OFF...
YOUR WHO?
YOU TALKIN' ABOUT THIS BOY?
PERCIVAL!
GRKK
ZWIP
WHEN DID YOU...
SNOOORE
HUH?

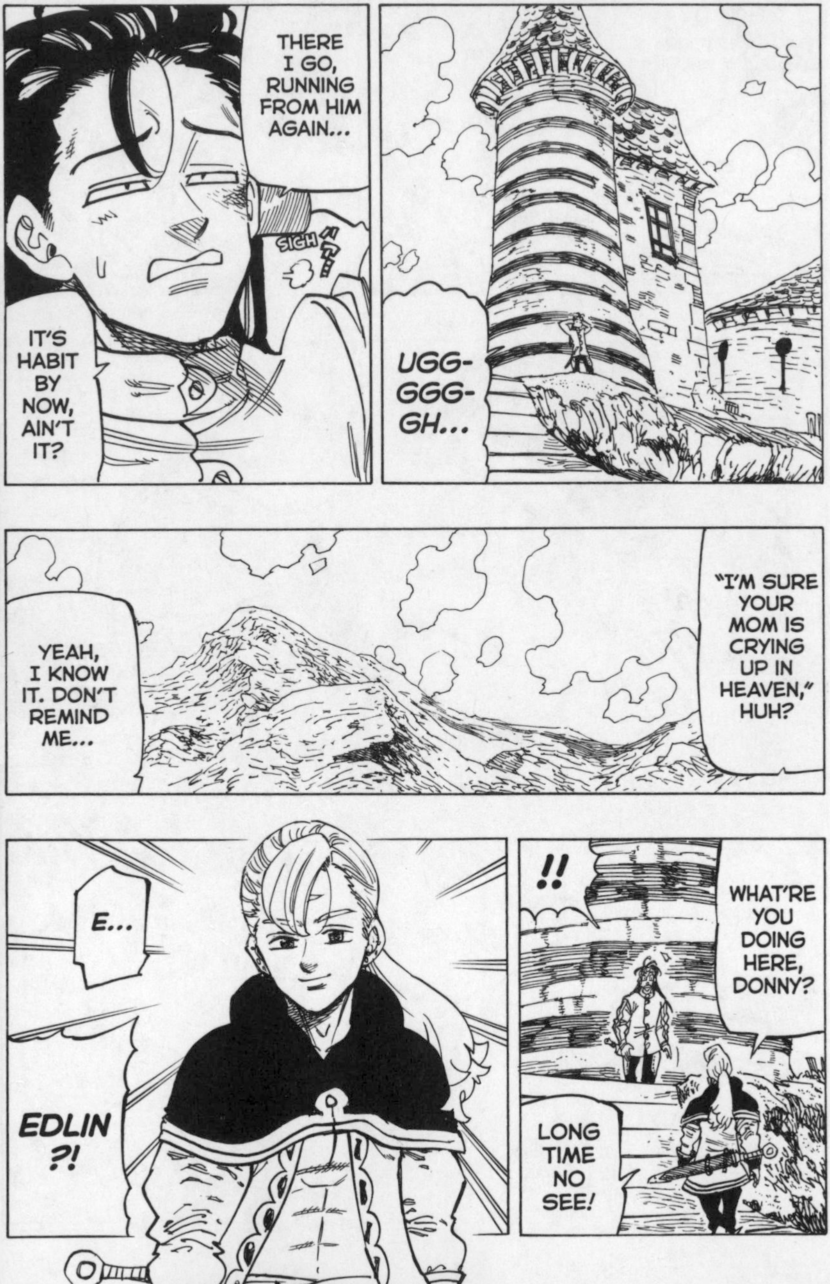
UGG-GGG-GH...
THERE I GO, RUNNING FROM HIM AGAIN...
SIGH
IT'S HABIT BY NOW, AIN'T IT?
"I'M SURE YOUR MOM IS CRYING UP IN HEAVEN," HUH?
YEAH, I KNOW IT. DON'T REMIND ME...
!!
WHAT'RE YOU DOING HERE, DONNY?
LONG TIME NO SEE!
E...
EDLIN ?!

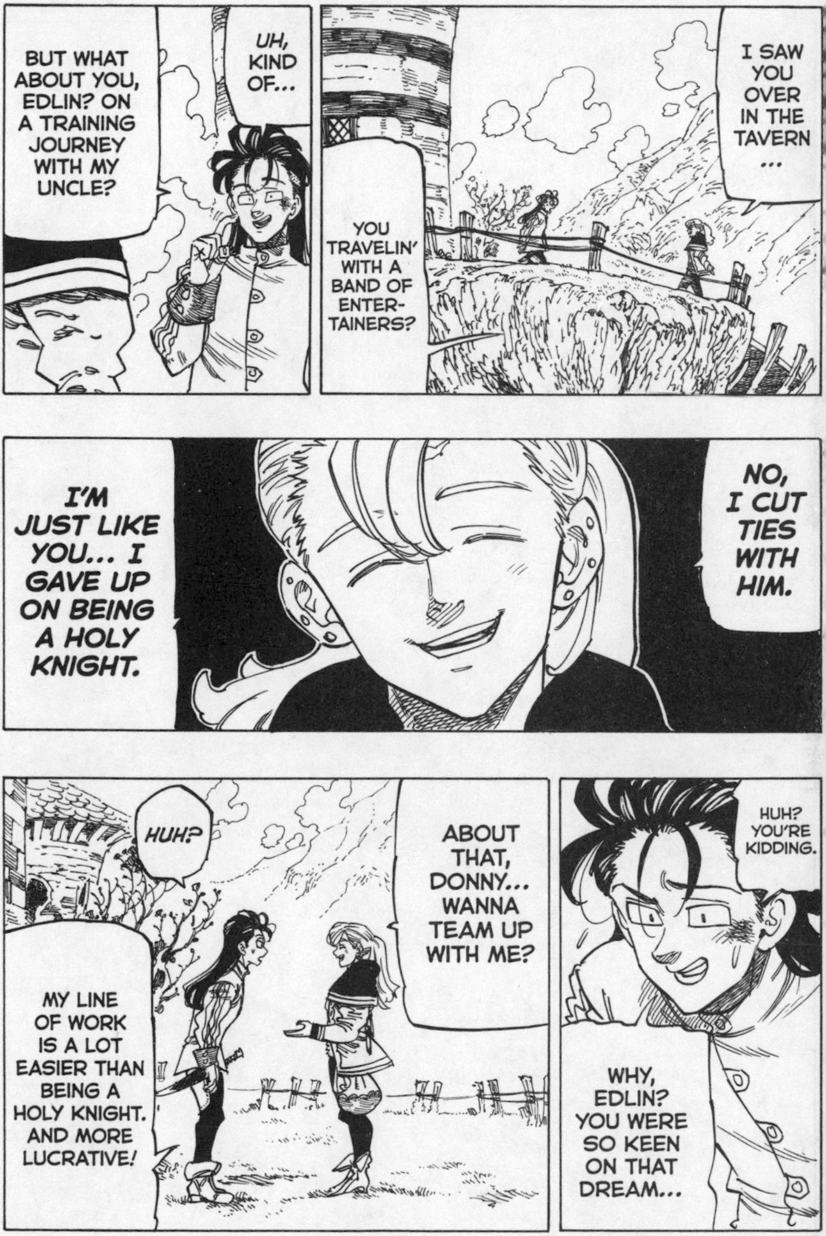
I SAW YOU OVER IN THE TAVERN...
YOU TRAVELIN' WITH A BAND OF ENTERTAINERS?
UH, KIND OF...
BUT WHAT ABOUT YOU, EDLIN? ON A TRAINING JOURNEY WITH MY UNCLE?
NO, I CUT TIES WITH HIM.
I'M JUST LIKE YOU... I GAVE UP ON BEING A HOLY KNIGHT.
HUH? YOU'RE KIDDING.
WHY, EDLIN? YOU WERE SO KEEN ON THAT DREAM...
ABOUT THAT, DONNY... WANNA TEAM UP WITH ME?
HUH?
MY LINE OF WORK IS A LOT EASIER THAN BEING A HOLY KNIGHT. AND MORE LUCRATIVE!

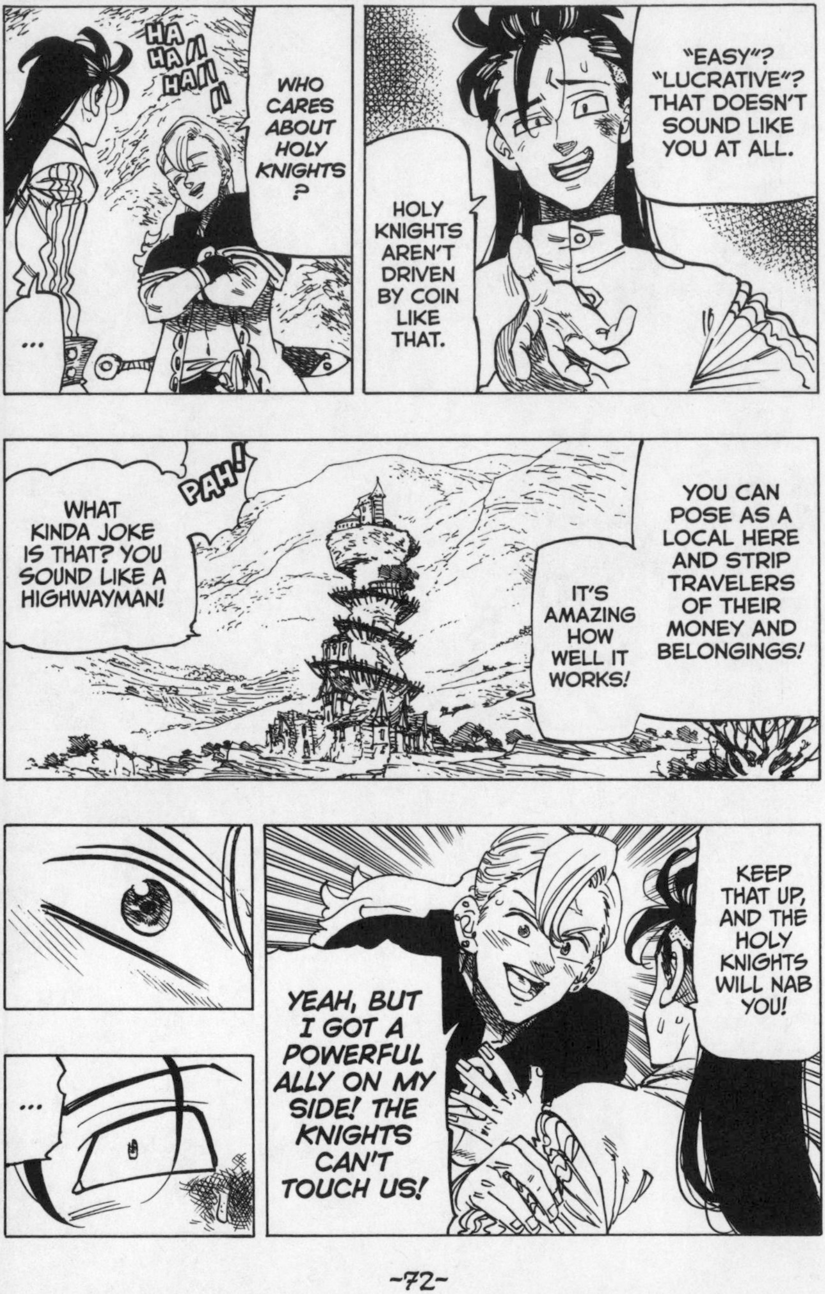
"EASY"? "LUCRATIVE"? THAT DOESN'T SOUND LIKE YOU AT ALL.
HOLY KNIGHTS AREN'T DRIVEN BY COIN LIKE THAT.
HA HA HA!!
WHO CARES ABOUT HOLY KNIGHTS?
...
YOU CAN POSE AS A LOCAL HERE AND STRIP TRAVELERS OF THEIR MONEY AND BELONGINGS!
IT'S AMAZING HOW WELL IT WORKS!
PAH!
WHAT KINDA JOKE IS THAT? YOU SOUND LIKE A HIGHWAYMAN!
KEEP THAT UP, AND THE HOLY KNIGHTS WILL NAB YOU!
YEAH, BUT I GOT A POWERFUL ALLY ON MY SIDE! THE KNIGHTS CAN'T TOUCH US!
...

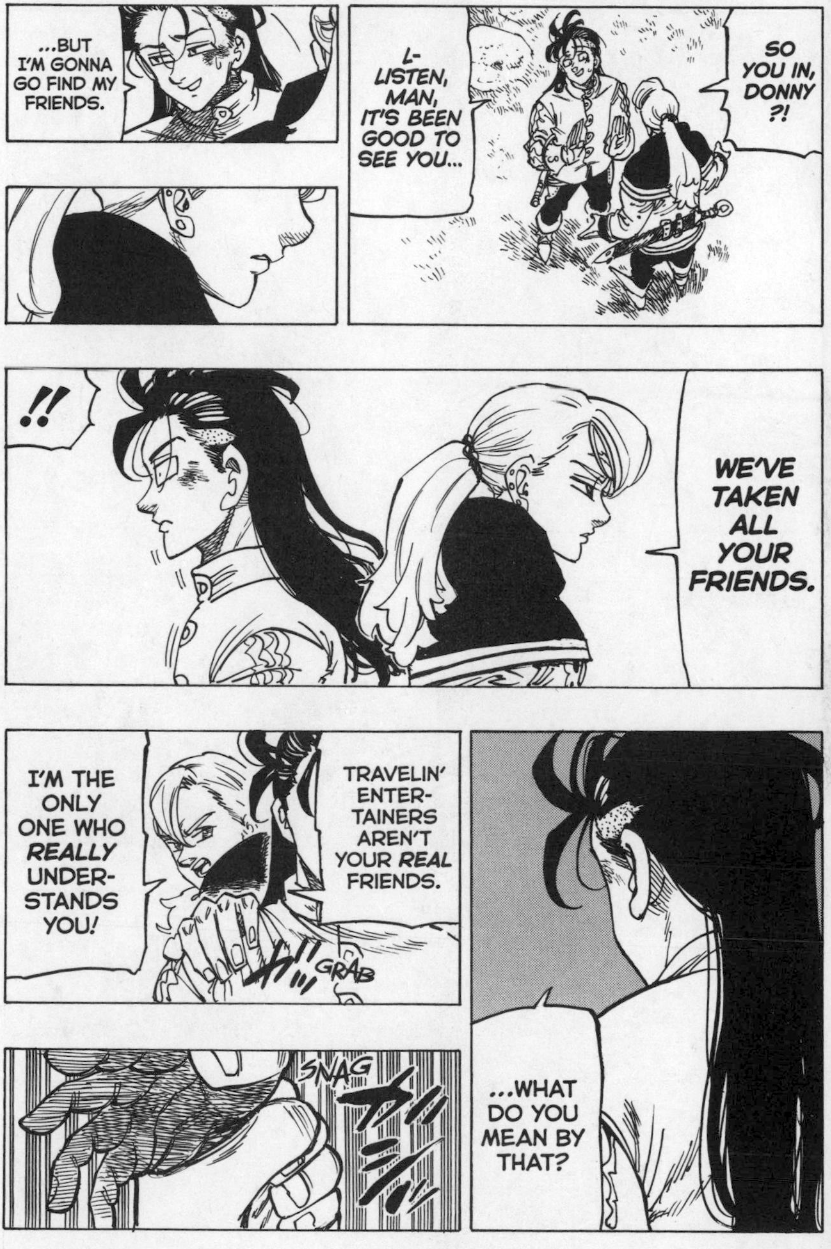
SO YOU IN, DONNY?!
L-LISTEN, MAN, IT'S BEEN GOOD TO SEE YOU...
...BUT I'M GONNA GO FIND MY FRIENDS.
WE'VE TAKEN ALL YOUR FRIENDS.
!!
...WHAT DO YOU MEAN BY THAT?
TRAVELIN' ENTERTAINERS AREN'T YOUR REAL FRIENDS.
I'M THE ONLY ONE WHO REALLY UNDERSTANDS YOU!
GRAB
SNAG

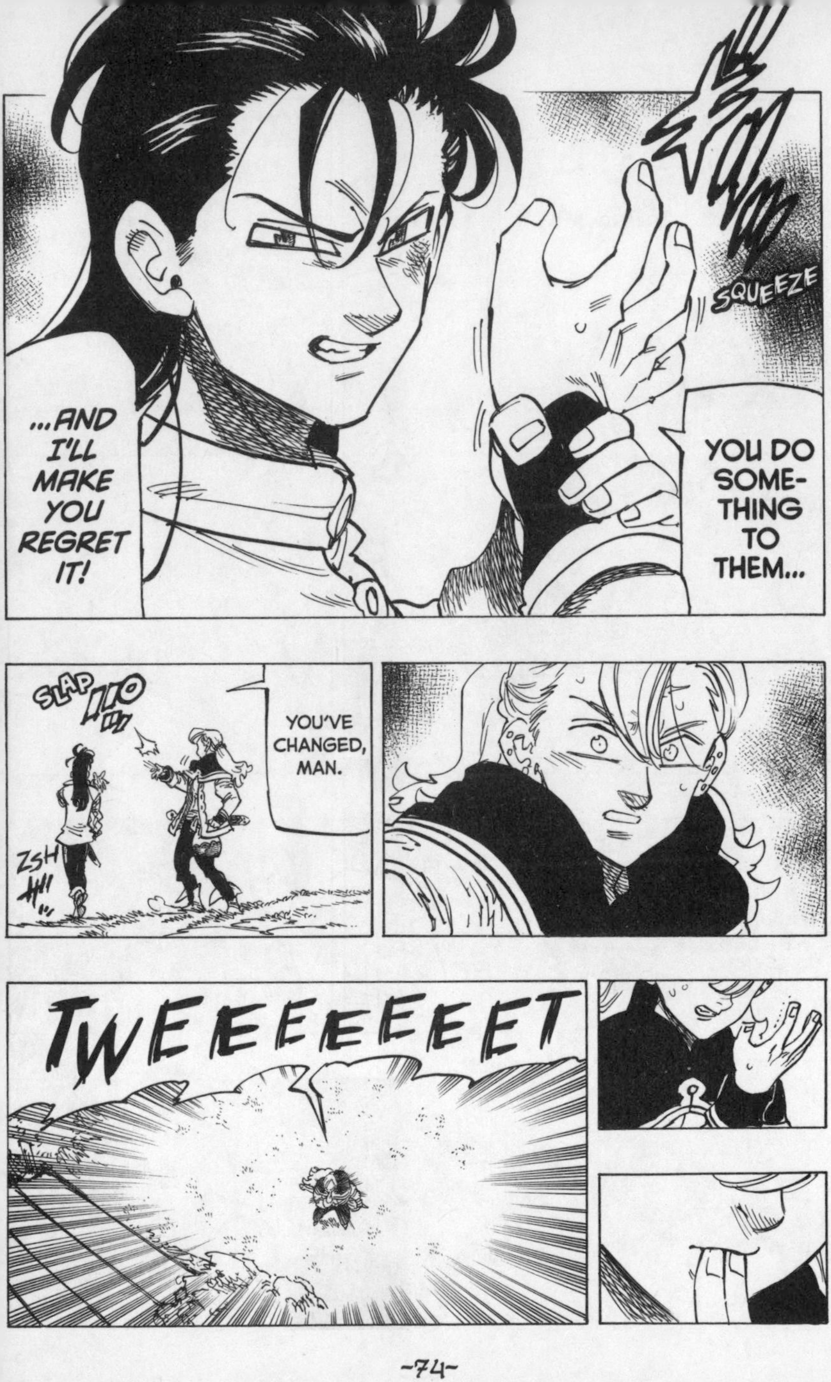
SQUEEZE
YOU DO SOME-THING TO THEM...
...AND I'LL MAKE YOU REGRET IT!
YOU'VE CHANGED, MAN.
SLAP
ZSH
TWEEEEEEET

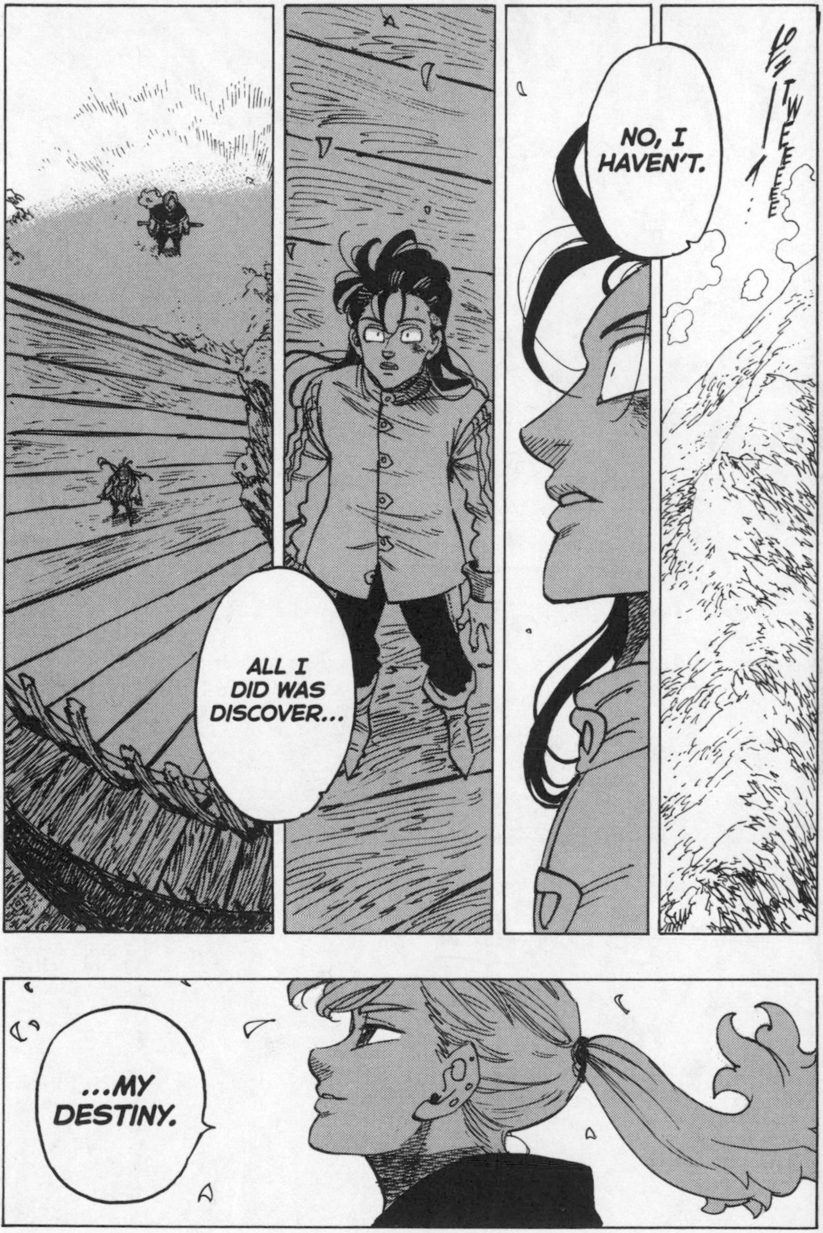
TWEEEE
NO, I HAVEN'T.
ALL I DID WAS DISCOVER...
...MY DESTINY.

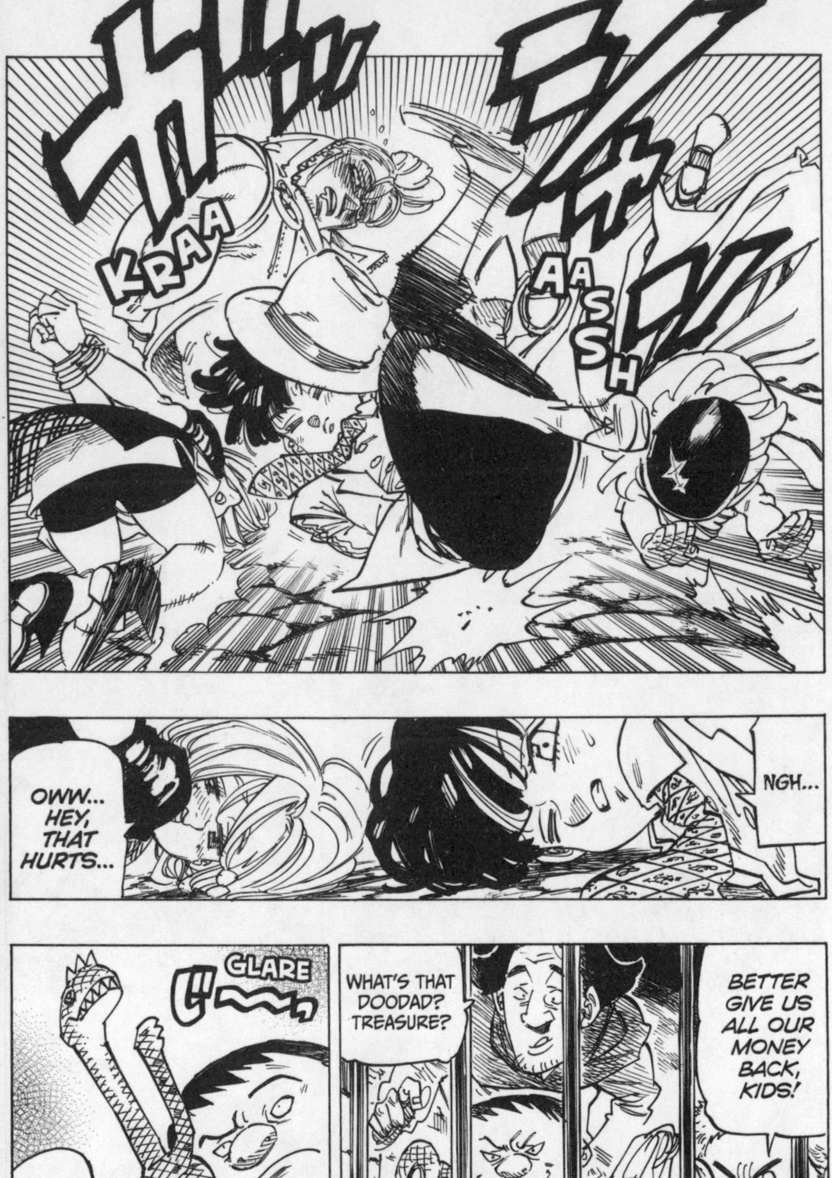
AASSH
KRAA
NGH...
OWW... HEY, THAT HURTS...
BETTER GIVE US ALL OUR MONEY BACK, KIDS!
WHAT'S THAT DOODAD? TREASURE?
GLARE
HMM...

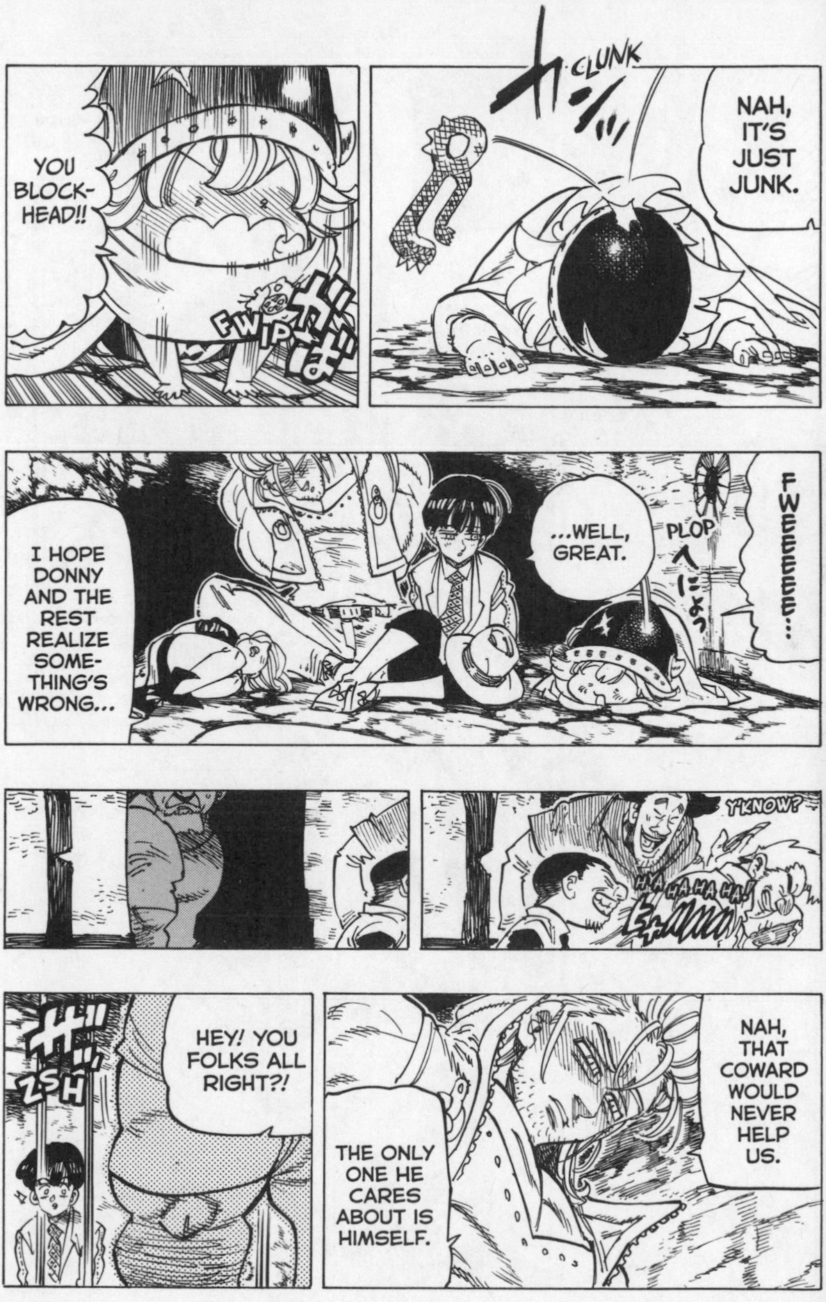
CLUNK
NAH, IT'S JUST JUNK.
YOU BLOCKHEAD!!
FWIP
FWEEEEE...
PLOP
...WELL, GREAT.
I HOPE DONNY AND THE REST REALIZE SOMETHING'S WRONG...
Y'KNOW?
HA HA HA HA!
NAH, THAT COWARD WOULD NEVER HELP US.
THE ONLY ONE HE CARES ABOUT IS HIMSELF.
HEY! YOU FOLKS ALL RIGHT?!
ZSH

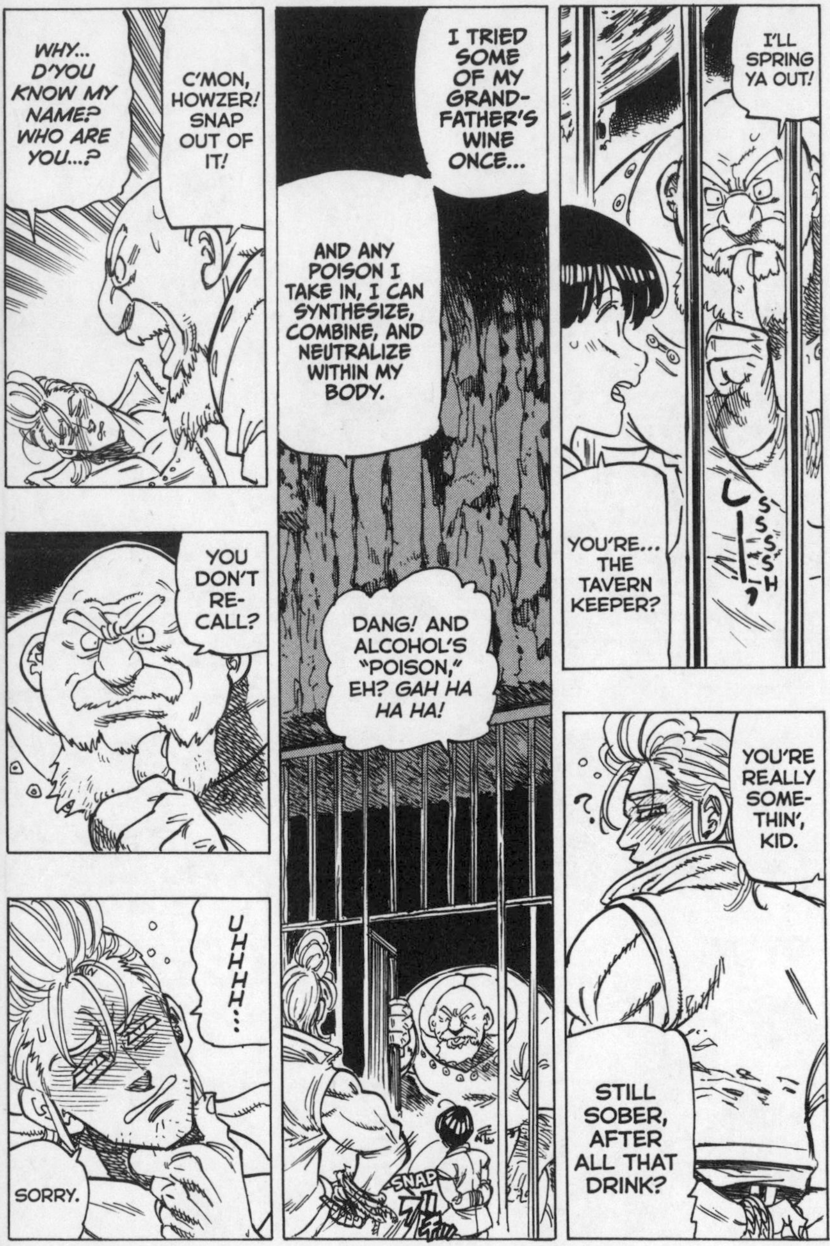
I'LL SPRING YA OUT!
YOU'RE... THE TAVERN KEEPER?
SSSSH
YOU'RE REALLY SOME-THIN', KID.
STILL SOBER, AFTER ALL THAT DRINK?
I TRIED SOME OF MY GRAND-FATHER'S WINE ONCE...
AND ANY POISON I TAKE IN, I CAN SYNTHESIZE, COMBINE, AND NEUTRALIZE WITHIN MY BODY.
DANG! AND ALCOHOL'S "POISON," EH? GAH HA HA HA!
SNAP
C'MON, HOWZER! SNAP OUT OF IT!
WHY... D'YOU KNOW MY NAME? WHO ARE YOU...?
YOU DON'T RE-CALL?
UHHHH...
SORRY.

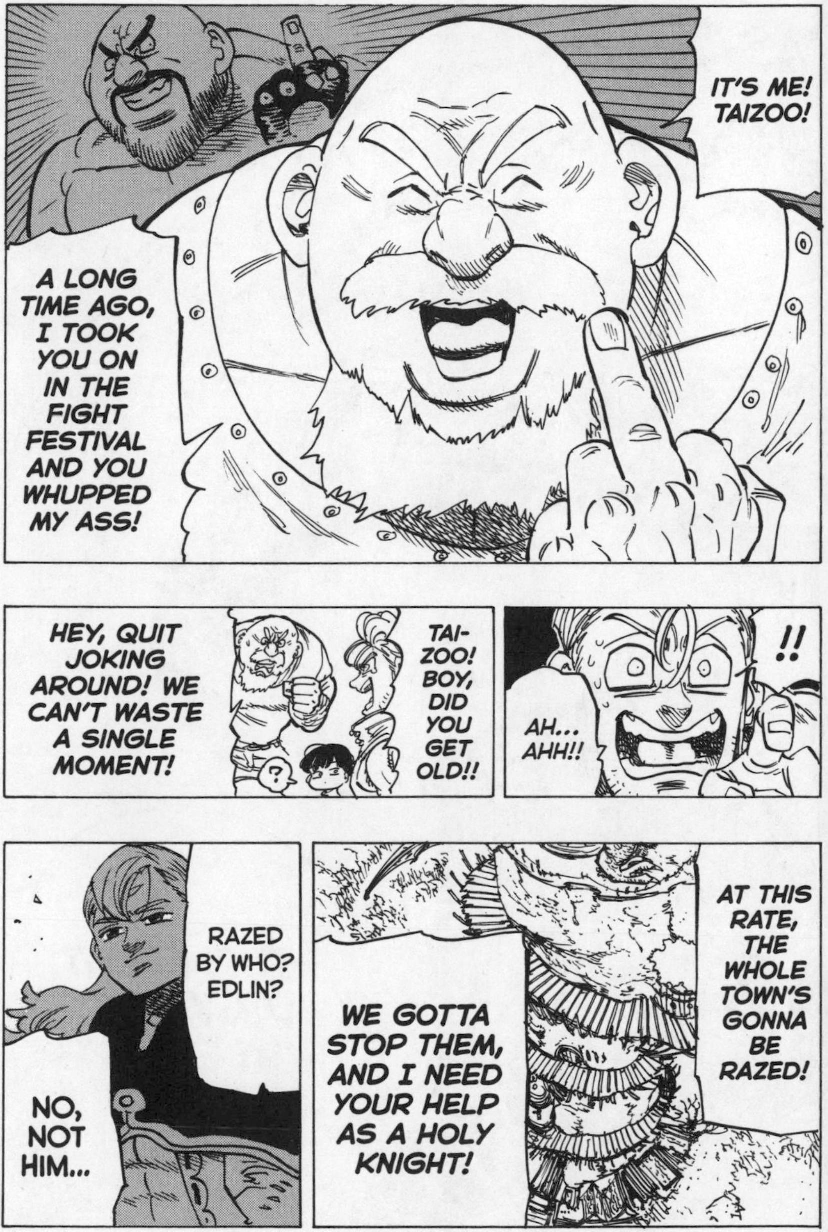
IT'S ME! TAIZOO!
A LONG TIME AGO, I TOOK YOU ON IN THE FIGHT FESTIVAL AND YOU WHUPPED MY ASS!
!!
AH... AHH!!
TAI-ZOO! BOY, DID YOU GET OLD!!
HEY, QUIT JOKING AROUND! WE CAN'T WASTE A SINGLE MOMENT!
?
AT THIS RATE, THE WHOLE TOWN'S GONNA BE RAZED!
WE GOTTA STOP THEM, AND I NEED YOUR HELP AS A HOLY KNIGHT!
RAZED BY WHO? EDLIN?
NO, NOT HIM...

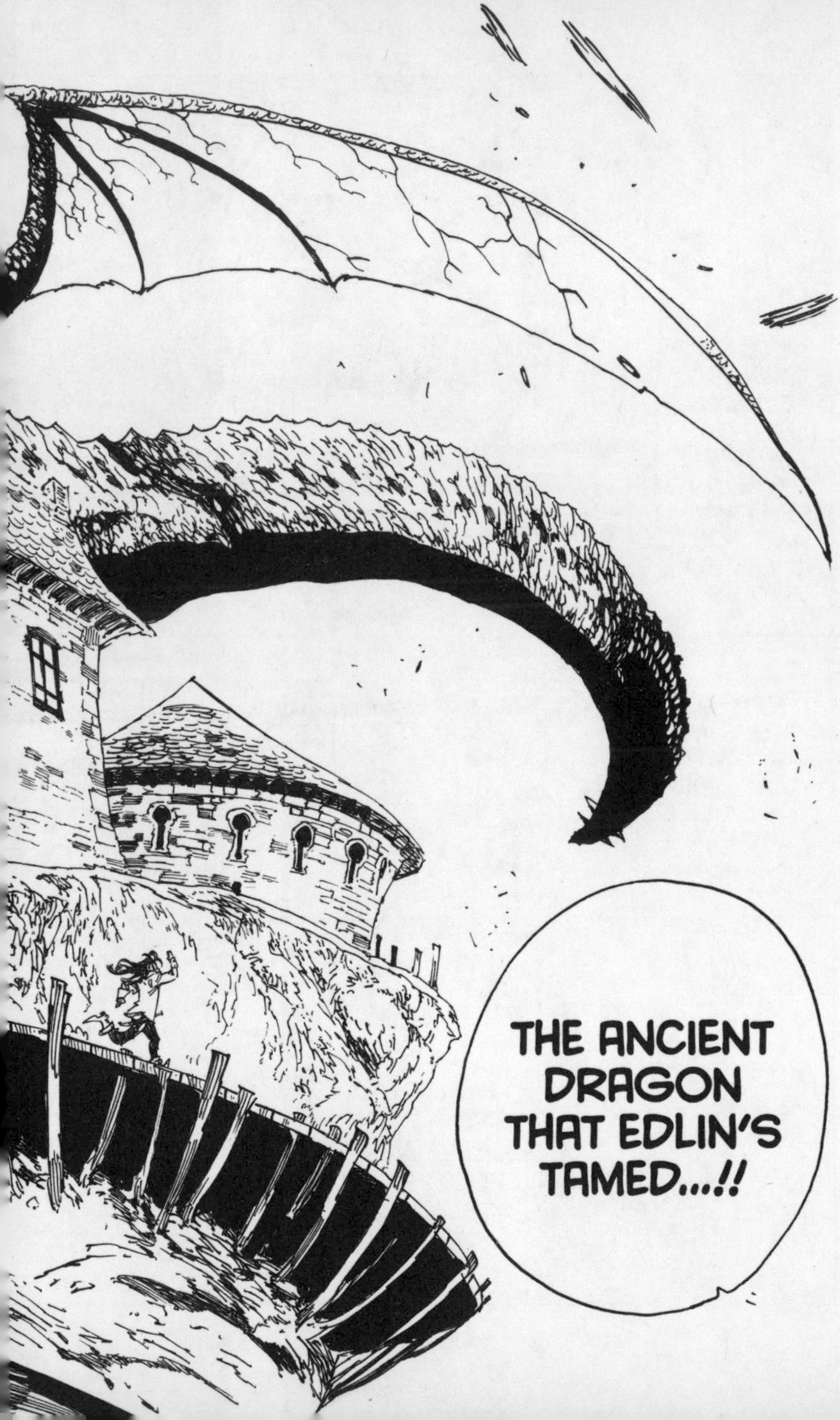
THE ANCIENT DRAGON THAT EDLIN'S TAMED...!!

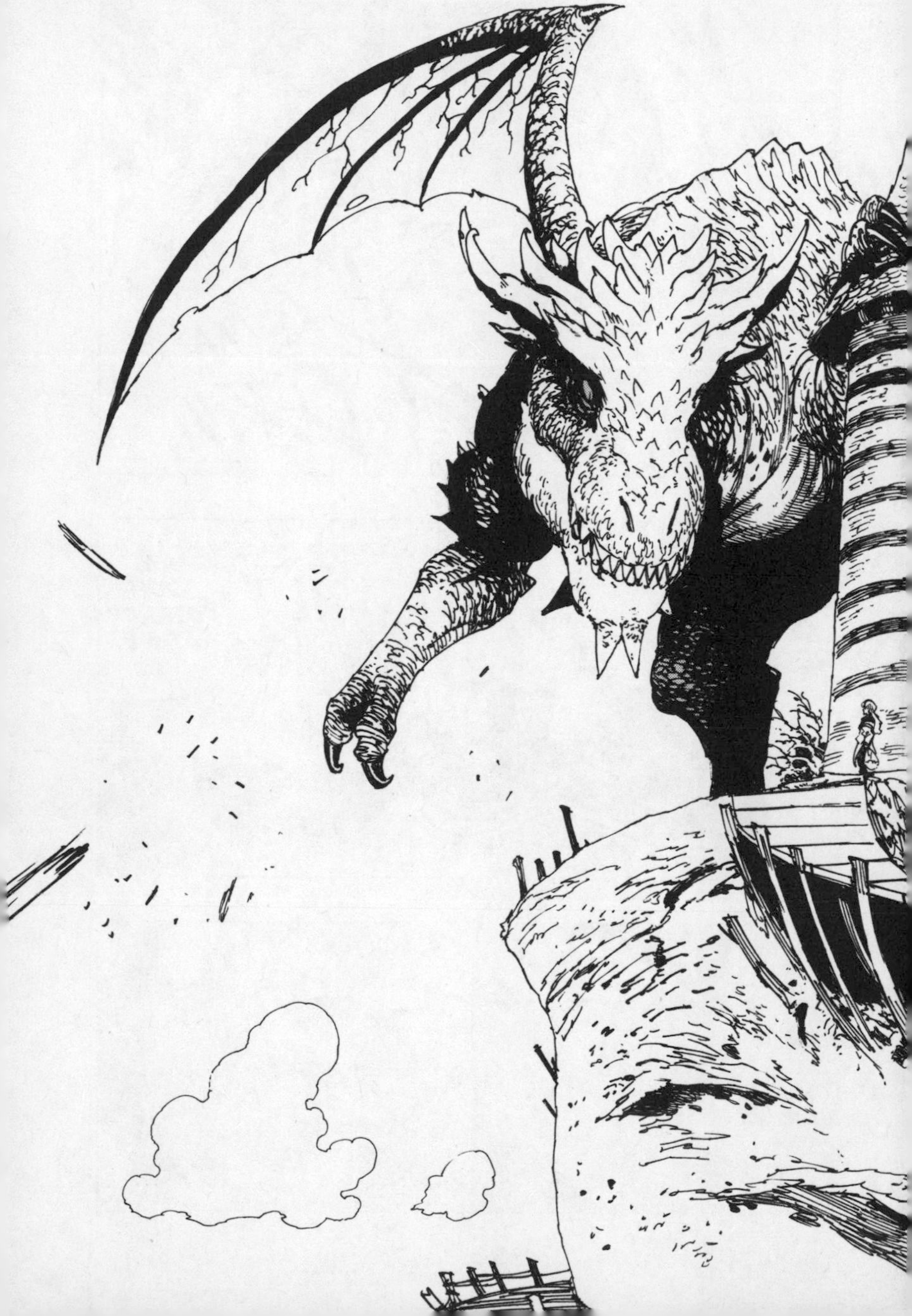

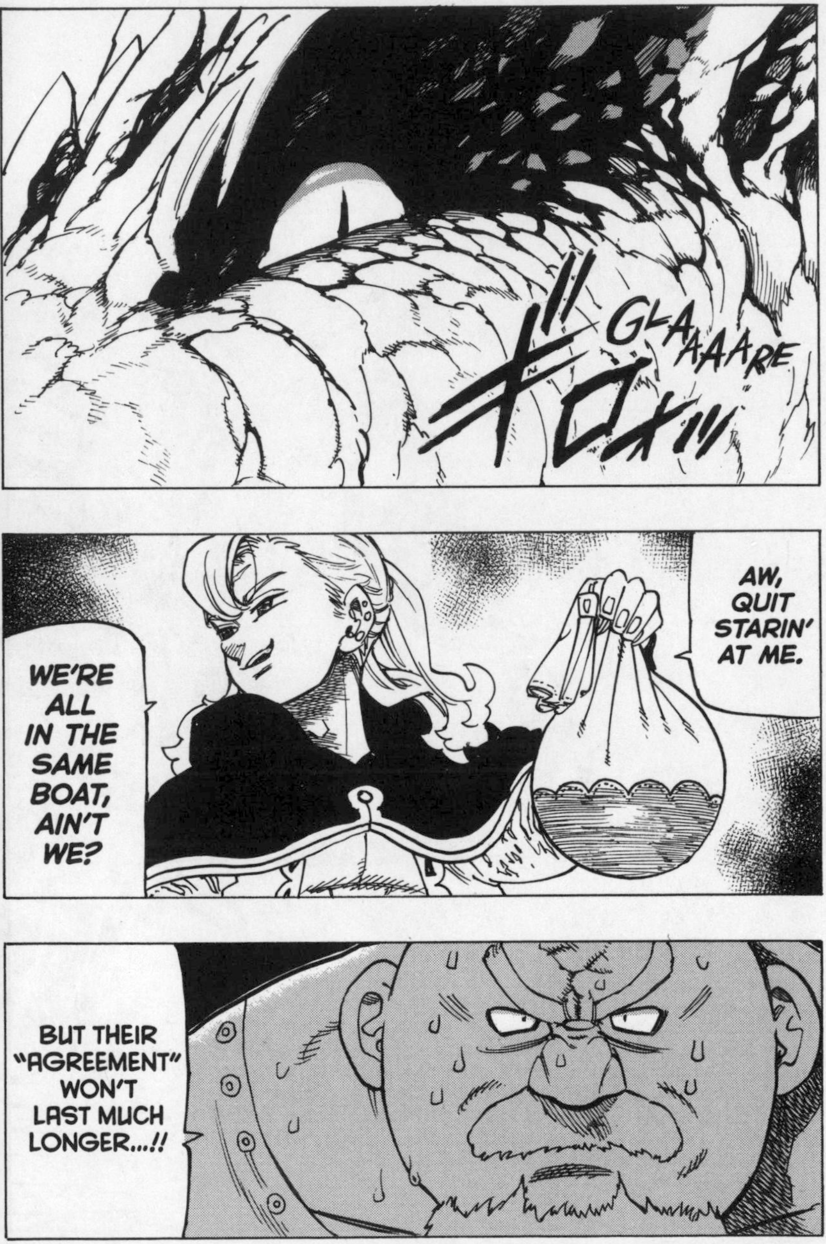
GLAAAARE
AW, QUIT STARIN' AT ME.
WE'RE ALL IN THE SAME BOAT, AIN'T WE?
BUT THEIR "AGREEMENT" WON'T LAST MUCH LONGER...!!

Four Knights of the Apocalypse

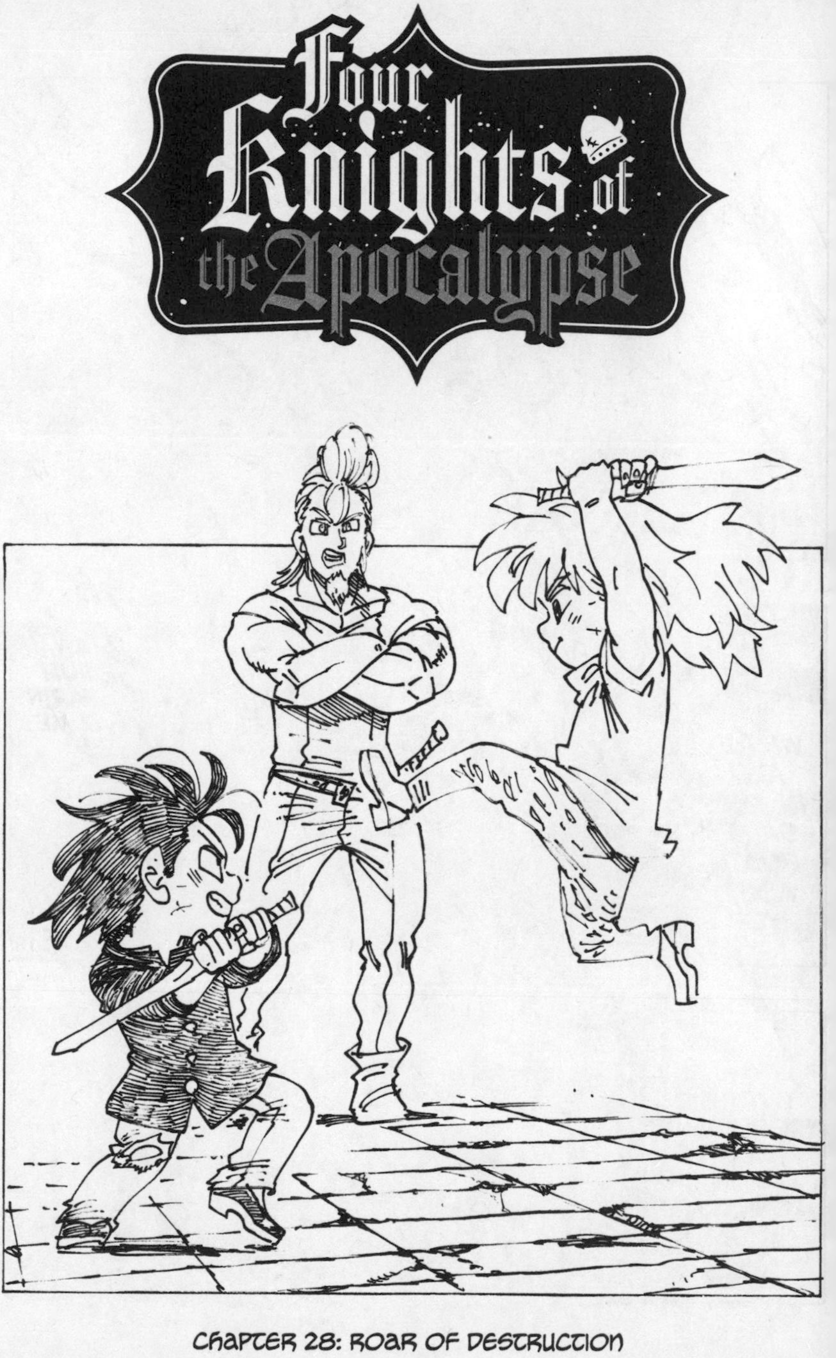

CHAPTER 28: ROAR OF DESTRUCTION

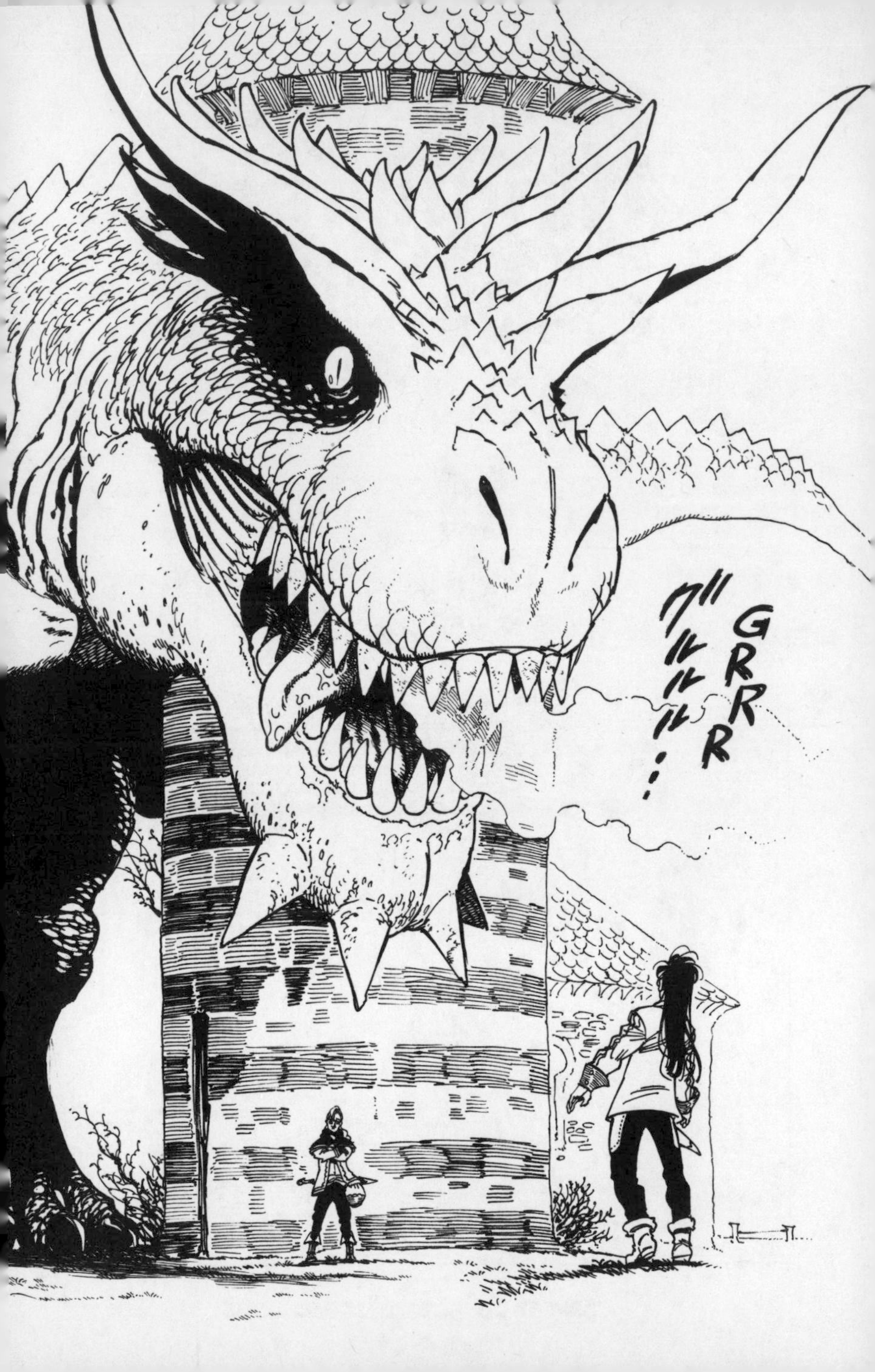
グルルルル…
GRRR

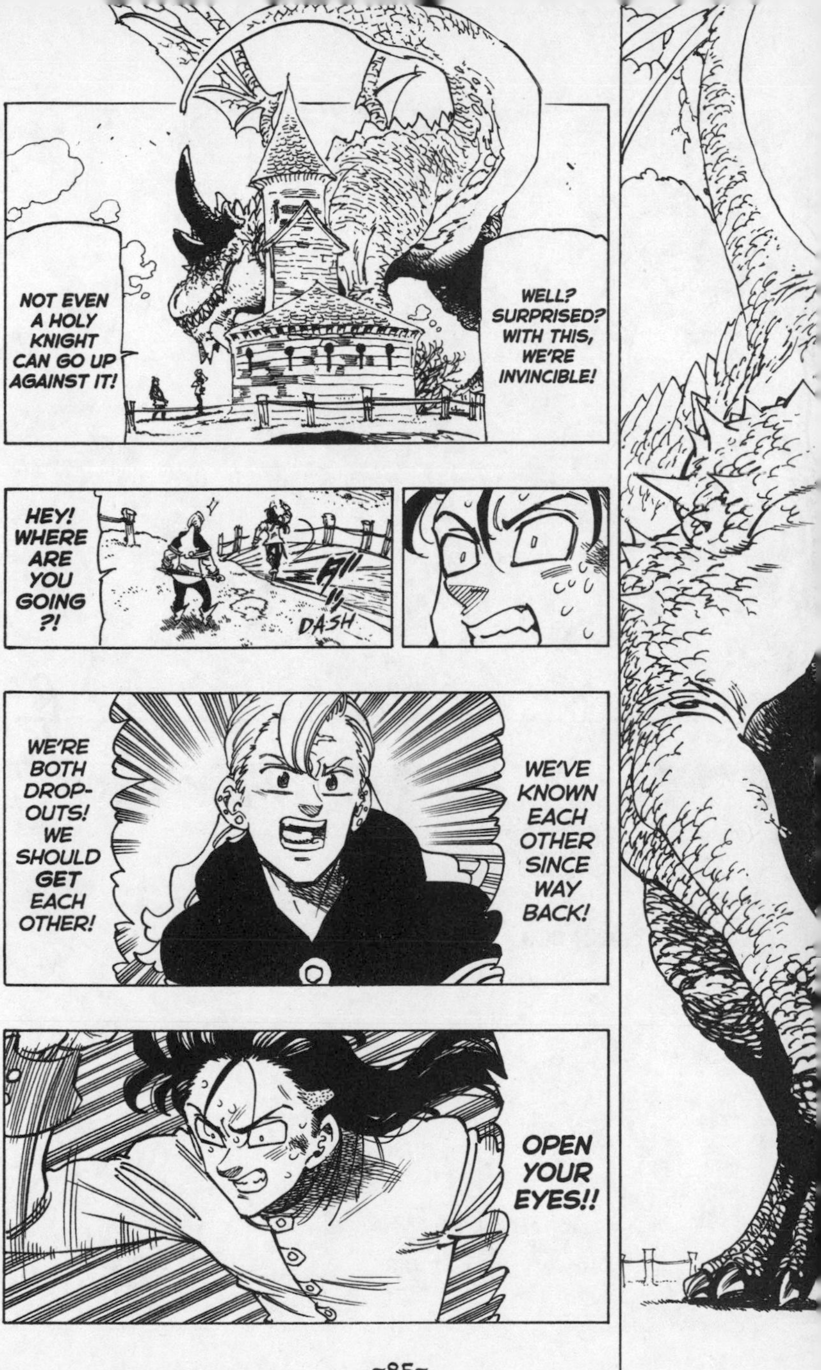
WELL? SURPRISED? WITH THIS, WE'RE INVINCIBLE!
NOT EVEN A HOLY KNIGHT CAN GO UP AGAINST IT!
HEY! WHERE ARE YOU GOING?!
DASH
WE'VE KNOWN EACH OTHER SINCE WAY BACK!
WE'RE BOTH DROP-OUTS! WE SHOULD GET EACH OTHER!
OPEN YOUR EYES!!

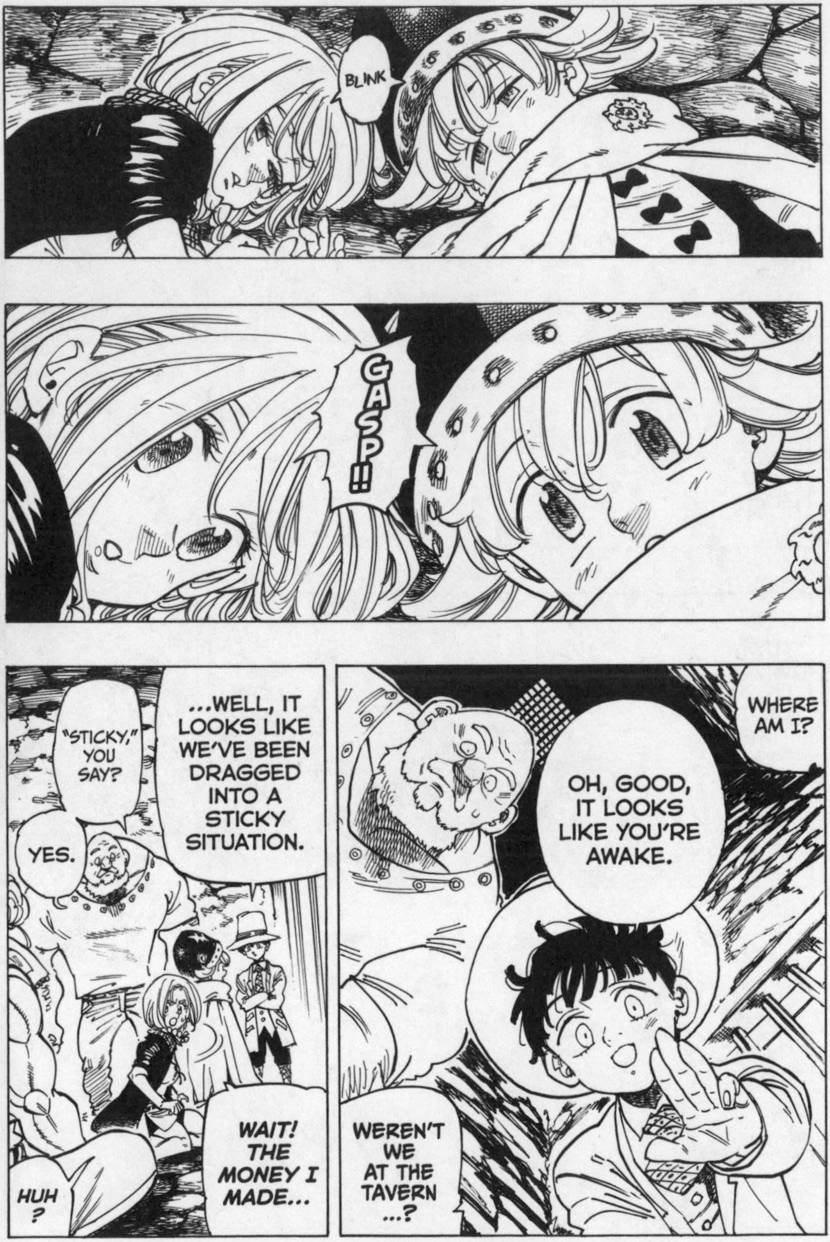
BLINK
GASP!!
WHERE AM I?
OH, GOOD, IT LOOKS LIKE YOU'RE AWAKE.
WEREN'T WE AT THE TAVERN ...?
...WELL, IT LOOKS LIKE WE'VE BEEN DRAGGED INTO A STICKY SITUATION.
"STICKY," YOU SAY?
YES.
WAIT! THE MONEY I MADE...
HUH?

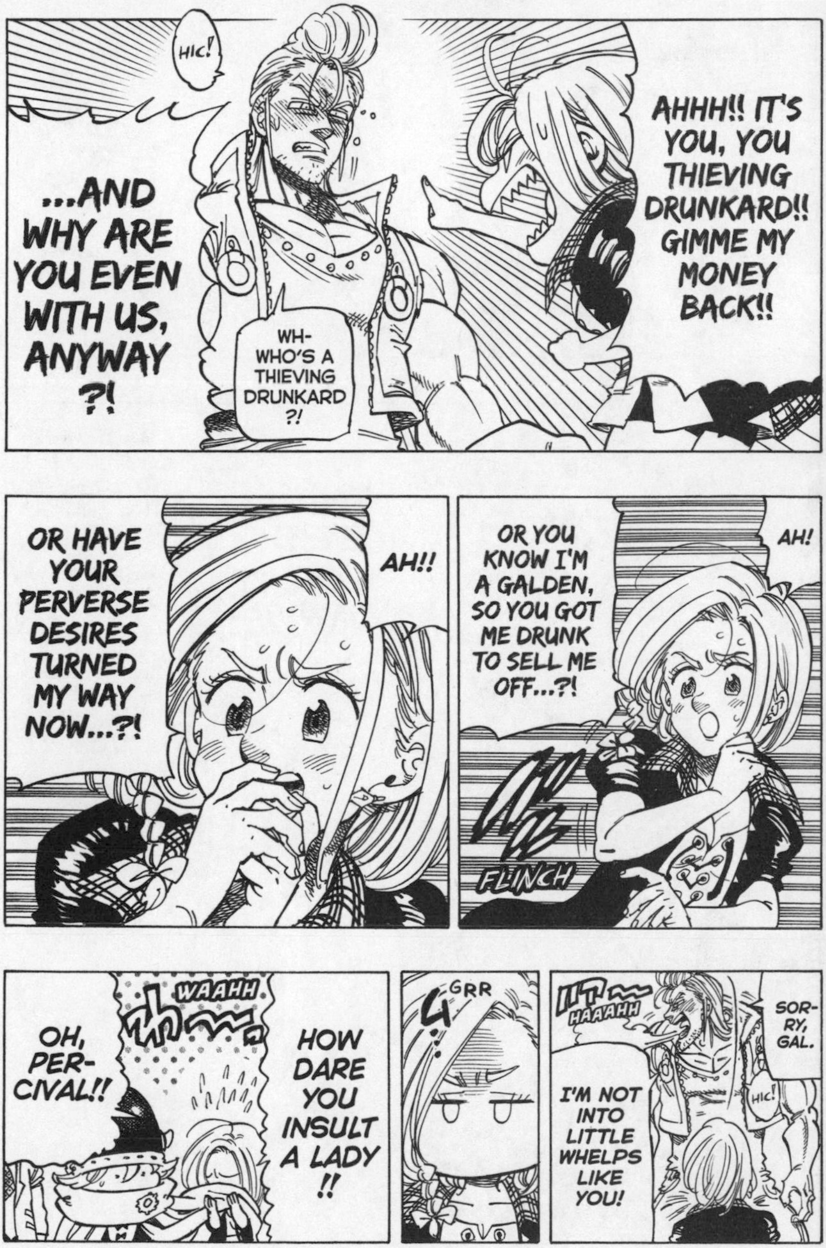
AHHH!! IT'S YOU, YOU THIEVING DRUNKARD!! GIMME MY MONEY BACK!!
HIC!
WH- WHO'S A THIEVING DRUNKARD ?!
...AND WHY ARE YOU EVEN WITH US, ANYWAY ?!
AH!
OR YOU KNOW I'M A GALDEN, SO YOU GOT ME DRUNK TO SELL ME OFF...?!
FLINCH
AH!!
OR HAVE YOUR PERVERSE DESIRES TURNED MY WAY NOW...?!
SOR-RY, GAL.
HAAAAH
HIC!
I'M NOT INTO LITTLE WHELPS LIKE YOU!
GRR
WAAHH
HOW DARE YOU INSULT A LADY !!
OH, PER-CIVAL!!

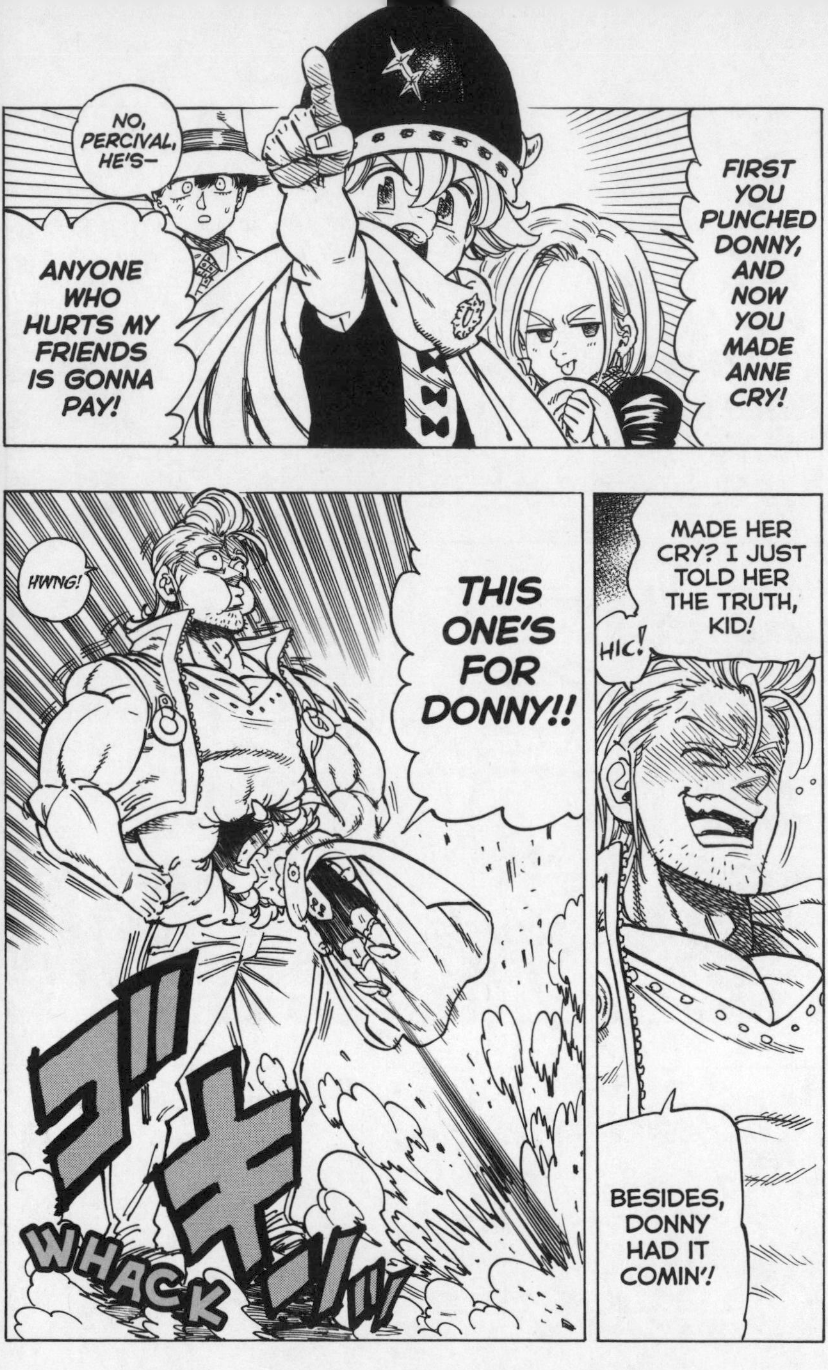
FIRST YOU PUNCHED DONNY, AND NOW YOU MADE ANNE CRY!
NO, PERCIVAL, HE'S—
ANYONE WHO HURTS MY FRIENDS IS GONNA PAY!
MADE HER CRY? I JUST TOLD HER THE TRUTH, KID!
HIC!
BESIDES, DONNY HAD IT COMIN'!
THIS ONE'S FOR DONNY!!
HWNG!
WHACK

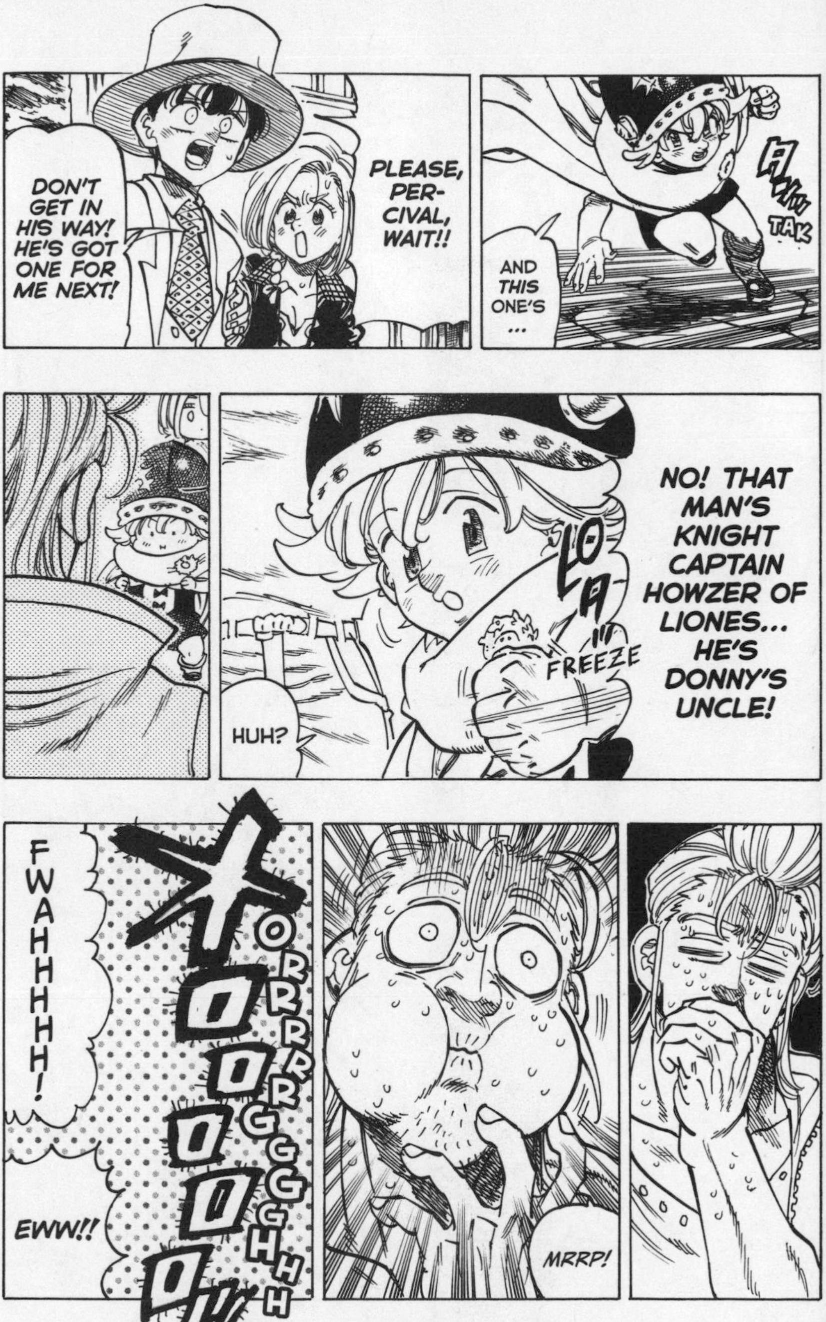

TAK
AND THIS ONE'S ...
PLEASE, PER-CIVAL, WAIT!!
DON'T GET IN HIS WAY! HE'S GOT ONE FOR ME NEXT!
NO! THAT MAN'S KNIGHT CAPTAIN HOWZER OF LIONES... HE'S DONNY'S UNCLE!
FREEZE
HUH?
MRRP!
ORRRRRGGGGHHHH
FWAHHHHH!
EWW!!

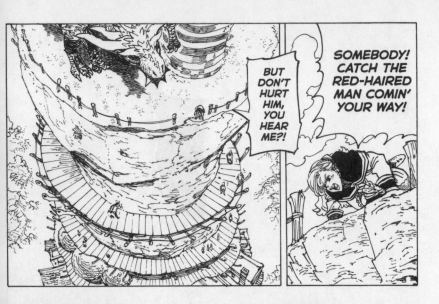

SOMEBODY! CATCH THE RED-HAIRED MAN COMIN' YOUR WAY!

BUT DON'T HURT HIM, YOU HEAR ME?!

"DON'T HURT HIM"? WE DON'T EVEN KNOW WHO HE IS!

PFFT! SCREW THAT! JUST KILL HIM!

T.OK T.OK A AI

BACK TO YOUR NEST. I'LL CALL YOU IF I NEED YOU.

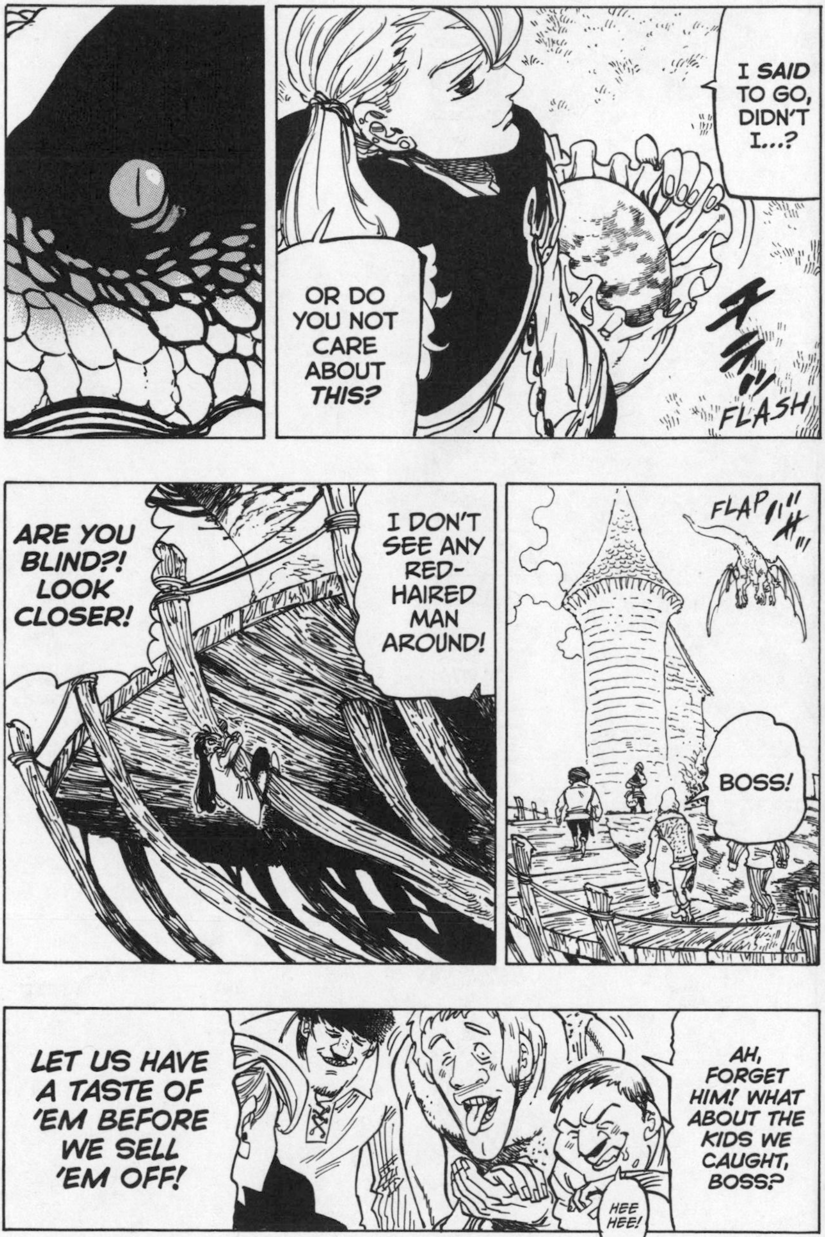
I SAID TO GO, DIDN'T I...?
OR DO YOU NOT CARE ABOUT THIS?
FLASH
FLAP
BOSS!
I DON'T SEE ANY RED-HAIRED MAN AROUND!
ARE YOU BLIND?! LOOK CLOSER!
AH, FORGET HIM! WHAT ABOUT THE KIDS WE CAUGHT, BOSS?
HEE HEE!
LET US HAVE A TASTE OF 'EM BEFORE WE SELL 'EM OFF!

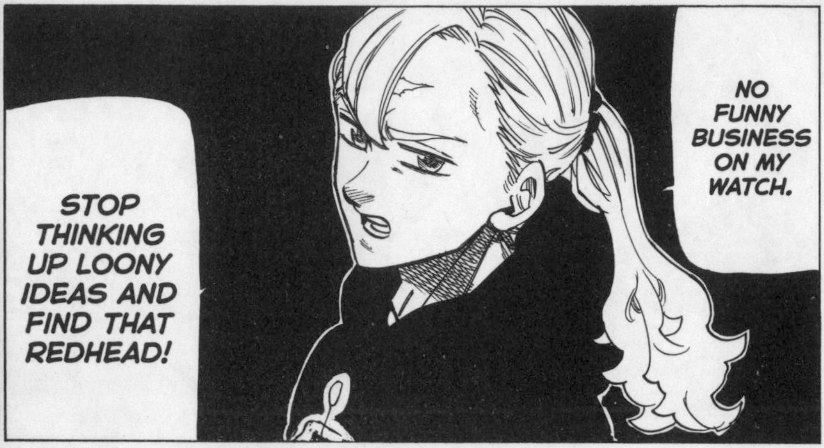
NO FUNNY BUSINESS ON MY WATCH.
STOP THINKING UP LOONY IDEAS AND FIND THAT REDHEAD!

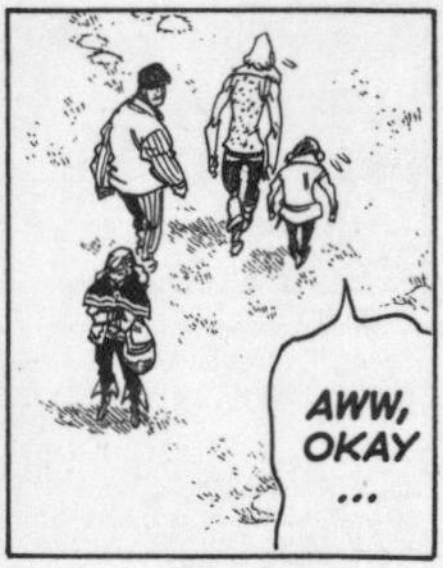
AWW, OKAY ...

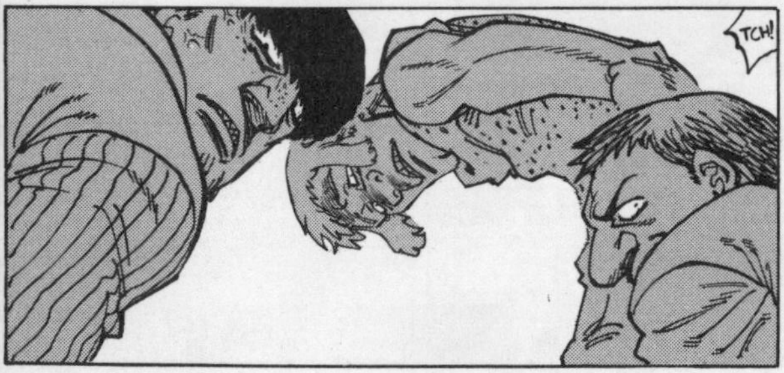
TCH!

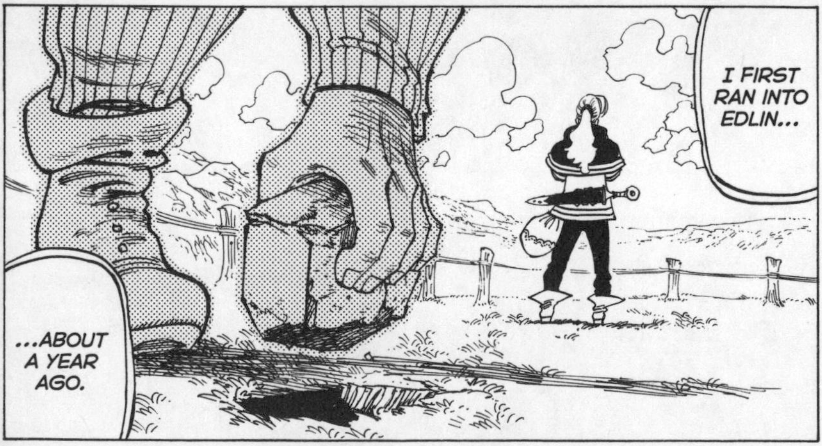
I FIRST RAN INTO EDLIN...
...ABOUT A YEAR AGO.

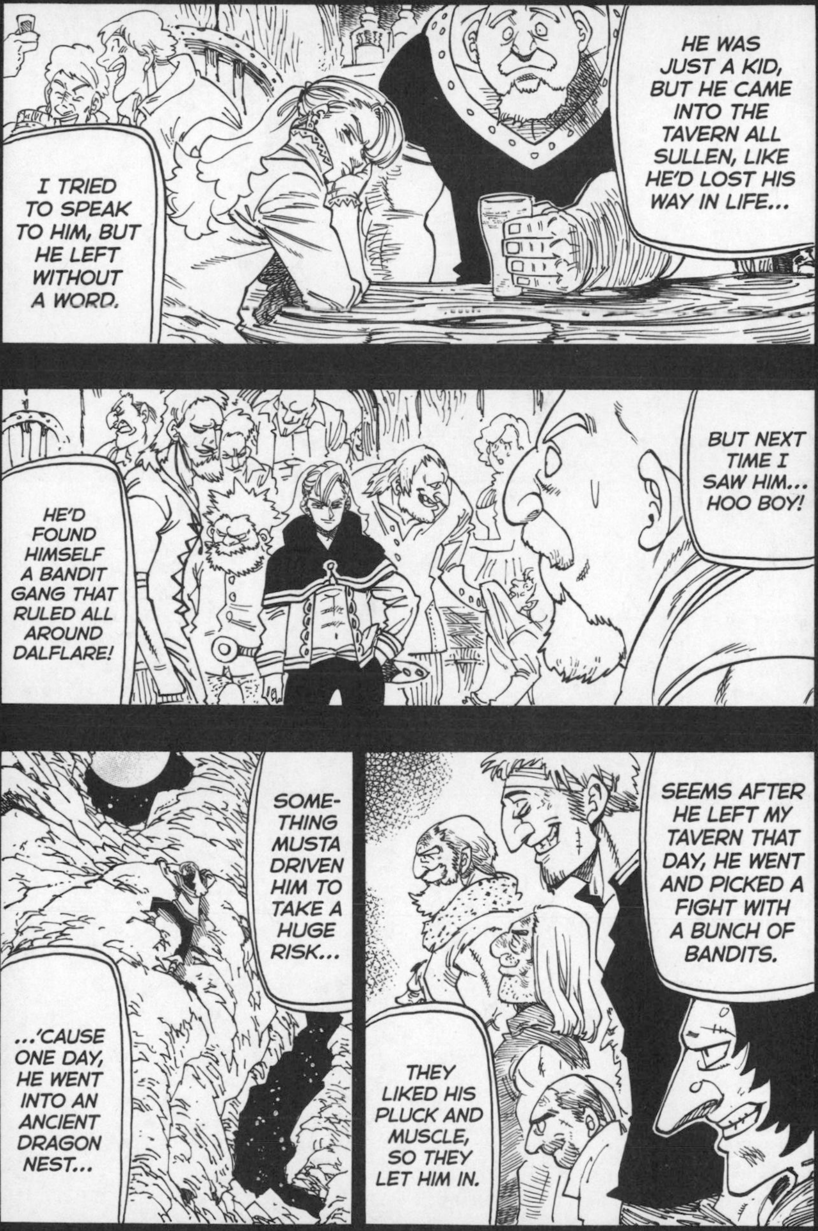
HE WAS JUST A KID, BUT HE CAME INTO THE TAVERN ALL SULLEN, LIKE HE'D LOST HIS WAY IN LIFE...
I TRIED TO SPEAK TO HIM, BUT HE LEFT WITHOUT A WORD.
BUT NEXT TIME I SAW HIM... HOO BOY!
HE'D FOUND HIMSELF A BANDIT GANG THAT RULED ALL AROUND DALFLARE!
SEEMS AFTER HE LEFT MY TAVERN THAT DAY, HE WENT AND PICKED A FIGHT WITH A BUNCH OF BANDITS.
THEY LIKED HIS PLUCK AND MUSCLE, SO THEY LET HIM IN.
SOME-THING MUSTA DRIVEN HIM TO TAKE A HUGE RISK...
...'CAUSE ONE DAY, HE WENT INTO AN ANCIENT DRAGON NEST...

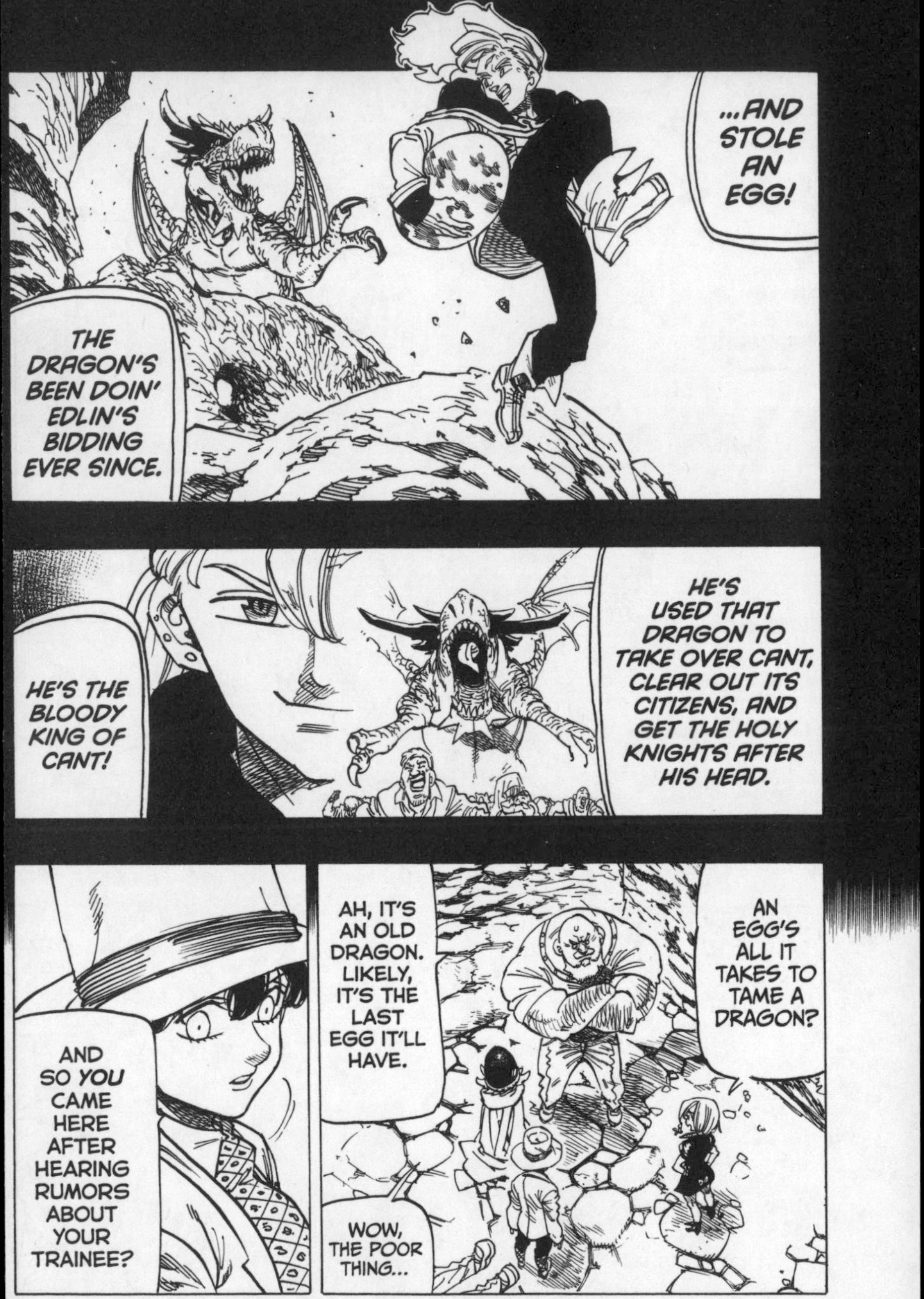
...AND STOLE AN EGG!
THE DRAGON'S BEEN DOIN' EDLIN'S BIDDING EVER SINCE.
HE'S USED THAT DRAGON TO TAKE OVER CANT, CLEAR OUT ITS CITIZENS, AND GET THE HOLY KNIGHTS AFTER HIS HEAD.
HE'S THE BLOODY KING OF CANT!
AN EGG'S ALL IT TAKES TO TAME A DRAGON?
AH, IT'S AN OLD DRAGON. LIKELY, IT'S THE LAST EGG IT'LL HAVE.
WOW, THE POOR THING...
AND SO *YOU* CAME HERE AFTER HEARING RUMORS ABOUT YOUR TRAINEE?

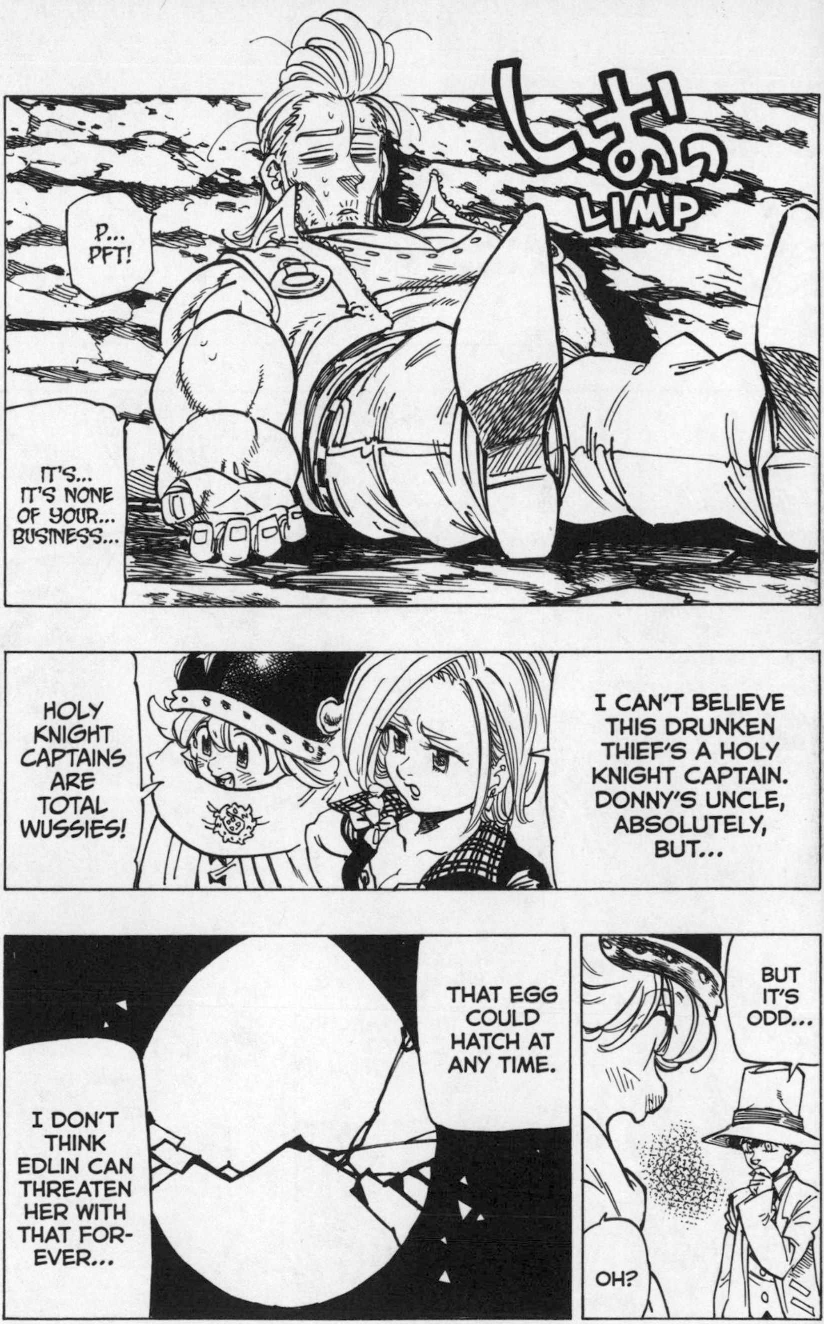
しおっ
LIMP
P... PFT!
IT'S... IT'S NONE OF YOUR... BUSINESS...
I CAN'T BELIEVE THIS DRUNKEN THIEF'S A HOLY KNIGHT CAPTAIN. DONNY'S UNCLE, ABSOLUTELY, BUT...
HOLY KNIGHT CAPTAINS ARE TOTAL WUSSIES!
BUT IT'S ODD...
OH?
THAT EGG COULD HATCH AT ANY TIME.
I DON'T THINK EDLIN CAN THREATEN HER WITH THAT FOR-EVER...

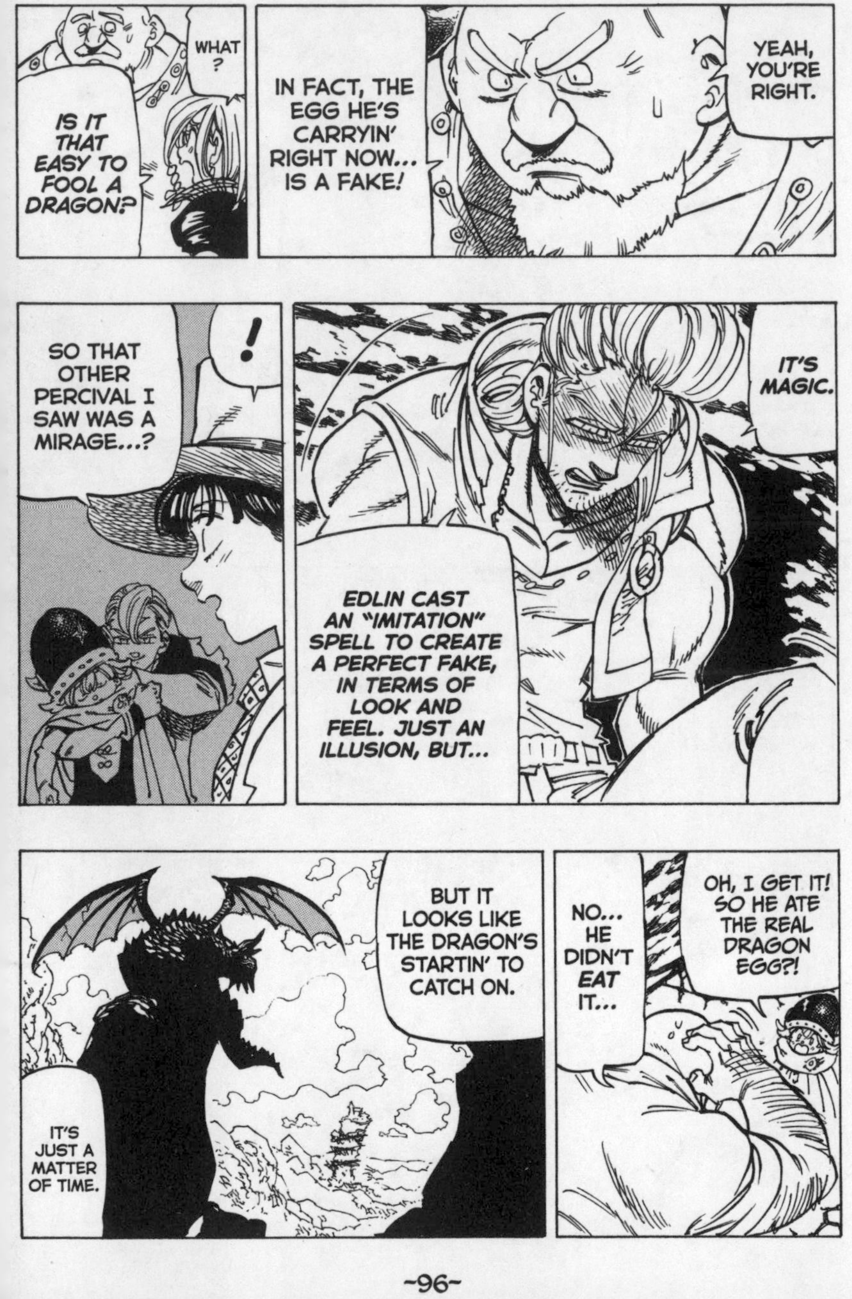
YEAH, YOU'RE RIGHT.
IN FACT, THE EGG HE'S CARRYIN' RIGHT NOW... IS A FAKE!
WHAT?
IS IT THAT EASY TO FOOL A DRAGON?
IT'S MAGIC.
EDLIN CAST AN "IMITATION" SPELL TO CREATE A PERFECT FAKE, IN TERMS OF LOOK AND FEEL. JUST AN ILLUSION, BUT...
!
SO THAT OTHER PERCIVAL I SAW WAS A MIRAGE...?
OH, I GET IT! SO HE ATE THE REAL DRAGON EGG?!
NO... HE DIDN'T EAT IT...
BUT IT LOOKS LIKE THE DRAGON'S STARTIN' TO CATCH ON.
IT'S JUST A MATTER OF TIME.

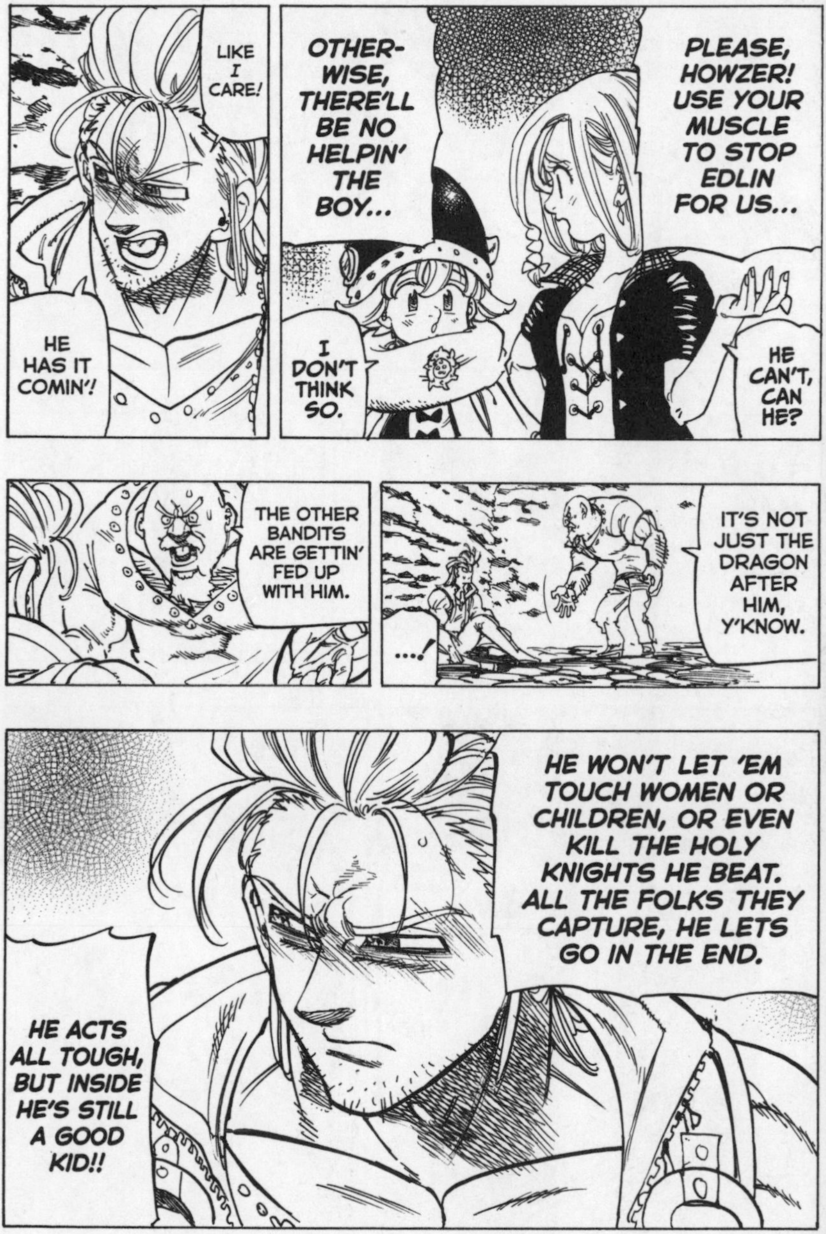
PLEASE, HOWZER! USE YOUR MUSCLE TO STOP EDLIN FOR US...
OTHER-WISE, THERE'LL BE NO HELPIN' THE BOY...
HE CAN'T, CAN HE?
I DON'T THINK SO.
LIKE I CARE!
HE HAS IT COMIN'!
IT'S NOT JUST THE DRAGON AFTER HIM, Y'KNOW.
....!
THE OTHER BANDITS ARE GETTIN' FED UP WITH HIM.
HE WON'T LET 'EM TOUCH WOMEN OR CHILDREN, OR EVEN KILL THE HOLY KNIGHTS HE BEAT. ALL THE FOLKS THEY CAPTURE, HE LETS GO IN THE END.
HE ACTS ALL TOUGH, BUT INSIDE HE'S STILL A GOOD KID!!

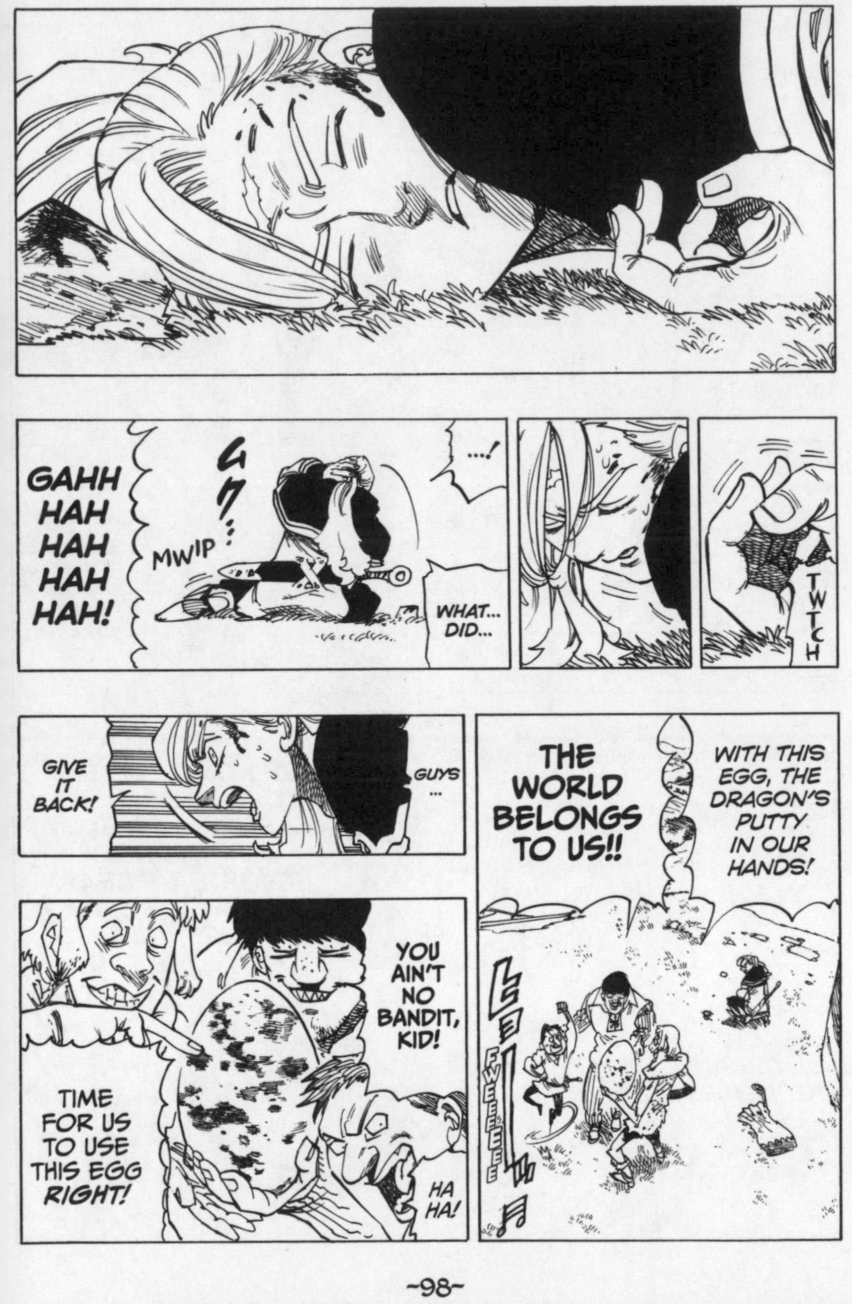
TWTCH
...!
WHAT... DID...
MWIP
GAHH HAH HAH HAH HAH!
WITH THIS EGG, THE DRAGON'S PUTTY IN OUR HANDS!
THE WORLD BELONGS TO US!!
FWEEEEEE
GUYS ...
GIVE IT BACK!
YOU AIN'T NO BANDIT, KID!
HA HA!
TIME FOR US TO USE THIS EGG RIGHT!

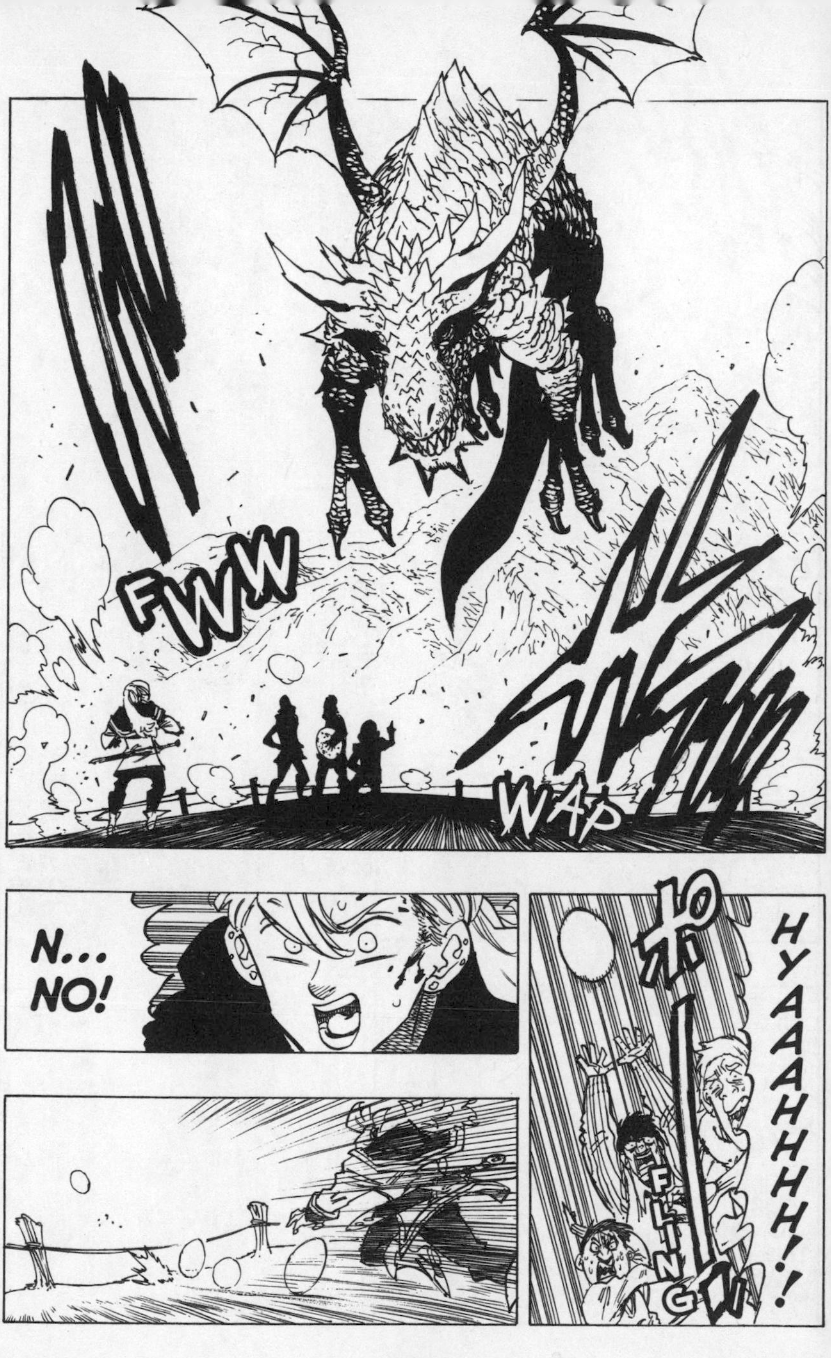
FWW
WAP
HYAAAHHHH!!
FLING
N... NO!

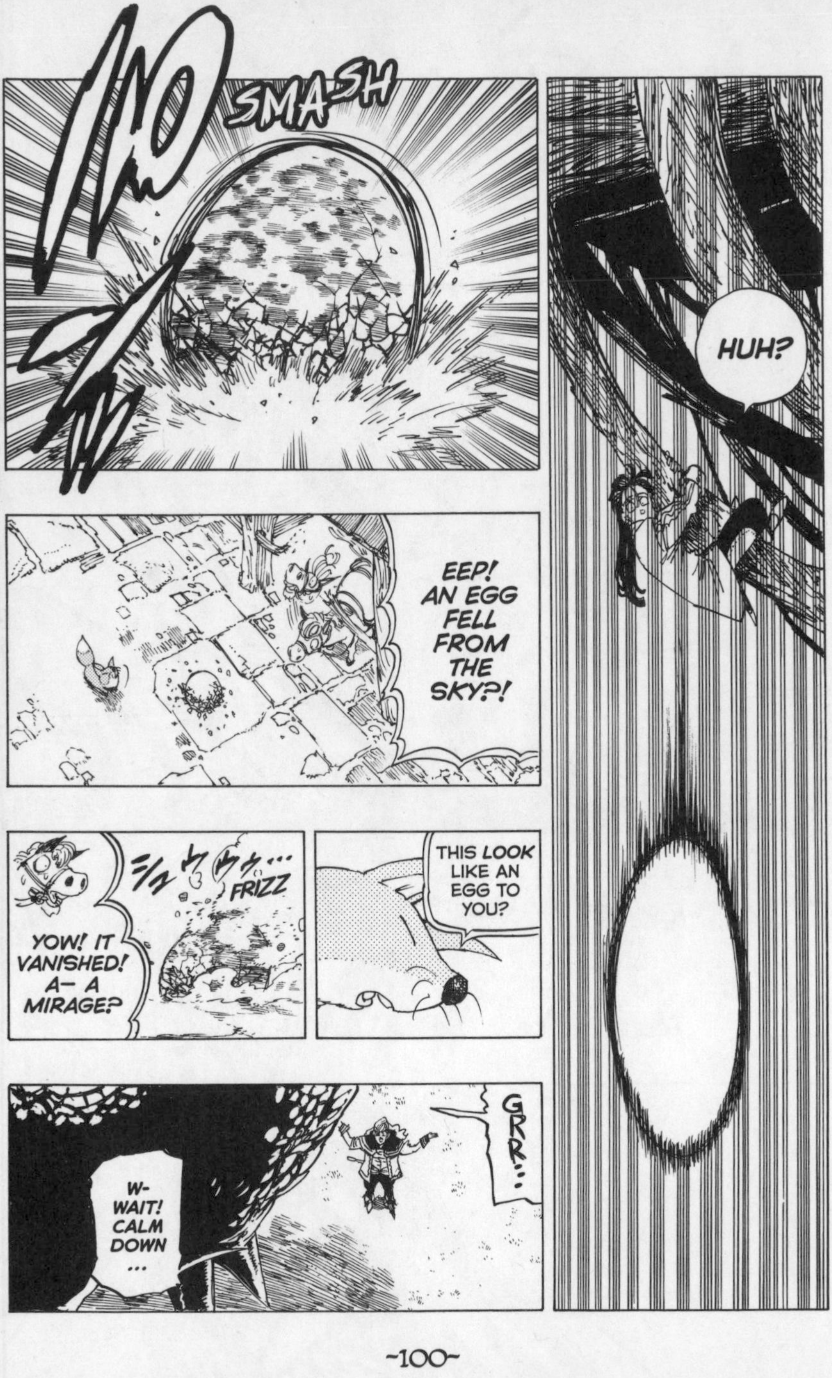
HUH?
SMASH
EEP! AN EGG FELL FROM THE SKY?!
THIS LOOK LIKE AN EGG TO YOU?
FRIZZ
YOW! IT VANISHED! A— A MIRAGE?
GRR...
W-WAIT! CALM DOWN ...

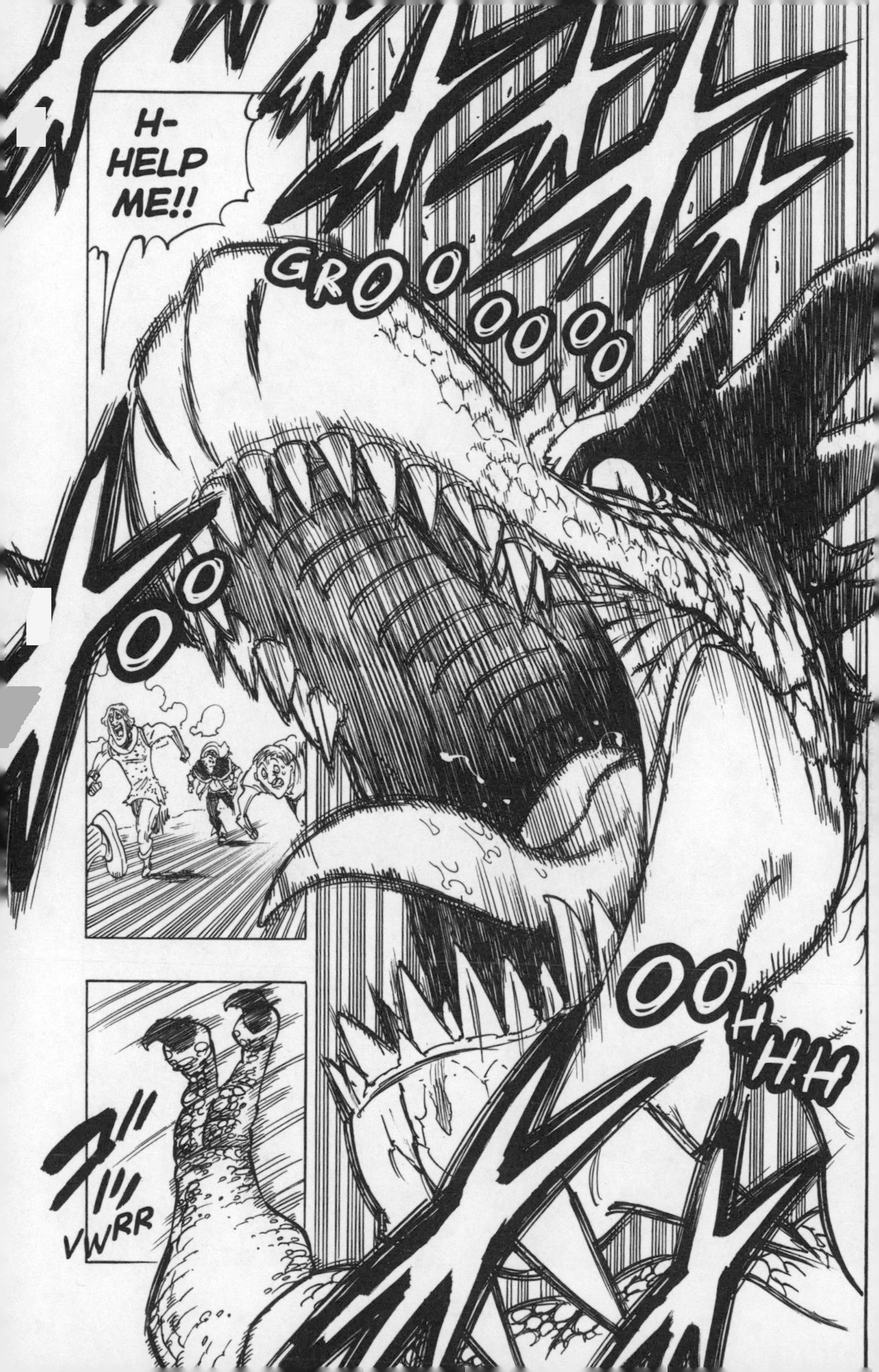
GROOOOOOO
OOHHHH
H-HELP ME!!
VWRR

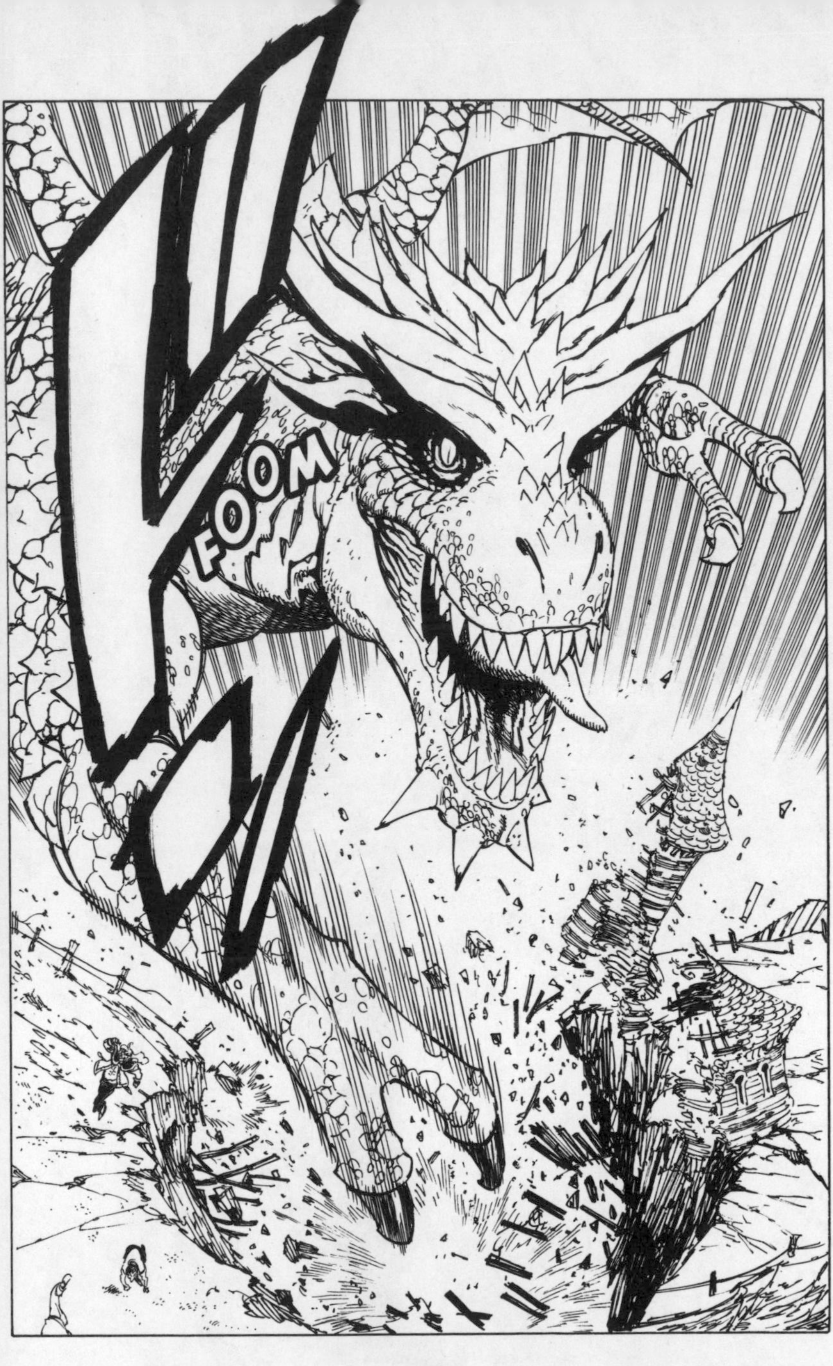
FOOM

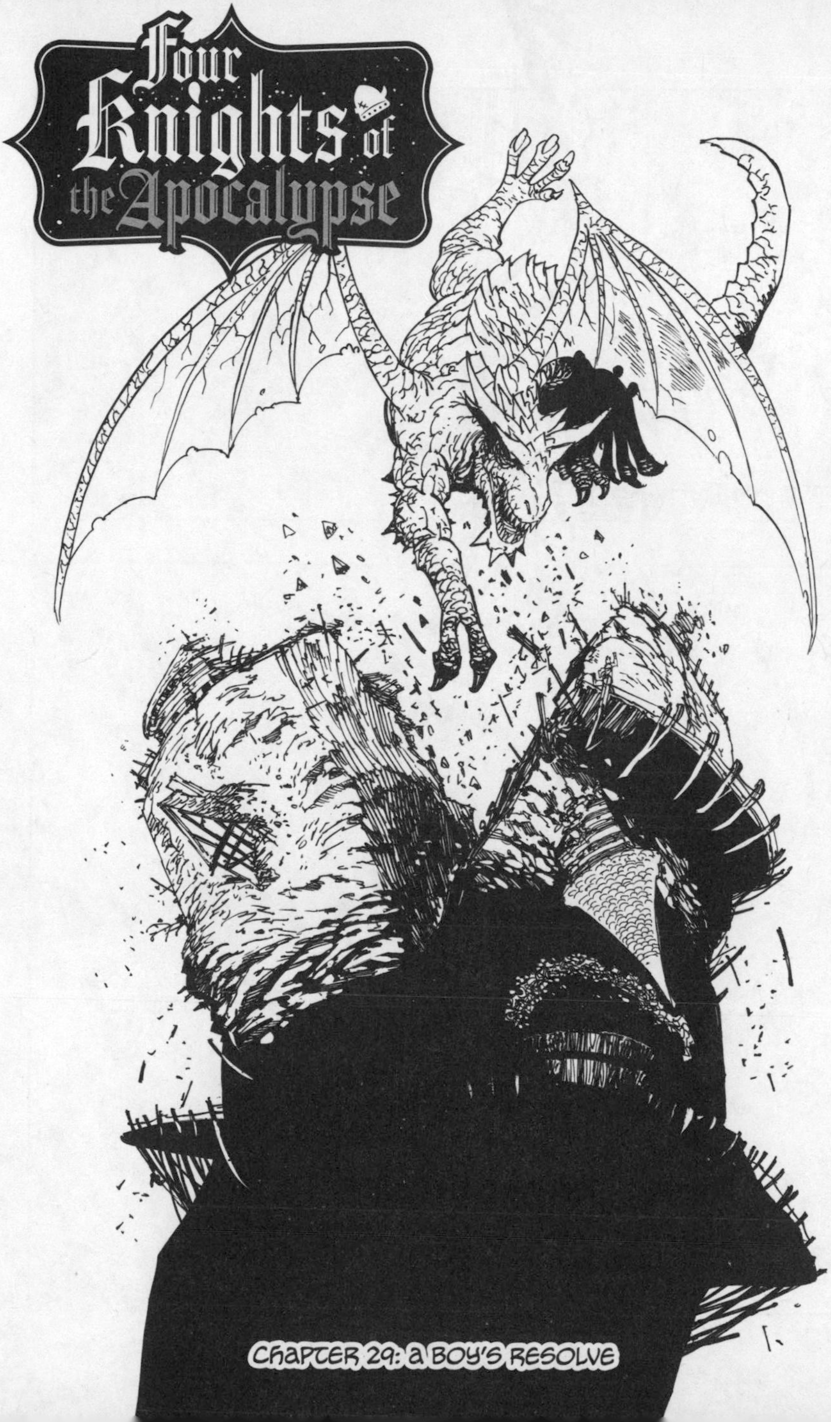
Four Knights of the Apocalypse
Chapter 29: A Boy's Resolve

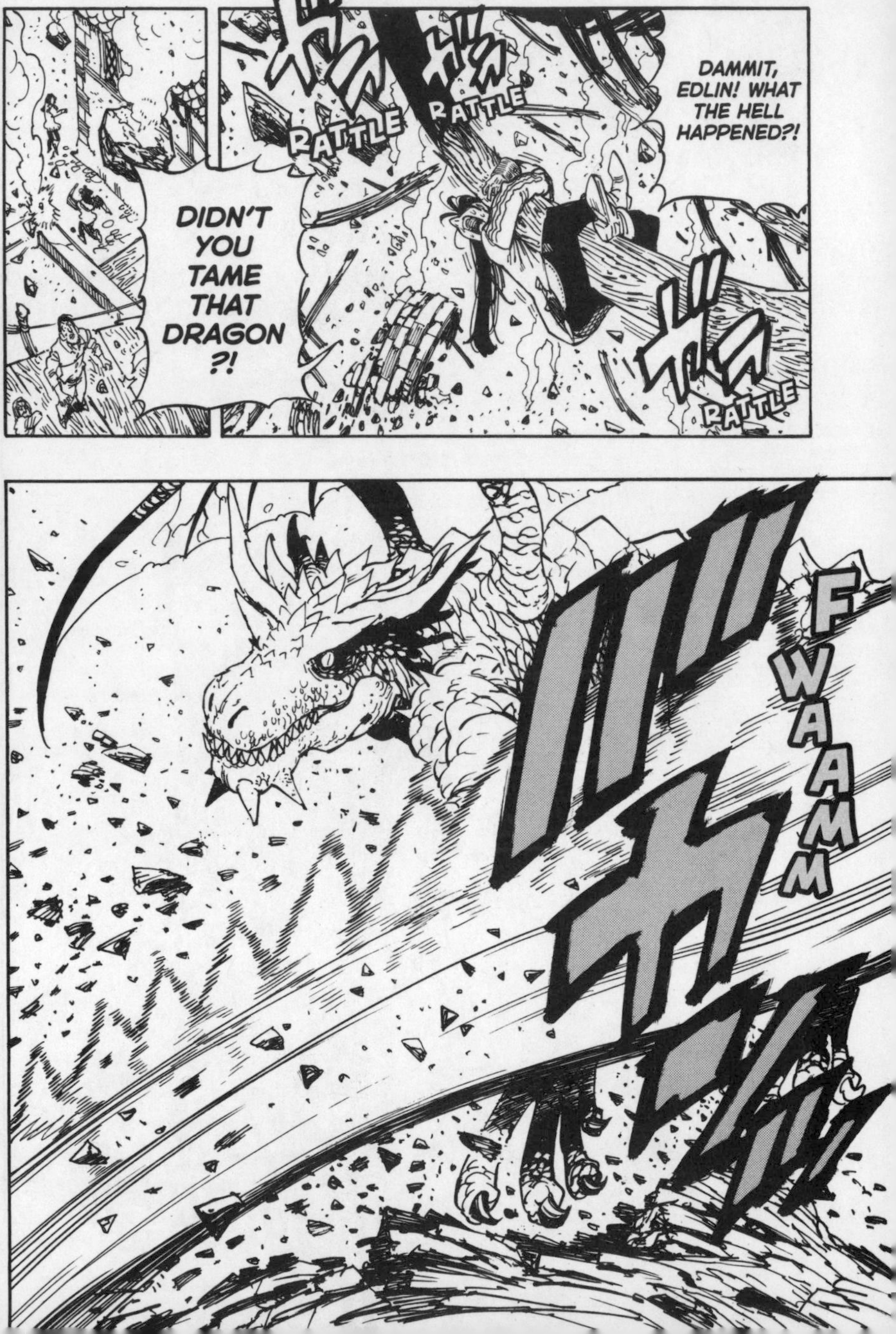
RATTLE RATTLE
DAMMIT, EDLIN! WHAT THE HELL HAPPENED?!
RATTLE
DIDN'T YOU TAME THAT DRAGON?!
FWAAMM

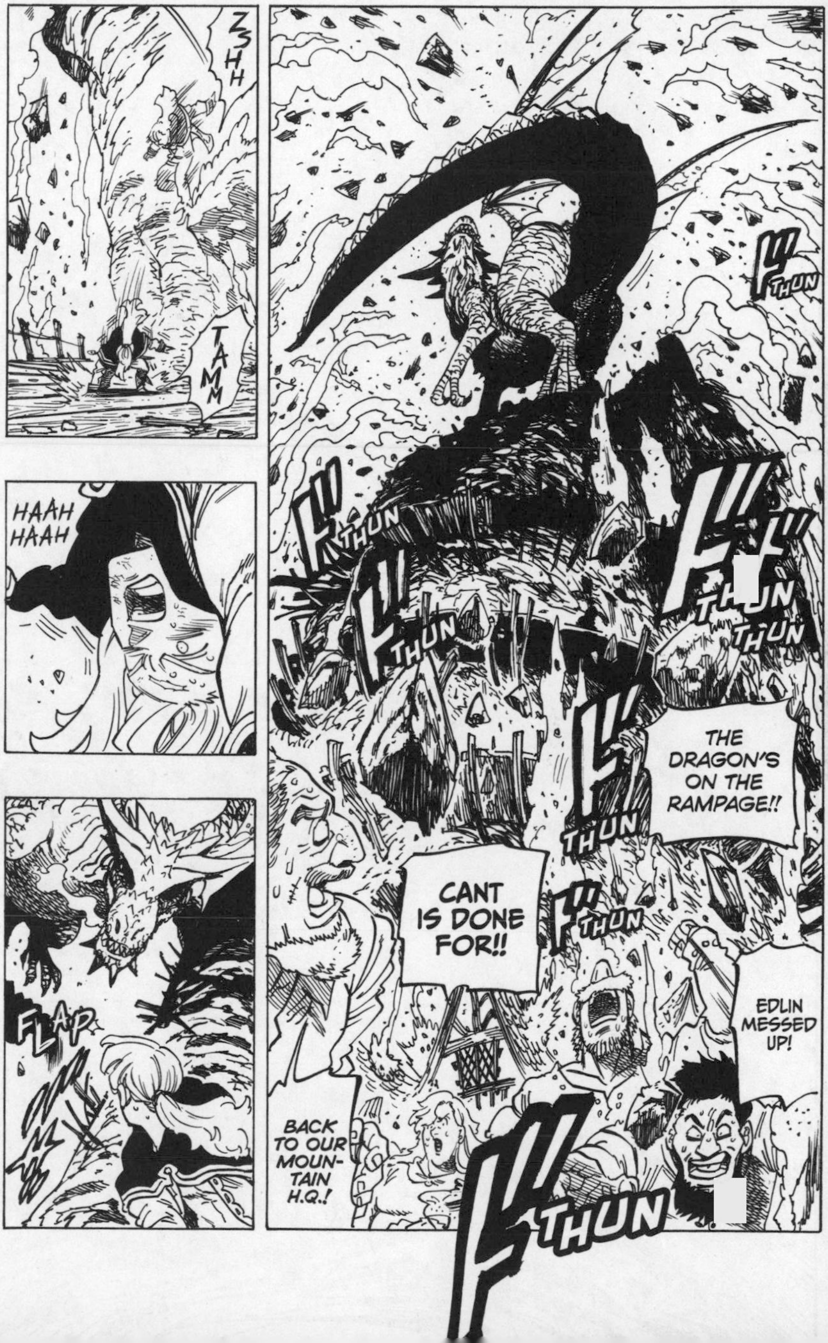
THUN
THUN
THUN
THUN
THUN
THUN
THE DRAGON'S ON THE RAMPAGE!!
THUN
CANT IS DONE FOR!!
THUN
EDLIN MESSED UP!
BACK TO OUR MOUN-TAIN H.Q.!
THUN
ZSHH
TAMM
HAAH HAAH
FLAP

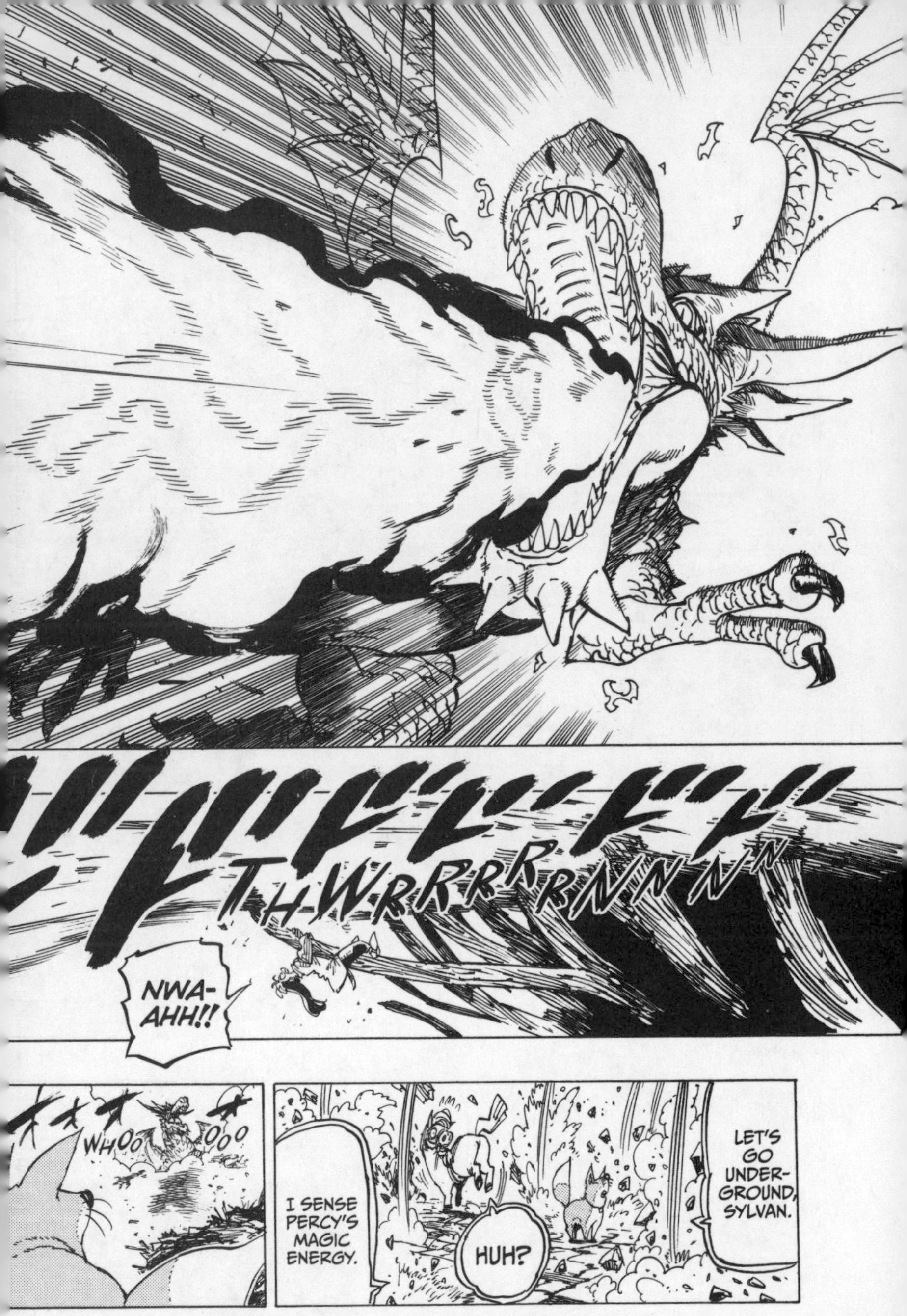
THWRRRRRNNNN
NWA-AHH!!
LET'S GO UNDERGROUND, SYLVAN.
HUH?
I SENSE PERCY'S MAGIC ENERGY.
WHOOOOOO

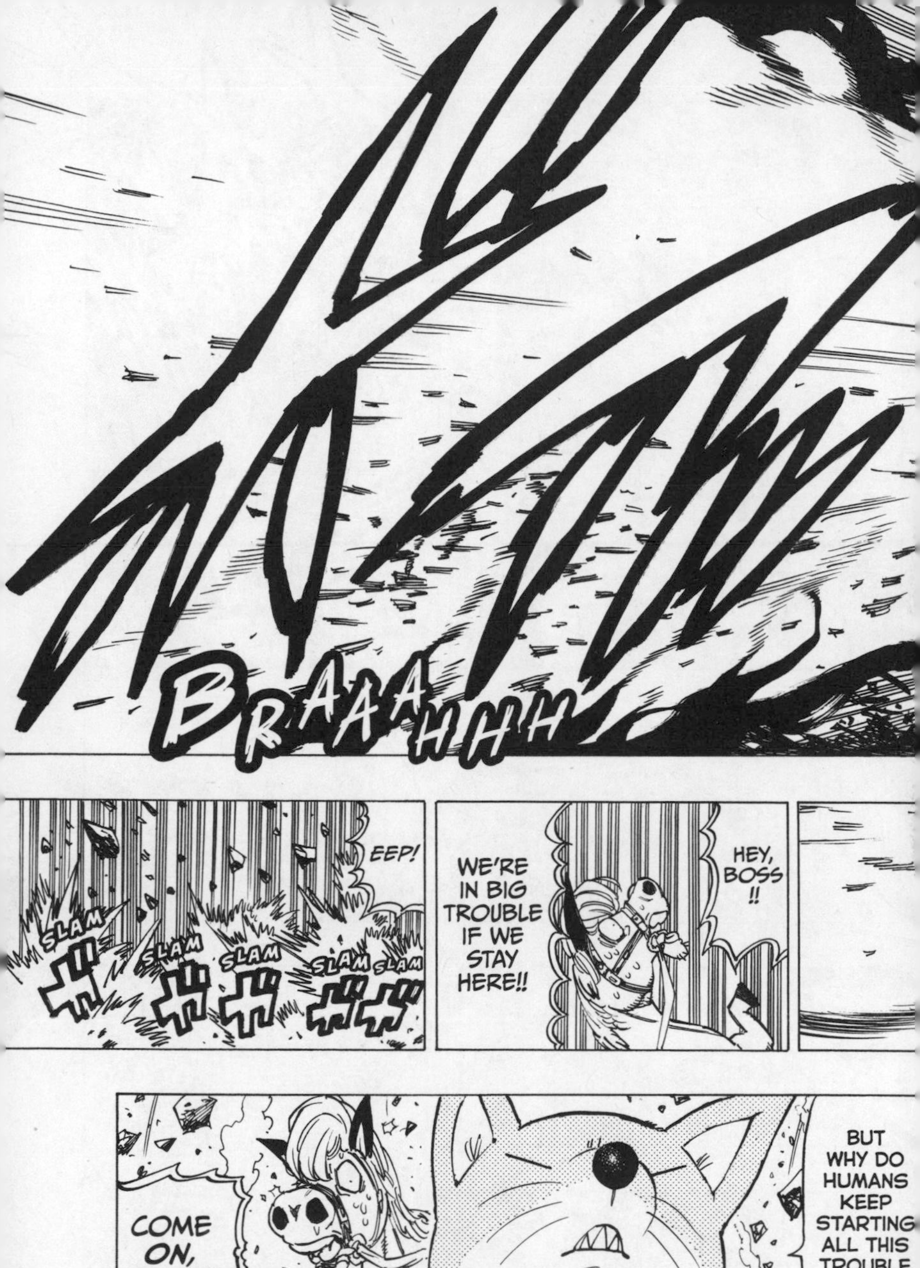
BRAAAHHH
HEY, BOSS!!
WE'RE IN BIG TROUBLE IF WE STAY HERE!!
EEP!
SLAM
SLAM
SLAM
SLAM
SLAM
BUT WHY DO HUMANS KEEP STARTING ALL THIS TROUBLE...?
COME ON, BOSS!!

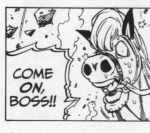

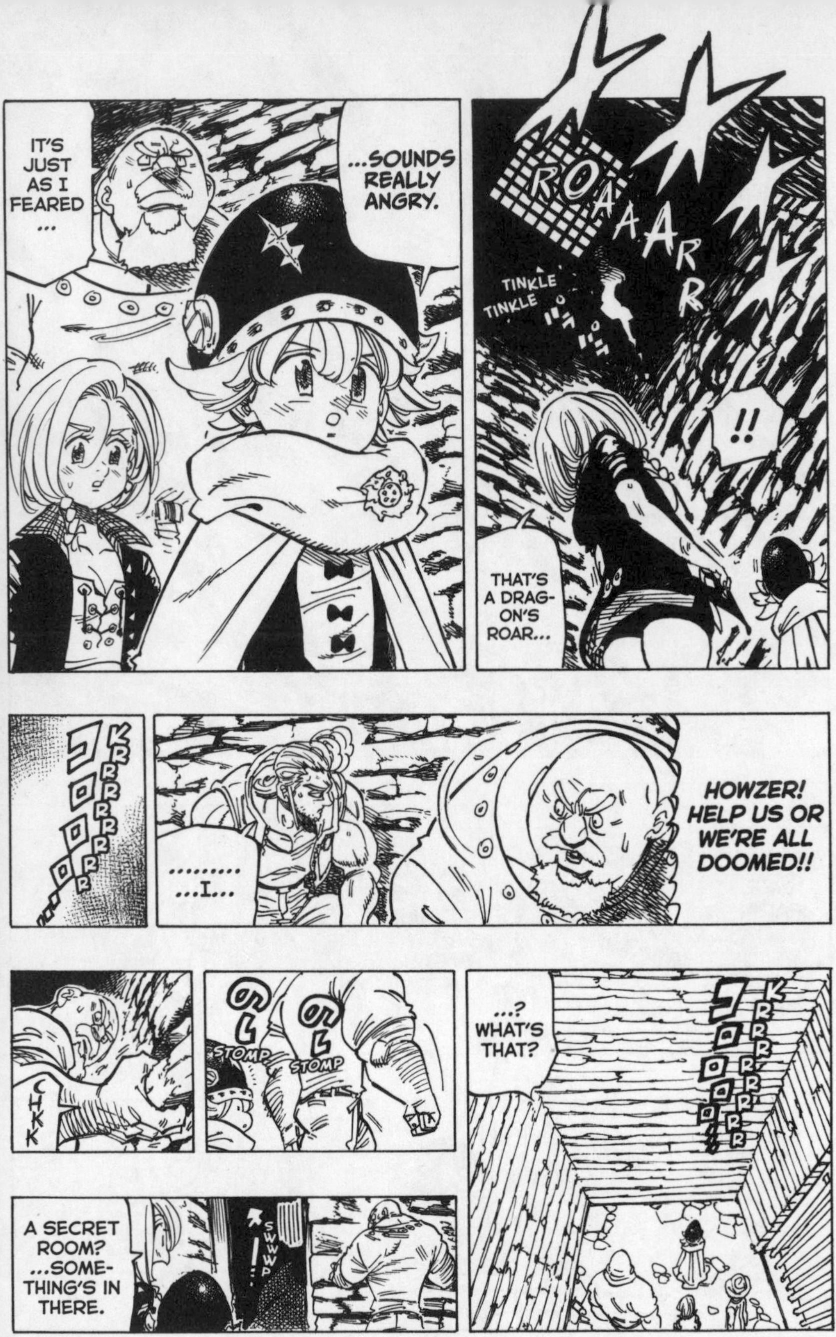
ROAAARR
TINKLE TINKLE
!!
THAT'S A DRAG-ON'S ROAR...
...SOUNDS REALLY ANGRY.
IT'S JUST AS I FEARED ...
HOWZER! HELP US OR WE'RE ALL DOOMED!!
....
...I...
KRRRRRRR
...? WHAT'S THAT?
KRRRRRRR
STOMP
STOMP
CHKK
SWWP
A SECRET ROOM? ...SOME-THING'S IN THERE.

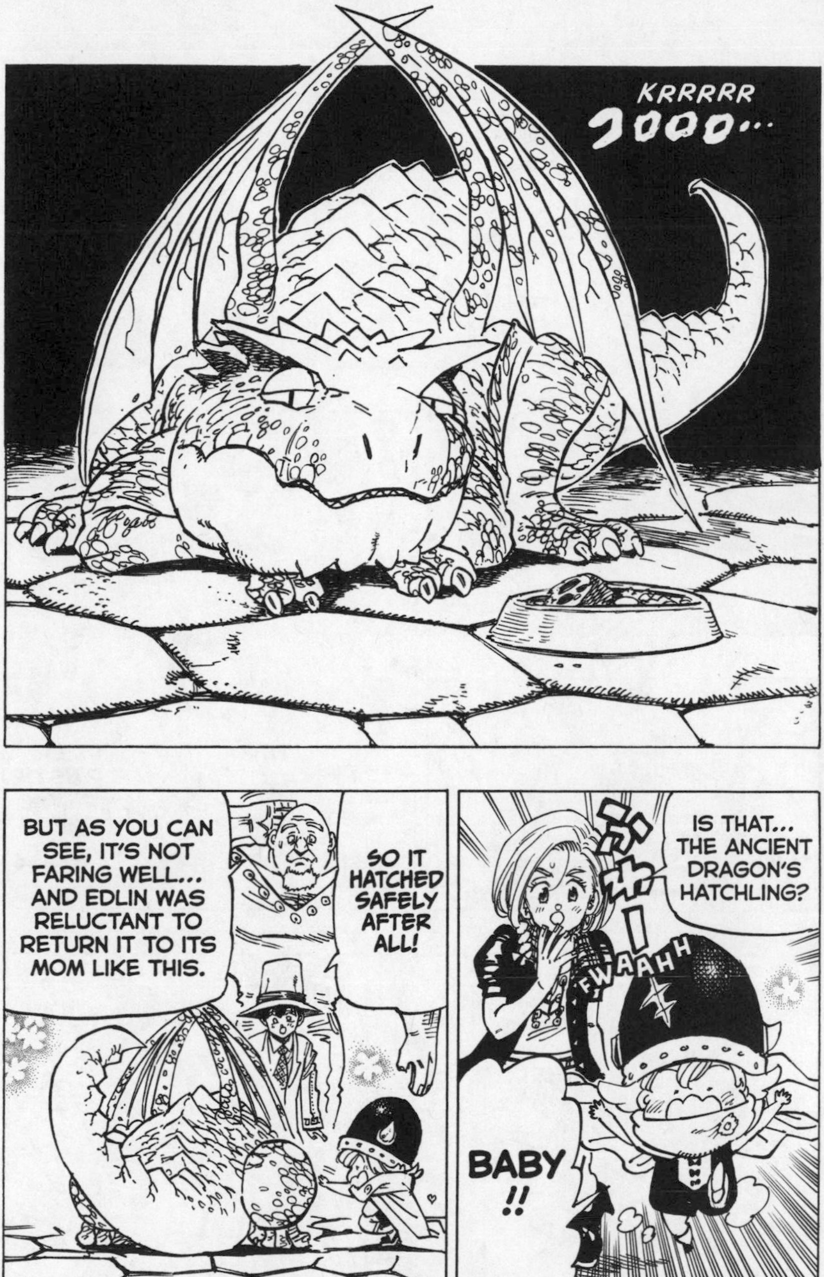
KRRRRR
IS THAT... THE ANCIENT DRAGON'S HATCHLING?
FWAAHH
BABY !!
SO IT HATCHED SAFELY AFTER ALL!
BUT AS YOU CAN SEE, IT'S NOT FARING WELL... AND EDLIN WAS RELUCTANT TO RETURN IT TO ITS MOM LIKE THIS.

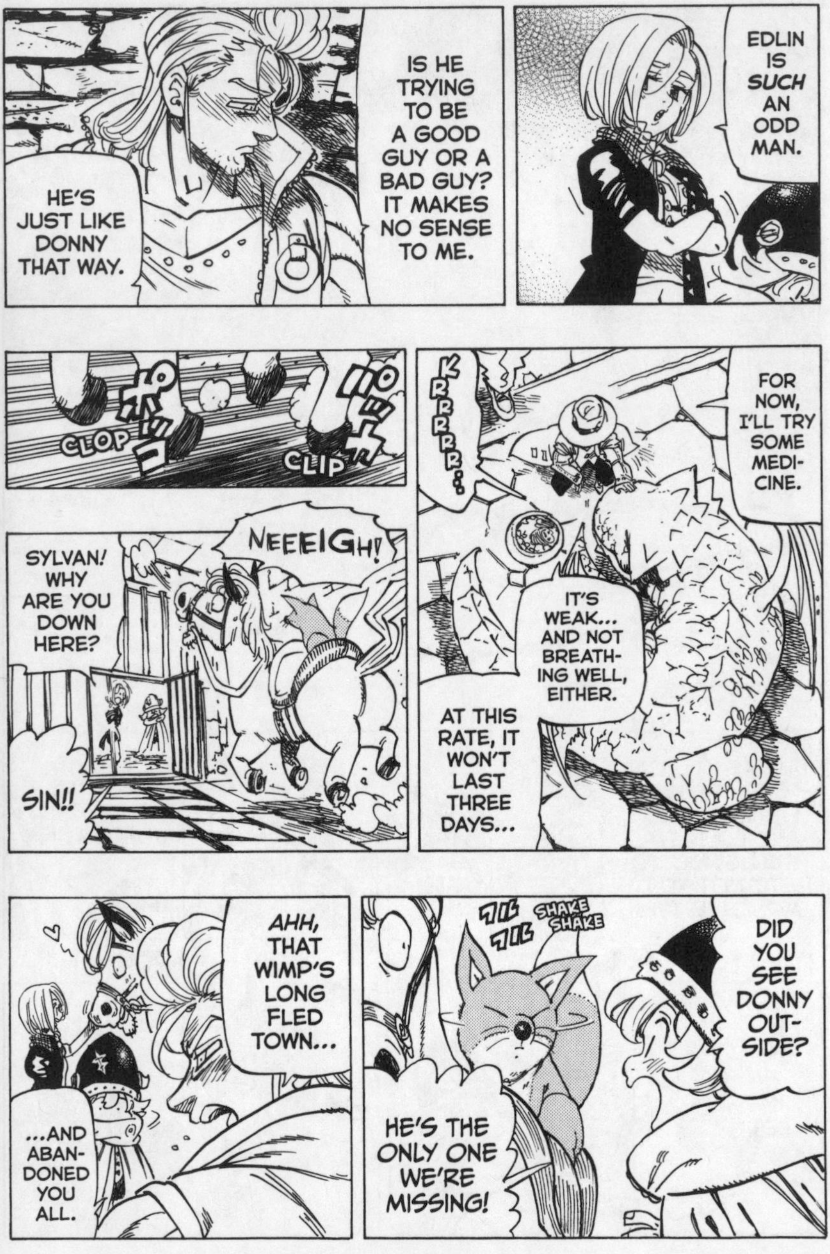
EDLIN IS SUCH AN ODD MAN.
IS HE TRYING TO BE A GOOD GUY OR A BAD GUY? IT MAKES NO SENSE TO ME.
HE'S JUST LIKE DONNY THAT WAY.
FOR NOW, I'LL TRY SOME MEDI-CINE.
KRRRRR...
IT'S WEAK... AND NOT BREATH-ING WELL, EITHER.
AT THIS RATE, IT WON'T LAST THREE DAYS...
CLIP
CLOP
NEEEIGH!
SYLVAN! WHY ARE YOU DOWN HERE?
SIN!!
DID YOU SEE DONNY OUT-SIDE?
SHAKE SHAKE
HE'S THE ONLY ONE WE'RE MISSING!
AHH, THAT WIMP'S LONG FLED TOWN...
...AND ABAN-DONED YOU ALL.

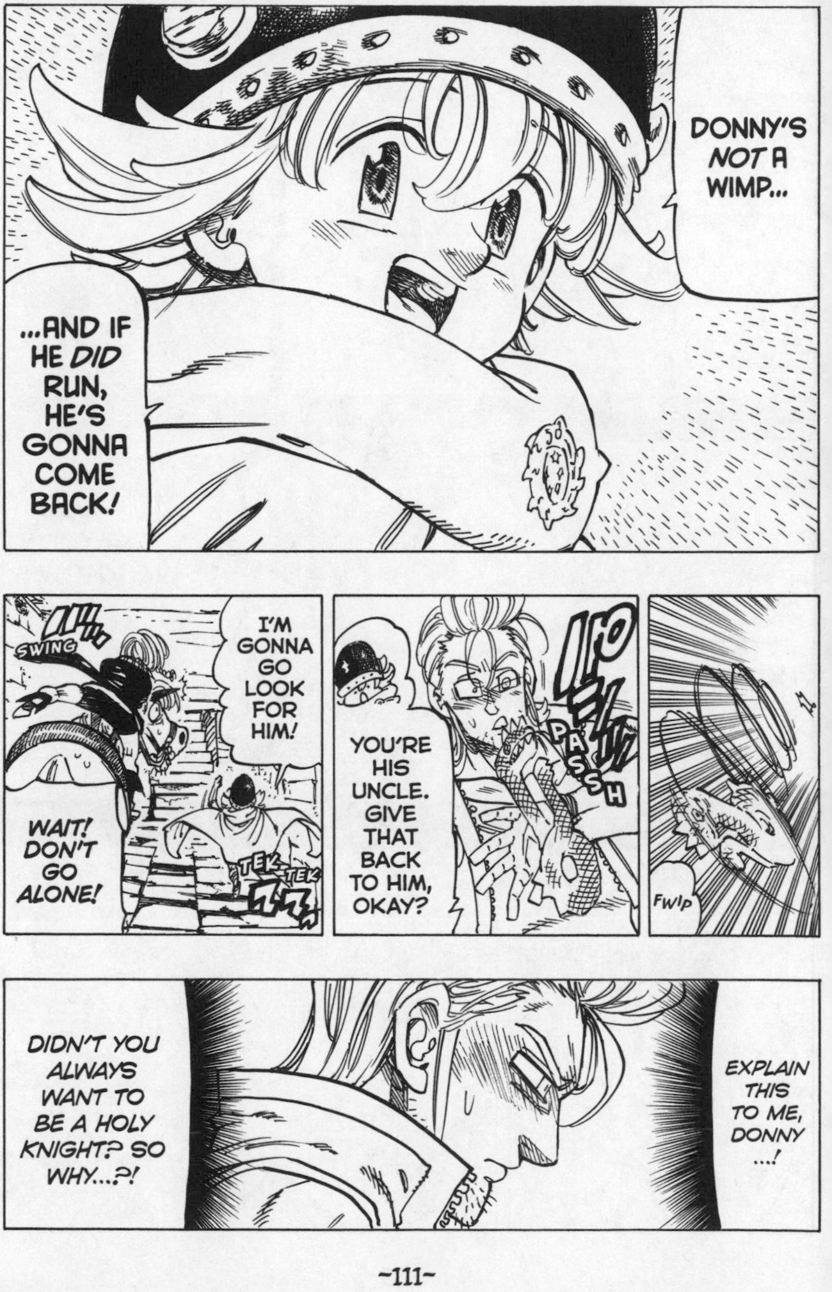
DONNY'S NOT A WIMP...
...AND IF HE DID RUN, HE'S GONNA COME BACK!
FWIP
PASSH
YOU'RE HIS UNCLE. GIVE THAT BACK TO HIM, OKAY?
I'M GONNA GO LOOK FOR HIM!
SWING
WAIT! DON'T GO ALONE!
TEK TEK
EXPLAIN THIS TO ME, DONNY ...!
DIDN'T YOU ALWAYS WANT TO BE A HOLY KNIGHT? SO WHY...?!

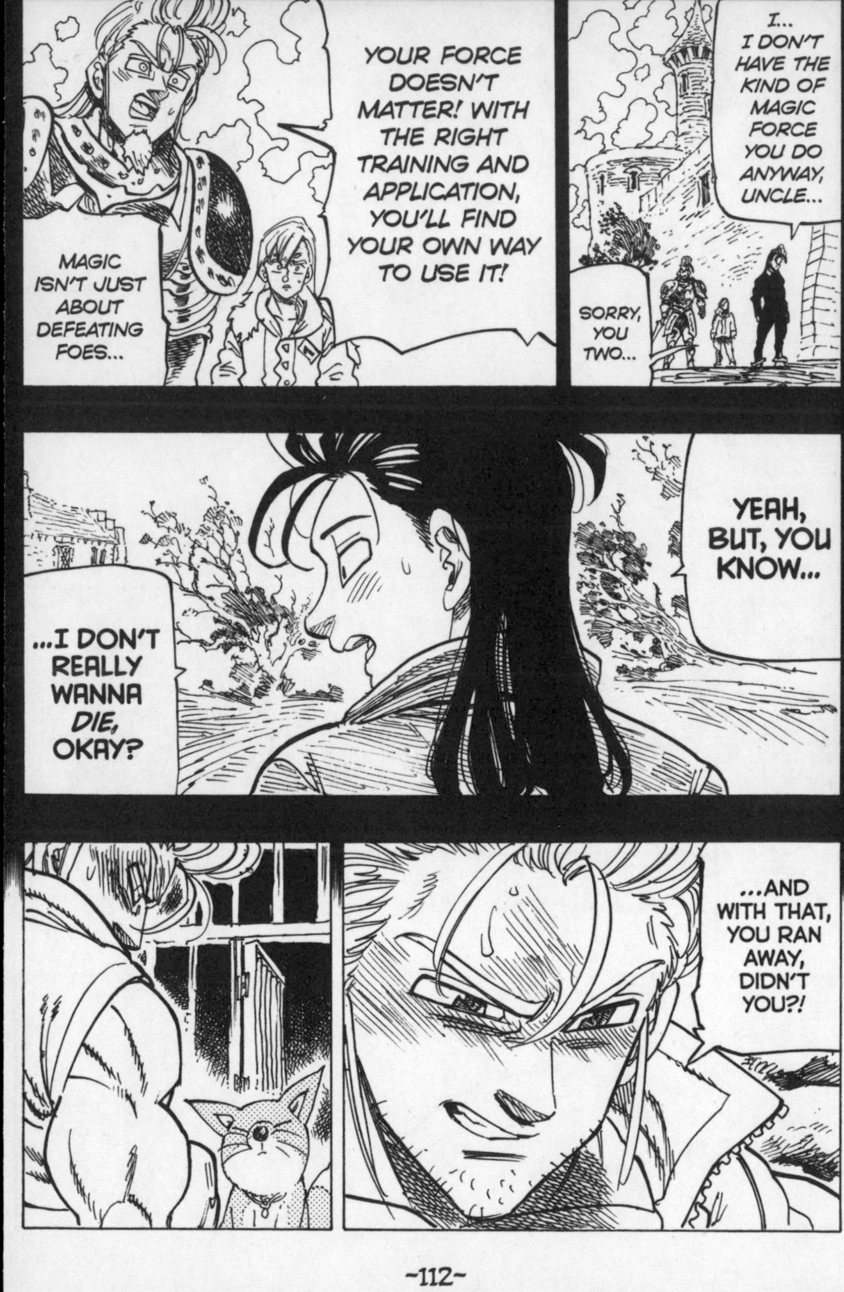
I... I DON'T HAVE THE KIND OF MAGIC FORCE YOU DO ANYWAY, UNCLE...
SORRY, YOU TWO...
YOUR FORCE DOESN'T MATTER! WITH THE RIGHT TRAINING AND APPLICATION, YOU'LL FIND YOUR OWN WAY TO USE IT!
MAGIC ISN'T JUST ABOUT DEFEATING FOES...
YEAH, BUT, YOU KNOW...
...I DON'T REALLY WANNA *DIE*, OKAY?
...AND WITH THAT, YOU RAN AWAY, DIDN'T YOU?!

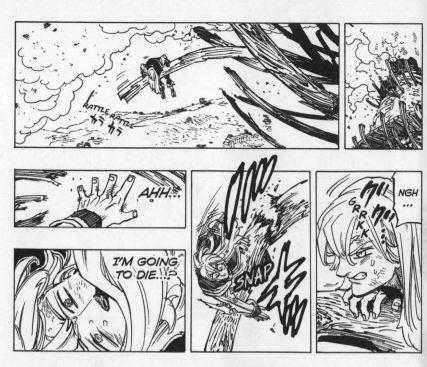

RATTLE RATTLE

AHH...

I'M GOING TO DIE...?

SNAP

NGH...

GRRKK

I'M FLOATING...?

...HUH?

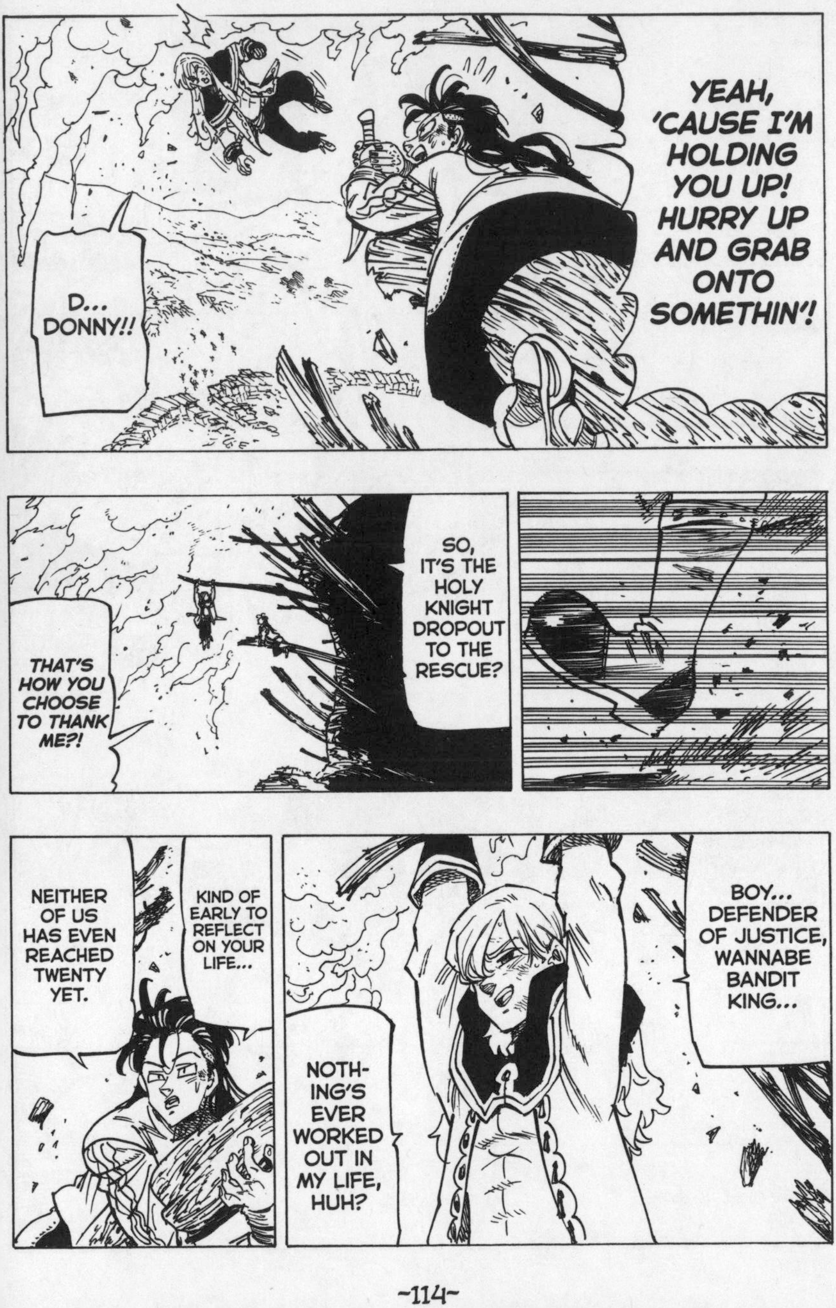
YEAH, 'CAUSE I'M HOLDING YOU UP! HURRY UP AND GRAB ONTO SOMETHIN'!
D... DONNY!!
SO, IT'S THE HOLY KNIGHT DROPOUT TO THE RESCUE?
THAT'S HOW YOU CHOOSE TO THANK ME?!
BOY... DEFENDER OF JUSTICE, WANNABE BANDIT KING...
NOTH-ING'S EVER WORKED OUT IN MY LIFE, HUH?
KIND OF EARLY TO REFLECT ON YOUR LIFE...
NEITHER OF US HAS EVEN REACHED TWENTY YET.

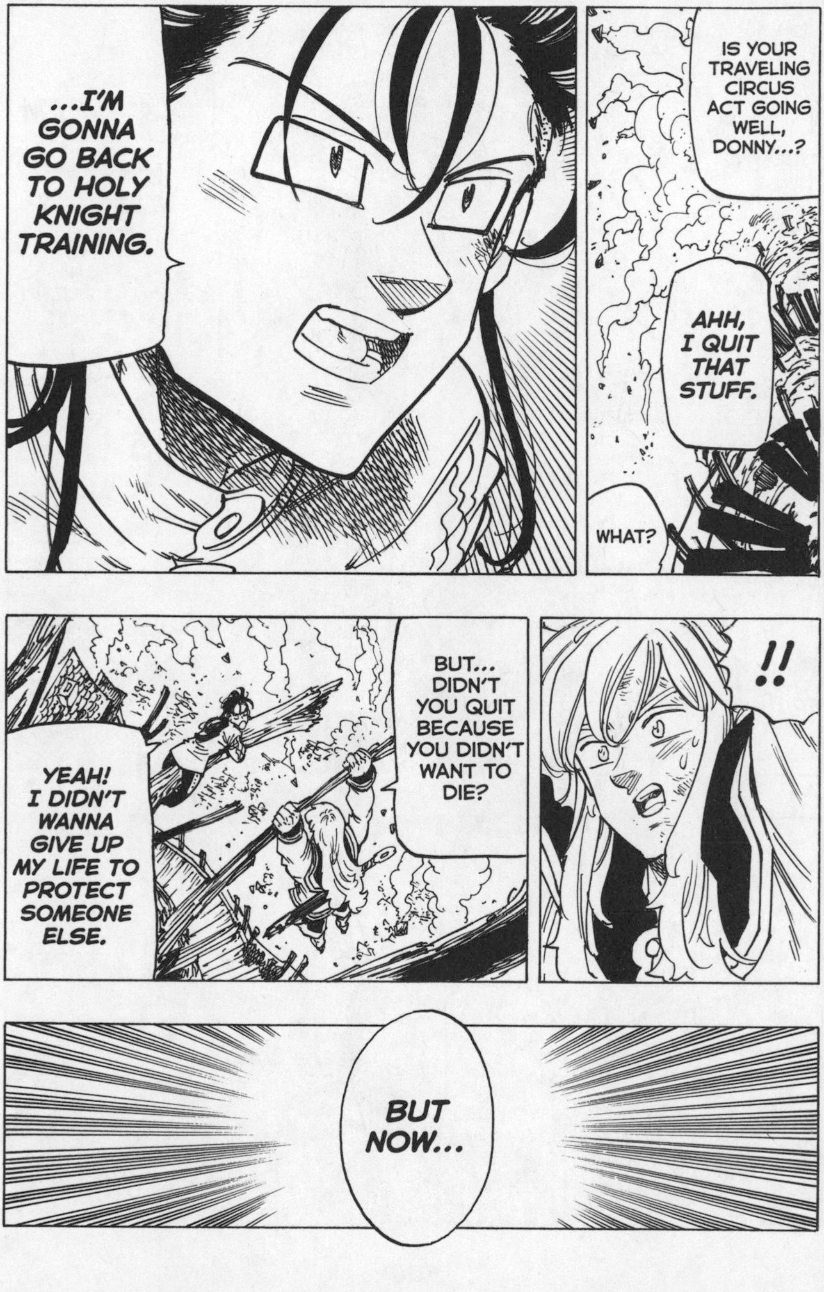
IS YOUR TRAVELING CIRCUS ACT GOING WELL, DONNY...?
AHH, I QUIT THAT STUFF.
WHAT?
...I'M GONNA GO BACK TO HOLY KNIGHT TRAINING.
!!
BUT... DIDN'T YOU QUIT BECAUSE YOU DIDN'T WANT TO DIE?
YEAH! I DIDN'T WANNA GIVE UP MY LIFE TO PROTECT SOMEONE ELSE.
BUT NOW...

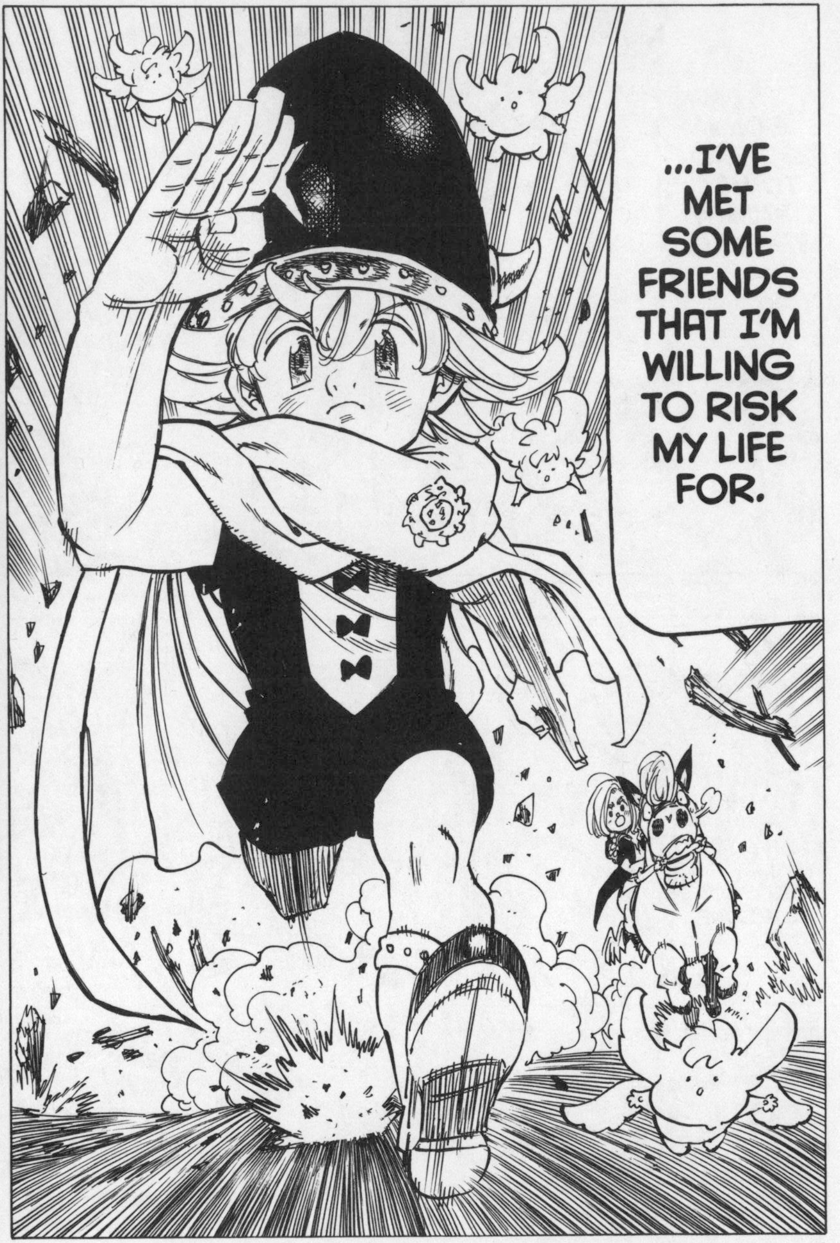
...I'VE MET SOME FRIENDS THAT I'M WILLING TO RISK MY LIFE FOR.

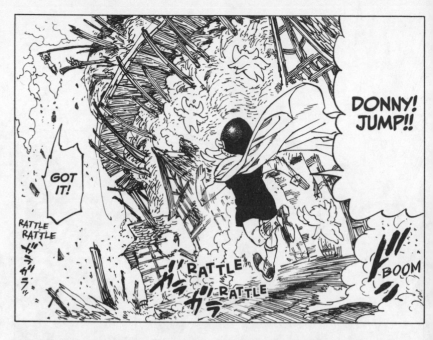

DONNY! JUMP!!

GOT IT!

RATTLE RATTLE

RATTLE RATTLE

BOOM

LET GO, EDLIN!

I'VE GOT YOU!

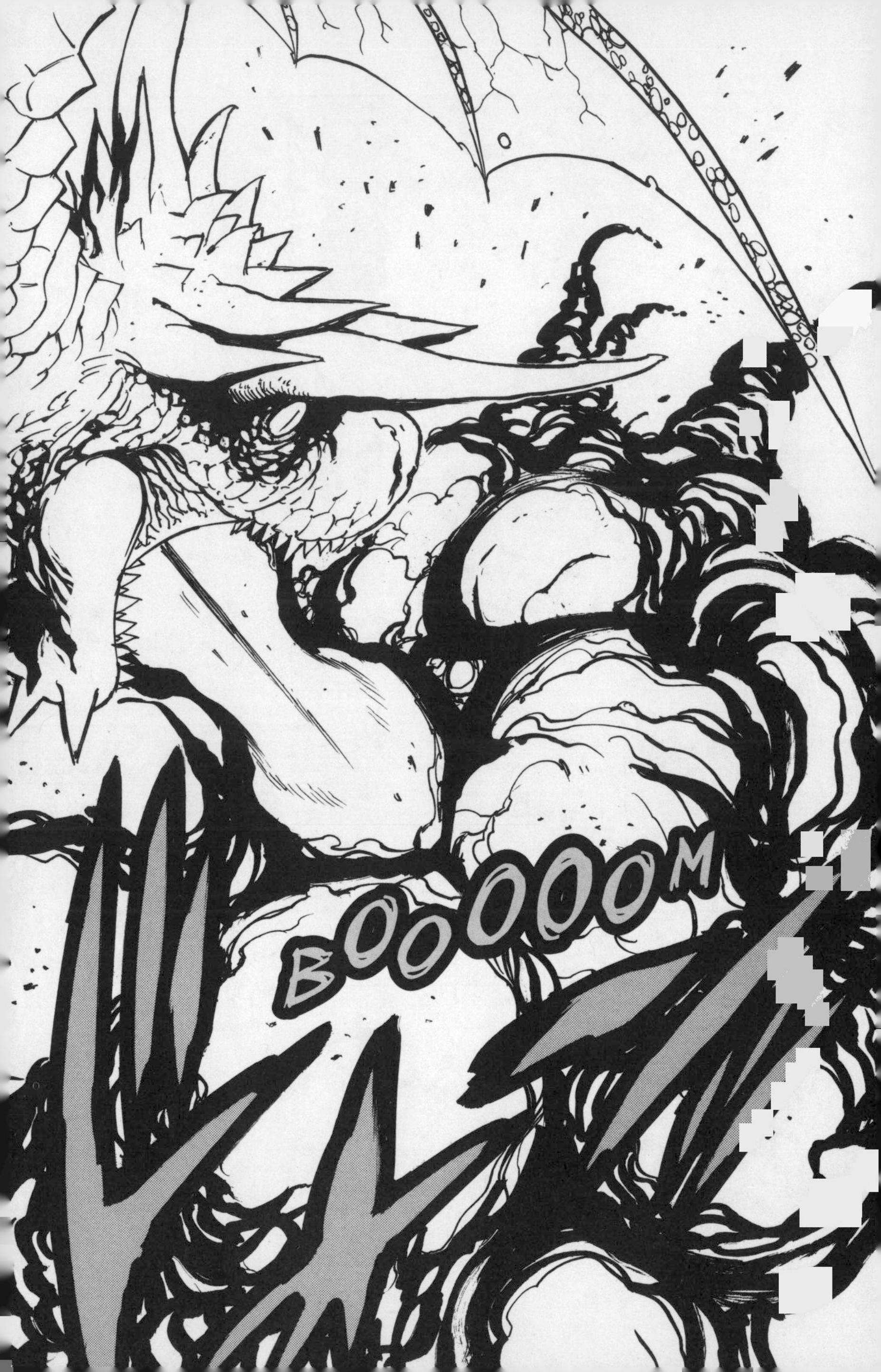
BOOOOOM

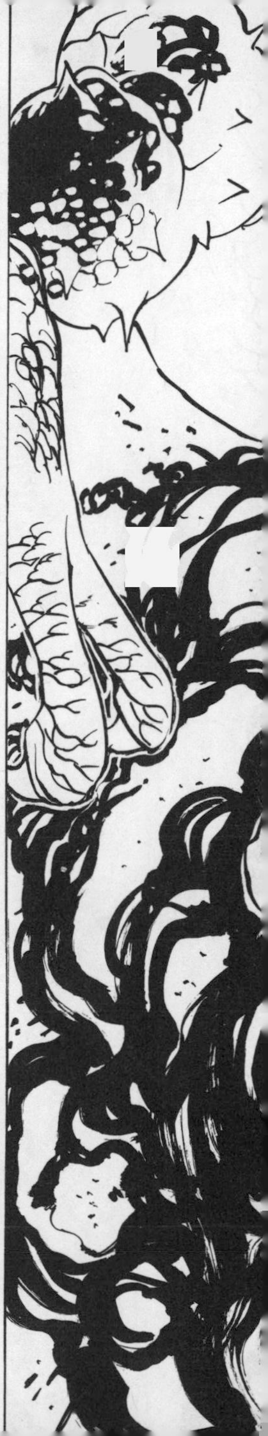

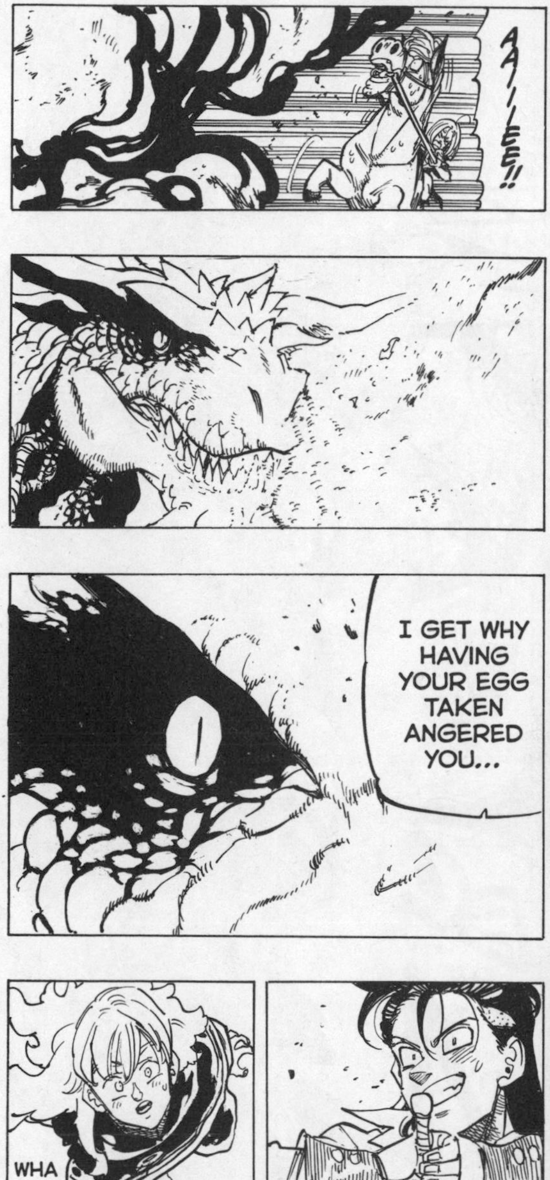
AAIIEE!!
I GET WHY HAVING YOUR EGG TAKEN ANGERED YOU...
WHA ...

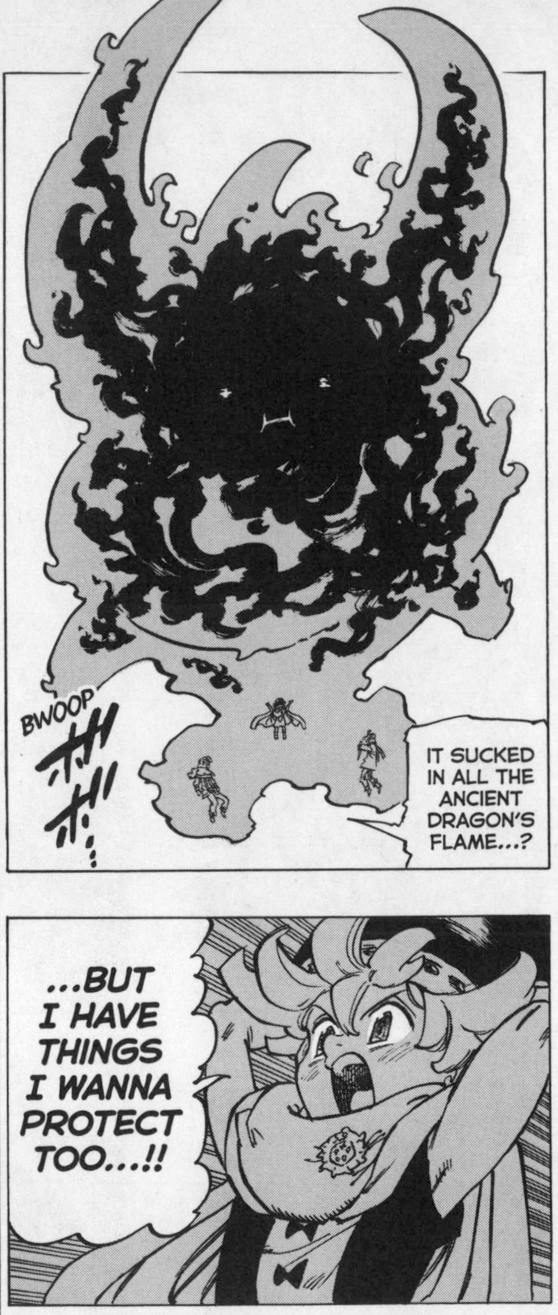
IT SUCKED IN ALL THE ANCIENT DRAGON'S FLAME...?
BWOOP
...BUT I HAVE THINGS I WANNA PROTECT TOO...!!

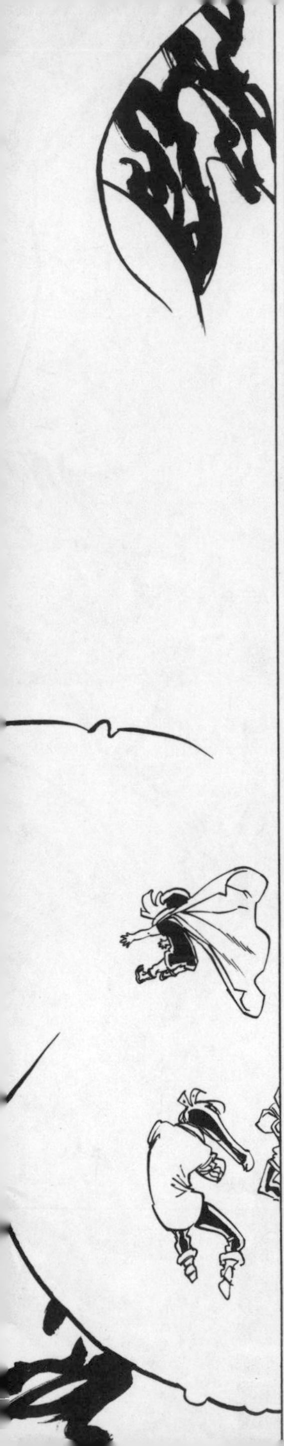

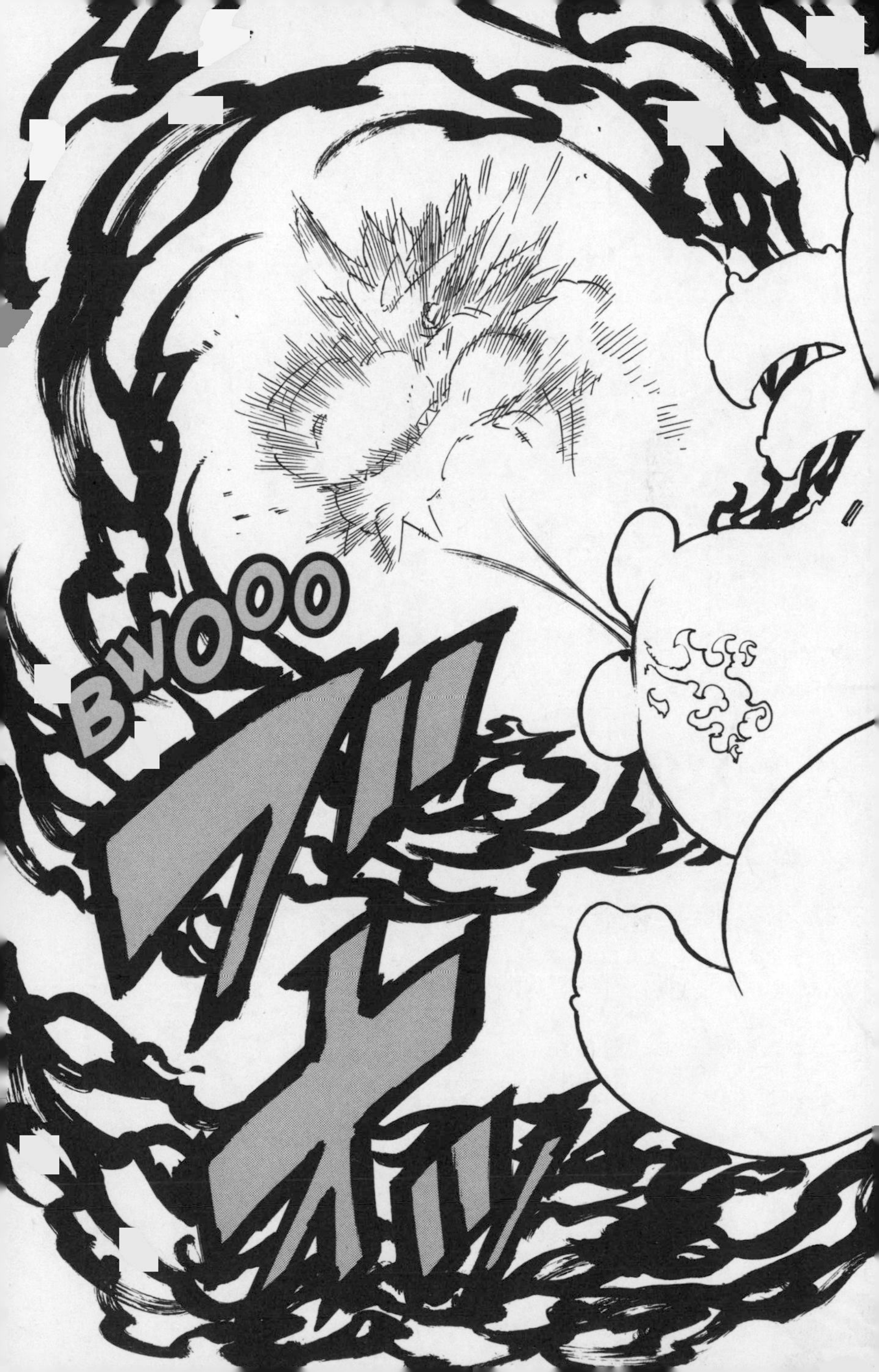
BWOOO

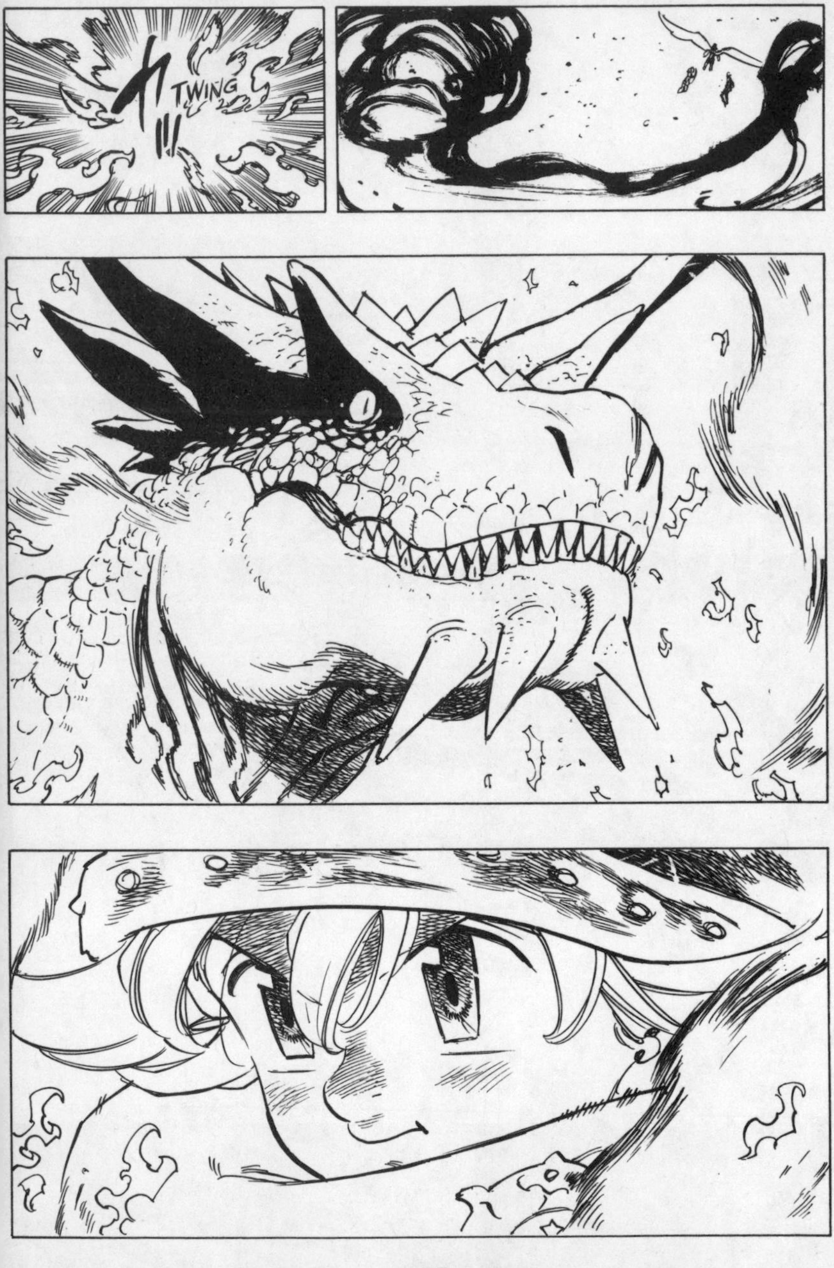
TWING

DONNY THE INFORMANT (1)

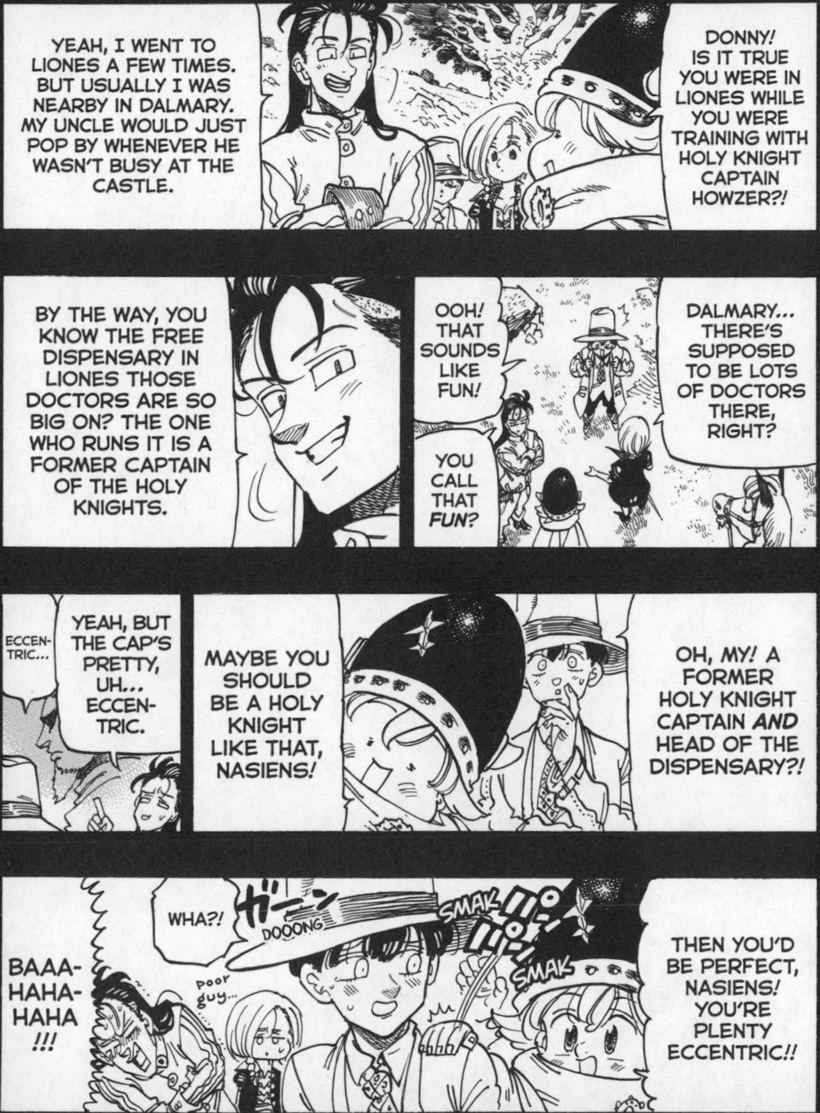
DONNY! IS IT TRUE YOU WERE IN LIONES WHILE YOU WERE TRAINING WITH HOLY KNIGHT CAPTAIN HOWZER?!
YEAH, I WENT TO LIONES A FEW TIMES. BUT USUALLY I WAS NEARBY IN DALMARY. MY UNCLE WOULD JUST POP BY WHENEVER HE WASN'T BUSY AT THE CASTLE.
DALMARY... THERE'S SUPPOSED TO BE LOTS OF DOCTORS THERE, RIGHT?
OOH! THAT SOUNDS LIKE FUN!
YOU CALL THAT *FUN*?
BY THE WAY, YOU KNOW THE FREE DISPENSARY IN LIONES THOSE DOCTORS ARE SO BIG ON? THE ONE WHO RUNS IT IS A FORMER CAPTAIN OF THE HOLY KNIGHTS.
OH, MY! A FORMER HOLY KNIGHT CAPTAIN *AND* HEAD OF THE DISPENSARY?!
MAYBE YOU SHOULD BE A HOLY KNIGHT LIKE THAT, NASIENS!
YEAH, BUT THE CAP'S PRETTY, UH... ECCEN-TRIC.
ECCEN-TRIC...
THEN YOU'D BE PERFECT, NASIENS! YOU'RE PLENTY ECCENTRIC!!
SMAK
SMAK
DOOONG
WHA?!
poor guy...
BAAA-HAHA-HAHA!!!

END

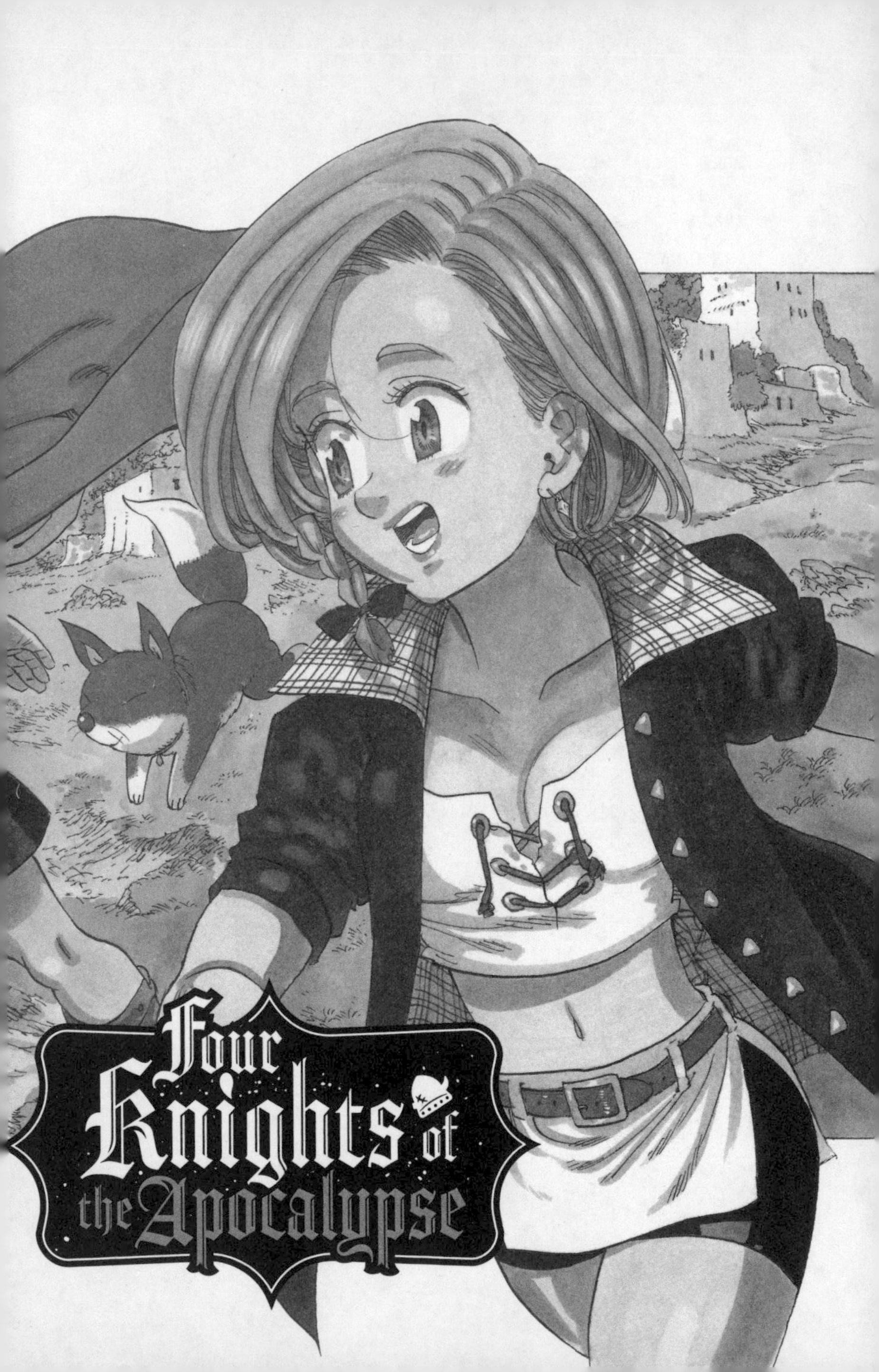
Four
Knights of
the Apocalypse

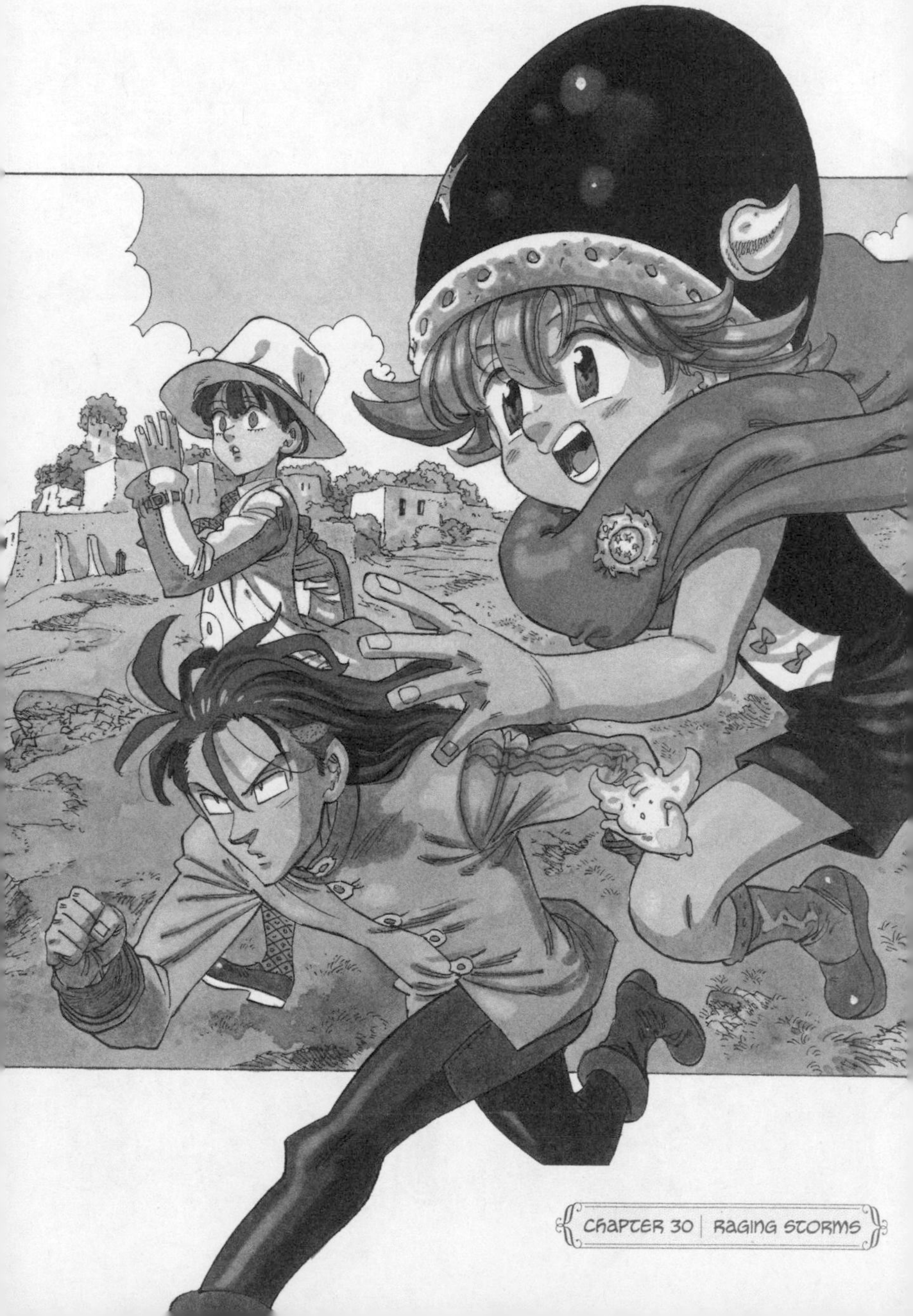

CHAPTER 30 | RAGING STORMS

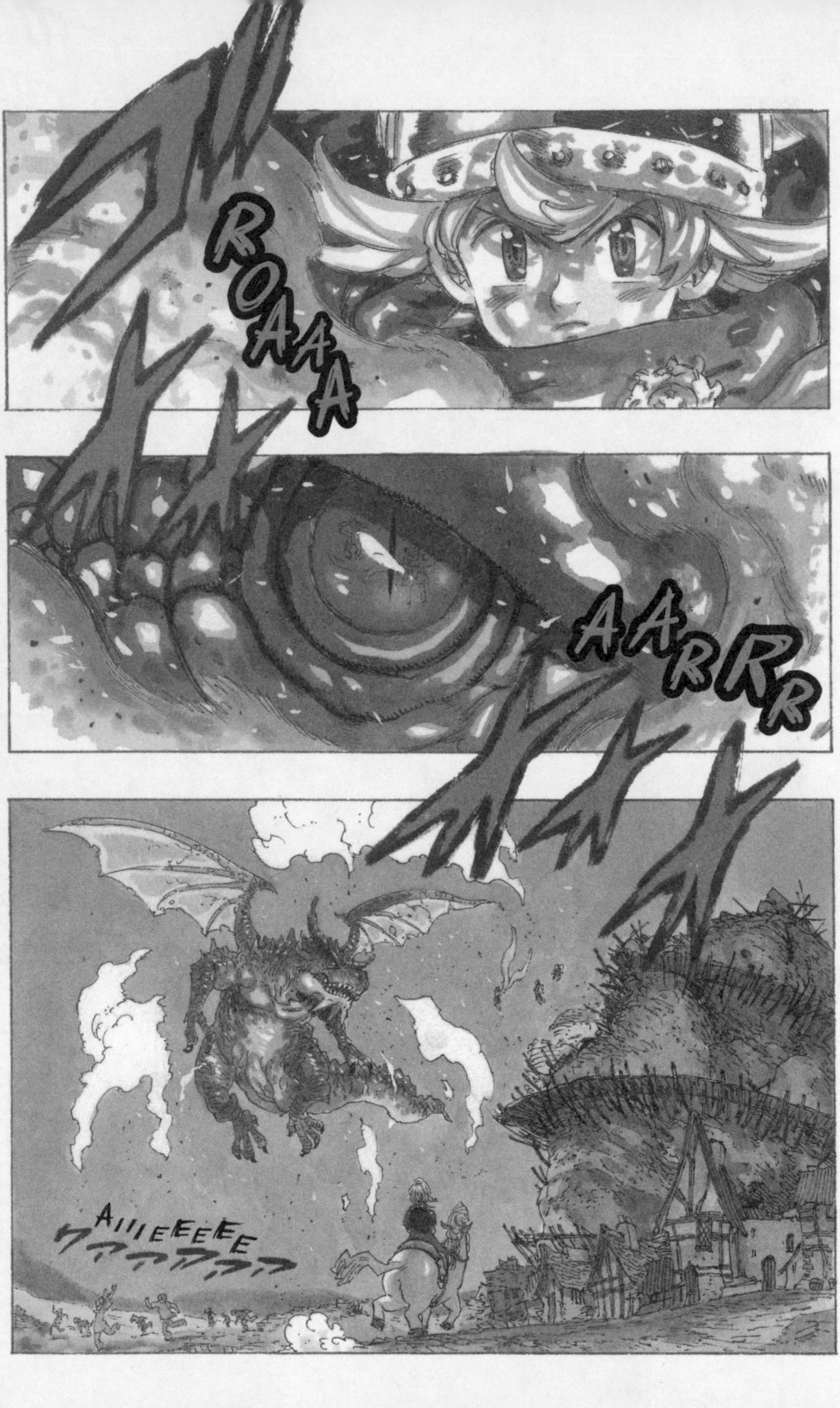
ROAAAA
AARRRR
AIIIEEEEE

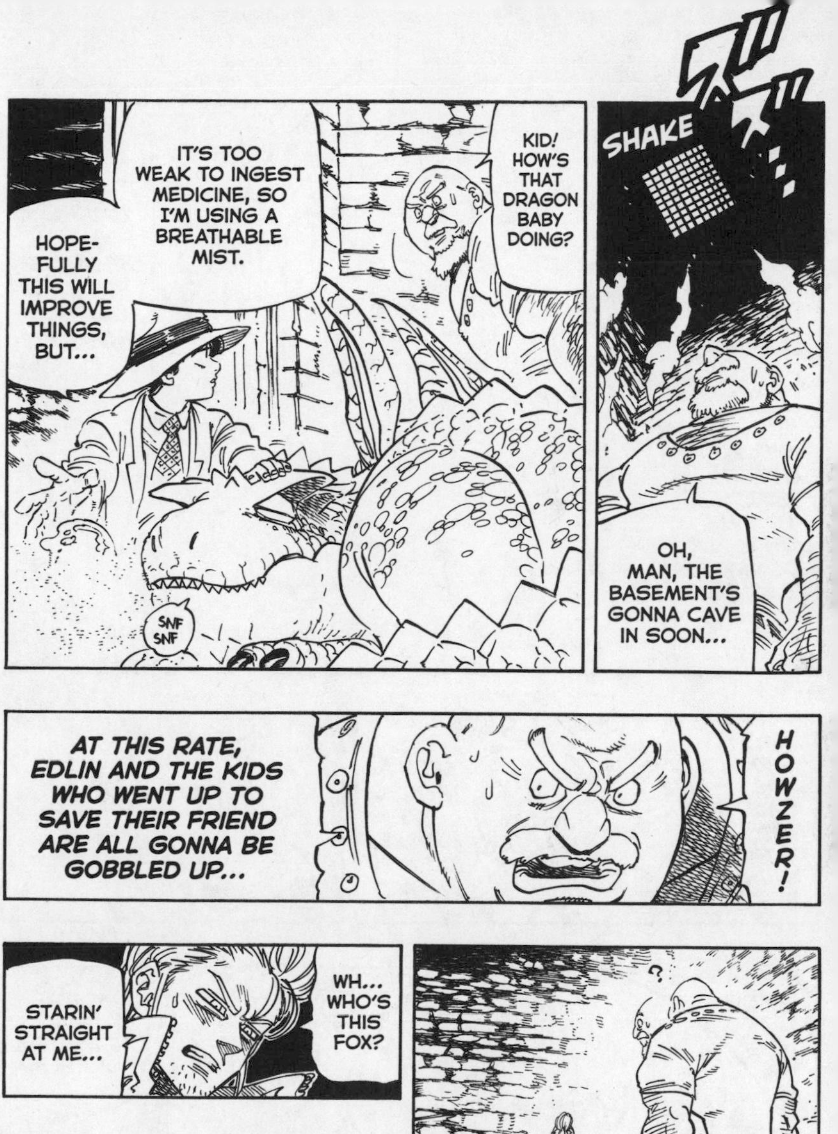
SHAKE
OH, MAN, THE BASEMENT'S GONNA CAVE IN SOON...
KID! HOW'S THAT DRAGON BABY DOING?
IT'S TOO WEAK TO INGEST MEDICINE, SO I'M USING A BREATHABLE MIST.
HOPE-FULLY THIS WILL IMPROVE THINGS, BUT...
SNF SNF
HOWZER!
AT THIS RATE, EDLIN AND THE KIDS WHO WENT UP TO SAVE THEIR FRIEND ARE ALL GONNA BE GOBBLED UP...
?
WH... WHO'S THIS FOX?
STARIN' STRAIGHT AT ME...

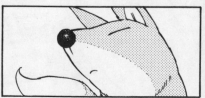

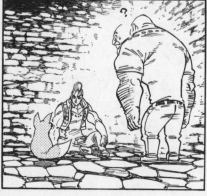

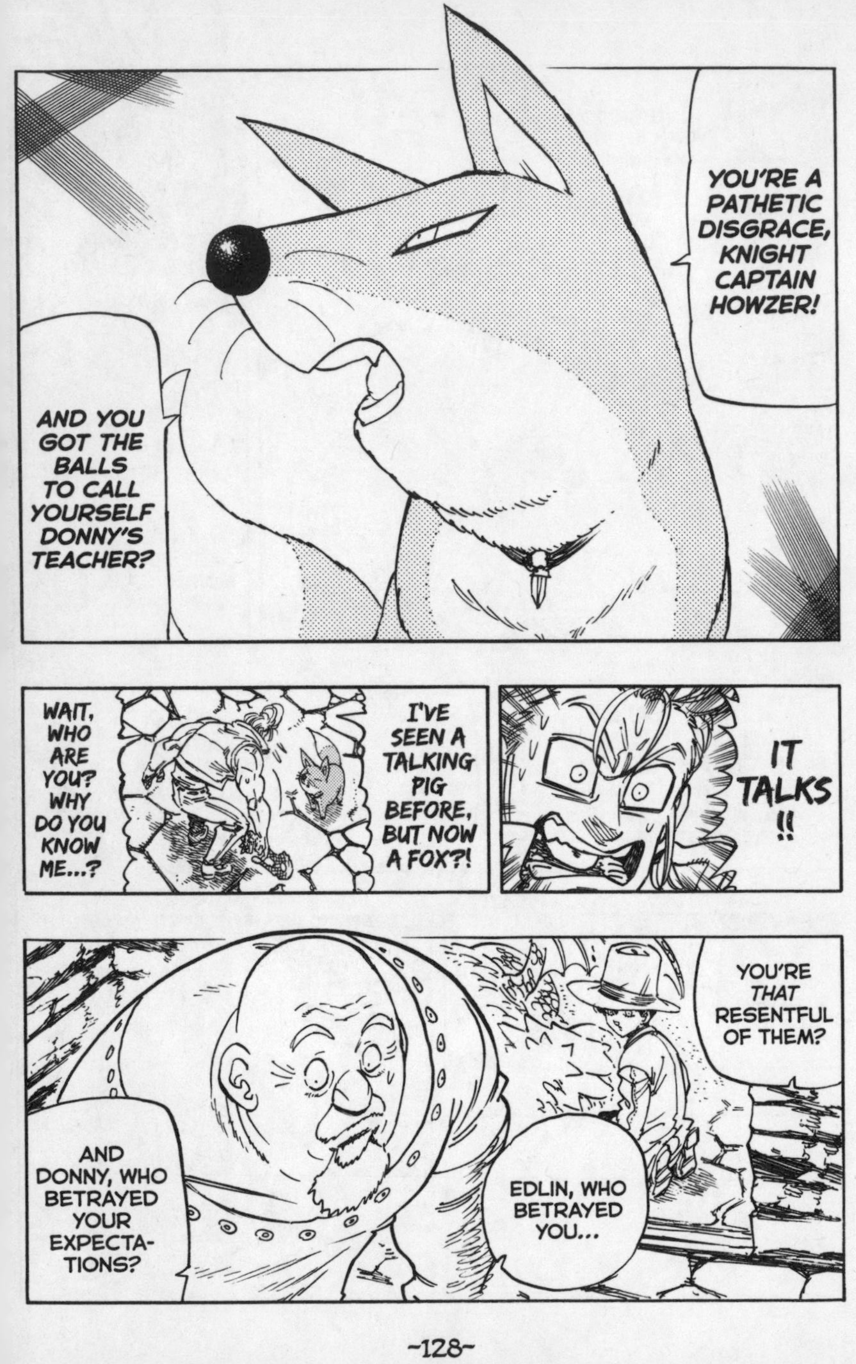
YOU'RE A PATHETIC DISGRACE, KNIGHT CAPTAIN HOWZER!
AND YOU GOT THE BALLS TO CALL YOURSELF DONNY'S TEACHER?
IT TALKS!!
I'VE SEEN A TALKING PIG BEFORE, BUT NOW A FOX?!
WAIT, WHO ARE YOU? WHY DO YOU KNOW ME...?
YOU'RE *THAT* RESENTFUL OF THEM?
EDLIN, WHO BETRAYED YOU...
AND DONNY, WHO BETRAYED YOUR EXPECTATIONS?

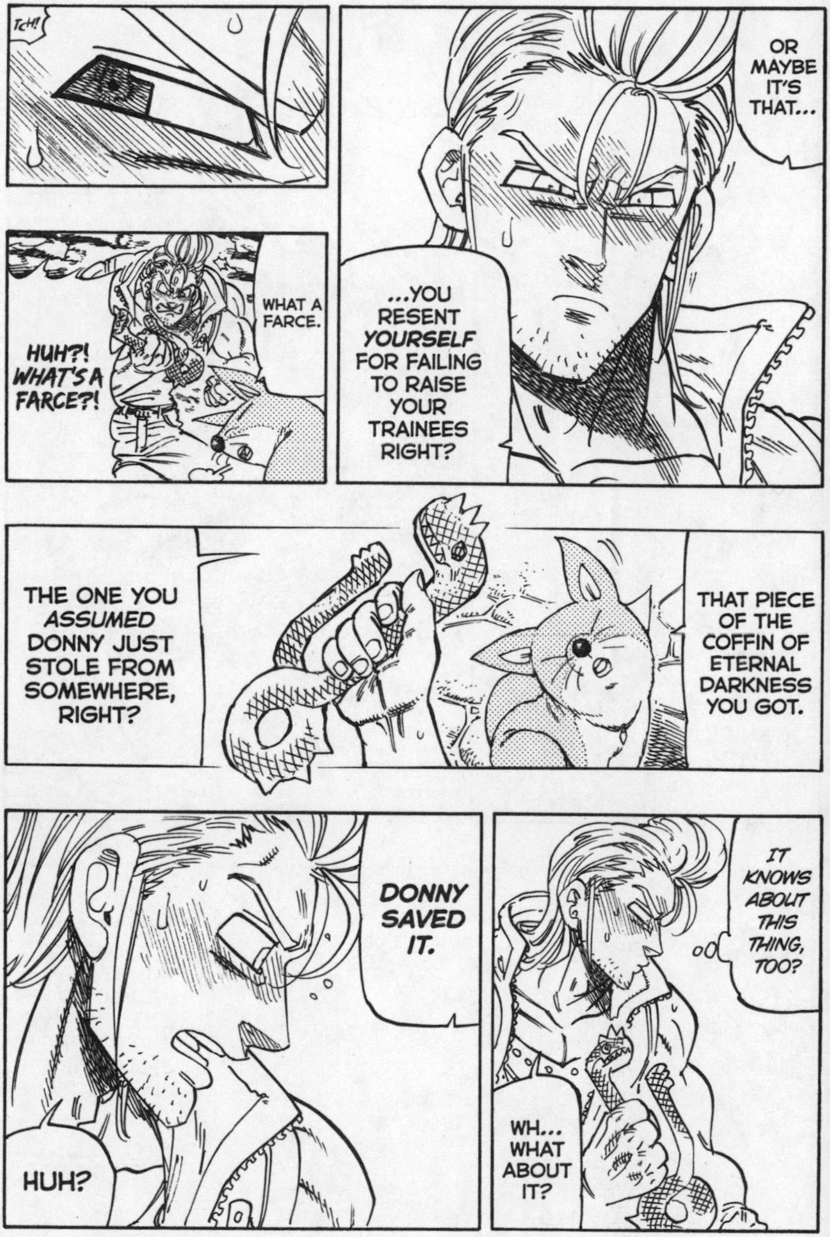
OR MAYBE IT'S THAT...
...YOU RESENT YOURSELF FOR FAILING TO RAISE YOUR TRAINEES RIGHT?
TCH!
WHAT A FARCE.
HUH?! WHAT'S A FARCE?!
THAT PIECE OF THE COFFIN OF ETERNAL DARKNESS YOU GOT.
THE ONE YOU ASSUMED DONNY JUST STOLE FROM SOMEWHERE, RIGHT?
IT KNOWS ABOUT THIS THING, TOO?
WH... WHAT ABOUT IT?
DONNY SAVED IT.
HUH?

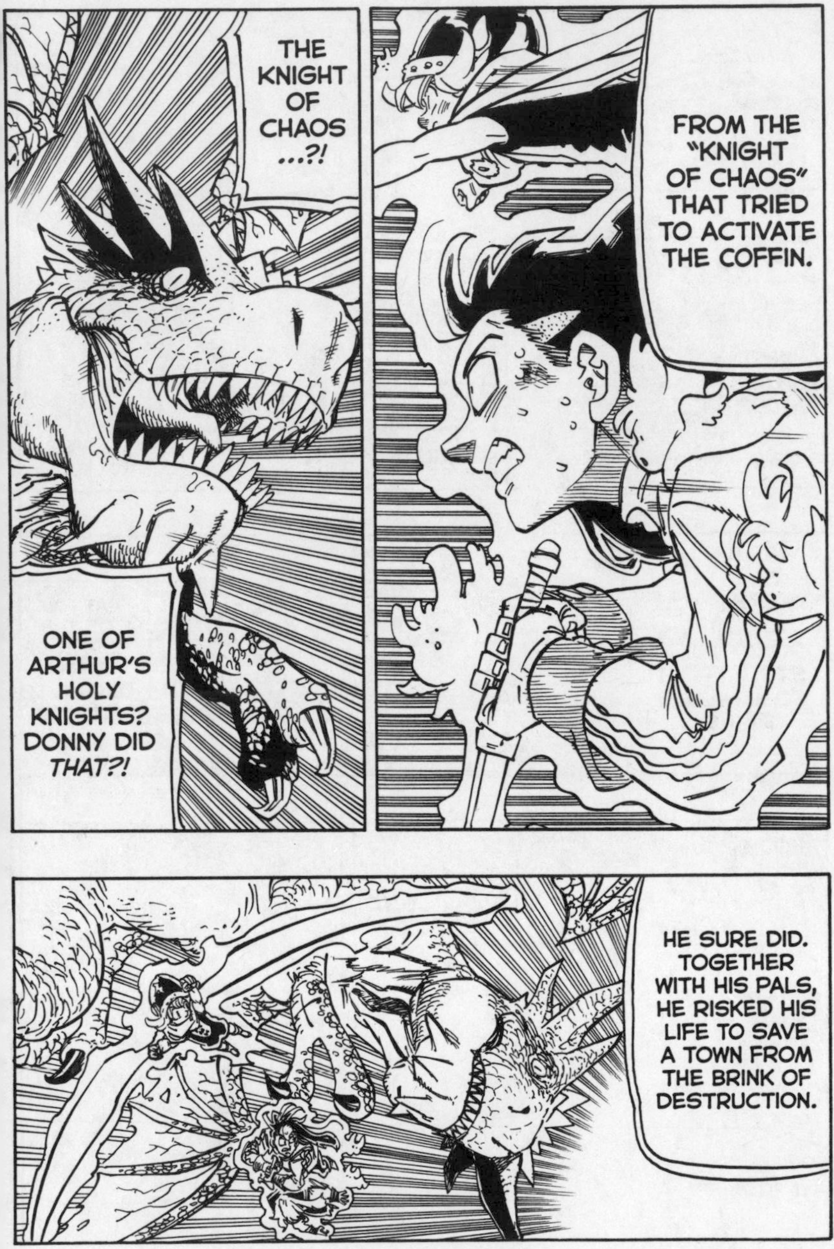
FROM THE "KNIGHT OF CHAOS" THAT TRIED TO ACTIVATE THE COFFIN.
THE KNIGHT OF CHAOS ...?!
ONE OF ARTHUR'S HOLY KNIGHTS? DONNY DID *THAT?!*
HE SURE DID. TOGETHER WITH HIS PALS, HE RISKED HIS LIFE TO SAVE A TOWN FROM THE BRINK OF DESTRUCTION.

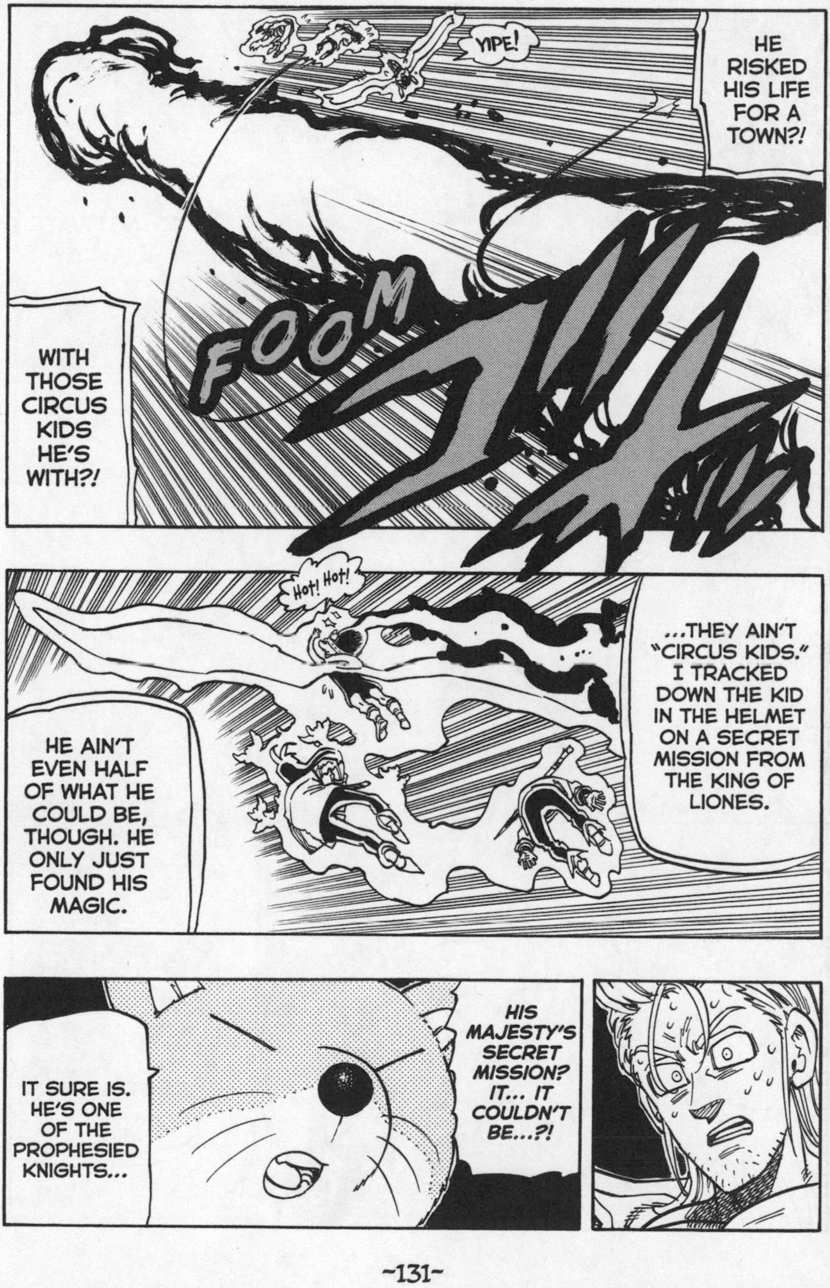
HE RISKED HIS LIFE FOR A TOWN?!
YIPE!
WITH THOSE CIRCUS KIDS HE'S WITH?!
FOOM
...THEY AIN'T "CIRCUS KIDS." I TRACKED DOWN THE KID IN THE HELMET ON A SECRET MISSION FROM THE KING OF LIONES.
Hot! Hot!
HE AIN'T EVEN HALF OF WHAT HE COULD BE, THOUGH. HE ONLY JUST FOUND HIS MAGIC.
HIS MAJESTY'S SECRET MISSION? IT... IT COULDN'T BE...?!
IT SURE IS. HE'S ONE OF THE PROPHESIED KNIGHTS...

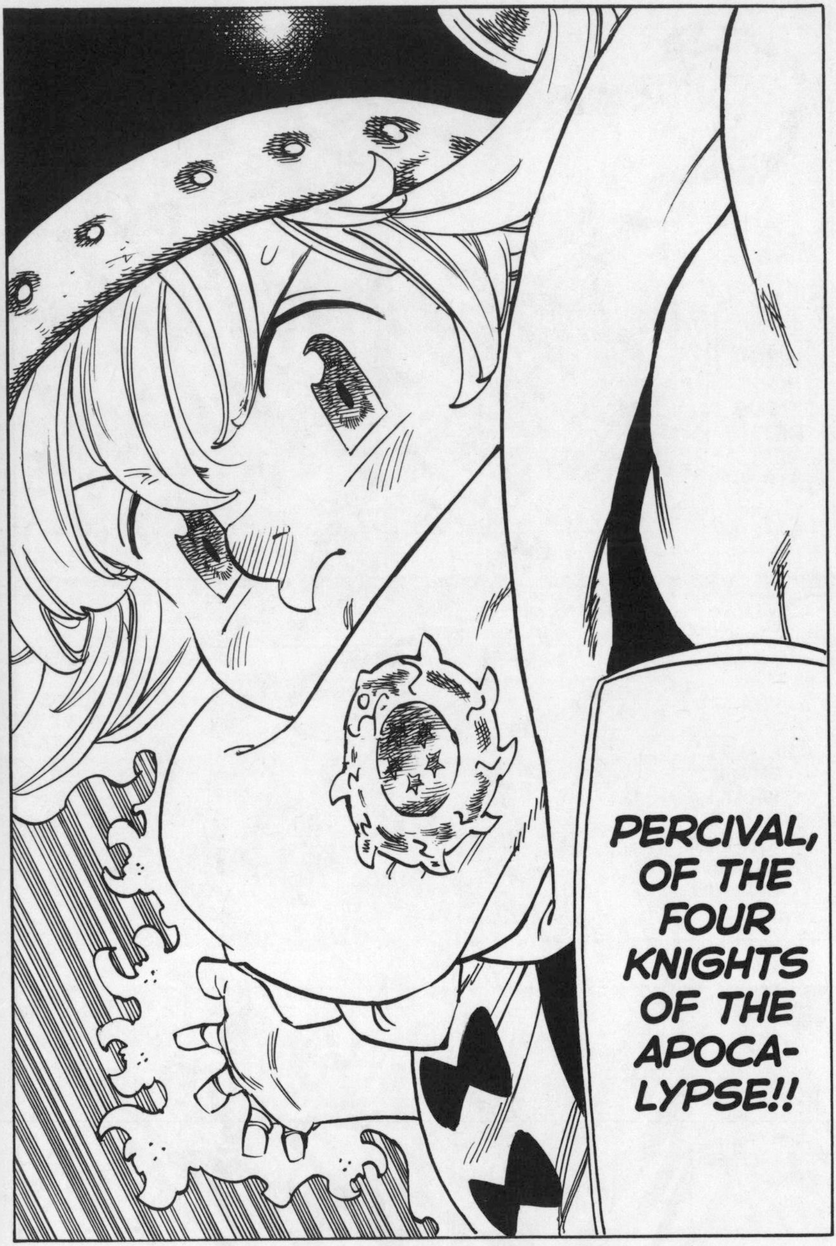
PERCIVAL, OF THE FOUR KNIGHTS OF THE APOCA-LYPSE!!

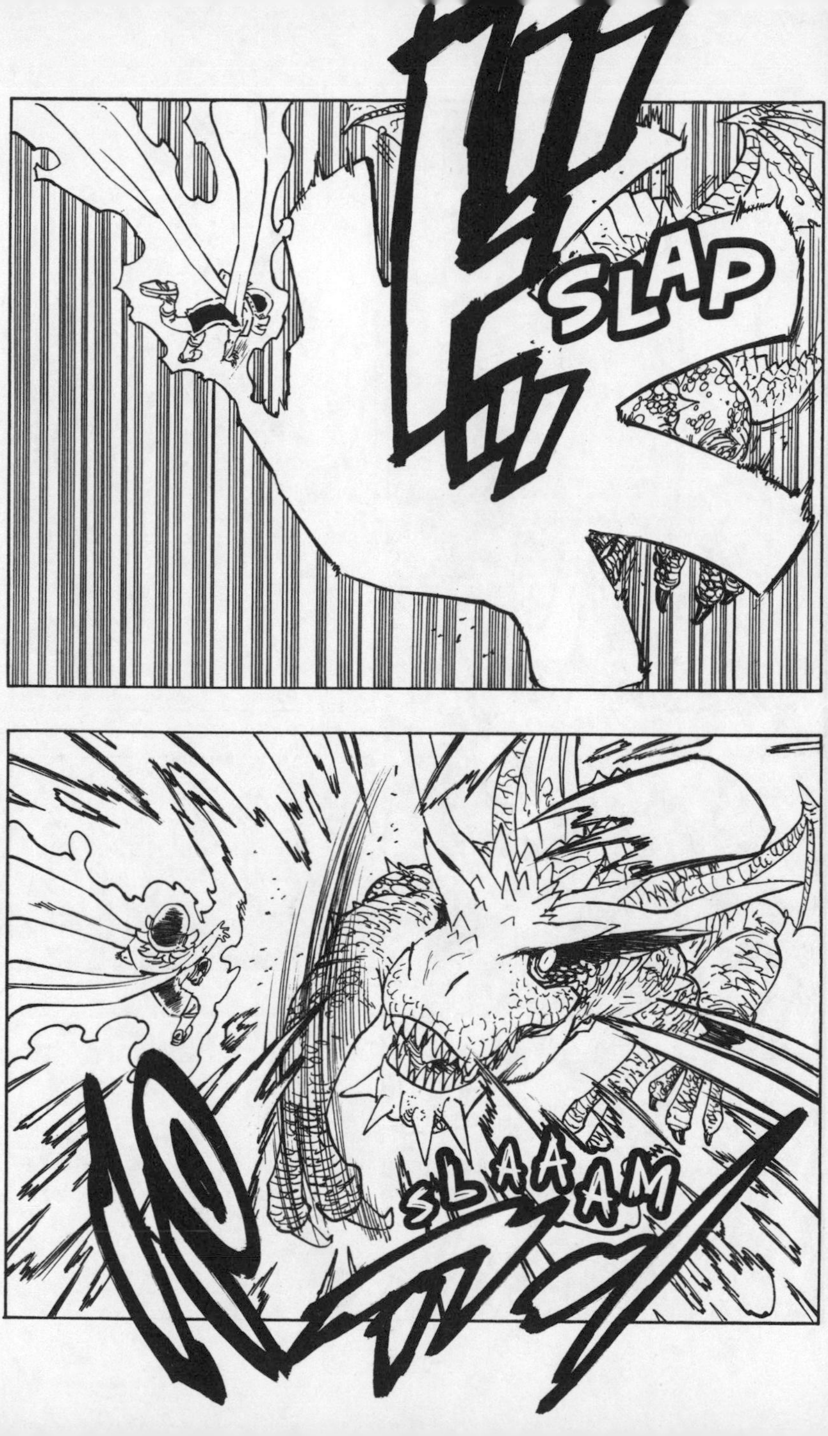
SLAP
SLAAAM

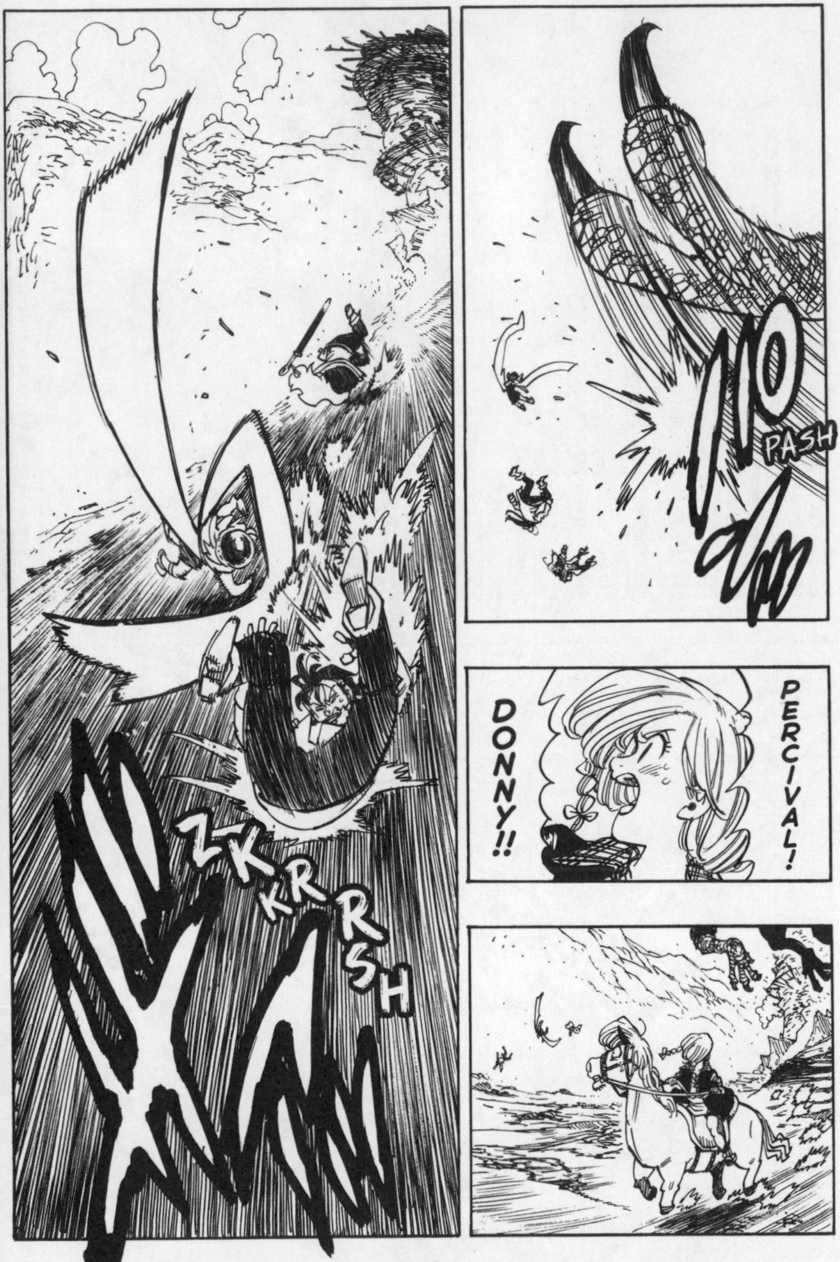
PASH
PERCIVAL!
DONNY!!
ZKKRRSH

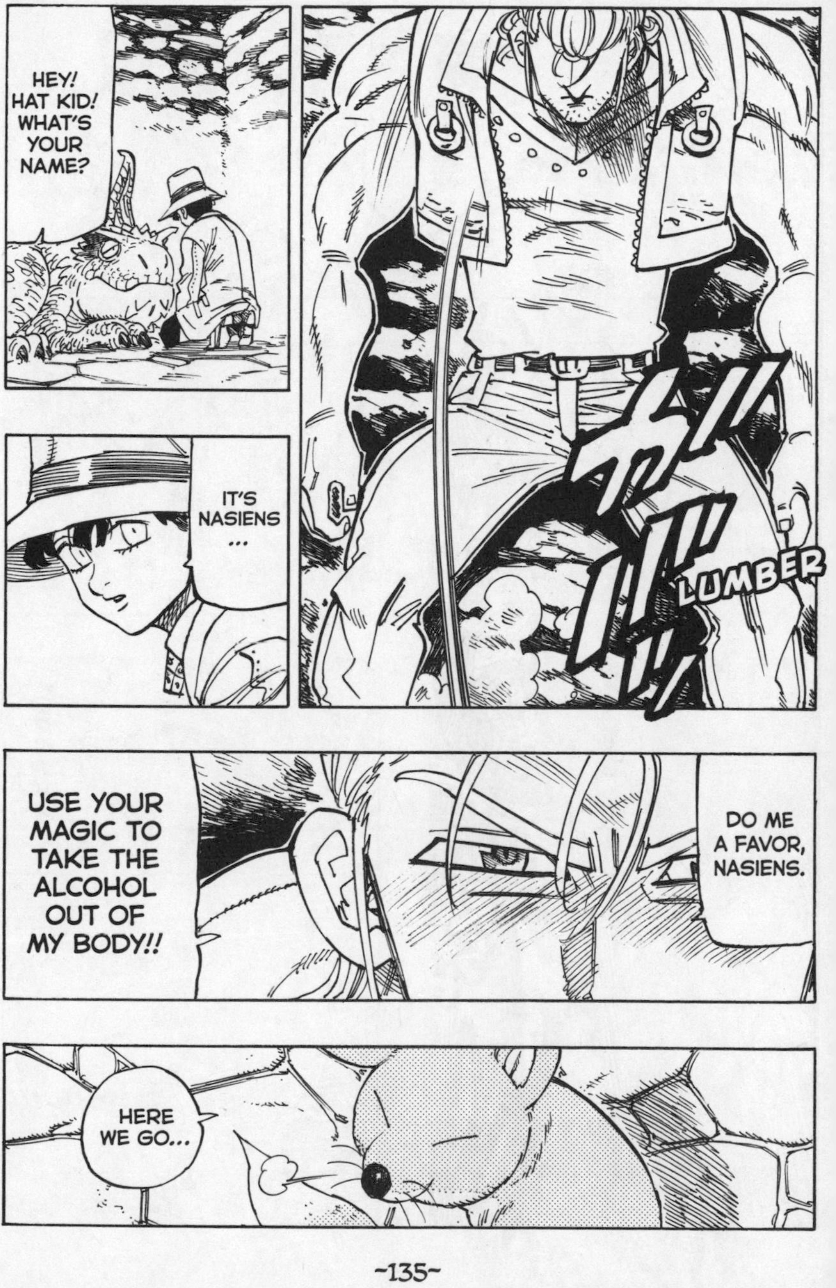
LUMBER
HEY! HAT KID! WHAT'S YOUR NAME?
IT'S NASIENS...
DO ME A FAVOR, NASIENS.
USE YOUR MAGIC TO TAKE THE ALCOHOL OUT OF MY BODY!!
HERE WE GO...

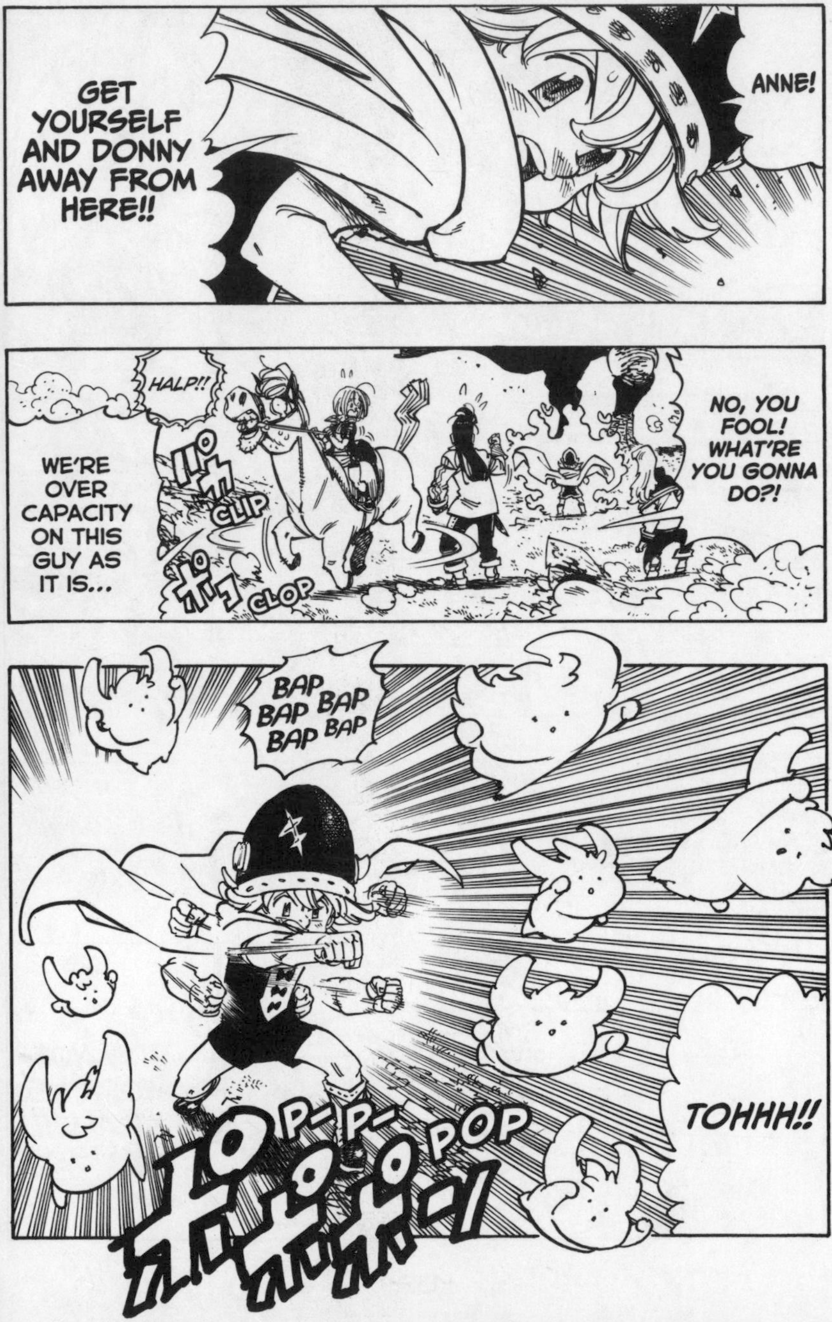
ANNE!
GET YOURSELF AND DONNY AWAY FROM HERE!!
NO, YOU FOOL! WHAT'RE YOU GONNA DO?!
HALP!!
WE'RE OVER CAPACITY ON THIS GUY AS IT IS...
CLIP
CLOP
TOHHH!!
BAP BAP BAP BAP BAP
P-P-POP

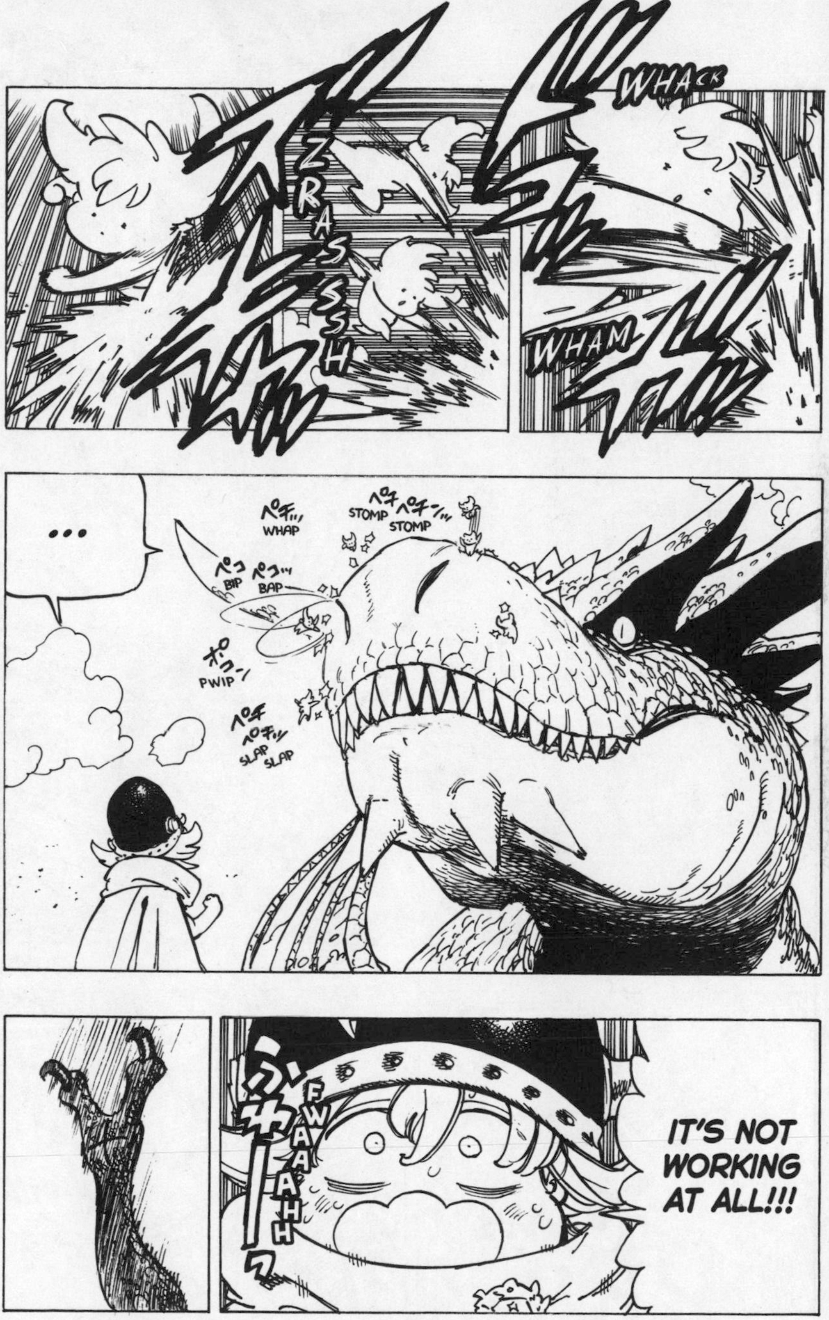
WHACK
WHAM
ZRASSSH
STOMP STOMP
WHAP
BIP BAP
PWIP
SLAP SLAP
...
FWAAAAHH
IT'S NOT WORKING AT ALL!!!

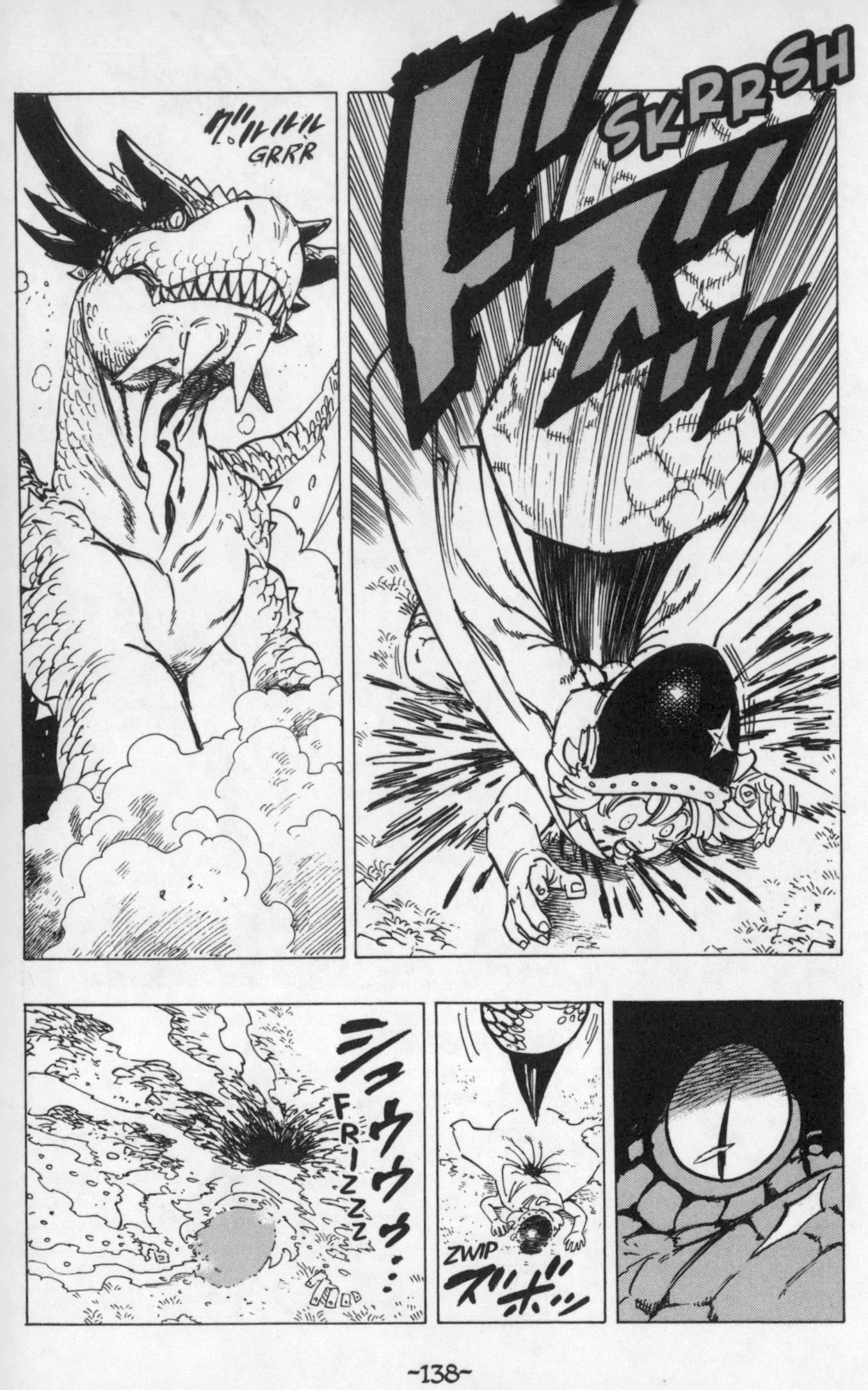
ドスッ
SKRRSH
グルルル
GRRR
ズボッ
ZWIP
シュウウウ…
FRIZZZ

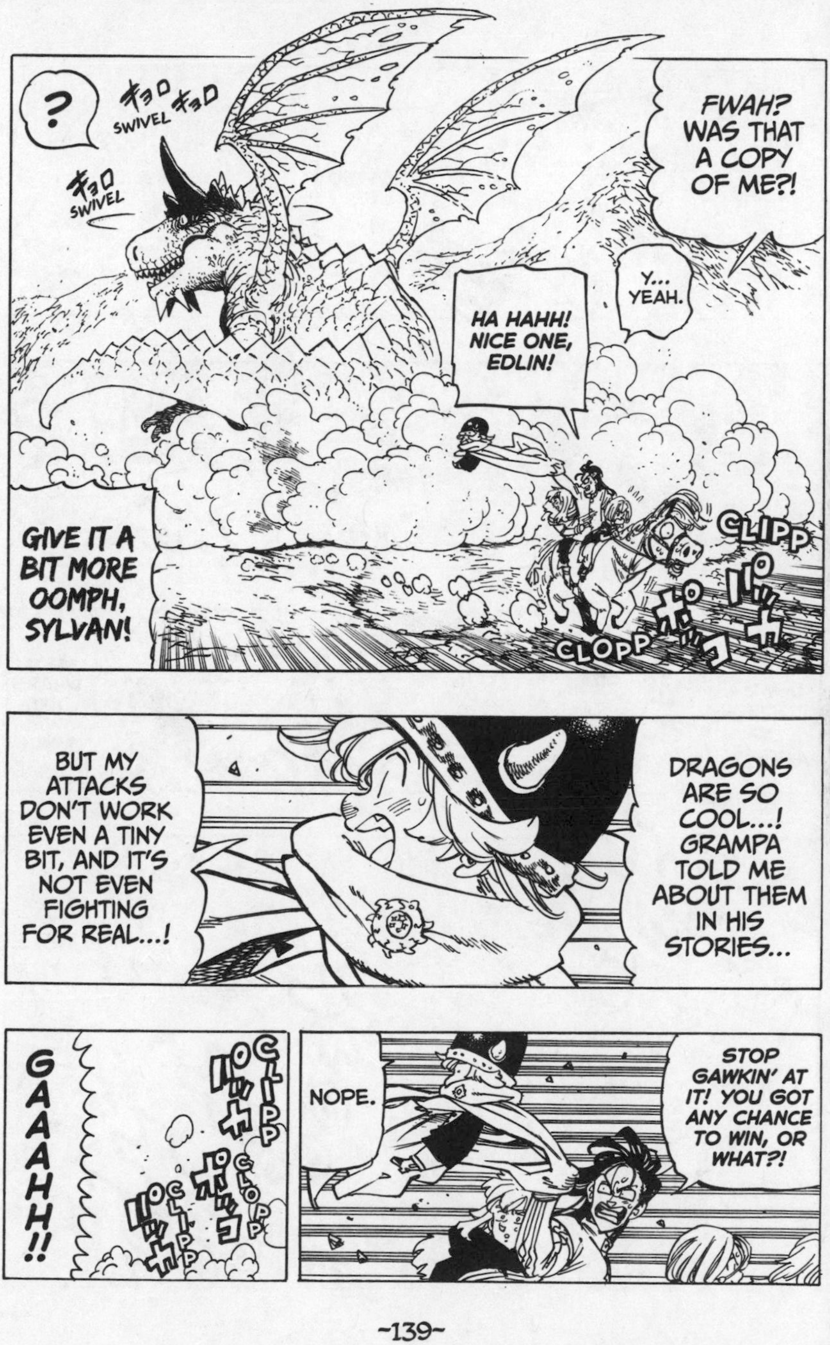
FWAH? WAS THAT A COPY OF ME?!
Y... YEAH.
HA HAHH! NICE ONE, EDLIN!
?
キョロ SWIVEL キョロ
キョロ SWIVEL
GIVE IT A BIT MORE OOMPH, SYLVAN!
パッカ CLIPP
ポッコ CLOPP
DRAGONS ARE SO COOL...! GRAMPA TOLD ME ABOUT THEM IN HIS STORIES...
BUT MY ATTACKS DON'T WORK EVEN A TINY BIT, AND IT'S NOT EVEN FIGHTING FOR REAL...!
STOP GAWKIN' AT IT! YOU GOT ANY CHANCE TO WIN, OR WHAT?!
NOPE.
パッカ CLIPP
ポッコ CLOPP
パッカ CLIPP
GAAAAHH!!

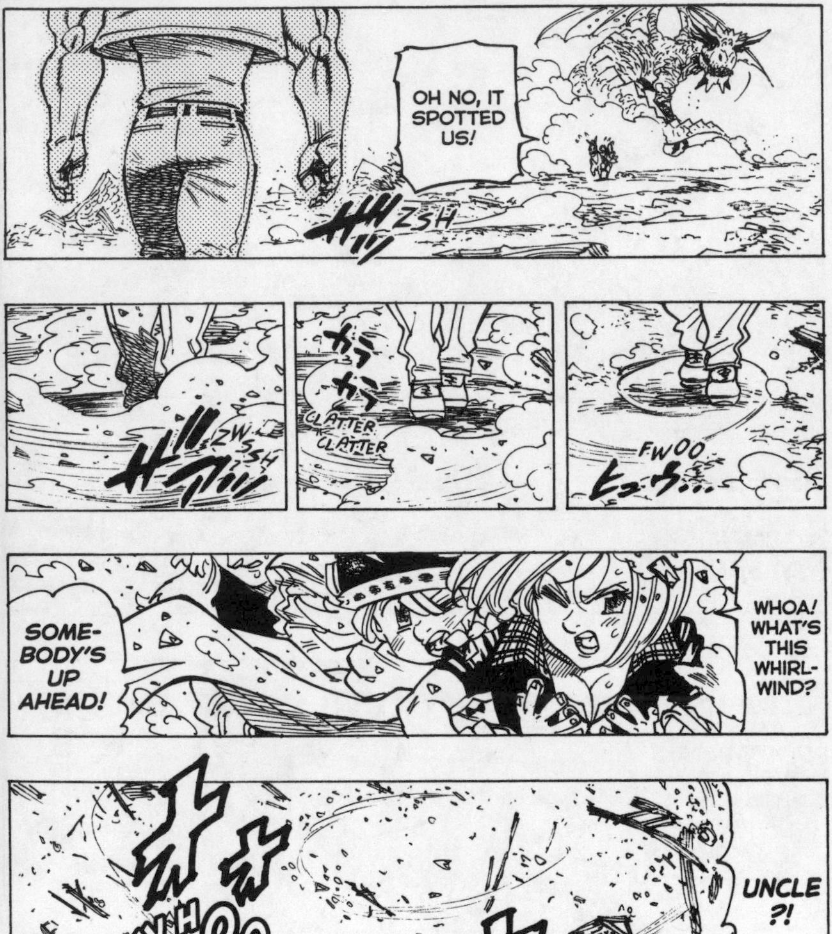
OH NO, IT SPOTTED US!
ZSH
FWOO
CLATTER CLATTER
ZWSSH
WHOA! WHAT'S THIS WHIRLWIND?
SOMEBODY'S UP AHEAD!
UNCLE ?!
MASTER HOWZER ?!
WHOOO

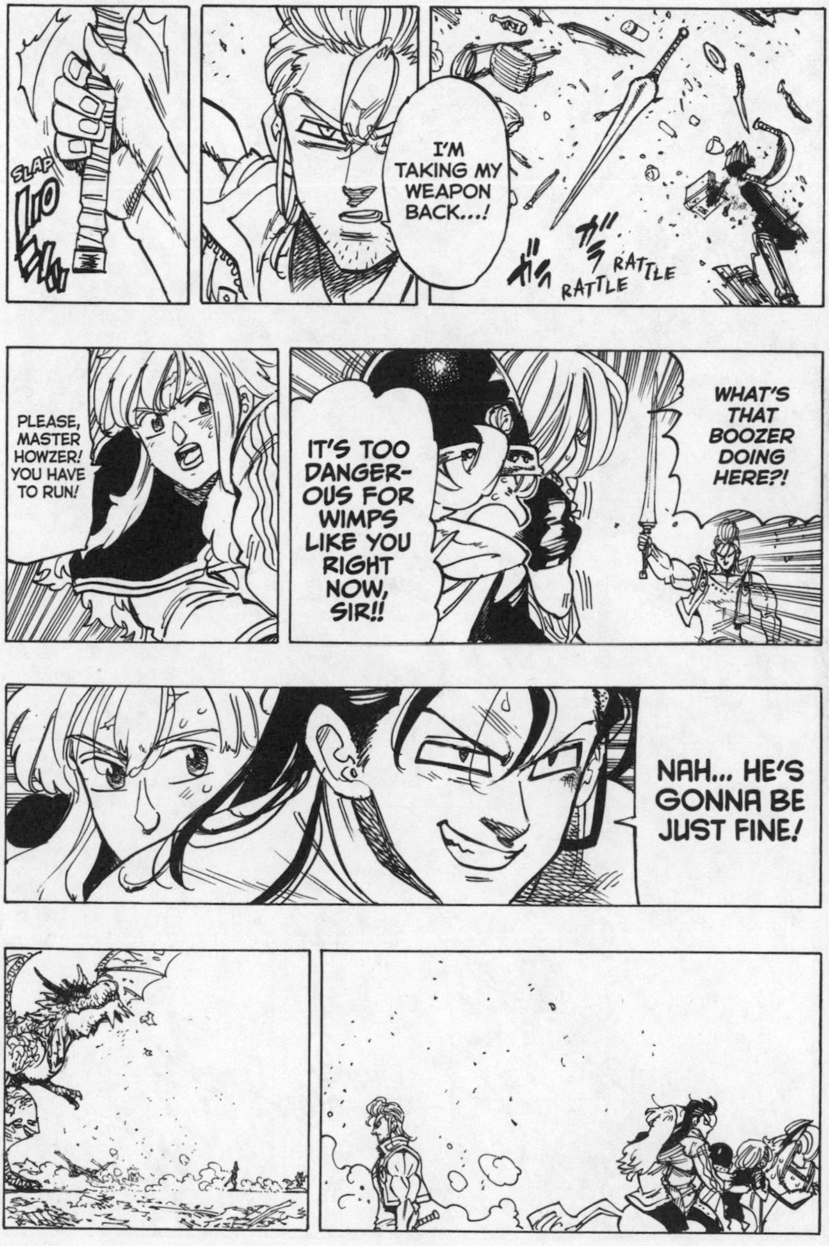

RATTLE RATTLE
I'M TAKING MY WEAPON BACK...!
SLAP
WHAT'S THAT BOOZER DOING HERE?!
IT'S TOO DANGEROUS FOR WIMPS LIKE YOU RIGHT NOW, SIR!!
PLEASE, MASTER HOWZER! YOU HAVE TO RUN!
NAH... HE'S GONNA BE JUST FINE!

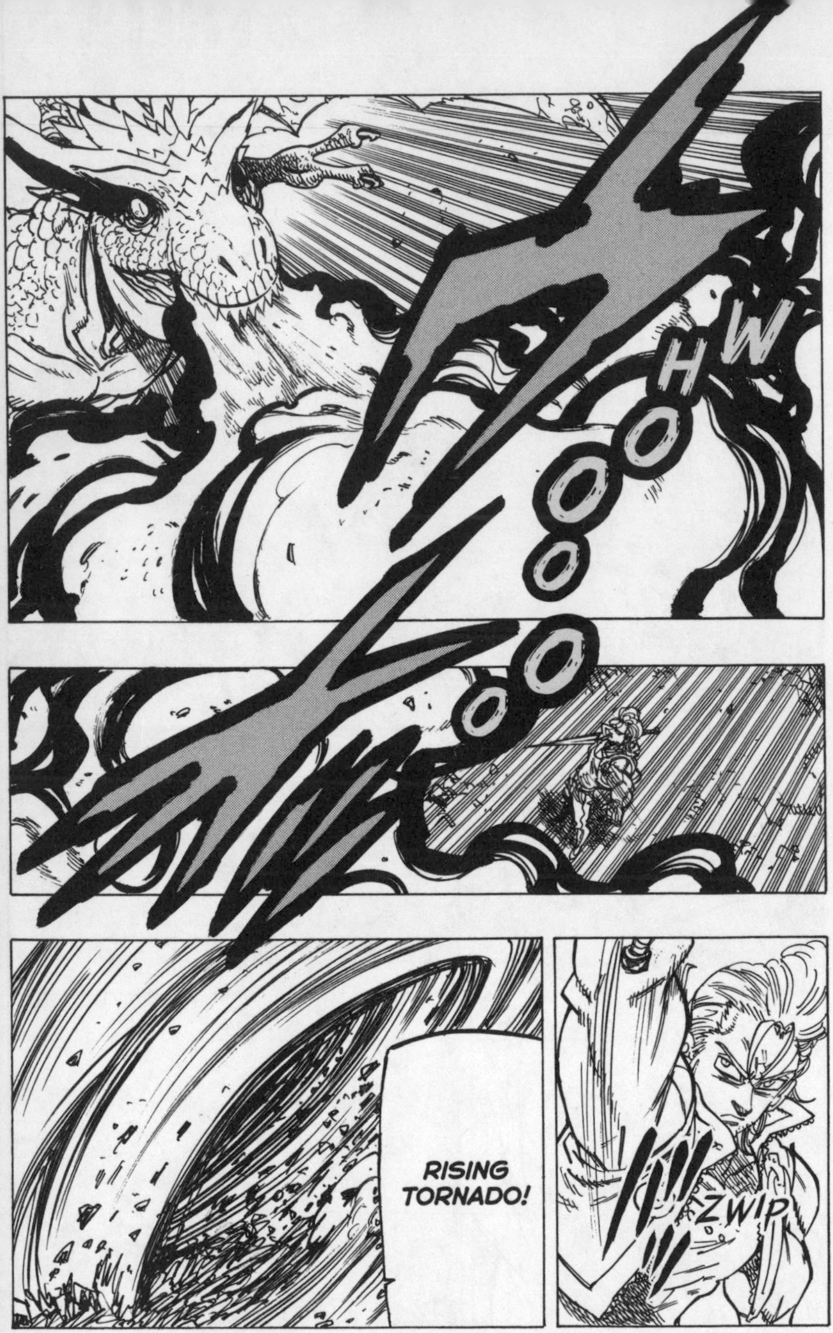
WHOOOOO
ZWIP
RISING TORNADO!

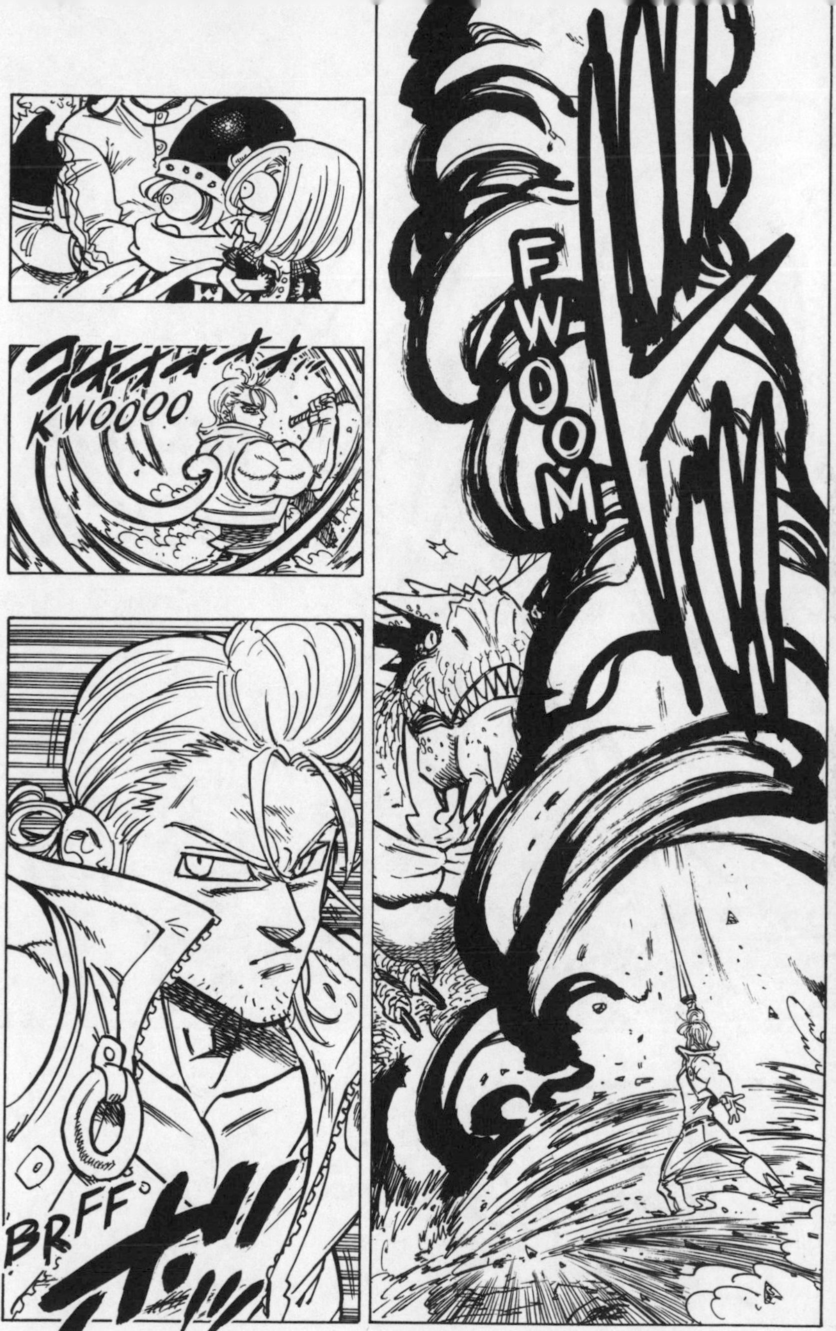
FWOOM
KWOOOO
BRFF

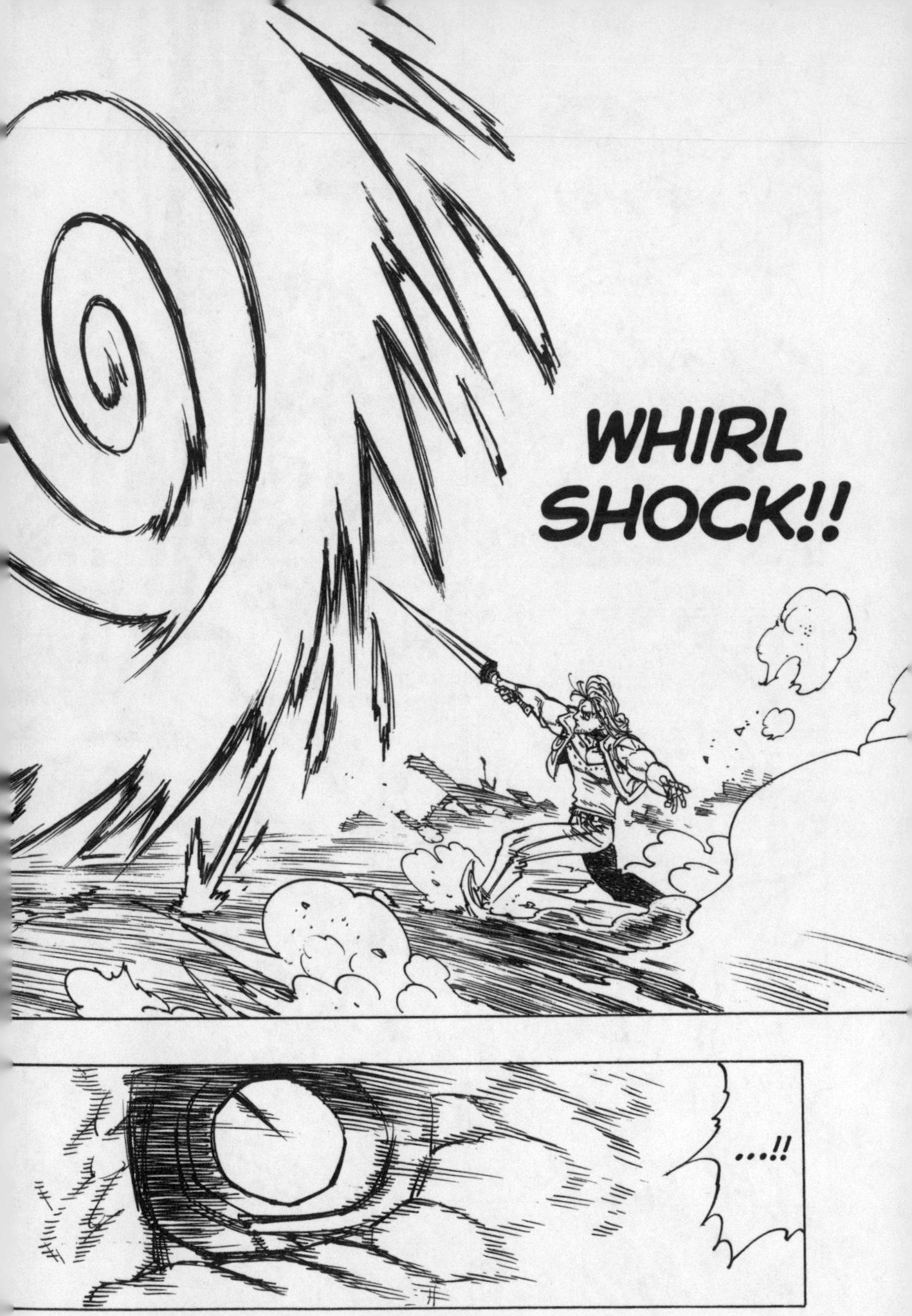
WHIRL SHOCK!!
...!!

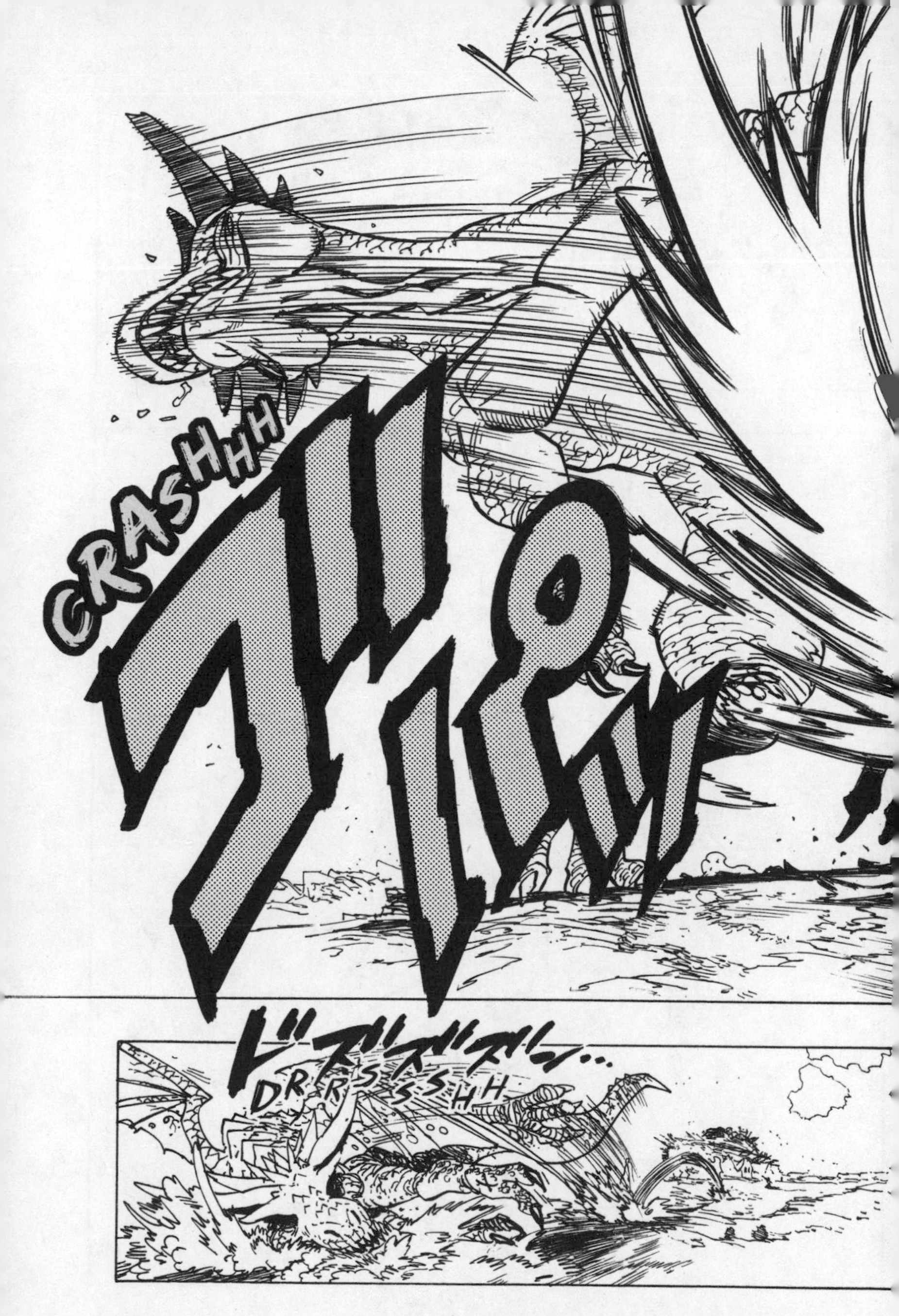
CRASHHH
DRRSSSHH

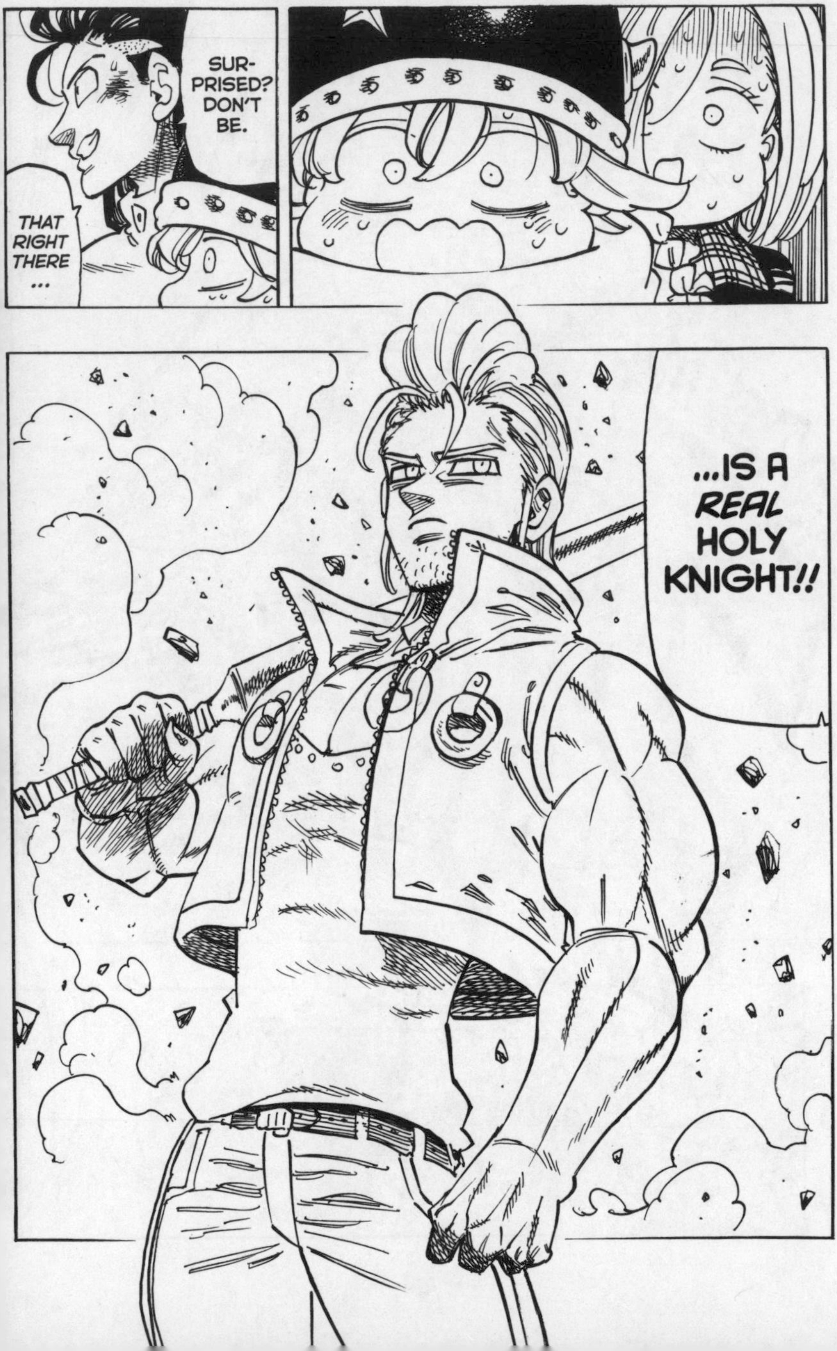
SUR-PRISED? DON'T BE.
THAT RIGHT THERE ...
...IS A *REAL* HOLY KNIGHT!!

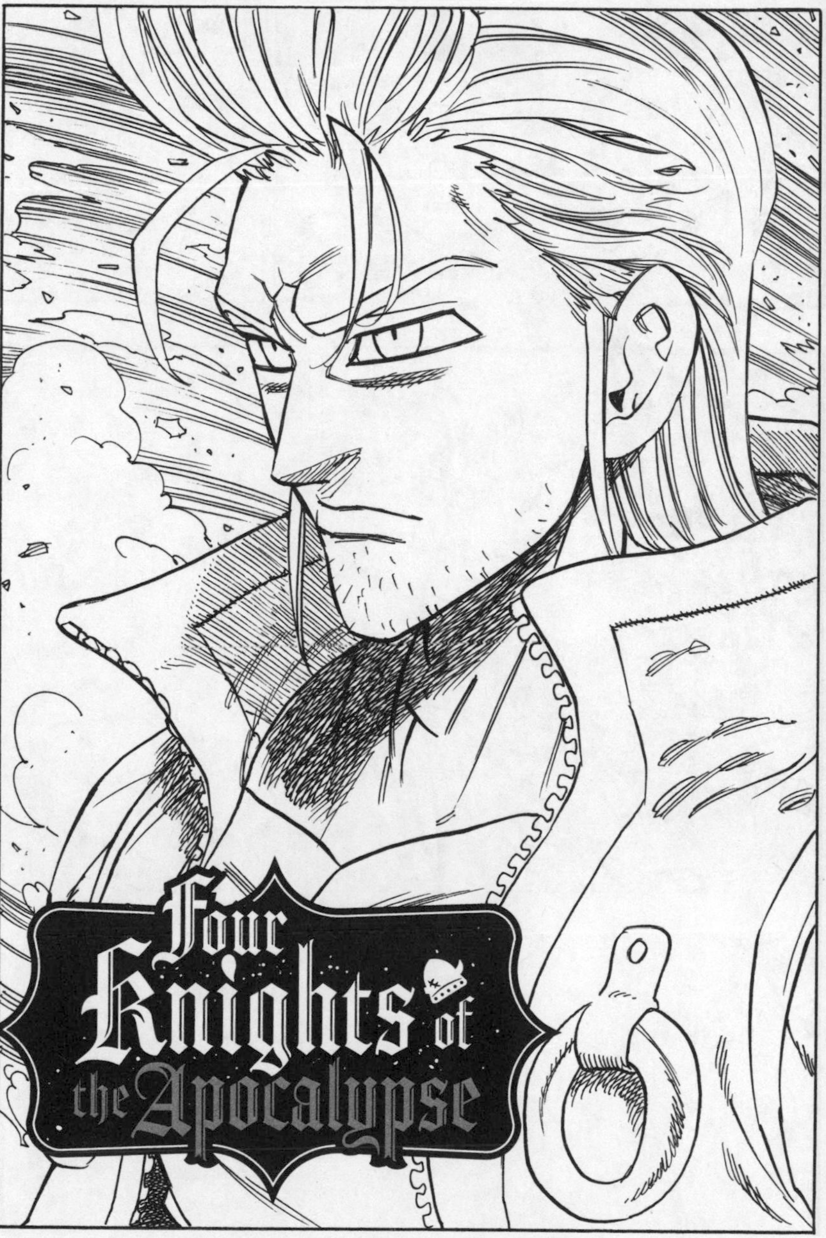
Four Knights of the Apocalypse

CHAPTER 31: A REAL HOLY KNIGHT

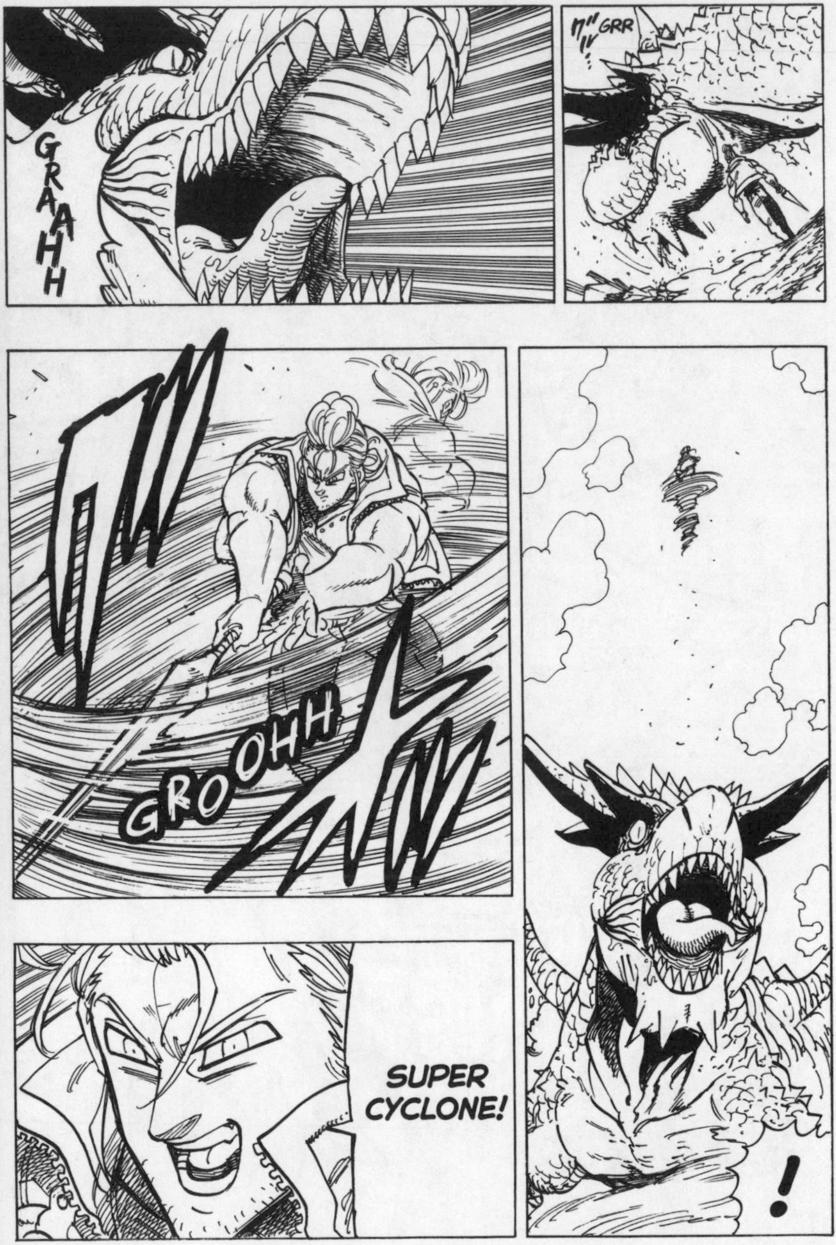
GRR
GRAAHH
!
GROOHH
SUPER CYCLONE!

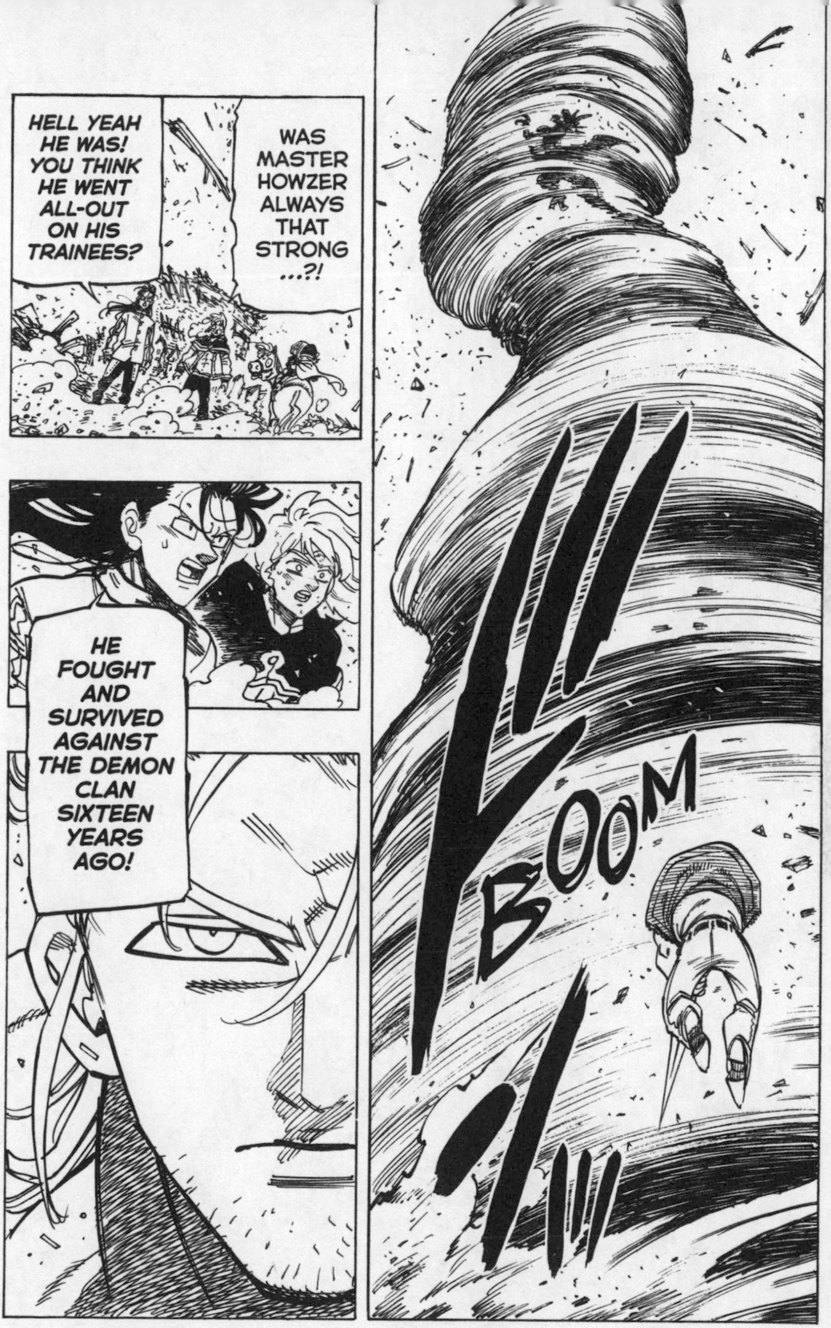
BOOM
WAS MASTER HOWZER ALWAYS THAT STRONG ...?!
HELL YEAH HE WAS! YOU THINK HE WENT ALL-OUT ON HIS TRAINEES?
HE FOUGHT AND SURVIVED AGAINST THE DEMON CLAN SIXTEEN YEARS AGO!

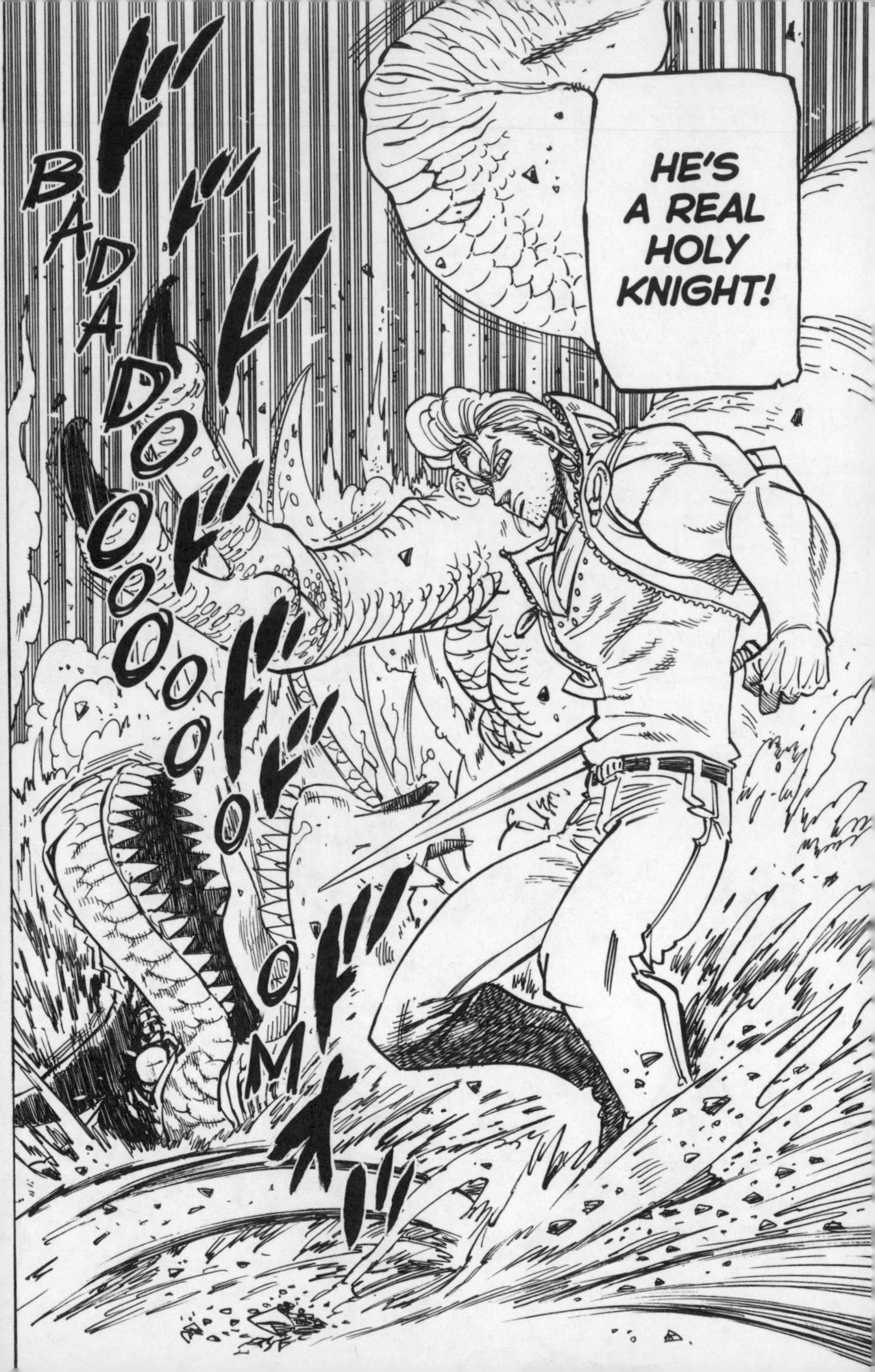
HE'S A REAL HOLY KNIGHT!
BADADOOOOOOOOOM

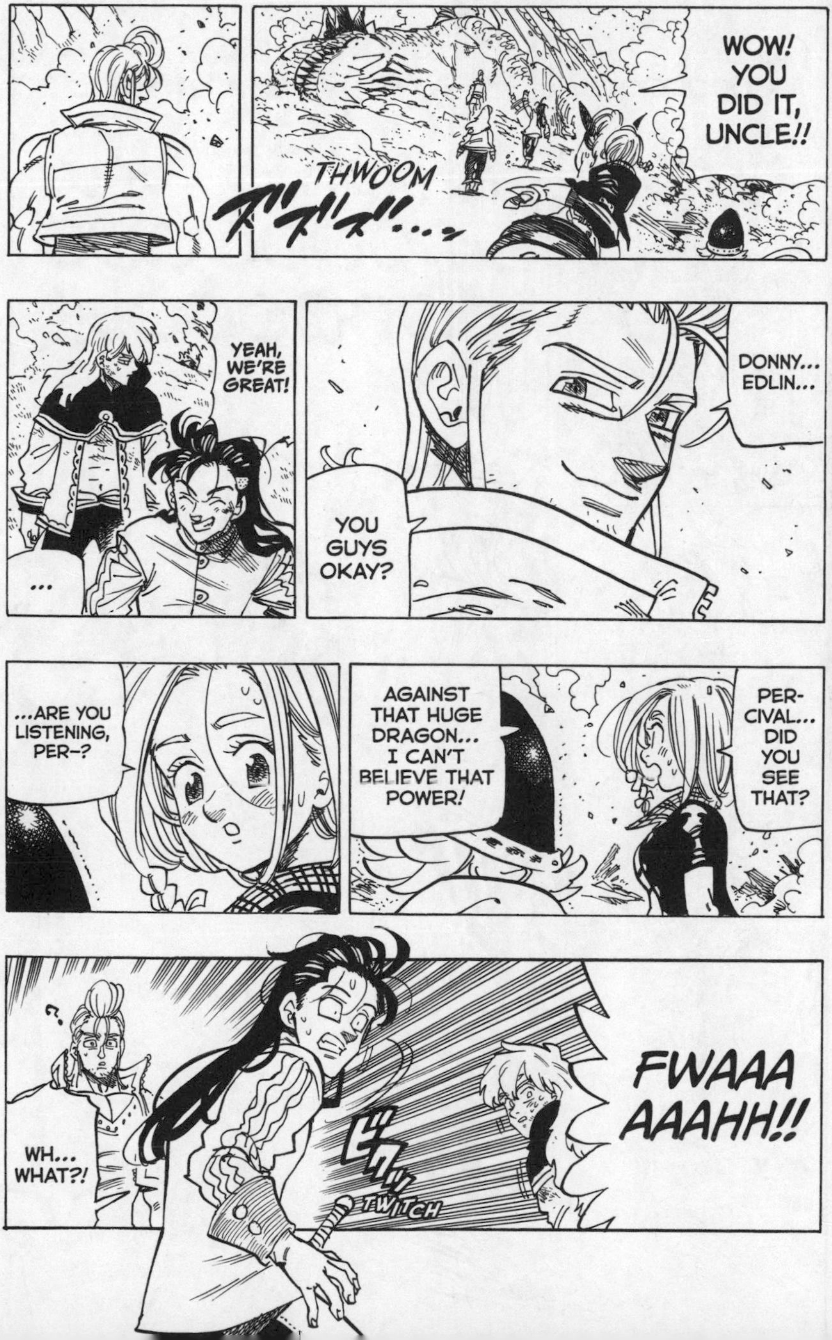
WOW! YOU DID IT, UNCLE!!
THWOOM
DONNY... EDLIN...
YOU GUYS OKAY?
YEAH, WE'RE GREAT!
...
PER-CIVAL... DID YOU SEE THAT?
AGAINST THAT HUGE DRAGON... I CAN'T BELIEVE THAT POWER!
...ARE YOU LISTENING, PER-?
FWAAA AAAHH!!
TWITCH
WH... WHAT?!

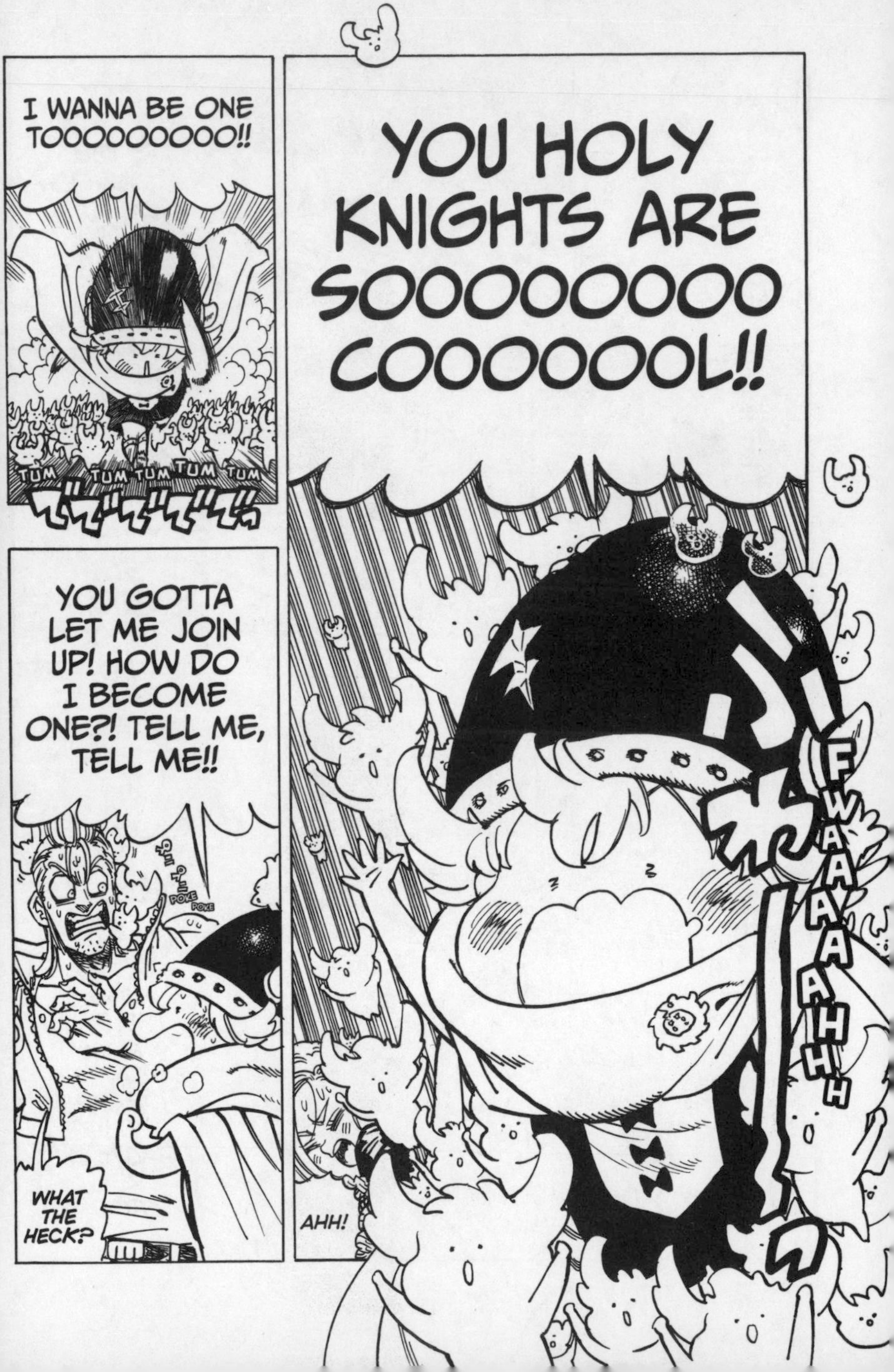
YOU HOLY KNIGHTS ARE SOOOOOOOOO COOOOOOOL!!
FWAAAAAAHHH
AHH!
I WANNA BE ONE TOOOOOOOOO!!
TUM TUM TUM TUM TUM
YOU GOTTA LET ME JOIN UP! HOW DO I BECOME ONE?! TELL ME, TELL ME!!
POKE POKE
WHAT THE HECK?

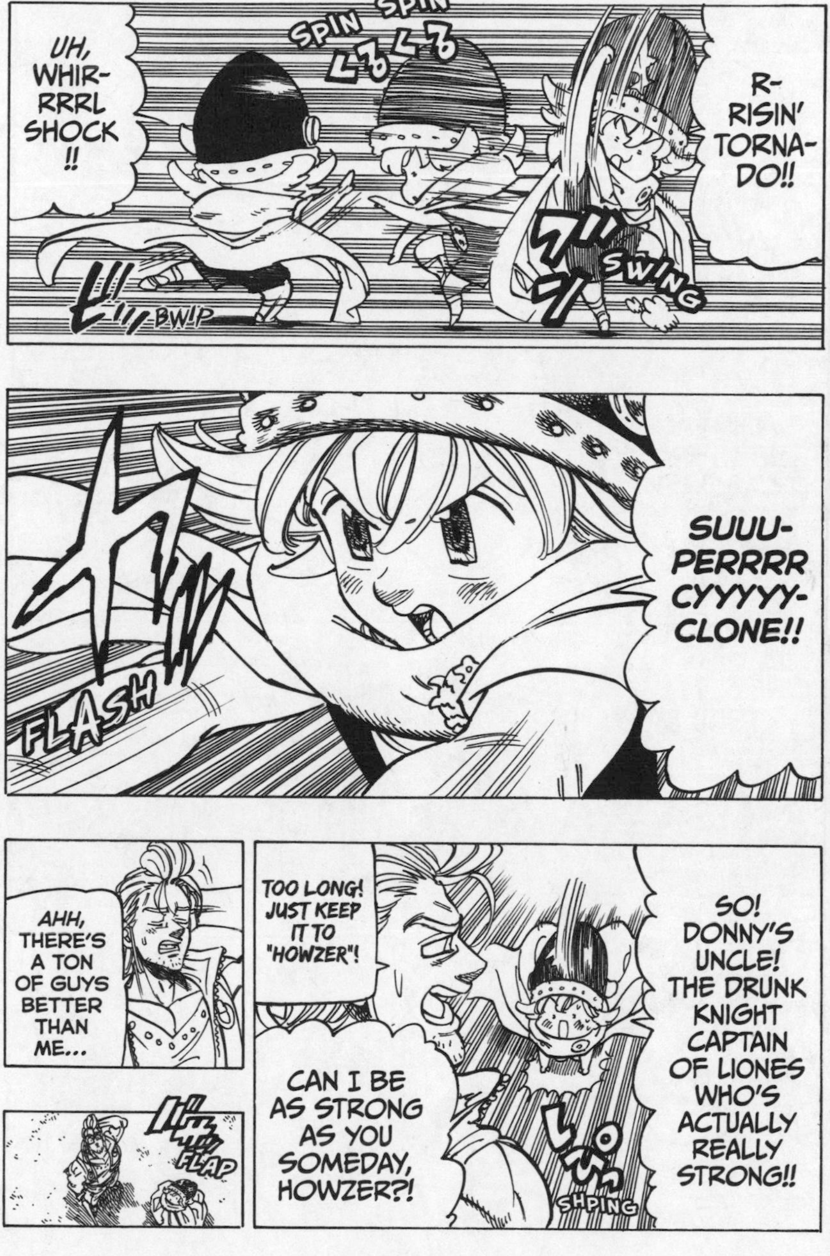
R-RISIN' TORNADO!!
SWING
SPIN SPIN
UH, WHIR-RRRL SHOCK!!
BWIP
SUUU-PERRRR CYYYYY-CLONE!!
FLASH
SO! DONNY'S UNCLE! THE DRUNK KNIGHT CAPTAIN OF LIONES WHO'S ACTUALLY REALLY STRONG!!
SHPING
CAN I BE AS STRONG AS YOU SOMEDAY, HOWZER?!
TOO LONG! JUST KEEP IT TO "HOWZER"!
AHH, THERE'S A TON OF GUYS BETTER THAN ME...
FLAP

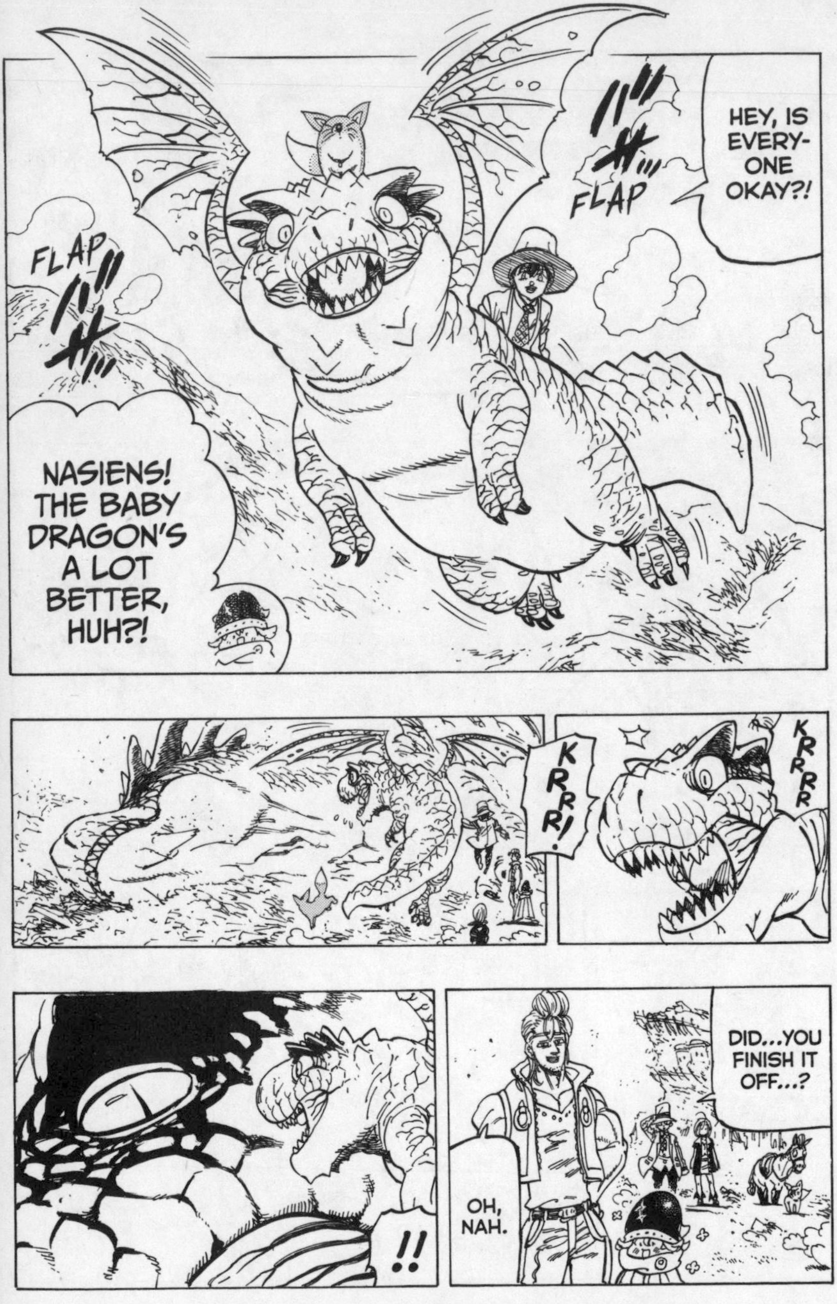
HEY, IS EVERYONE OKAY?!
FLAP
FLAP
NASIENS! THE BABY DRAGON'S A LOT BETTER, HUH?!
KRRRR
KRRR!
DID...YOU FINISH IT OFF...?
OH, NAH.
!!

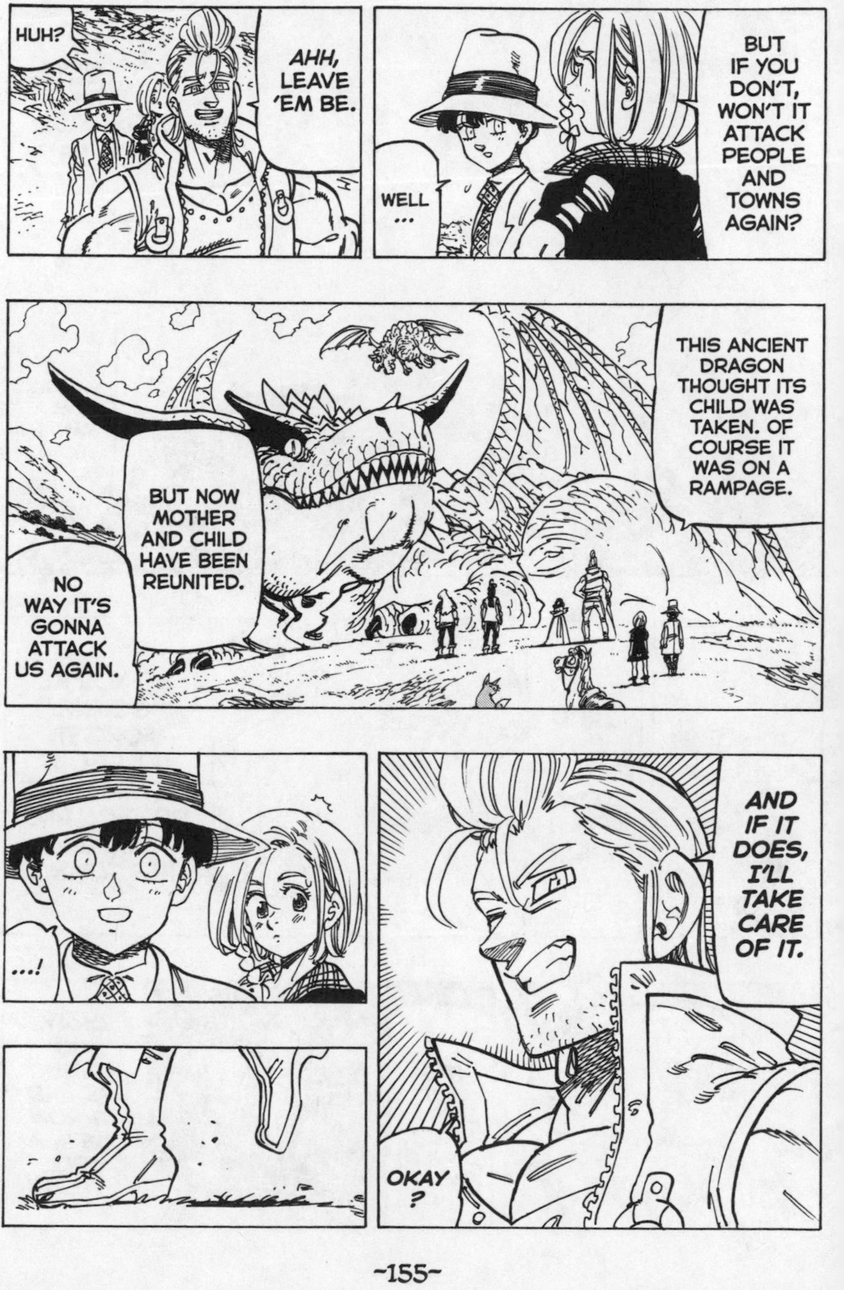
BUT IF YOU DON'T, WON'T IT ATTACK PEOPLE AND TOWNS AGAIN?
WELL ...
AHH, LEAVE 'EM BE.
HUH?
THIS ANCIENT DRAGON THOUGHT ITS CHILD WAS TAKEN. OF COURSE IT WAS ON A RAMPAGE.
BUT NOW MOTHER AND CHILD HAVE BEEN REUNITED.
NO WAY IT'S GONNA ATTACK US AGAIN.
AND IF IT DOES, I'LL TAKE CARE OF IT.
OKAY ?
...!

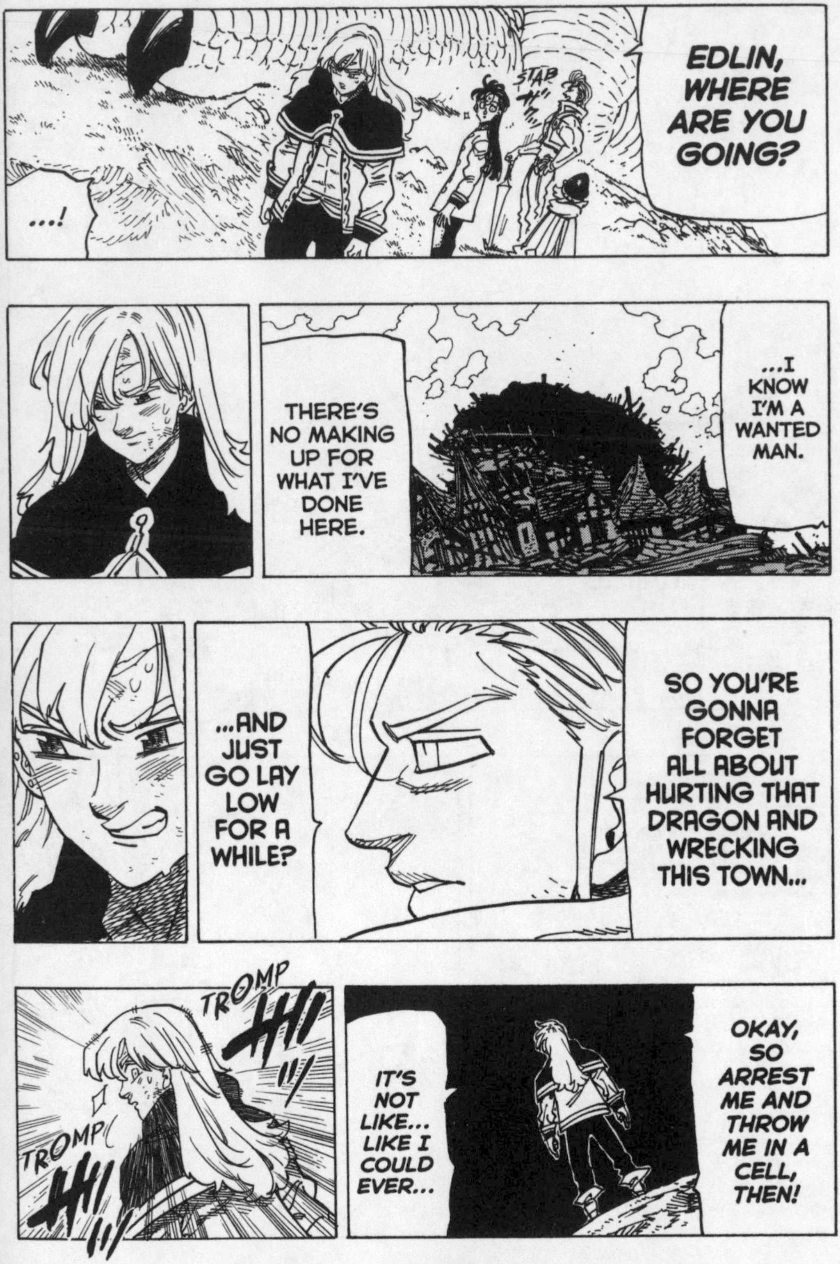
EDLIN, WHERE ARE YOU GOING?
STAB
...!
...I KNOW I'M A WANTED MAN.
THERE'S NO MAKING UP FOR WHAT I'VE DONE HERE.
SO YOU'RE GONNA FORGET ALL ABOUT HURTING THAT DRAGON AND WRECKING THIS TOWN...
...AND JUST GO LAY LOW FOR A WHILE?
OKAY, SO ARREST ME AND THROW ME IN A CELL, THEN!
IT'S NOT LIKE... LIKE I COULD EVER...
TROMP
TROMP

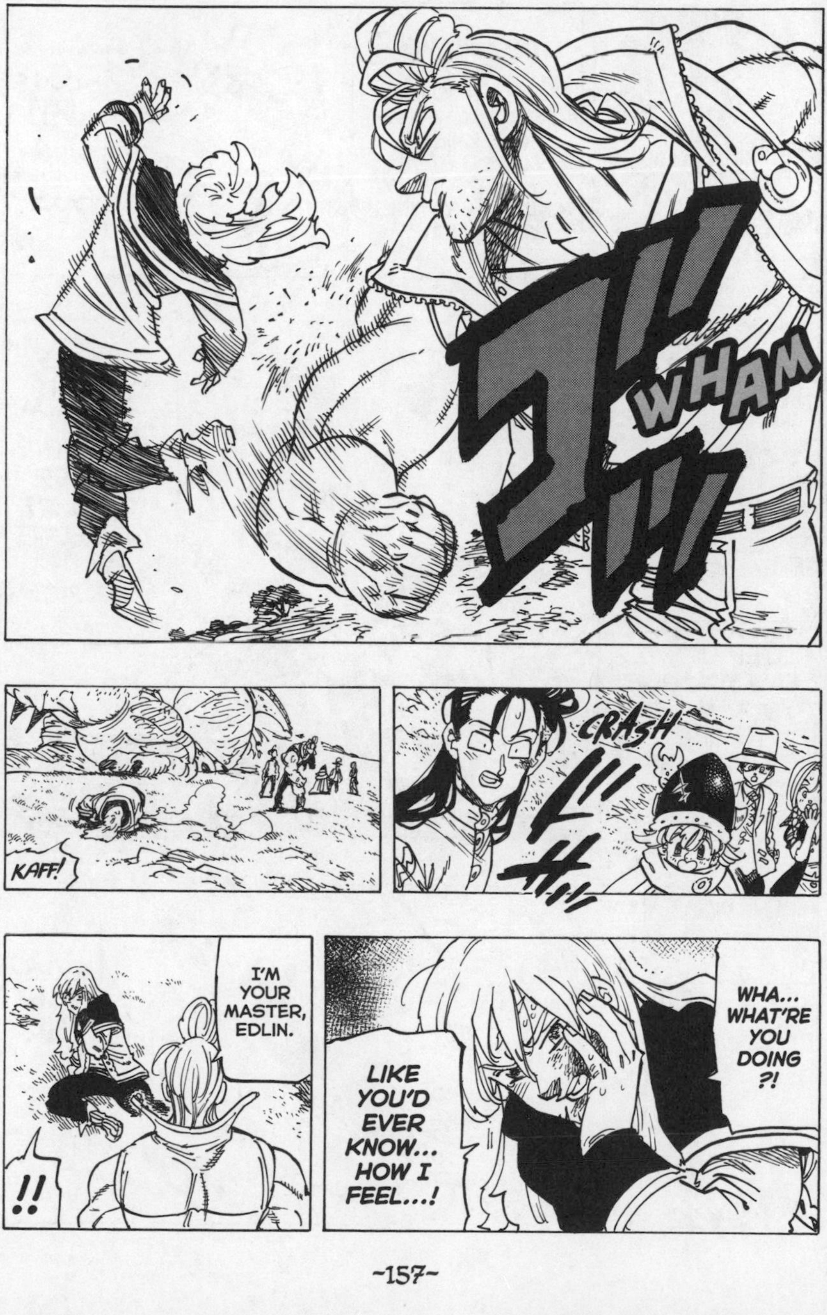
WHAM
CRASH
KAFF!
WHA... WHAT'RE YOU DOING?!
LIKE YOU'D EVER KNOW... HOW I FEEL...!
I'M YOUR MASTER, EDLIN.
!!

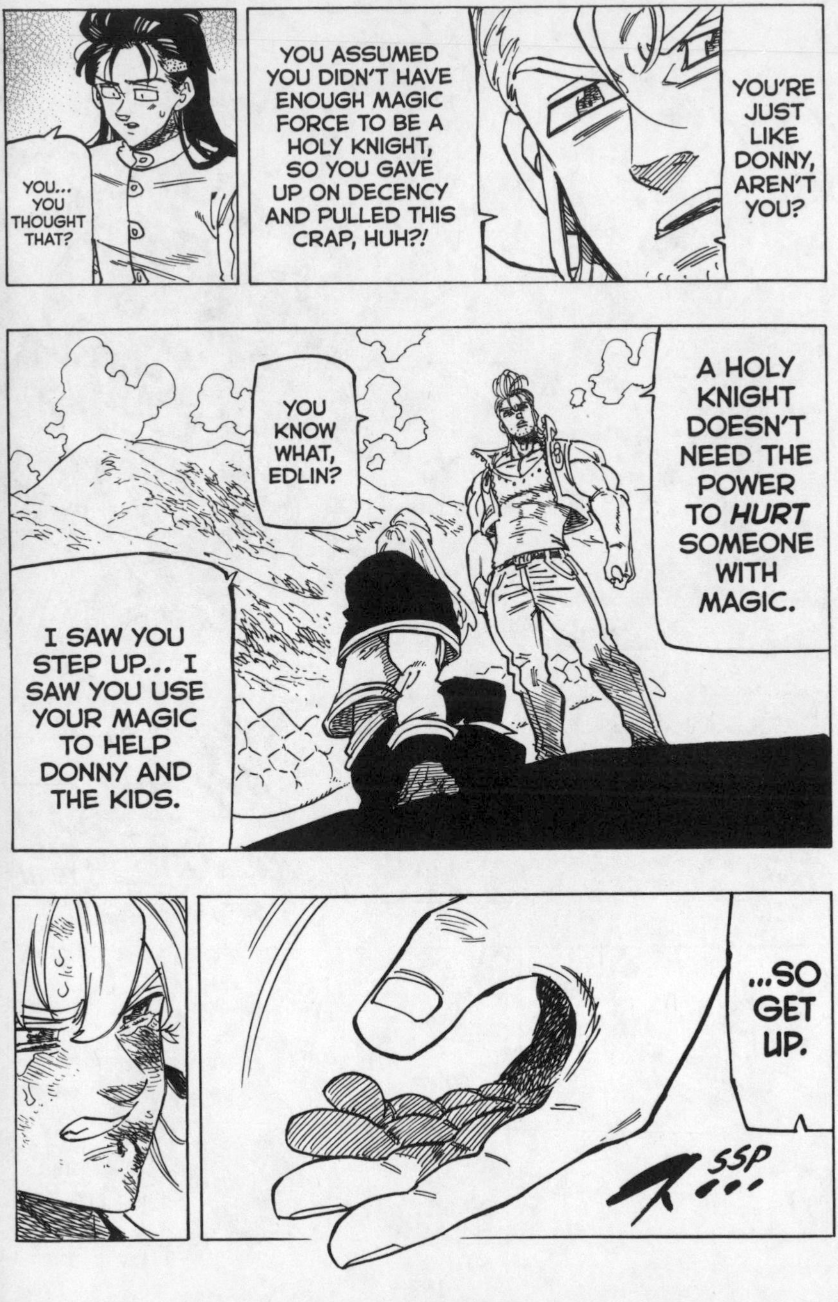
YOU'RE JUST LIKE DONNY, AREN'T YOU?
YOU ASSUMED YOU DIDN'T HAVE ENOUGH MAGIC FORCE TO BE A HOLY KNIGHT, SO YOU GAVE UP ON DECENCY AND PULLED THIS CRAP, HUH?!
YOU... YOU THOUGHT THAT?
A HOLY KNIGHT DOESN'T NEED THE POWER TO *HURT* SOMEONE WITH MAGIC.
YOU KNOW WHAT, EDLIN?
I SAW YOU STEP UP... I SAW YOU USE YOUR MAGIC TO HELP DONNY AND THE KIDS.
...SO GET UP.
SSP...

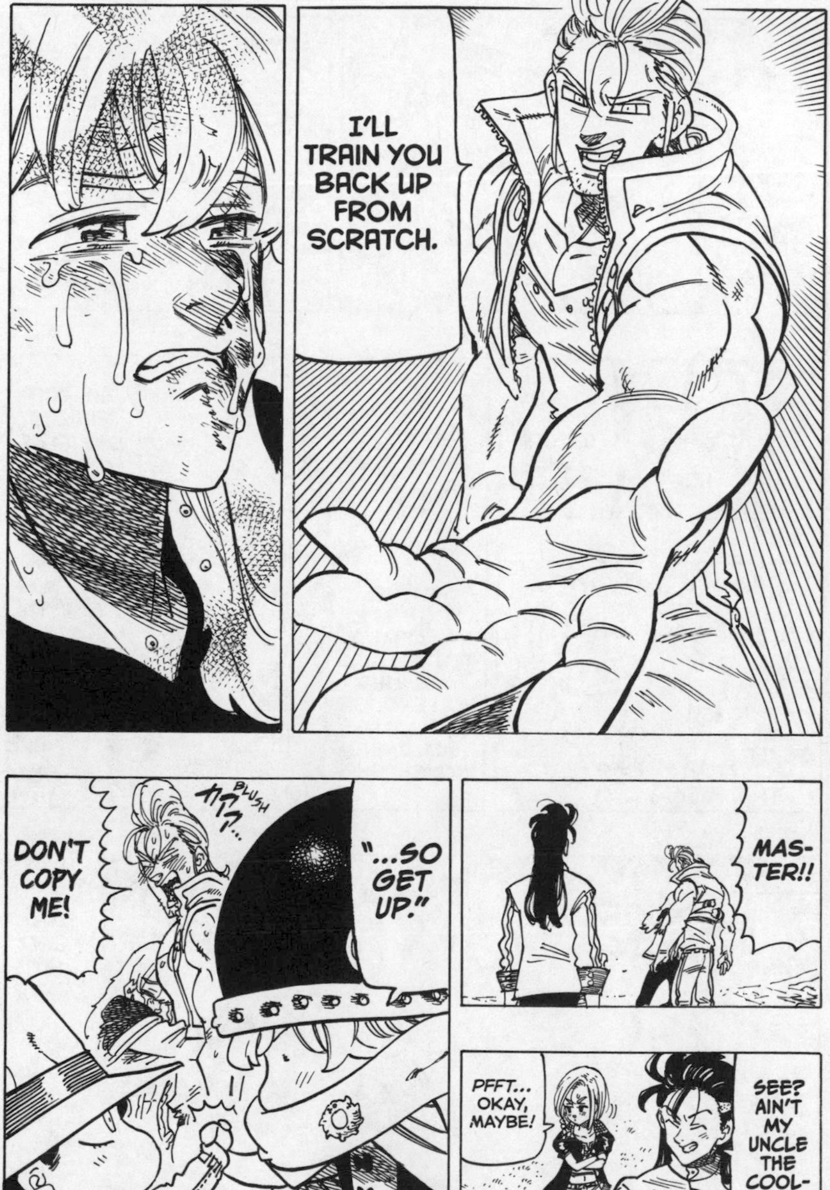
I'LL TRAIN YOU BACK UP FROM SCRATCH.
MAS-TER!!
SEE? AIN'T MY UNCLE THE COOL-EST?
PFFT... OKAY, MAYBE!
"...SO GET UP."
BLUSH
DON'T COPY ME!

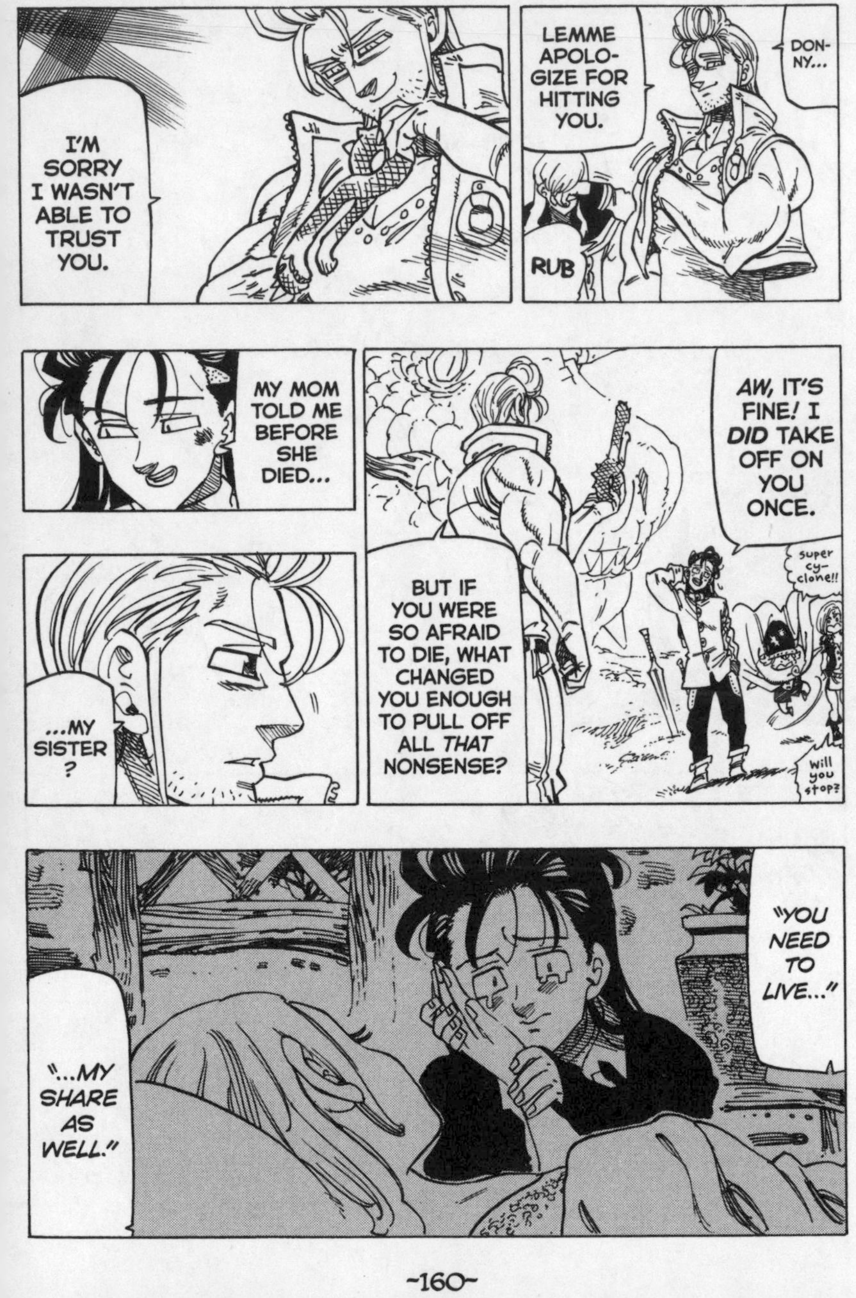
DON-NY...
LEMME APOLO-GIZE FOR HITTING YOU.
RUB
I'M SORRY I WASN'T ABLE TO TRUST YOU.
AW, IT'S FINE! I DID TAKE OFF ON YOU ONCE.
super cy-clone!!
will you stop?
BUT IF YOU WERE SO AFRAID TO DIE, WHAT CHANGED YOU ENOUGH TO PULL OFF ALL THAT NONSENSE?
MY MOM TOLD ME BEFORE SHE DIED...
...MY SISTER?
"YOU NEED TO LIVE..."
"...MY SHARE AS WELL."

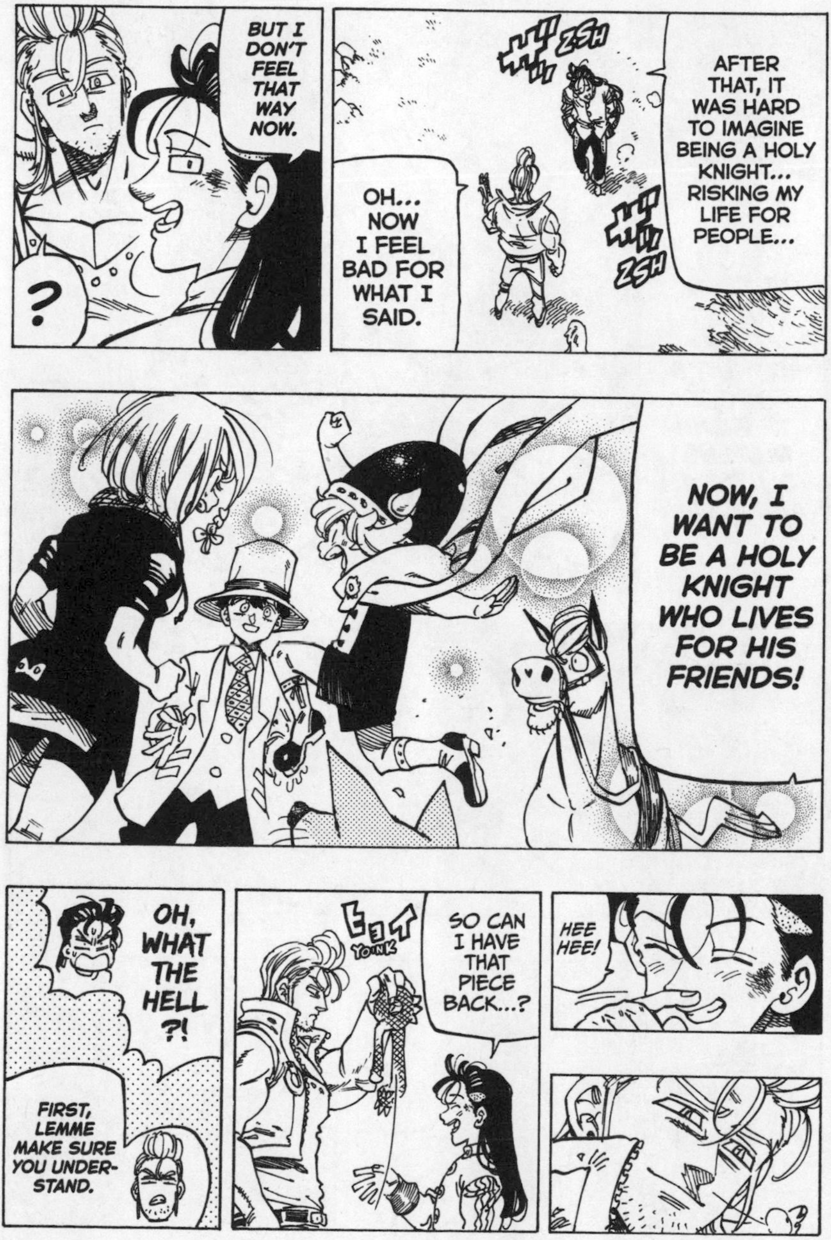
AFTER THAT, IT WAS HARD TO IMAGINE BEING A HOLY KNIGHT... RISKING MY LIFE FOR PEOPLE...
ZSH
ZSH
OH... NOW I FEEL BAD FOR WHAT I SAID.
BUT I DON'T FEEL THAT WAY NOW.
?
NOW, I WANT TO BE A HOLY KNIGHT WHO LIVES FOR HIS FRIENDS!
HEE HEE!
SO CAN I HAVE THAT PIECE BACK...?
YOINK
OH, WHAT THE HELL ?!
FIRST, LEMME MAKE SURE YOU UNDER-STAND.

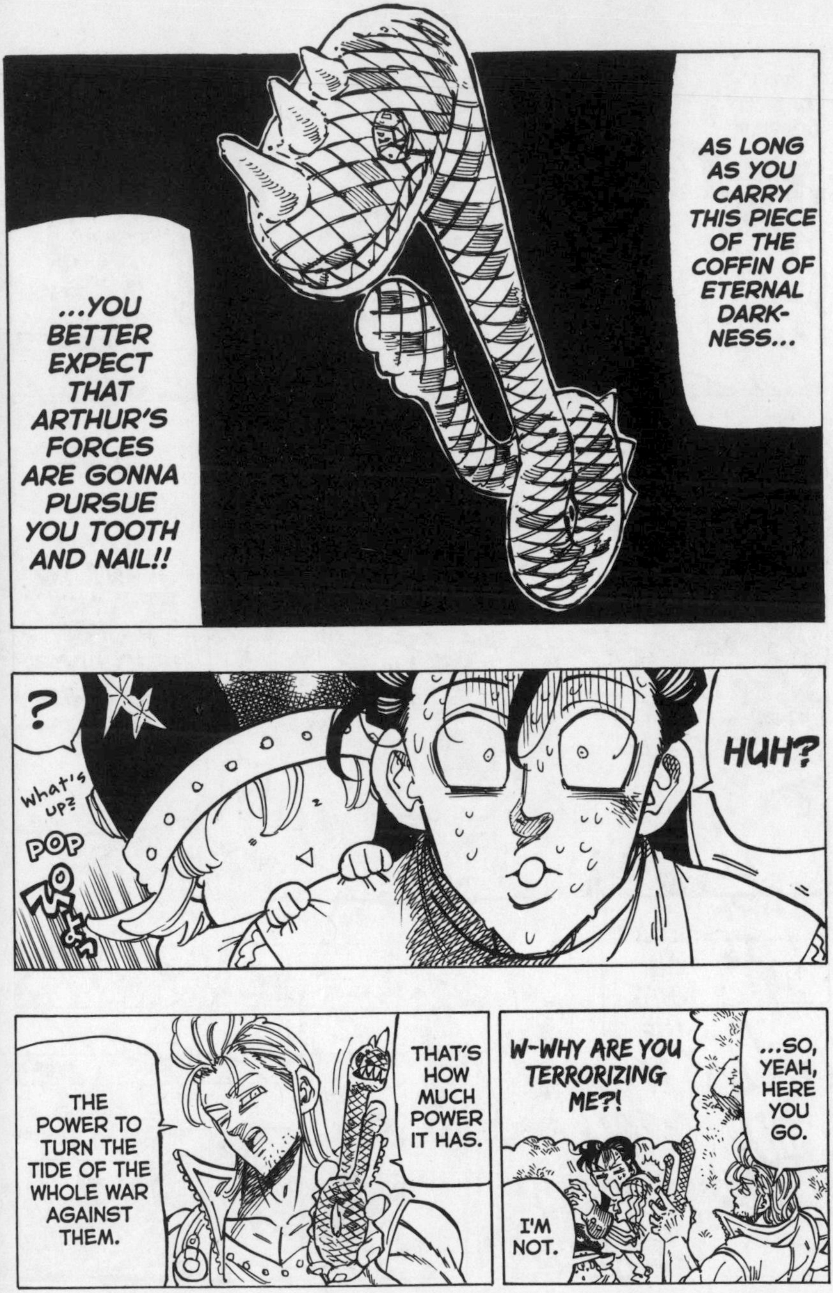
AS LONG AS YOU CARRY THIS PIECE OF THE COFFIN OF ETERNAL DARKNESS...
...YOU BETTER EXPECT THAT ARTHUR'S FORCES ARE GONNA PURSUE YOU TOOTH AND NAIL!!
HUH?
?
what's up?
POP
...SO, YEAH, HERE YOU GO.
W-WHY ARE YOU TERRORIZING ME?!
I'M NOT.
THAT'S HOW MUCH POWER IT HAS.
THE POWER TO TURN THE TIDE OF THE WHOLE WAR AGAINST THEM.

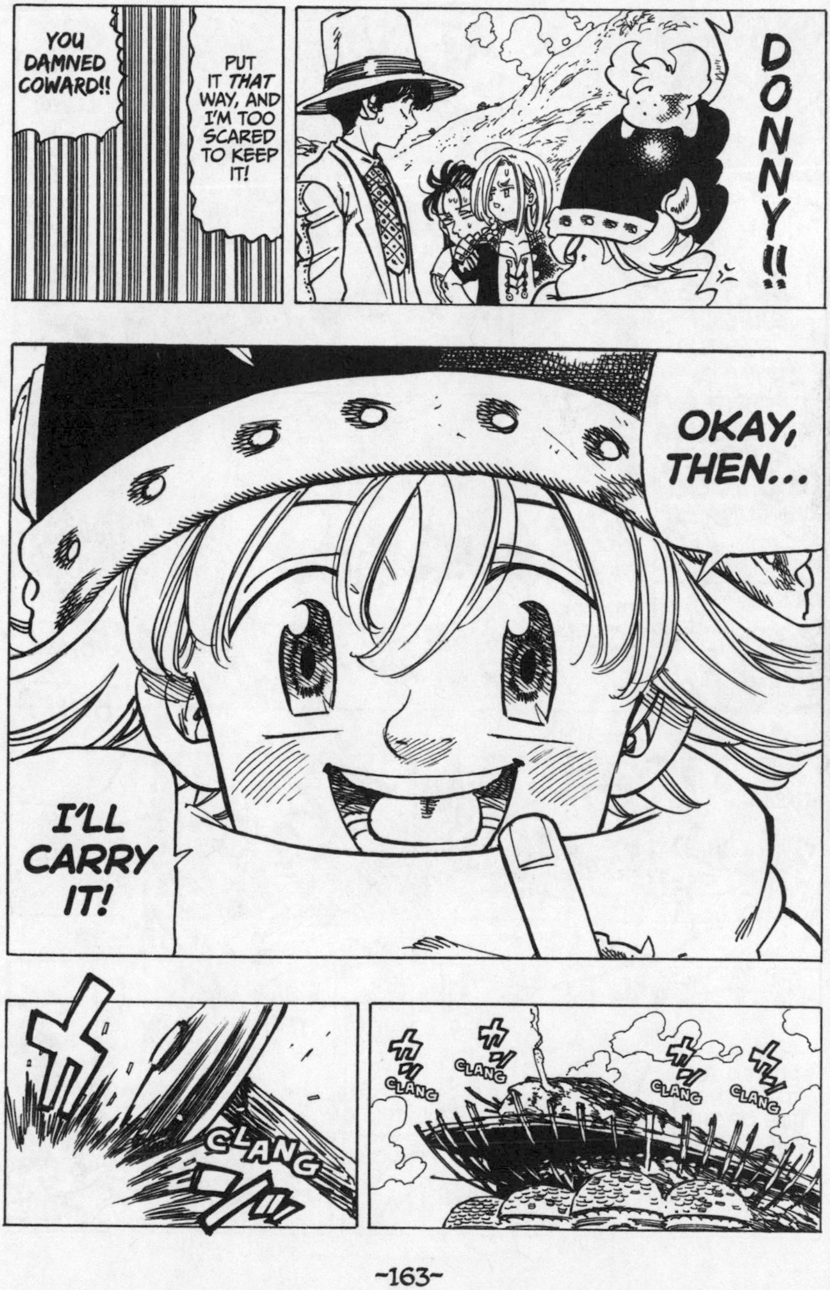
DONNY!!
PUT IT *THAT* WAY, AND I'M TOO SCARED TO KEEP IT!
YOU DAMNED COWARD!!
OKAY, THEN...
I'LL CARRY IT!
CLANG
CLANG
CLANG
CLANG
CLANG

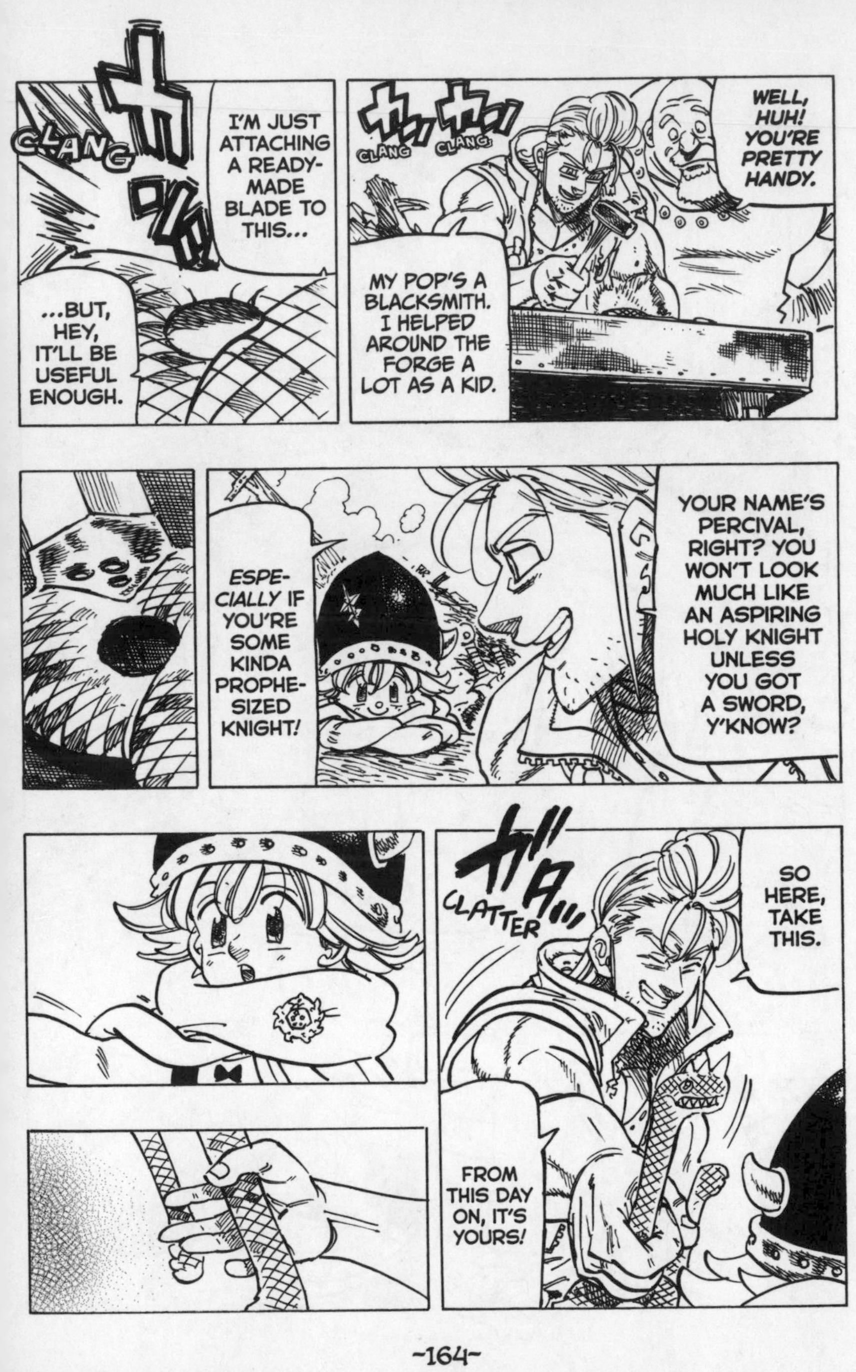
CLANG
CLANG
WELL, HUH! YOU'RE PRETTY HANDY.
MY POP'S A BLACKSMITH. I HELPED AROUND THE FORGE A LOT AS A KID.
CLANG
I'M JUST ATTACHING A READY-MADE BLADE TO THIS...
...BUT, HEY, IT'LL BE USEFUL ENOUGH.
YOUR NAME'S PERCIVAL, RIGHT? YOU WON'T LOOK MUCH LIKE AN ASPIRING HOLY KNIGHT UNLESS YOU GOT A SWORD, Y'KNOW?
ESPECIALLY IF YOU'RE SOME KINDA PROPHESIZED KNIGHT!
CLATTER
SO HERE, TAKE THIS.
FROM THIS DAY ON, IT'S YOURS!

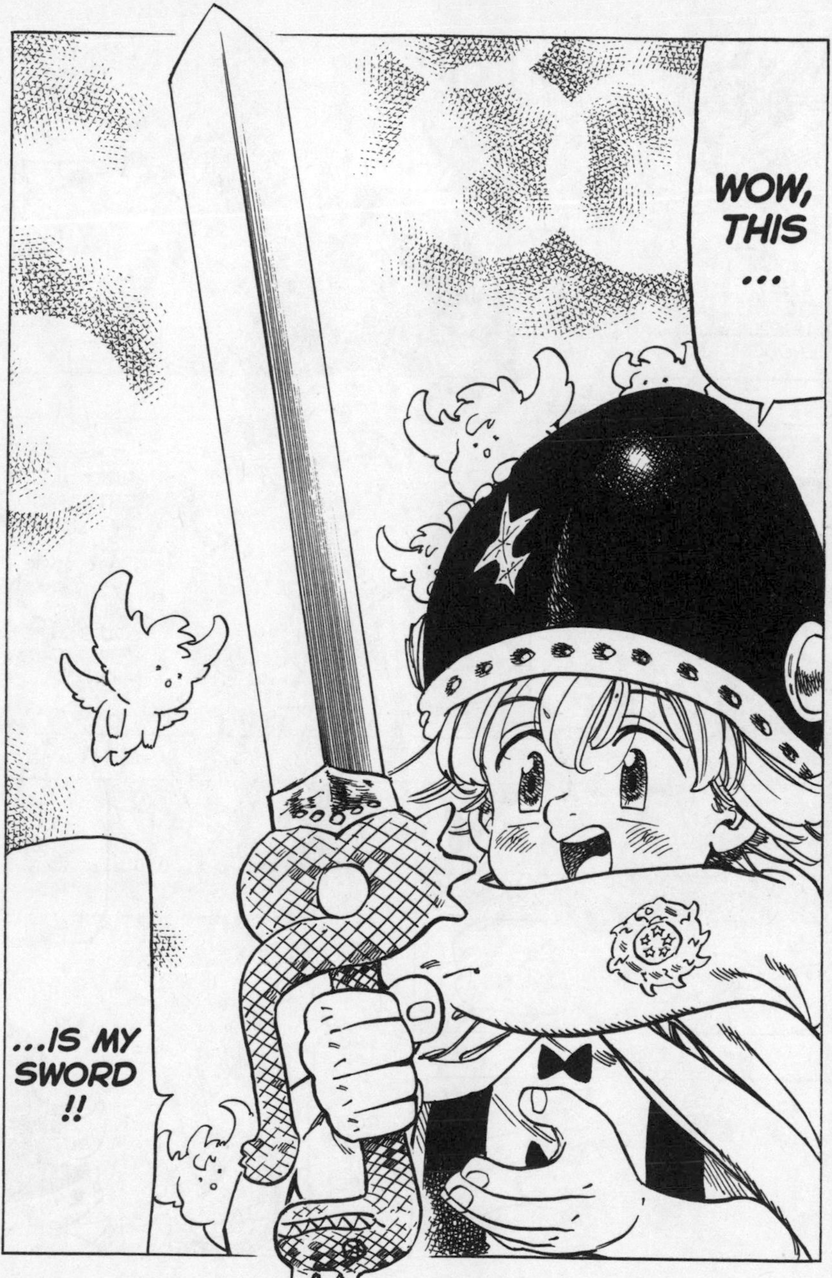
WOW, THIS ...
...IS MY SWORD !!

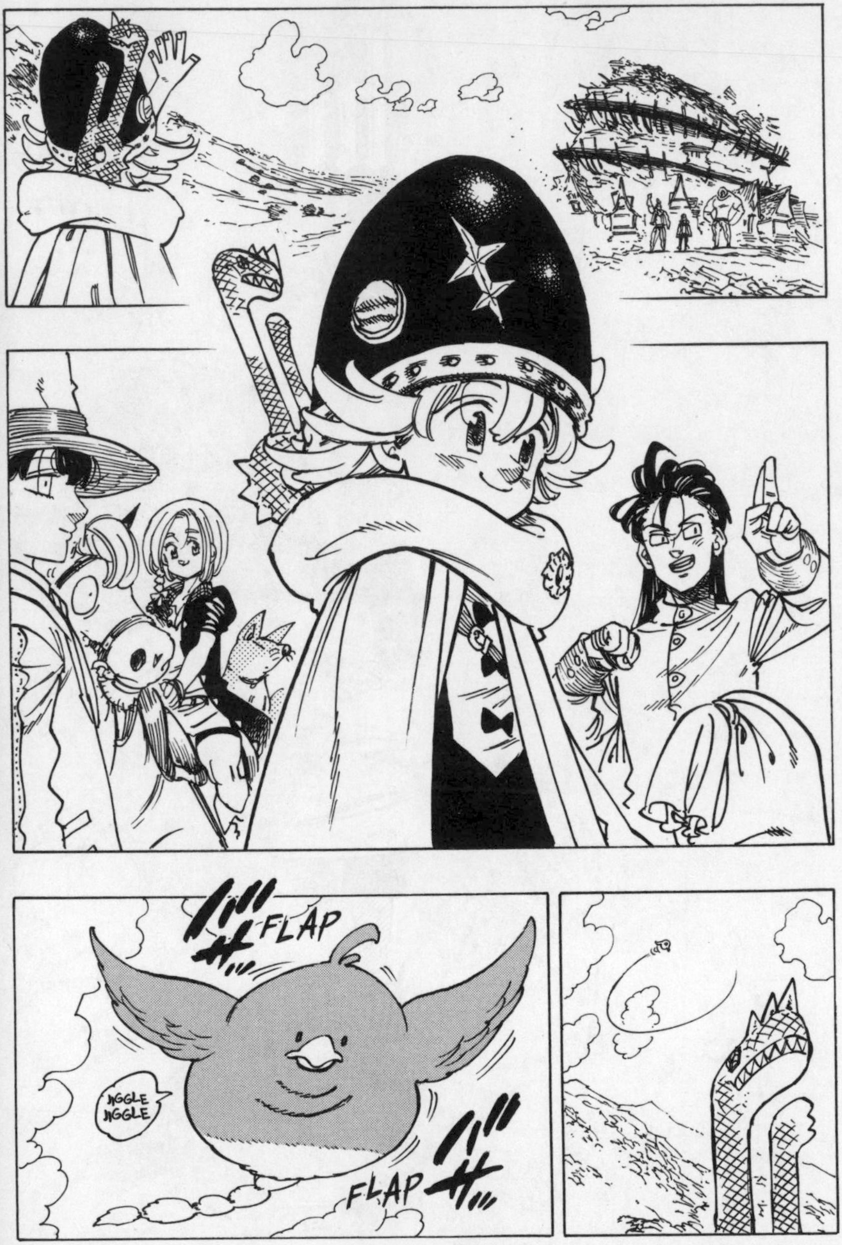
FLAP
JIGGLE JIGGLE
FLAP

Four Knights of the Apocalypse

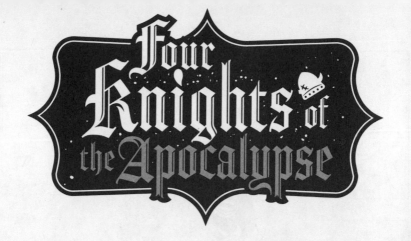

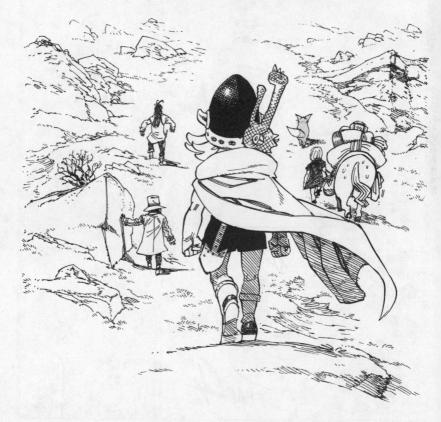

CHAPTER 32: THE PEAKS OF FEAR

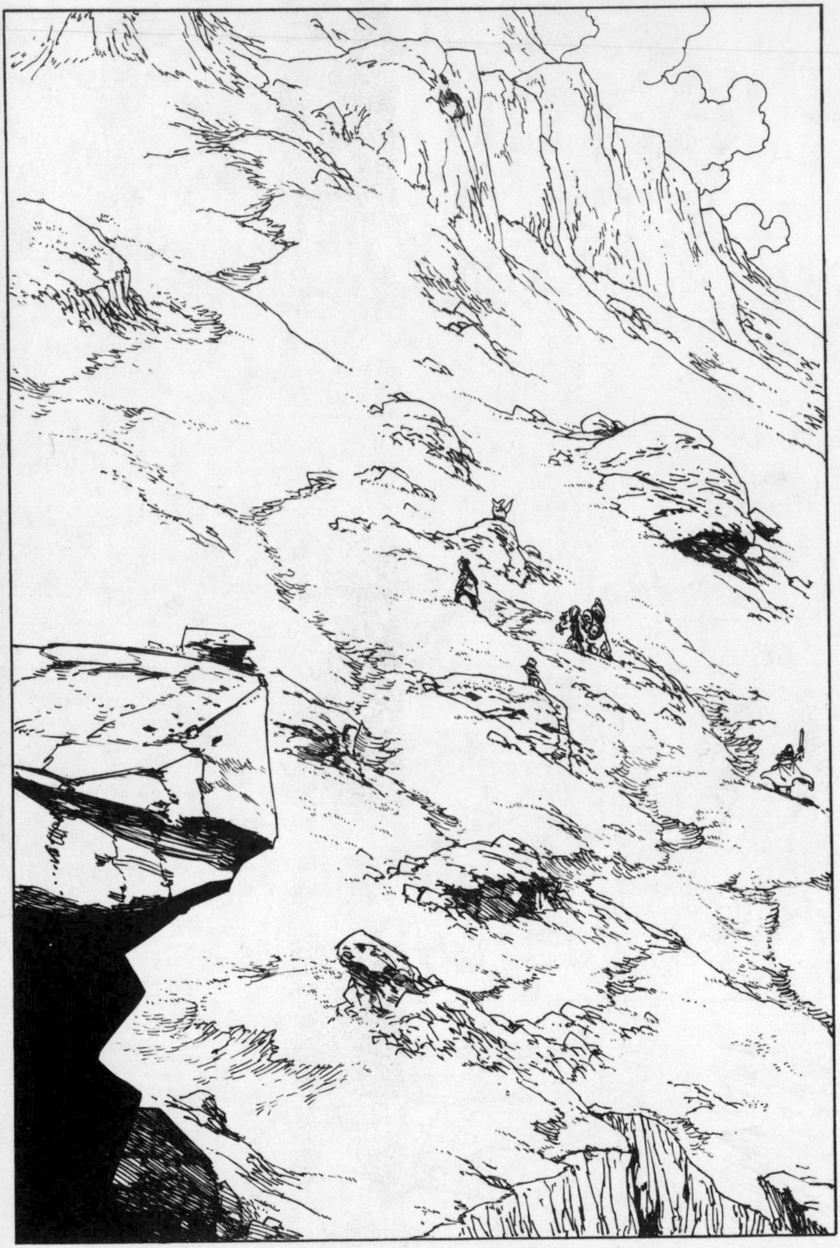

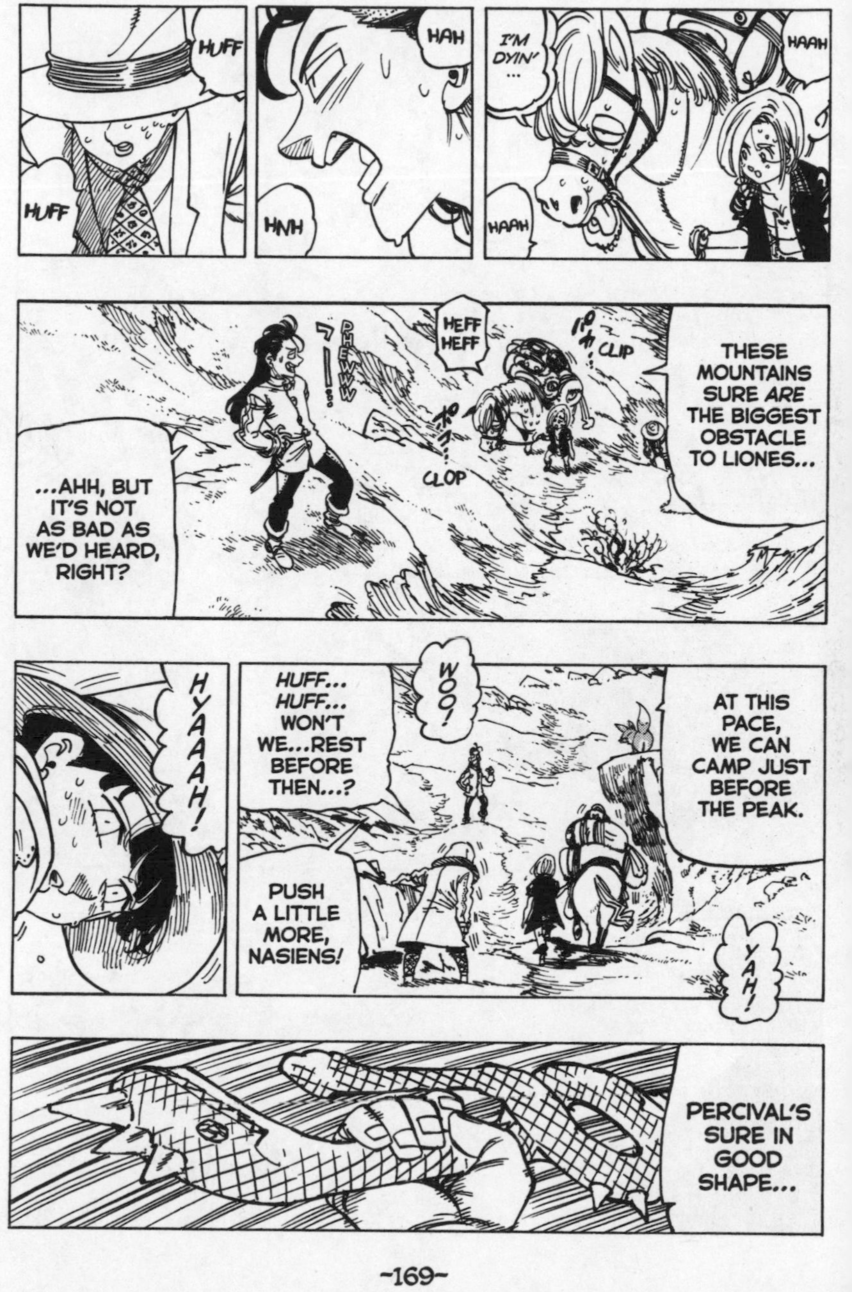
HAAH
I'M DYIN' ...
HAAH
HAH
HNH
HUFF
HUFF
THESE MOUNTAINS SURE ARE THE BIGGEST OBSTACLE TO LIONES...
CLIP
HEFF HEFF
PHEWWW
CLOP
...AHH, BUT IT'S NOT AS BAD AS WE'D HEARD, RIGHT?
AT THIS PACE, WE CAN CAMP JUST BEFORE THE PEAK.
WOO!
HUFF... HUFF... WON'T WE...REST BEFORE THEN...?
YAH!
PUSH A LITTLE MORE, NASIENS!
HYAAAAH!
PERCIVAL'S SURE IN GOOD SHAPE...

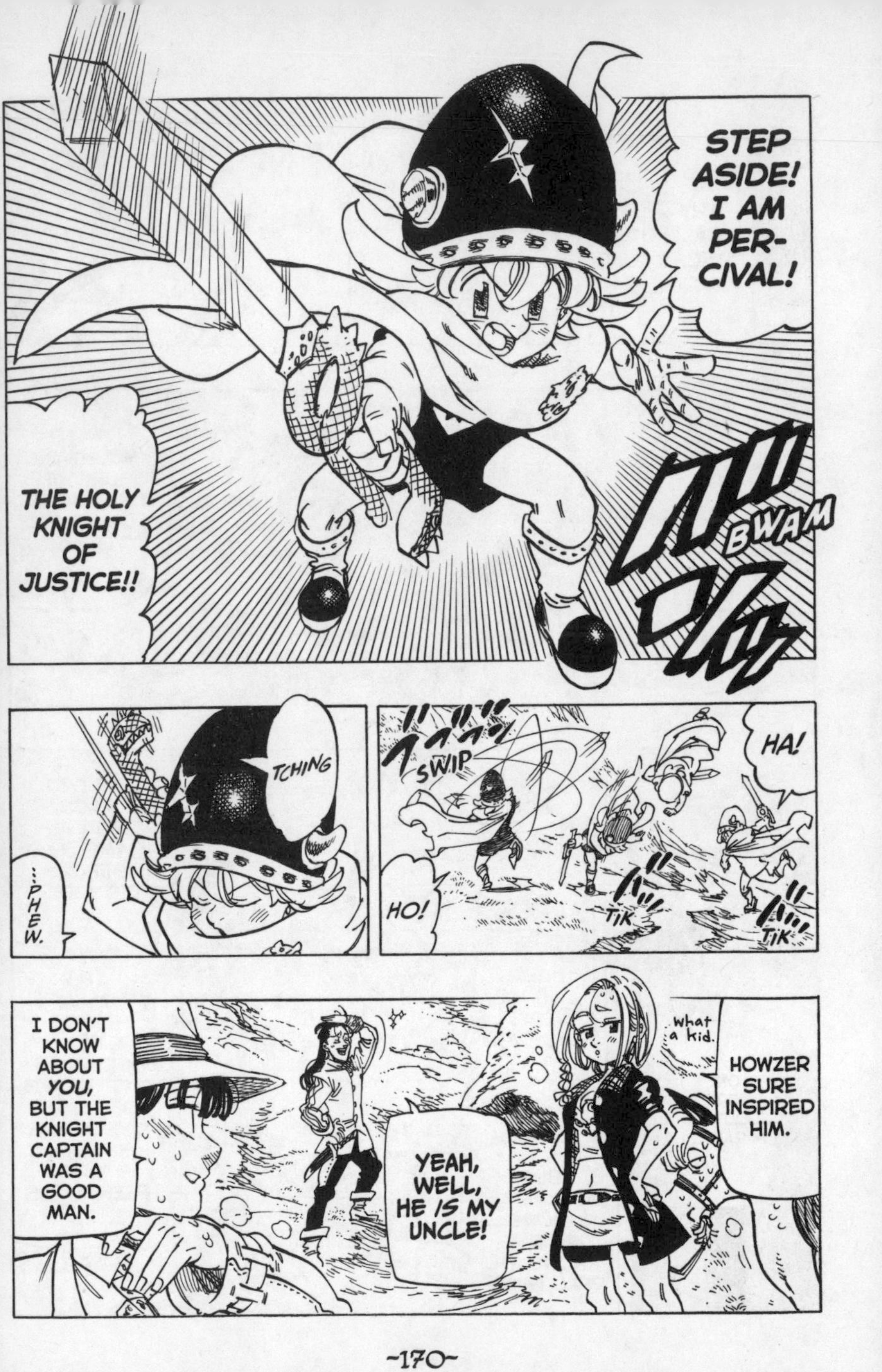
STEP ASIDE! I AM PERCIVAL!
THE HOLY KNIGHT OF JUSTICE!!
BWAM
HA!
SWIP
TIK
TIK
HO!
TCHING
...PHEW.
what a kid.
HOWZER SURE INSPIRED HIM.
YEAH, WELL, HE IS MY UNCLE!
I DON'T KNOW ABOUT YOU, BUT THE KNIGHT CAPTAIN WAS A GOOD MAN.

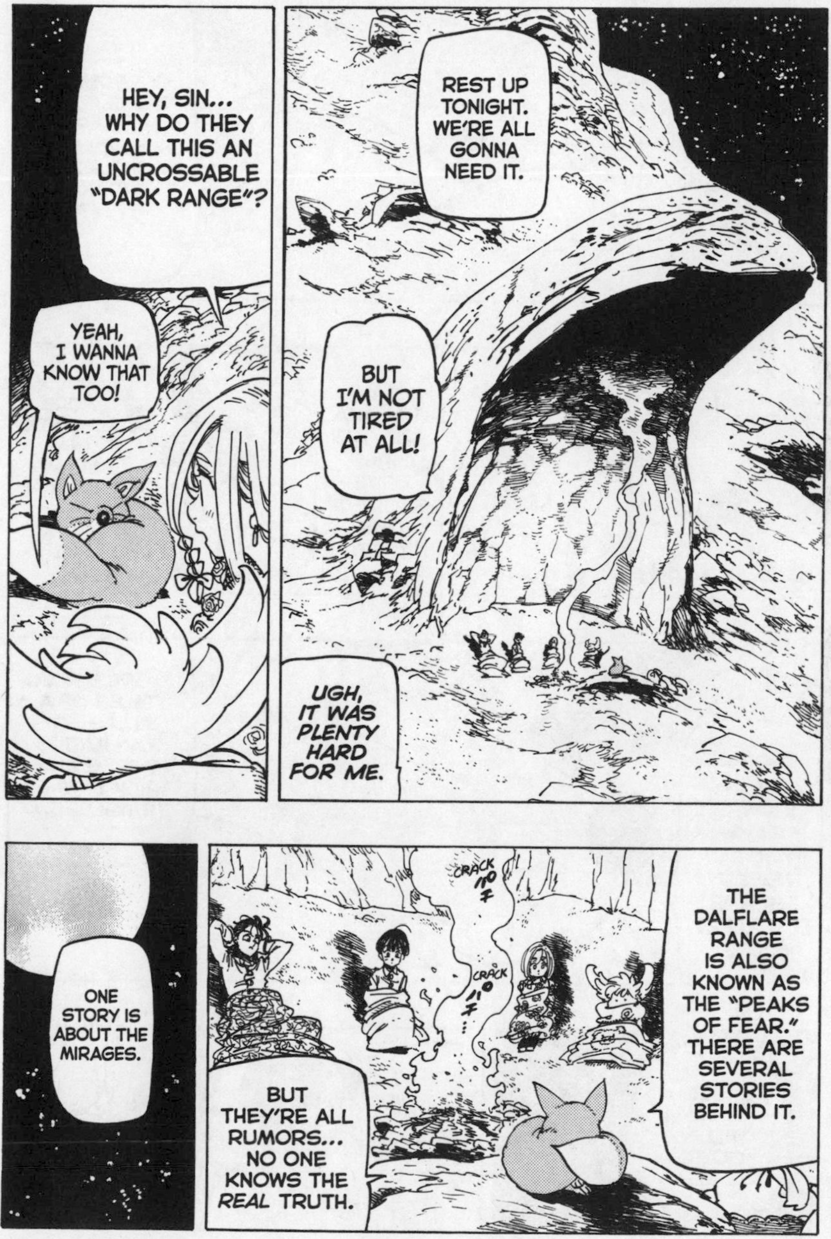
REST UP TONIGHT. WE'RE ALL GONNA NEED IT.
BUT I'M NOT TIRED AT ALL!
UGH, IT WAS PLENTY HARD FOR ME.
HEY, SIN... WHY DO THEY CALL THIS AN UNCROSSABLE "DARK RANGE"?
YEAH, I WANNA KNOW THAT TOO!
CRACK
CRACK
THE DALFLARE RANGE IS ALSO KNOWN AS THE "PEAKS OF FEAR." THERE ARE SEVERAL STORIES BEHIND IT.
BUT THEY'RE ALL RUMORS... NO ONE KNOWS THE REAL TRUTH.
ONE STORY IS ABOUT THE MIRAGES.

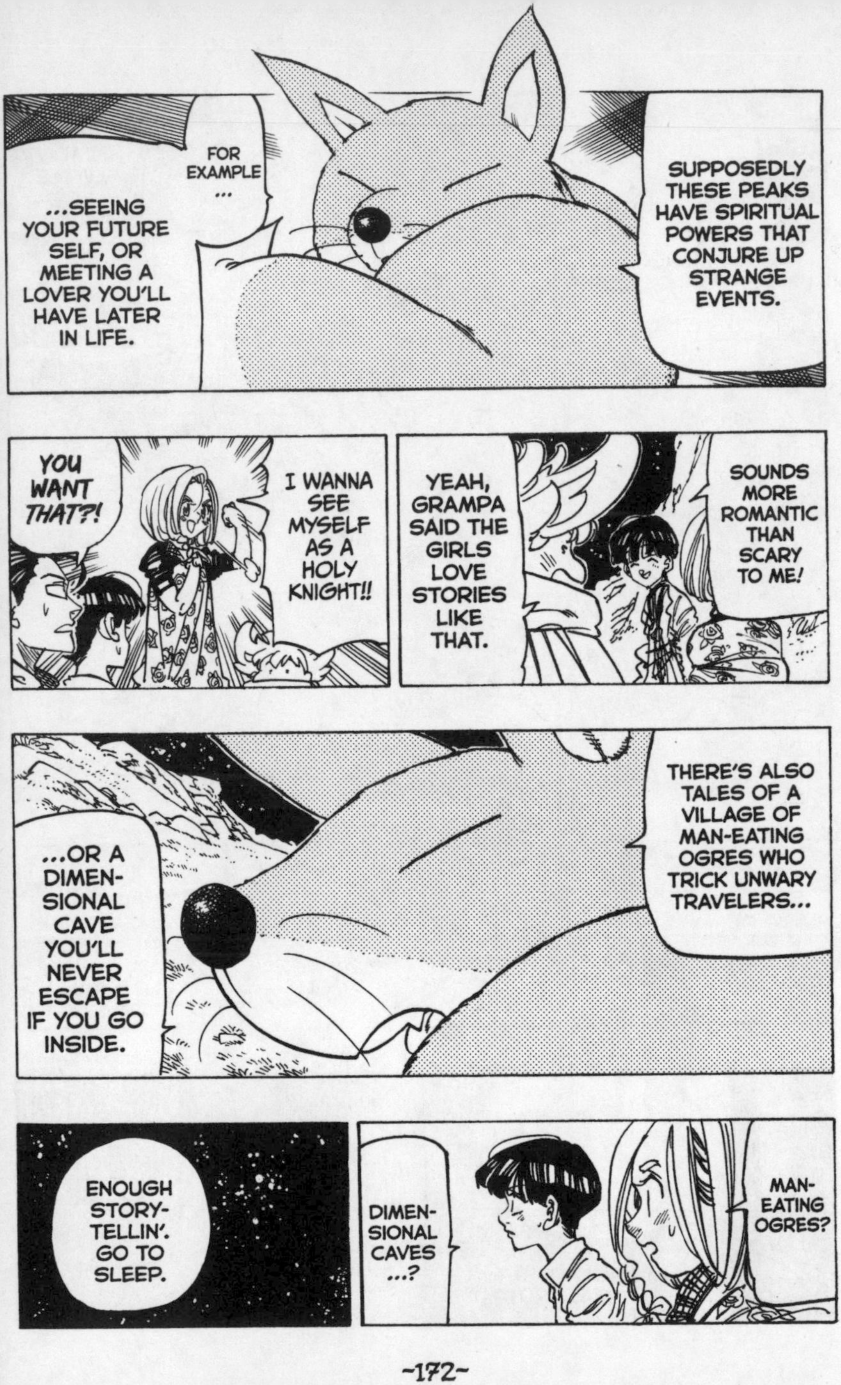
SUPPOSEDLY THESE PEAKS HAVE SPIRITUAL POWERS THAT CONJURE UP STRANGE EVENTS.
FOR EXAMPLE ...
...SEEING YOUR FUTURE SELF, OR MEETING A LOVER YOU'LL HAVE LATER IN LIFE.
SOUNDS MORE ROMANTIC THAN SCARY TO ME!
YEAH, GRAMPA SAID THE GIRLS LOVE STORIES LIKE THAT.
I WANNA SEE MYSELF AS A HOLY KNIGHT!!
YOU WANT THAT?!
THERE'S ALSO TALES OF A VILLAGE OF MAN-EATING OGRES WHO TRICK UNWARY TRAVELERS...
...OR A DIMEN-SIONAL CAVE YOU'LL NEVER ESCAPE IF YOU GO INSIDE.
MAN-EATING OGRES?
DIMEN-SIONAL CAVES ...?
ENOUGH STORY-TELLIN'. GO TO SLEEP.

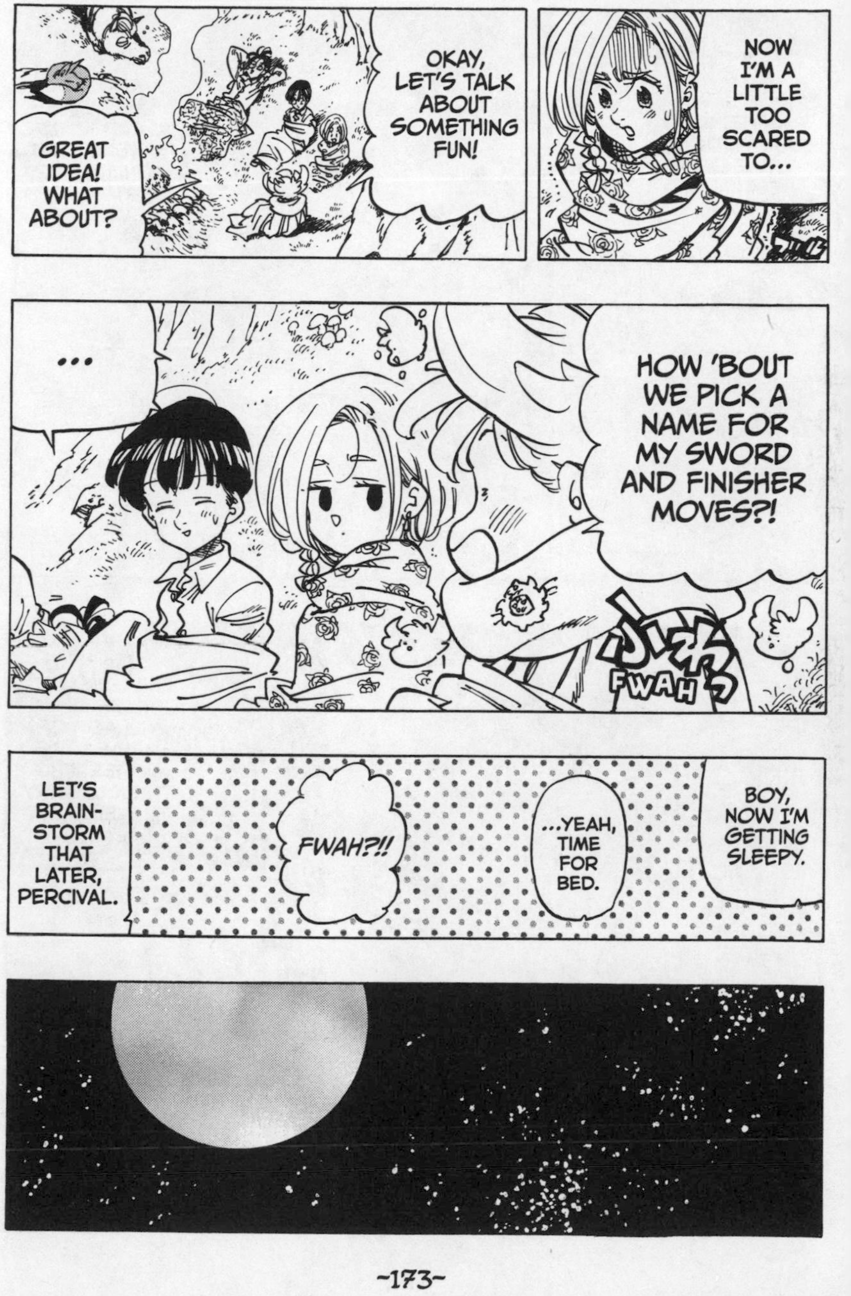
NOW I'M A LITTLE TOO SCARED TO...
OKAY, LET'S TALK ABOUT SOMETHING FUN!
GREAT IDEA! WHAT ABOUT?
HOW 'BOUT WE PICK A NAME FOR MY SWORD AND FINISHER MOVES?!
FWAH
...
BOY, NOW I'M GETTING SLEEPY.
...YEAH, TIME FOR BED.
FWAH?!!
LET'S BRAIN-STORM THAT LATER, PERCIVAL.

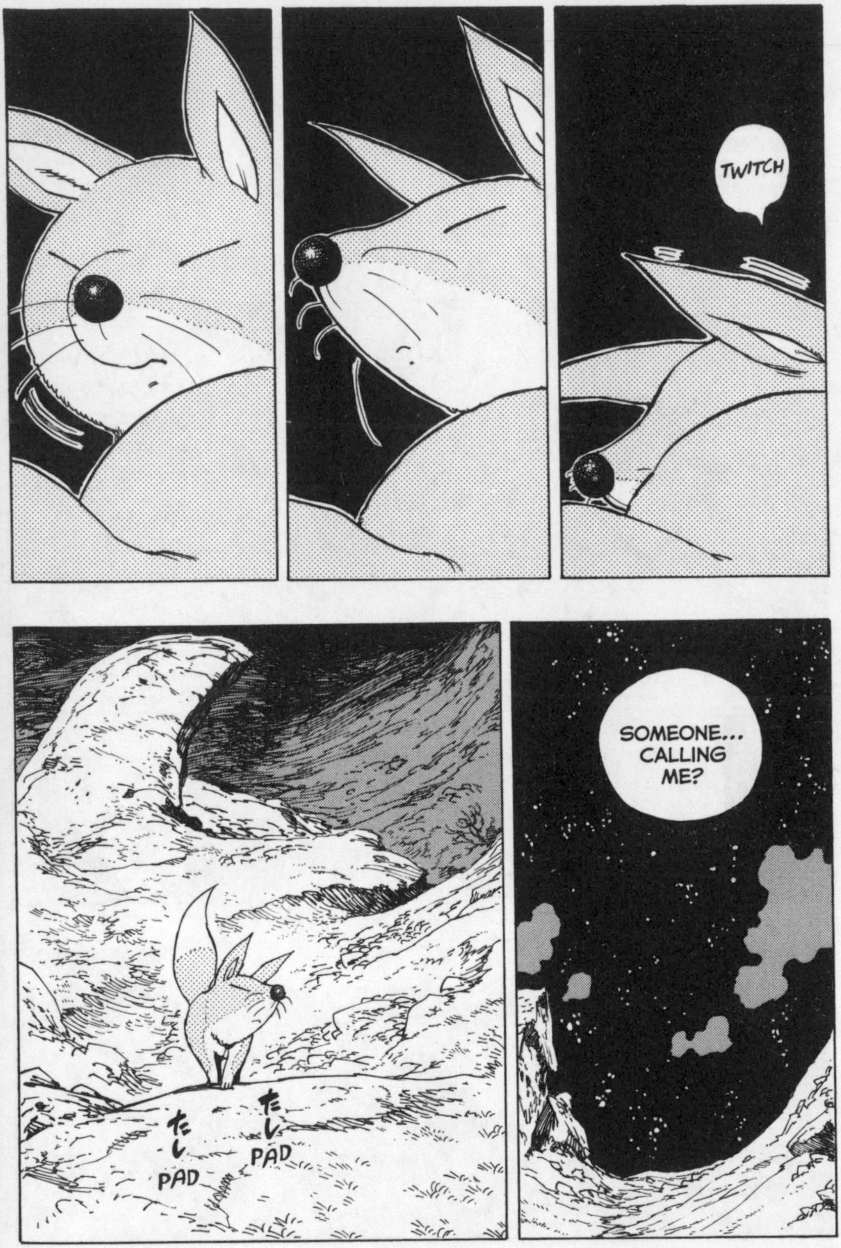
TWITCH
SOMEONE... CALLING ME?
たし PAD
たし PAD

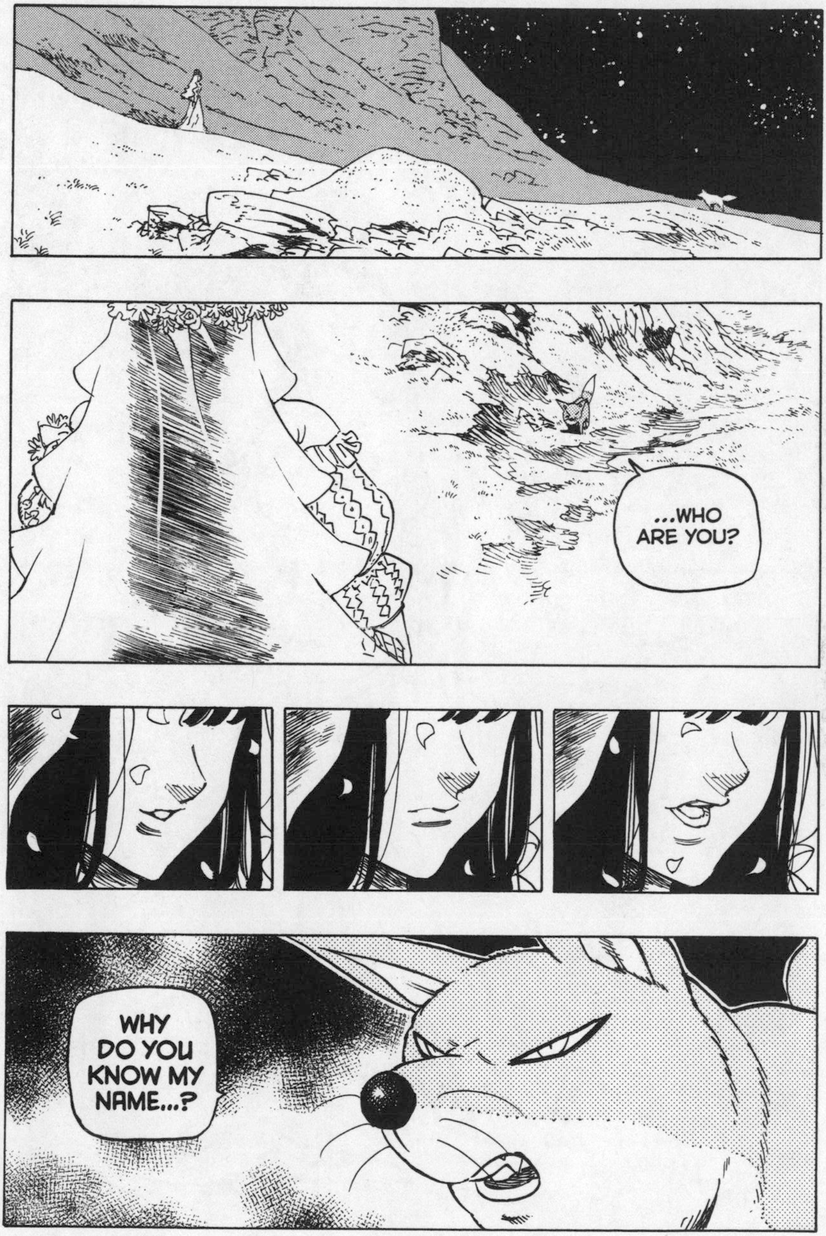
...WHO ARE YOU?
WHY DO YOU KNOW MY NAME...?

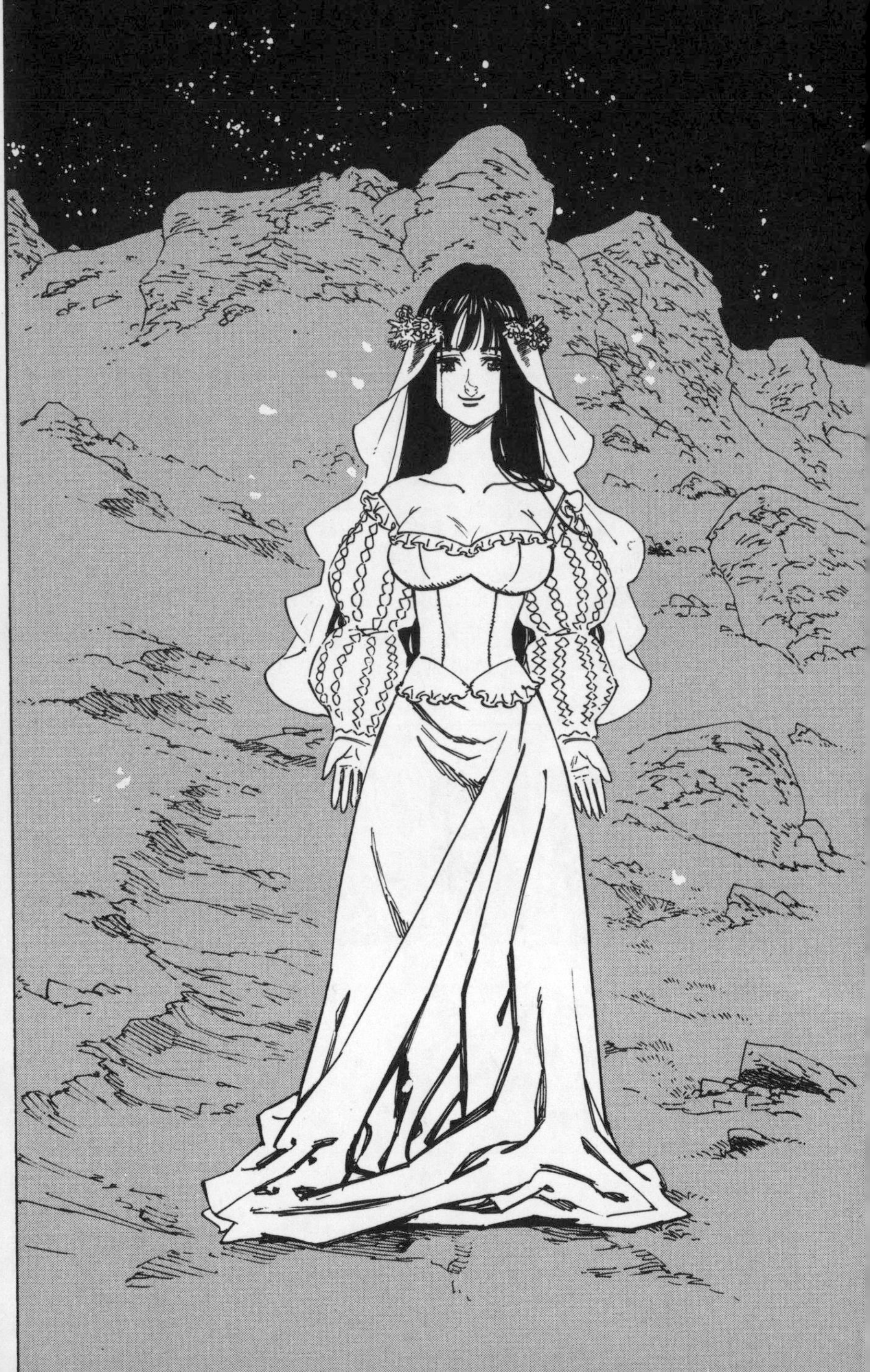

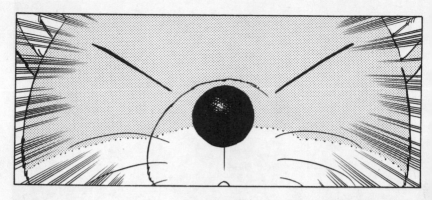

EH-CHOO!!

YAWN

MMPH

SHIVER

UGH, I'M FREEZING...

A GIRL WALKING AROUND BY HERSELF AT NIGHT?

HUH?

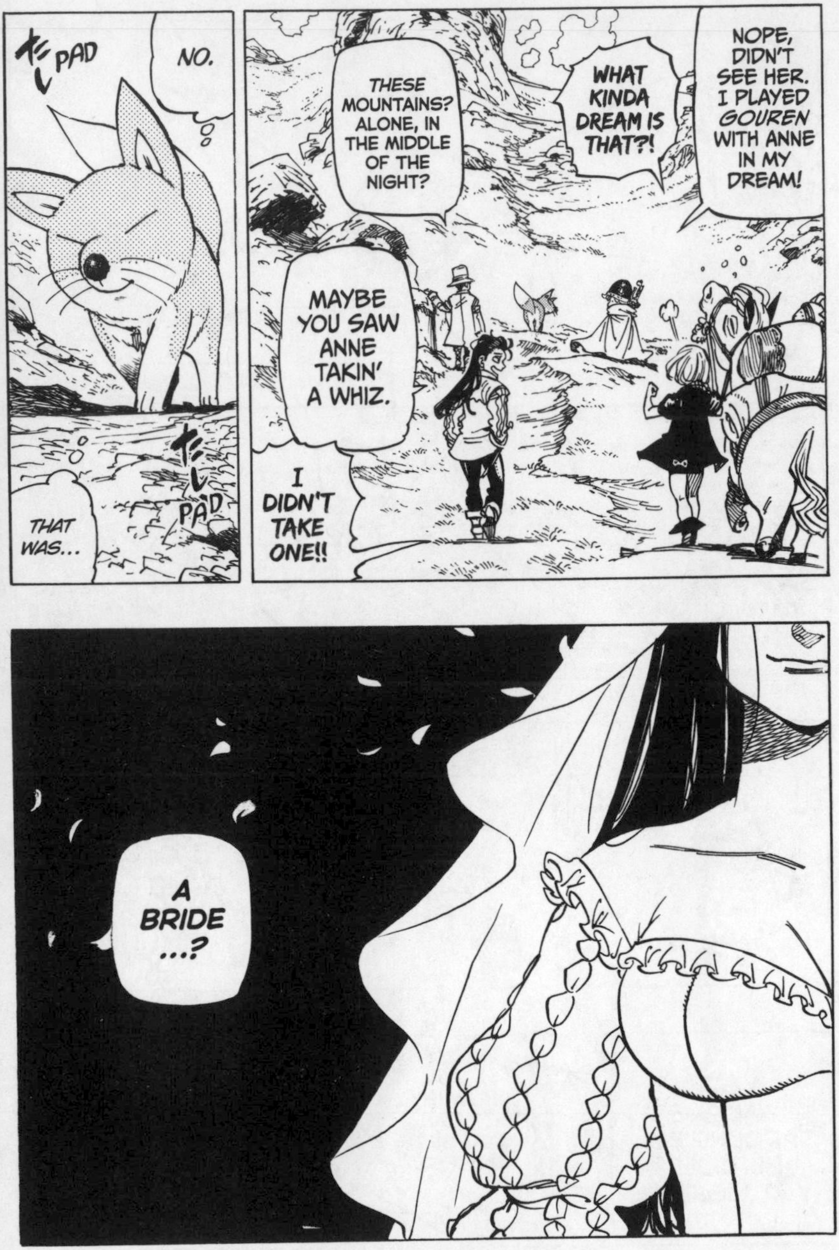
NOPE, DIDN'T SEE HER. I PLAYED GOUREN WITH ANNE IN MY DREAM!
WHAT KINDA DREAM IS THAT?!
THESE MOUNTAINS? ALONE, IN THE MIDDLE OF THE NIGHT?
MAYBE YOU SAW ANNE TAKIN' A WHIZ.
I DIDN'T TAKE ONE!!
NO.
PAD
PAD
THAT WAS...
A BRIDE ...?

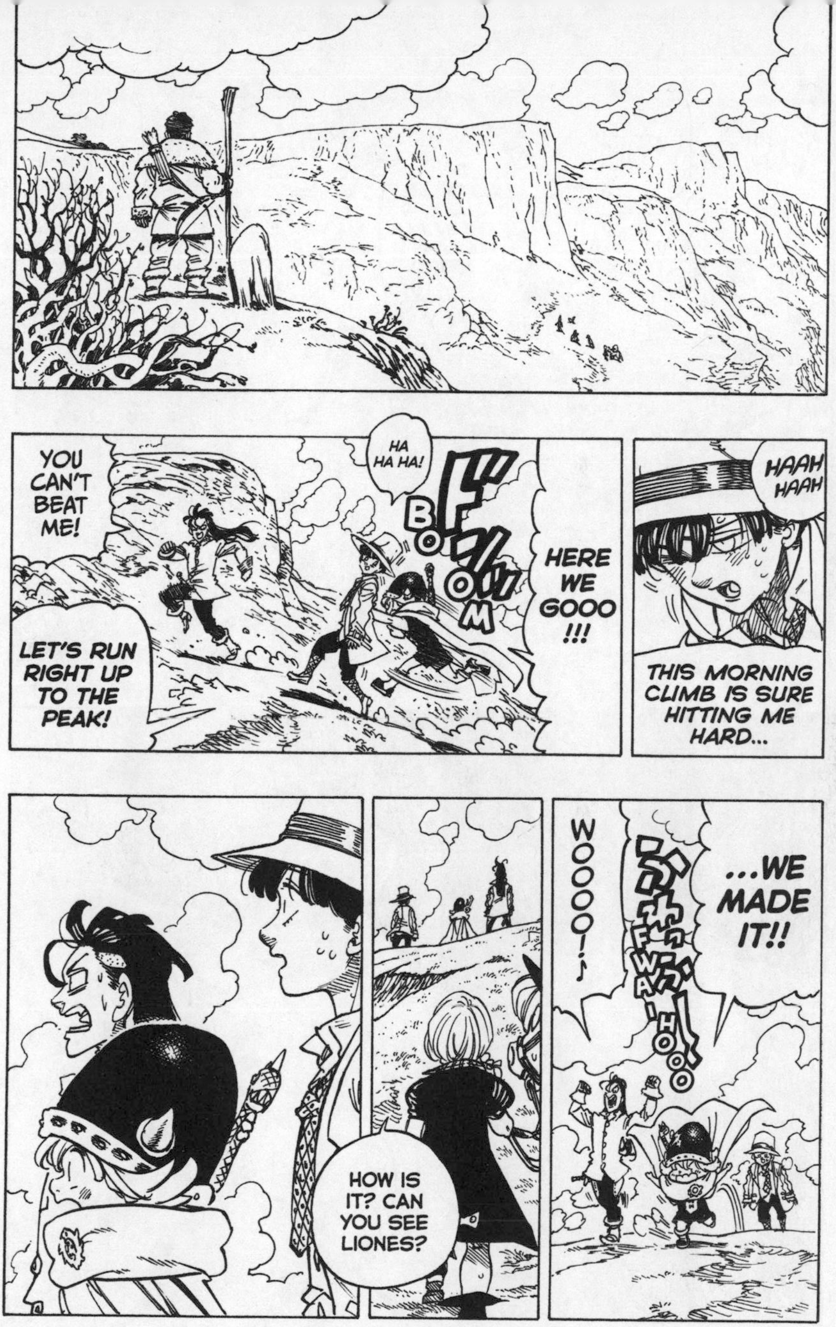
HAAH HAAH
THIS MORNING CLIMB IS SURE HITTING ME HARD...
HA HA HA!
BOOM
HERE WE GOOO!!!
YOU CAN'T BEAT ME!
LET'S RUN RIGHT UP TO THE PEAK!
...WE MADE IT!!
FWAH-HOOO
WOOOO!!♪
HOW IS IT? CAN YOU SEE LIONES?

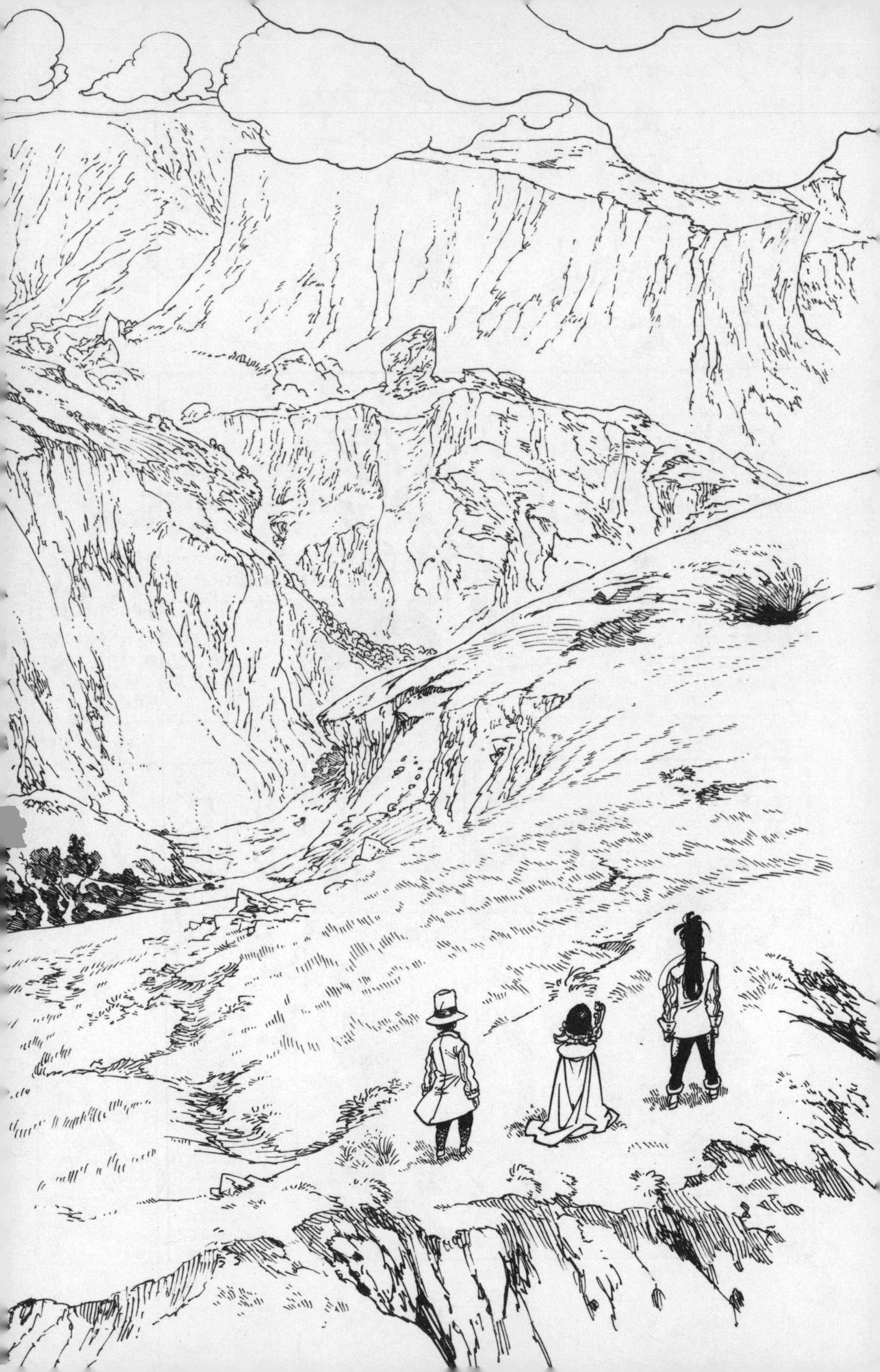

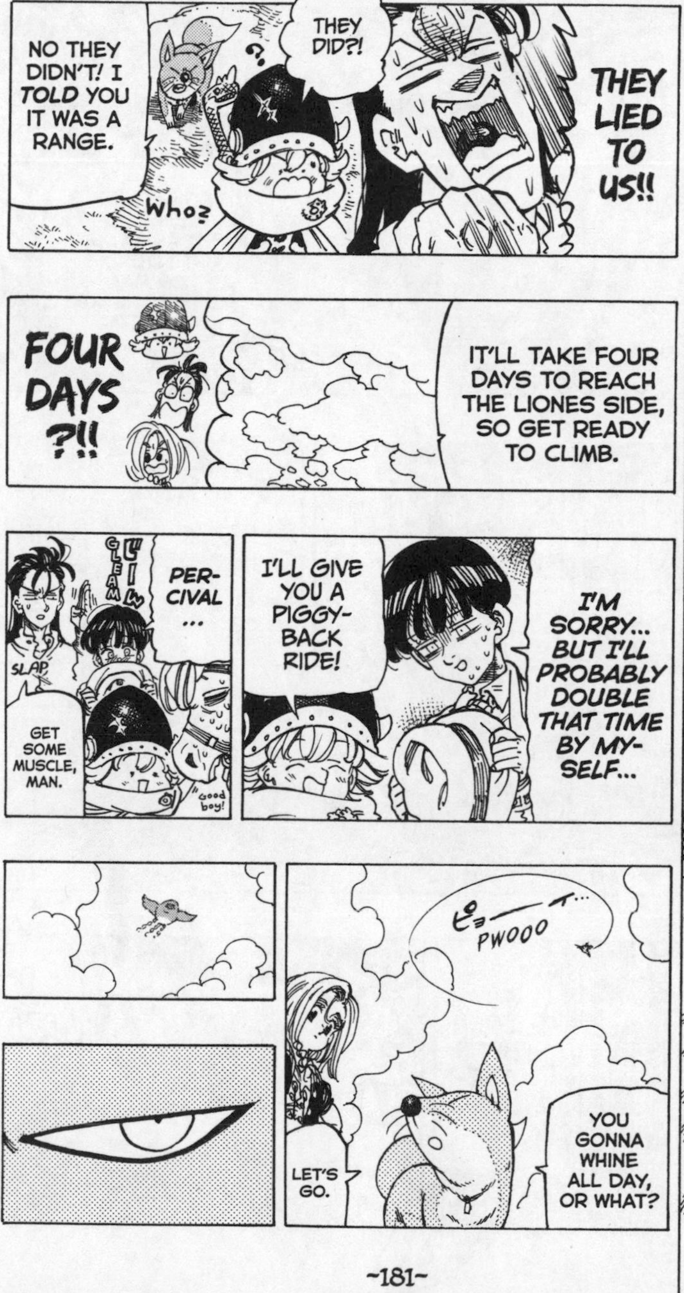
THEY LIED TO US!!
THEY DID?!
NO THEY DIDN'T! I TOLD YOU IT WAS A RANGE.
Who?
IT'LL TAKE FOUR DAYS TO REACH THE LIONES SIDE, SO GET READY TO CLIMB.
FOUR DAYS ?!!
I'M SORRY... BUT I'LL PROBABLY DOUBLE THAT TIME BY MY-SELF...
I'LL GIVE YOU A PIGGY-BACK RIDE!
PER-CIVAL ...
GLEAM
SLAP
GET SOME MUSCLE, MAN.
Good boy!
ピョ——イ…
PWOOO
YOU GONNA WHINE ALL DAY, OR WHAT?
LET'S GO.
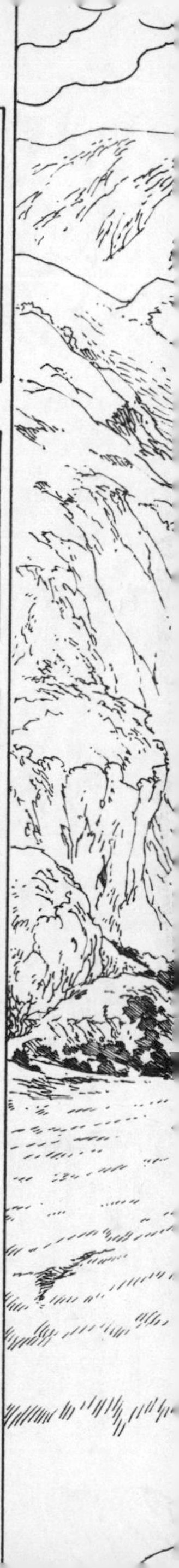

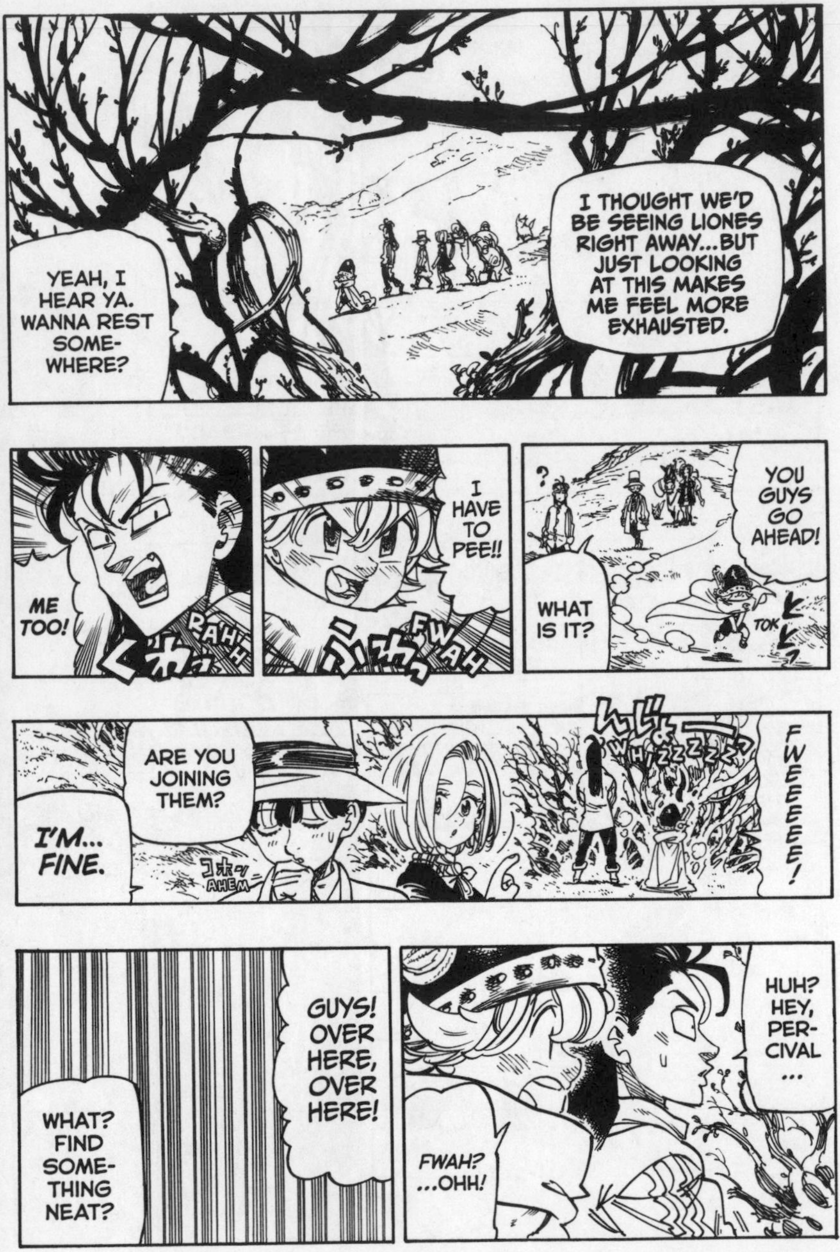
I THOUGHT WE'D BE SEEING LIONES RIGHT AWAY...BUT JUST LOOKING AT THIS MAKES ME FEEL MORE EXHAUSTED.
YEAH, I HEAR YA. WANNA REST SOME-WHERE?
YOU GUYS GO AHEAD!
?
WHAT IS IT?
TOK
I HAVE TO PEE!!
FWAH
ME TOO!
RAHH
FWEEEEEE!
WHIZZZZZZ
ARE YOU JOINING THEM?
I'M... FINE.
AHEM
HUH? HEY, PER-CIVAL ...
FWAH? ...OHH!
GUYS! OVER HERE, OVER HERE!
WHAT? FIND SOME-THING NEAT?

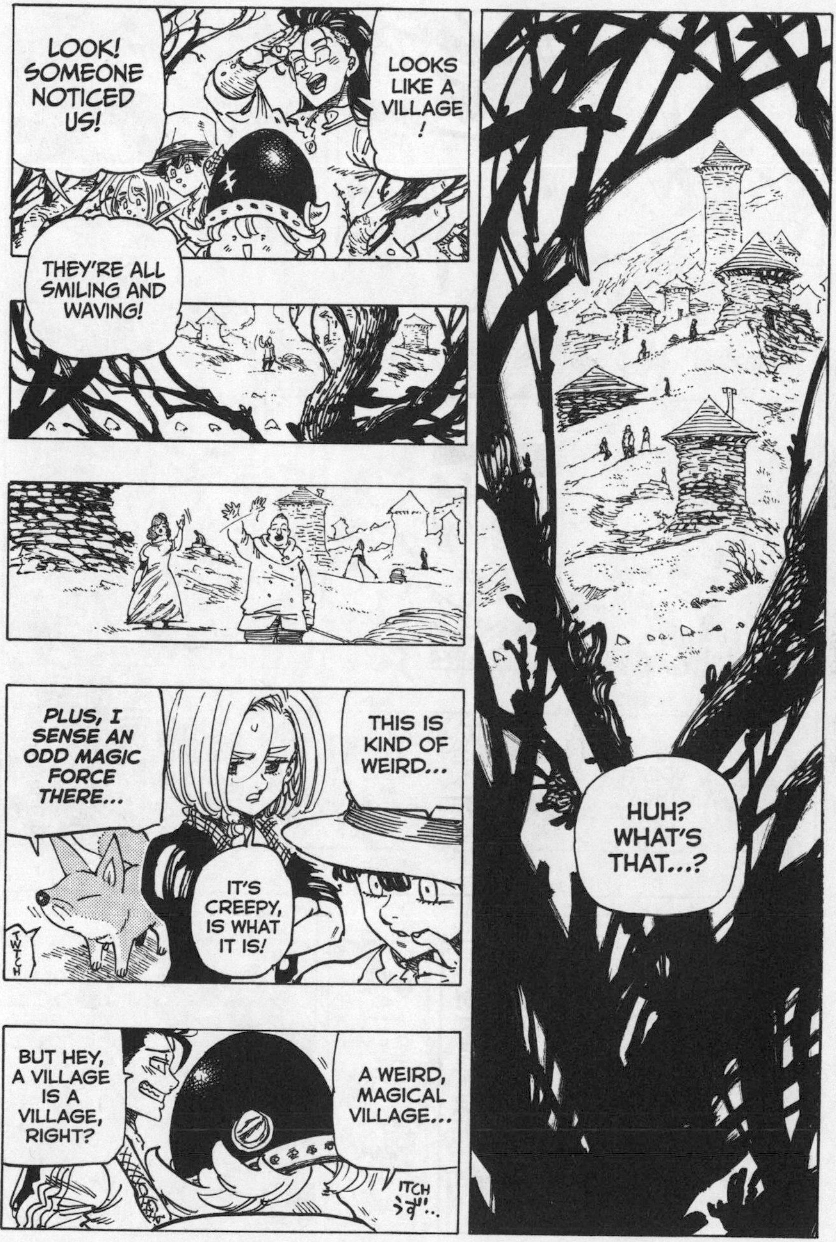

HUH? WHAT'S THAT...?
LOOKS LIKE A VILLAGE!
LOOK! SOMEONE NOTICED US!
THEY'RE ALL SMILING AND WAVING!
THIS IS KIND OF WEIRD...
PLUS, I SENSE AN ODD MAGIC FORCE THERE...
IT'S CREEPY, IS WHAT IT IS!
TWITCH
A WEIRD, MAGICAL VILLAGE...
BUT HEY, A VILLAGE IS A VILLAGE, RIGHT?
ITCH

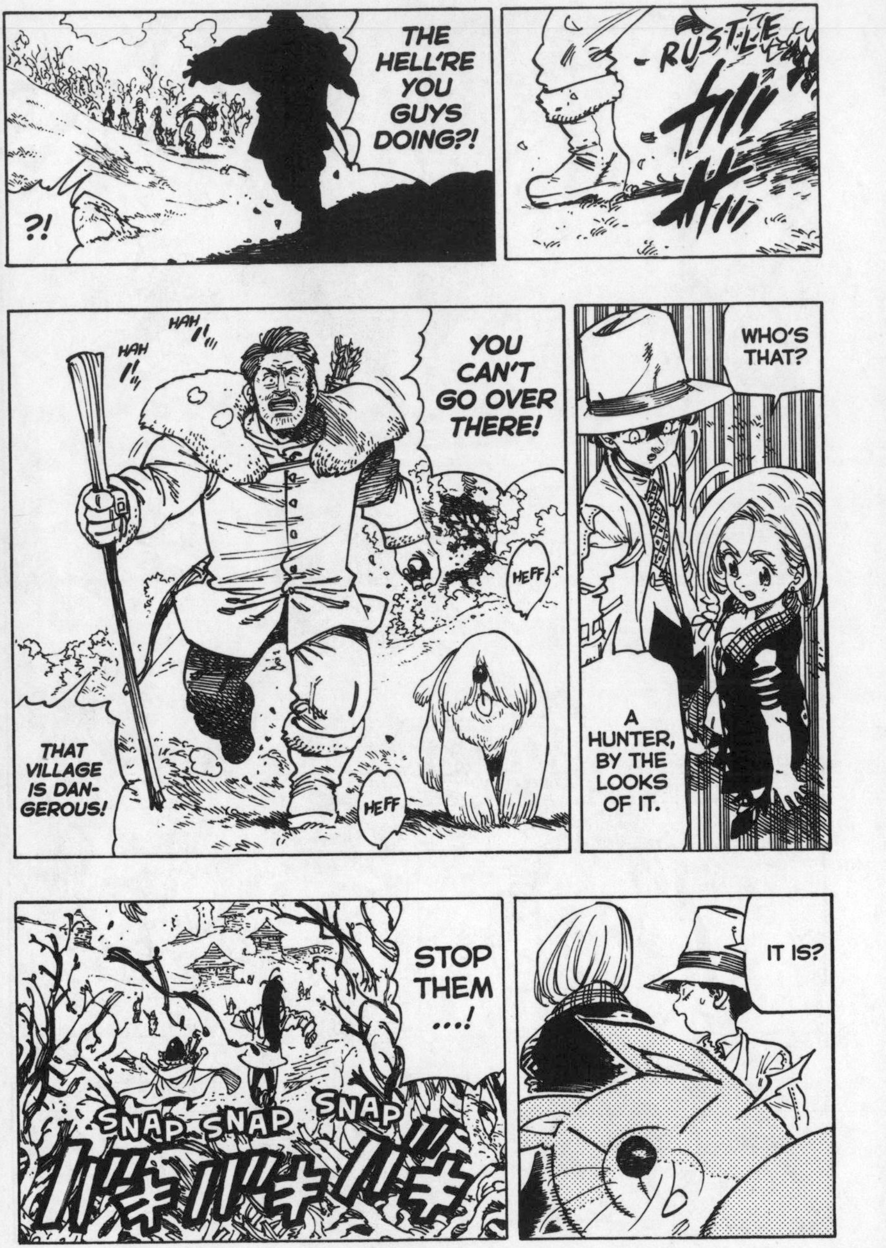
RUSTLE
THE HELL'RE YOU GUYS DOING?!
?!
WHO'S THAT?
A HUNTER, BY THE LOOKS OF IT.
YOU CAN'T GO OVER THERE!
HAH HAH
HEFF
THAT VILLAGE IS DANGEROUS!
HEFF
IT IS?
STOP THEM ...!
SNAP SNAP SNAP

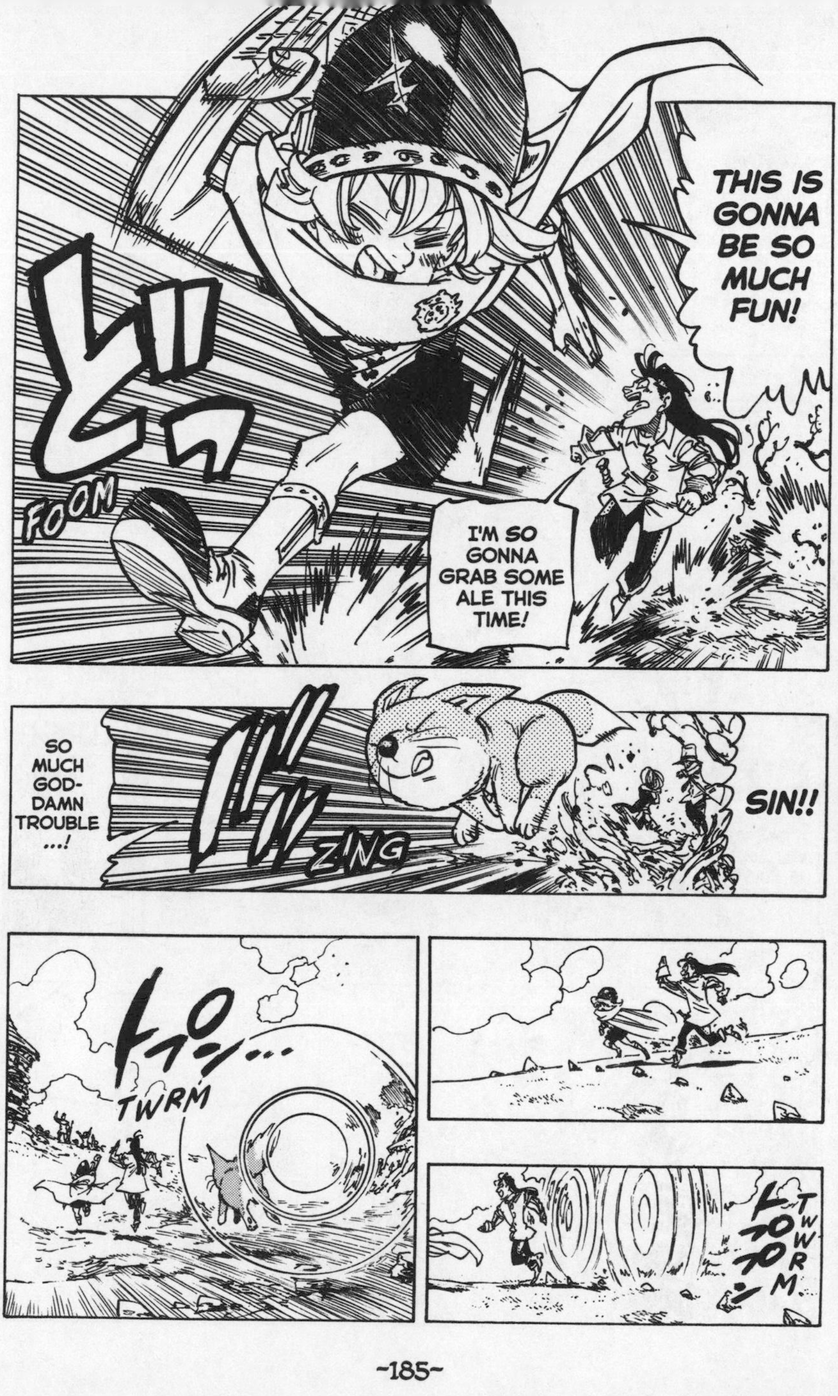
THIS IS GONNA BE SO MUCH FUN!
I'M SO GONNA GRAB SOME ALE THIS TIME!
FOOM
SIN!!
ZING
SO MUCH GOD-DAMN TROUBLE ...!
TWWRM.
TWRM

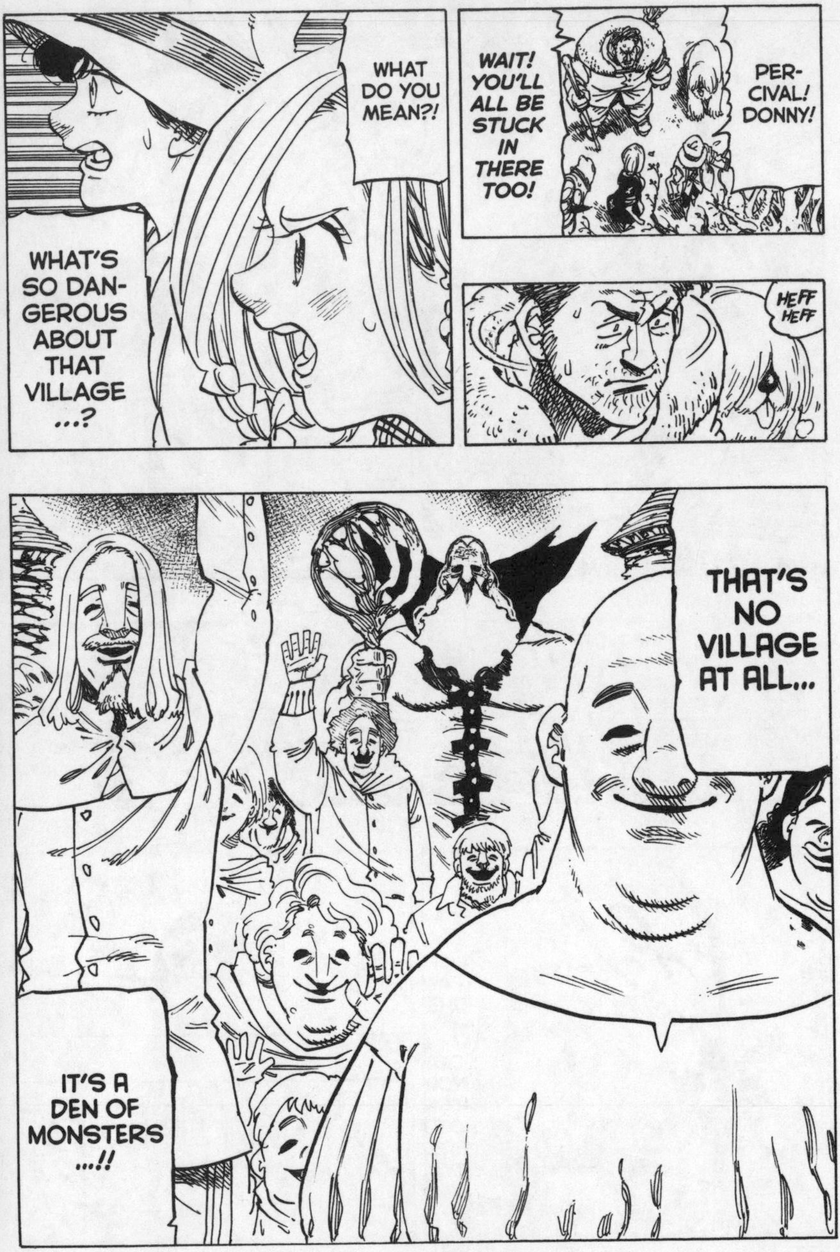
PER-CIVAL! DONNY!
WAIT! YOU'LL ALL BE STUCK IN THERE TOO!
HEFF HEFF
WHAT DO YOU MEAN?!
WHAT'S SO DAN-GEROUS ABOUT THAT VILLAGE ...?
THAT'S NO VILLAGE AT ALL...
IT'S A DEN OF MONSTERS ...!!

Four Knights of the Apocalypse Art Corner

Artist Knights' Chamber

DON'T FORGET TO INCLUDE YOUR NAME AND ADDRESS ON YOUR POSTCARD!

P = D = S = N = A =

SPECIAL AWARD

WE CAN BEAT ANYONE WHO WANTS A PIECE OF US!!

WE'RE GONNA HAVE TO FIGHT MORE OF THESE GUYS? I DON'T KNOW WHICH HURTS WORSE—MY HEAD OR MY STOMACH...

キャメロットの聖騎士。
黙示録の四騎士

Munière – Tokyo Prefecture

叔父さんかっこいい!!

P DONNY, YOUR UNCLE IS SO COOL!

A YEAH! UNLIKE DONNY! IT'S LIKE NIGHT AND DAY!

N LIKE A FEAST... AND LEFTOVERS!

Taiishi – Yamaguchi Prefecture

S PERCIVAL SUCKS AT DRAWING, HUH?

N I DON'T KNOW. I THINK HE'S GOT A PERSONAL STYLE.

D NO. IT'S JUST BAD.

Mitsuki Saito – Kanagawa Prefecture

P NASIENS SURE KNOWS ABOUT SOME WILD MEDICINES, HUH?!

S I THINK *HE* MIGHT NEED THEM MORE THAN ANYONE...

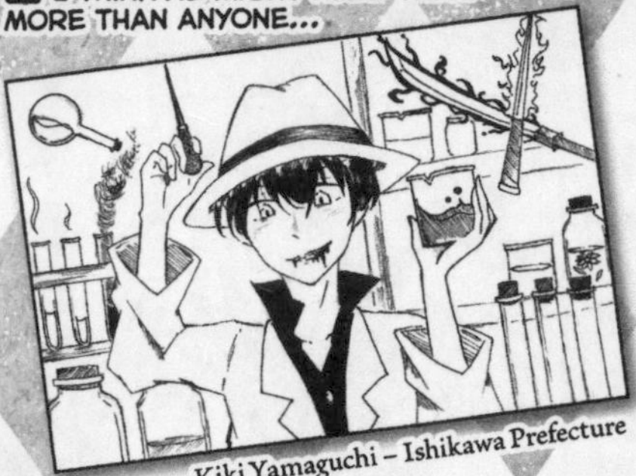

Kiki Yamaguchi – Ishikawa Prefecture

A CAN'T BELIEVE SUCH AN AWFUL GUY MADE A KID LIKE PERCIVAL!

D&N AGREED!

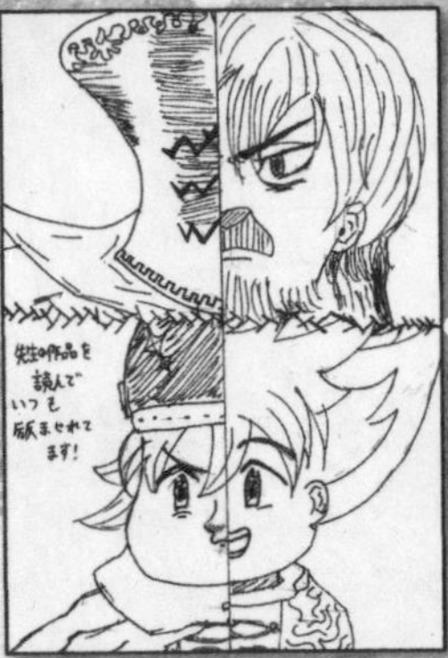

Akio Hayashi – Osaka Prefecture

P ANNE IS SO STALWART AND RELIABLE!

D YEAH! SHE'S THE DEFINITION OF *MANLY!* (LAFF)

N DONNY! ANNE IS RIGHT BEHIND YOU AND GLARING...

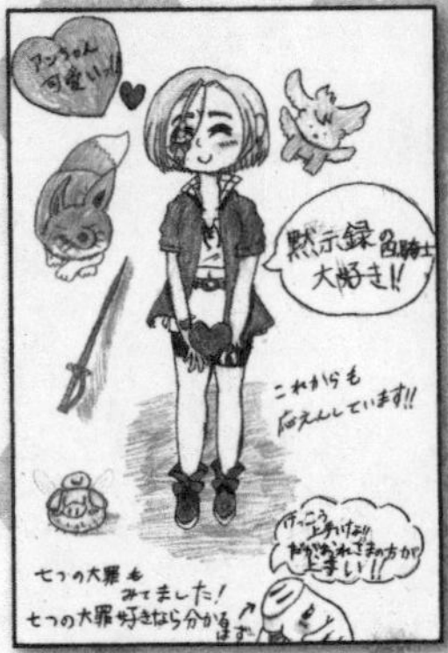
黙示録の四騎士大好き!!
これからも応援しています!!
七つの大罪もみてました!

Omochi – Aichi Prefecture

P AWESOME! LET'S ALL FOUR OF US WORK TO BECOME HOLY KNIGHTS!

N UH... I'M AIMING FOR APOTHE-CARY...

P A HOLY APOTHECARY KNIGHT, THEN!!

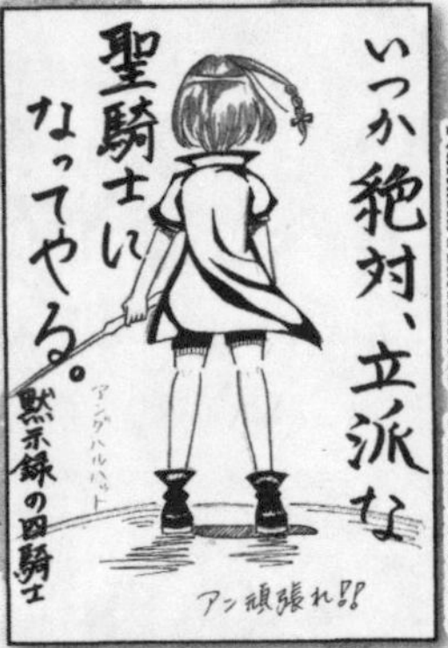
いつか絶対、立派な聖騎士になってやる。
黙示録の四騎士
アン頑張れ!!

Nanaka Hashimoto – Nara Prefecture

P MAN, I'D LIKE A MINI-PERCIVAL PLUSH OR SOME-THING...

D Y'KNOW... I KNOW WHAT YOU MEAN.

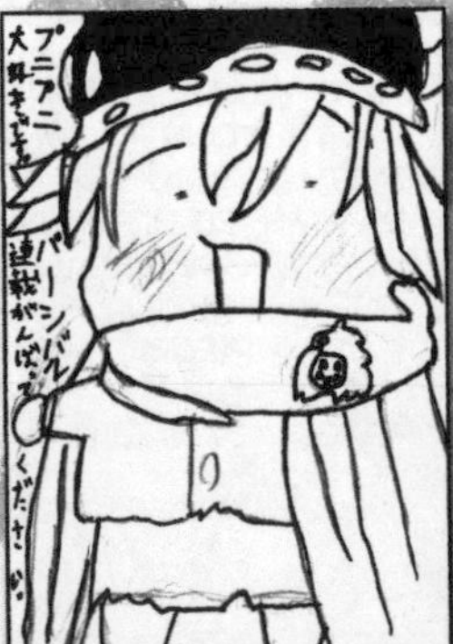

HawksMyFavorite – Kyoto Prefecture

P SIN'S A REAL FUNNY ONE... ARE ALL FOXES LIKE HIM?

N UH, I DON'T THINK SO.

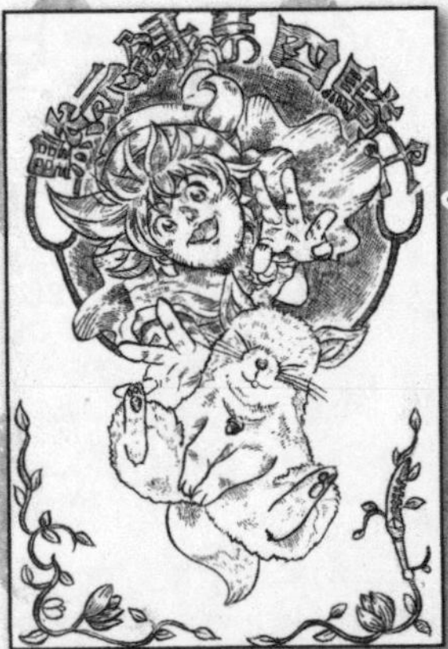

Kazuyuki Nakaeda – Ishikawa Prefecture

I KNOW! I THINK MAYBE I LOOK THE MOST GROWN-UP.

I CAN'T BELIEVE EVERYONE IN THIS PICTURE IS SUPPOSED TO BE THE SAME AGE.

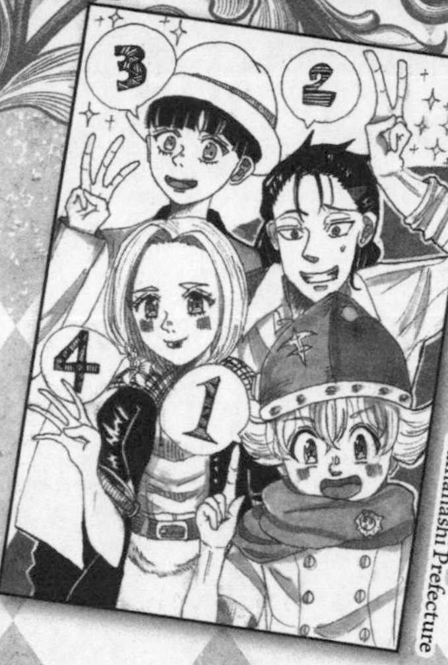
3
2
4
1

Waka Ishikawa – Yamanashi Prefecture

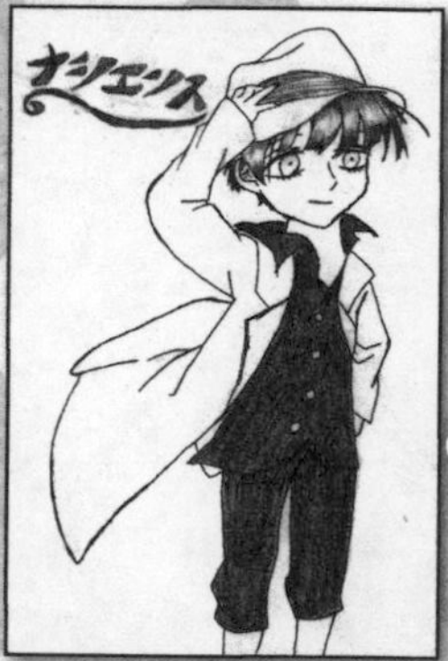
ナシエンス

Minako Matsui – Kanagawa Prefecture

A IS NASIENS A BOY? A GIRL? WHICH IS IT?

D WELL, IN TERMS OF LOOKS AND VOICE... YEAH, IT COULD GO EITHER WAY.

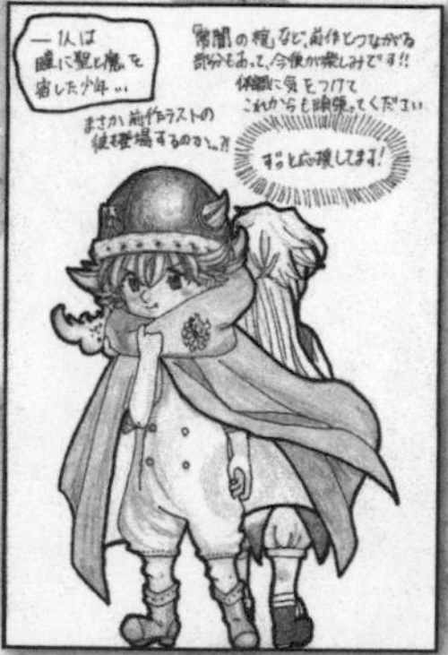
—1人は
瞳に聖と魔を
宿した少年…
「常闇の棺」など、前作とつながる部分もあって、今後が楽しみです!!
体調に気をつけて
これからも頑張ってください
まさか前作ラストの
彼も登場するのか…?!
ずっと応援してます!

Haruka Asamura – Akita Prefecture

D WHO'S THAT BEHIND PERCIVAL?

N IS THAT... A GIRL WITH SILVER HAIR?

A WHO SAYS IT HAS TO BE A GIRL?

Submit Your Drawing!

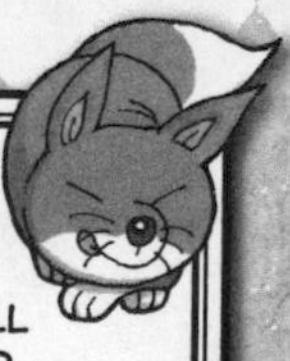

• ART MUST BE ON A POSTCARD OR POSTCARD-SIZED PAPER.
• WRITE YOUR NAME AND ADDRESS ON THE BACK OF YOUR PICTURE! YOU CAN INCLUDE COMMENTS IF YOU WANT. ALL ART WILL BE PRINTED IN BLACK AND WHITE, EVEN IF YOU SUBMIT IT IN COLOR.
• COPYING NAKABA SUZUKI'S ART STYLE IS FINE, OF COURSE, BUT COPYING PICTURES DRAWN BY OTHER FANS IS DEFINITELY NOT OKAY.

IF YOUR PIECE IS PRINTED, YOU'LL GET SPECIAL MERCH!
THE BEST PIECE IN EACH VOLUME WILL RECEIVE THE "SPECIAL AWARD" AND AN AUTOGRAPH!

SEND SUBMISSIONS TO:
KODANSHA WEEKLY SHONEN MAGAZINE
ATTN: FOUR KNIGHTS OF THE APOCALYPSE ART TROOP
2-12-21 OTOWA, BUNKYO WARD, TOKYO PREFECTURE 112-8001

NOTE: SUBMISSIONS WILL BE GIVEN TO THE ARTIST. PLEASE UNDERSTAND THAT THIS INCLUDES ANY ADDRESS, NAME, OR OTHER PERSONAL INFORMATION WRITTEN ON SAID SUBMISSIONS.

THE GREATEST OBSTACLE BETWEEN HIM AND LIONES!

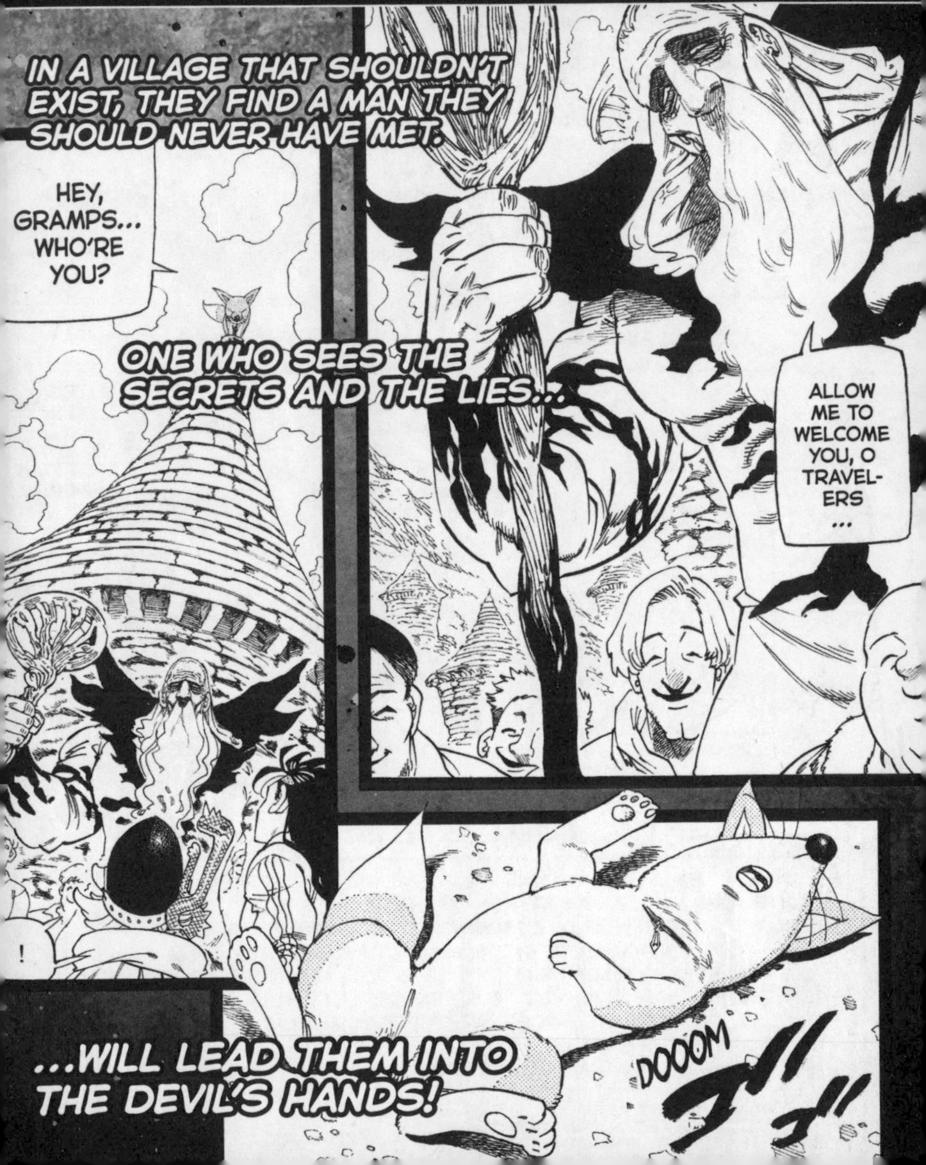
ALLOW ME TO WELCOME YOU, O TRAVELERS...
IN A VILLAGE THAT SHOULDN'T EXIST, THEY FIND A MAN THEY SHOULD NEVER HAVE MET.
HEY, GRAMPS... WHO'RE YOU?
ONE WHO SEES THE SECRETS AND THE LIES...
!
DOOOM
...WILL LEAD THEM INTO THE DEVIL'S HANDS!

PERCIVAL MUST CROSS THE DALFLARE MOUNTAINS,

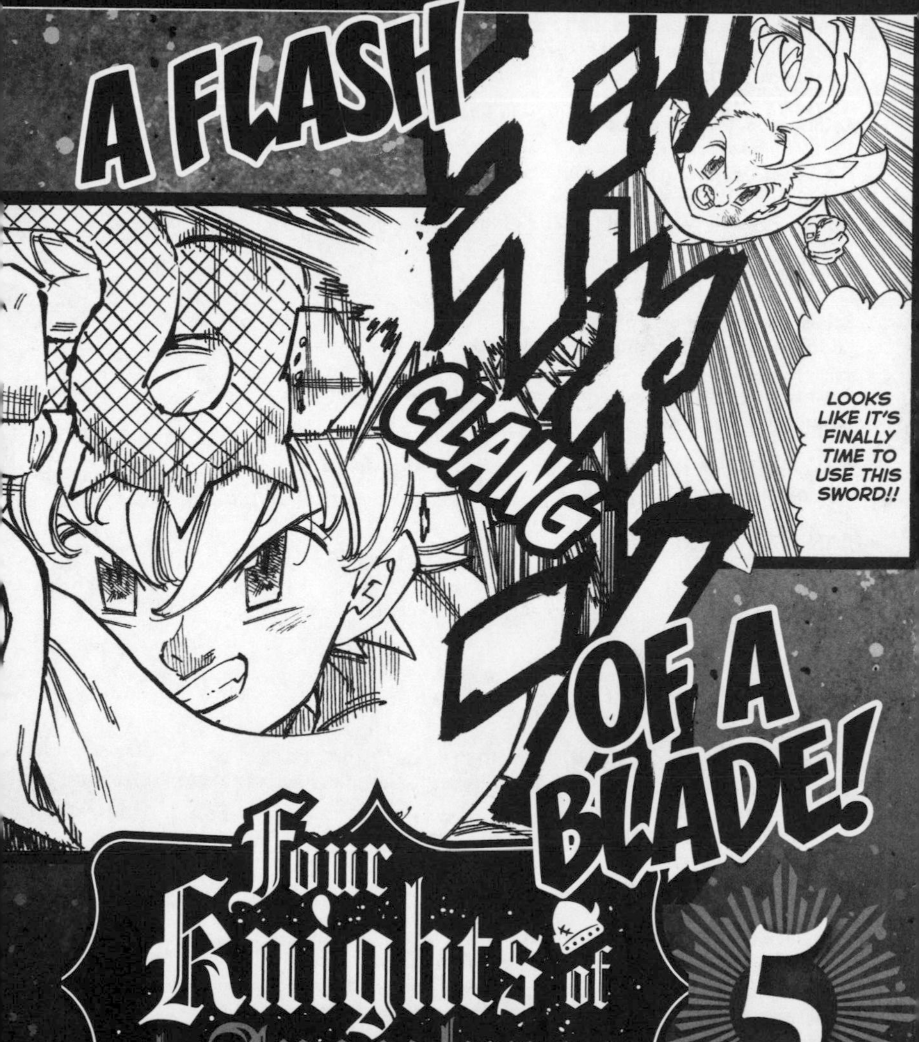
LOOKS LIKE IT'S FINALLY TIME TO USE THIS SWORD!!
A FLASH
CLANG
OF A BLADE!

Four Knights of the Apocalypse 5

A Kodansha Trade Paperback Original

The Seven Deadly Sins: Four Knights of the Apocalypse 4 copyright © 2021 Nakaba Suzuki
English translation copyright © 2022 Nakaba Suzuki

Published in the United States by
Kodansha USA Publishing, LLC, New York.

Publication rights for this English edition arranged through
Kodansha Ltd., Tokyo.

First published in Japan in 2021 by Kodansha Ltd., Tokyo
as *Mokushiroku no Yonkishi* 4.

ISBN 978-1-64651-604-9

Printed in the United States of America.

9 8 7 6 5 4 3 2 1

Translation: Kevin Gifford
Additional translation: Kevin Steinbach
Lettering: Darren Smith
Additional lettering and layout: AndWorld Design
Editing: Aimee Zink
YKS Services LLC/SKY Japan, Inc.
Kodansha USA Publishing edition cover design by Matt Akuginow

Publisher: Kiichiro Sugawara

Director of Publishing Services: Ben Applegate
Director of Publishing Operations: Dave Barrett
Associate Director of Publishing Operations: Stephen Pakula
Publishing Services Managing Editors: Alanna Ruse, Madison Salters
Production Managers: Jocelyn O'Dowd

KODANSHA.US

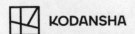
KODANSHA